KARL RAHNER

SERIES IN CONTINENTAL THOUGHT

EDITORIAL BOARD

Lester Embree, Chairman,
  Center President
  Duquesne University

Algis Mickunas
  Secretary
  Ohio University

Edward G. Ballard
  Tulane University

José Huertas-Jourda
  Wilfred Laurier University

Joseph J. Kockelmans
  Pennsylvania State University

William McKenna
  Miami University

J. N. Mohanty
  Temple University

Thomas M. Seebohn
  Johannes Gutenberg—Universität Mainz

Richard Zaner
  Vanderbilt University

INTERNATIONAL ADVISORY BOARD

Suzanne Bachelard
  Université de Paris

Rudolf Boehm
  Rijksuniversiteit-Gent

Albert Borgmann
  University of Montana

Amedeo P. Giorgi
  Duquesne University

Richard Grathoff
  Universität Bielefeld

Samuel Ijseling
  Husserl-Archief te Leuven

Alphonso Lingis
  Pennsylvania State University

Werner Marx
  Albert-Luwigs-Universität

David Rasmussen
  Boston College

John Sallis
  Loyola University, Chicago

John Scanlon
  Duquesne University

High J. Silverman
  State University of New York, Stony Brook

Carli Sini
  Universitá di Milano

Elisabeth Ströker
  Universität Köln

Jacques Taminiaux
  Louvain-la-Neuve

D. Lawrence Wieder
  University of Oklahoma

Dallas Willard
  University of Southern California

Sponsored by the Center for Advanced Research in Phenomenology, Inc.

ST. JOSEPH'S UNIVERSITY

3 9353 00238 2040

KARL RAHNER
THE PHILOSOPHICAL FOUNDATIONS

Thomas Sheehan

Preface by Karl Rahner, S.J.

PXQ

BT
40
S54
1987

OHIO UNIVERSITY PRESS
ATHENS

Copyright © 1987 by Thomas Sheehan.
Printed in the United States of America.
All rights reserved.

Library of Congress Cataloging-in-Publication Data

Sheehan, Thomas.
  Karl Rahner, the philosophical foundations.

  Includes bibliographies.
  1. Philosophical theology—History—20th century.
2. Rahner, Karl, 1904–   . I. Title.
BT40.S54 1987   193   86-19340
ISBN 0–8214–0684–1

DEDICATED TO
EWERT H. COUSINS
AND
JOSEPH DONCEEL, S.J.,
IN GRATITUDE AND RESPECT

TABLE OF CONTENTS

PREFACE[1]

On Martin Heidegger

Karl Rahner, S.J.

What should I, a student of Martin Heidegger, say of him? I am a theologian, and so much a theologian that I make no claim to being a philosopher. And yet, although I am a theologian, I respect him as my master.

I might say that Catholic theology, as it is today, can no longer be thought of without Martin Heidegger, because even those who hope to go beyond him and ask questions different from his, nonetheless owe their origin to him.

I might very simply and modestly acknowledge that although I had many good professors in the classroom, there is only *one* whom I can revere as my *teacher*, and he is Martin Heidegger.

I might also say that such an acknowledgement does not strike me as a simple and obvious matter, for I hope that the subject matter of philosophy and theology has always been more important to me than the persons who pursue these disciplines.

Or I might try to say, with equal measures of soberness and hope, that I am convinced that a great deal of Heidegger's work remains yet to be done, that it will have even further effect in the future history of thought, even though today very little is being said about him in that marketplace that pretends to be the tribunal of the intellect.

Or I might simply offer him my thanks and best wishes from out of a quiet inner relationship that has remained alive in me for over thirty years, even though I have had only very few personal contacts with him during that period.

Be that as it may, even as I do offer him, gratefully and respectfully, my best wishes, I am not precisely sure what that actually means. But surely he has taught us *one thing:* that everywhere and in everything we can and must seek out that *unutterable mystery* which *disposes* over us, even though we can hardly name it with words. And this we must do even if, in his own work and in a way that would be strange for a theologian, Heidegger himself abstains from *speech* about this mystery, speech which the theologian must *utter*.

Notes

1. When Professor Rahner was asked, before his death, to contribute a Foreword to this work, he responded that poor health prevented him from honoring the request but that the author could use the preceding text as a Preface. It was written for a 1969 *Festschrift* for Heidegger and is one of the few texts in which Rahner explicitly remarks on his own relation to Heidegger; hence it is particularly relevant to the present study, which, in some measure, is a critical commentary on that relation. The text is translated with permission from *Martin Heidegger im Gespräch*, ed. Richard Wisser (Freiburg and Munich: Alber, 1970), pp. 48–49. Two brief phrases which refer to Heidegger's eightieth birthday have been omitted.

INTRODUCTION

Karl Rahner, 1904-1984, was perhaps the most creative and certainly the most prolific scholar ever to have studied under Martin Heidegger. Today Rahner is known mostly as a theologian, the author of some sixteen volumes of *Schriften zur Theologie* (in English: *Theological Investigations*). However, he first gained his reputation as a philosopher when, in 1939, three years after completing his studies under Heidegger at Freiburg University, he published *Geist in Welt (Spirit in the World)*, his groundbreaking work on Thomas Aquinas' metaphysics of knowledge. The present essay is a critical examination of that book, with a particular focus on Rahner's debts to and arguments against the thought of Martin Heidegger.[1]

Geist in Welt (hereafter GW) is the most important work on Aquinas' theory of cognition to have appeared in contemporary philosophy. Strictly speaking, it is neither a commentary on nor a straight-forward explanation of what Aquinas said. Rather, it is what Heidegger called a "retrieval" or *Wiederholung*, an effort to articulate what remains "unsaid" but potentially sayable in a philosophical text—in this case, an article from the *Summa Theologiae*, Part One, Question Eighty-four, Article Seven. This article is a mere 700 words in length, and it argues that man can know nothing in this life, not even metaphysical objects, without being "turned to the phantasm," that is, without having sense intuition. But Rahner spends over 400 pages pulling out of this brief text the whole groundwork for Aquinas' metaphysics, and, what is most striking, he retrieves from the passage a transcendental turn to the subject as a new foundation for metaphysics. He freely admits that his own interpretation in many cases can be found only implicitly in the medieval article, and yet he insists that "the ideas expressed in *Geist in Welt* are truly Thomistic."[2]

Clearly, Rahner had no intention of serving up a warmed-over St. Thomas in the fashion of so many neo-Scholastic commentaries. "The past can only be preserved in its purity," he later wrote, "by someone who accepts responsibility for the future, who preserves insofar as he overcomes."[3] And for Rahner, preserving Aquinas meant overcoming his

1

objectivistic language and restating his insights in the framework of an existential-transcendental "Copernican Revolution." In the Introduction to GW, Rahner affirms that the book is "conditioned by the problematic of *today's* philosophy"; indeed, "I would know of no other reason to be occupied with Thomas than for the sake of those questions which stimulate *my* philosophy and that of my time."[4]

For Rahner the modern philosophy in terms of which he rereads Aquinas is fundamentally characterized by what he calls the turn to the subject. "Modern times (especially in the centuries-long process that reaches from Descartes through Kant and German Idealism to today's existential philosophy) is the process of man's understanding himself as subject, even where—as in contemporary Heideggerian philosophy—he will not admit this of himself."[5] In order to find the turn to the subject in Thomas Aquinas (others would accuse Rahner of reading it into him), Rahner takes up the Angelic Doctor's metaphysics of cognition—not, however, for itself but for the purpose of showing, against Kant, that a metaphysics of being as being is possible on the basis of the restriction of human knowledge to the objects of the sensible world without any vision of a spiritual "beyond." At stake in GW is the nature of subjectivity and the range of its intentional correlate once all closet Platonism, otherworldliness, and intellect intuitionism have been exorcised from the Thomistic tradition. Having precluded any Janus-head double vision whereby man would supposedly "take a look" at transcendent being and then take a look back at the world, Rahner masterfully shows, with considerable help from Heidegger, that man projectively *anticipates* (but never grasps) the ever elusive unity of being-as-such every time he knows a worldly entity. Man has no vision of God, only a knowledge of the world. But the condition of the possibility of that knowledge is an ontological premonition of the unlimited ground of the real. The science of metaphysics, according to Rahner, is not some kind of "news from nowhere" but only the thematization or explicitation of this *unified bivalence* of human cognition, indeed of human being. That is, metaphysics merely spells out the *de facto* nature of man: his projective anticipation of the wholeness of being (this constitutes man's "spirituality") as the basis for his access to material things (his "worldliness"). Rahner calls it a metaphysics of "spirit in the world." In Heidegger's language it would be called a "hermeneutics of facticity."

The Thomistic term that Rahner uses to name man's restriction to sense intuition is *conversio ad phantasma*, the condition of being always turned to the sensible. When Aquinas says that this is man's condition "in the present state of life" *(secundum praesentis vitae statum)*, one might be led to think that he promises some metaphysical intuition in an angelic afterlife, in which case the conversion to the phantasm would only be a passing necessity, a temporary drag, during the present vale of tears. But in Rahner's interpretation, the "present state of life," that is, the constant turnedness to the world, is the *only* state of life, and if there is immortality, it will not be an absolution from the physical. Much of the revolutionary quality of Rahner's work lies in this relentless affirmation of man's worldliness as over against all bloodless yearnings for the angelic. For Rahner, "the free spirit becomes, and must become, sensibility in order to be spirit, and thus it exposes itself to the whole destiny of the earth." More prosaically but just as forcefully: "All thought [therefore, even thought in a possible afterlife] exists only for sense intuition."[6]

Rahner's transcendental grounding of metaphysics on the foundation of human cognition had, from the very beginning, a theological teleology. Even though GW is strictly a philosophical work, it is scored in a hidden key: that of showing how man in his worldliness is open to a possible revelation of God in space and time. After GW had demonstrated that man is a cognitive anticipation of the ground of reality—a movement *towards* the divine while being always a movement *within* the world—Rahner's next work, *Hörer des Wortes (Hearers of the Word;* hereafter HW), published in 1941, was an extension of the themes of GW into the area of philosophy of religion, specifically in order to show the *a priori* possibility of man's capacity to hear a revelation that might possibly proceed from God.[7] There again the method was transcendental, an analysis of the structure of subjectivity with regard to the range of its possible objects. And the manifold essays that made up Rahner's theological production over the forty-five years of his career were a continuation of the transcendental approach into the area of Catholic dogmatics. For Rahner, "Dogmatic theology today has to be theological anthropology. . . . Such an anthropology must, of course, be a transcendental anthropology," and this entails "that every theological question must also be considered from a transcendental point of view." That is, "the *a priori* conditions for the knowledge of a particular object of faith are to be explicitly dealt with, and. . . the concepts used to describe these theological objects are to be determined by this reflection."[8]

In this essay I am not concerned with Rahner's theology in any way, nor with his philosophy of religion. My aim is simply to examine his metaphysics of human knowledge as a supposed foundation for metaphysics. I propose to show both the *similarity* of GW to certain major aspects of Heidegger's early work and its *divergence* from Heidegger's program as a whole. In the first case I will exhibit the parallels between, on the one hand, agent intellect and possible intellect in Rahner's rereading of Aquinas and, on the other hand, the two moments of Da-sein's bivalence according to Heidegger: existentiality and facticity, or projection and thrownness. Moreover, I will attempt to show that Rahner's interpretation of "cogitative sense" as the unity of abstraction and conversion to the phantasm parallels the central issue that Heidegger worked out in *Sein und Zeit*, namely, that the generation of human temporality is the unifying meaning of the bivalence of existentiality and facticity. To state this parallelism in other terms: the realm of intelligibility is opened up by man's ontological movement (temporality in Heidegger, cogitative sense in Rahner) in the twofold projectivity of agent intellect (existentiality: *nous poiētikos*) and possible intellect (facticity: *nous pathētikos*).

In the second case I will show that Rahner's transcendental grounding of metaphysics in human cognition continues to move within the parameters of the metaphysics which Heidegger adjudges to be "forgetful of being." What Rahner calls "being as self-presence" (*das Sein als Bei-sich-sein*) is, from Heidegger's perspective, only one more form of the "beingness of entities" (*die Seiendheit des Seienden*), and in fact is inserted within the formal structure of what Heidegger calls "onto-theo-logy." Nonetheless, I hope to show that the brilliance of Rahner's book lies in the fact that he bears onto-theo-logy to its very limits, to the point where the structure begins to come unglued.

Karl Rahner was born near Freiburg, Germany, in 1904 and entered the Society of Jesus in 1922.[9] He did his basic philosophical studies between 1924 and 1927 at Feldkirch, Austria (where in fact Heidegger had spent some weeks as a Jesuit seminarian in the fall of 1909), and at Pullach near Munich. The fare of these courses was the usual neo-Thomism, and, like many students before and since, Rahner was not impressed. He later called his teachers "learned, well-read and educated" but finally "relatively second-rate people."[10]

During those years Rahner set the groundwork for his own future philosophical work by an intense private study of Joseph Maréchal's *Le point de départ de la métaphysique*, especially the fifth volume, published in 1926, entitled *Le thomisme devant la philosophie critique*.[11] Maréchal, a Belgian Jesuit, was the first Catholic philosopher to enter seriously and sympathetically into Kant's work in order to rescore Aquinas' theory of knowledge in a transcendental key. Over against the formal synthetic function of the transcendental unity of apperception in Kant, Maréchal argued that the condition of the possibility of the objectivity of the contents of consciousness in affirmation is the movement of the knowing subject beyond all conceptual forms to the fullness of pure act. This work remained the abiding inspiration for Rahner's GW and the key to his reading of Heidegger.

Rahner was eventually singled out for a teaching position in the history of philosophy at the Philosophische Hochschule Berchmanskolleg in Pullach, and therefore, in 1934, two years after his ordination to the priesthood, he was sent to Freiburg University to take the Ph.D. in philosophy. There he followed a few courses under the neo-Thomist who held the chair of Catholic philosophy at Freiburg, Rev. Martin Honecker: one course in Greek philosophy, two courses in ethics, and a seminar in Franz Brentano. But Rahner's real enthusiasm was for Martin Heidegger, the *enfant terrible* of the new existential phenomenology, who had published *Sein und Zeit* in 1927 (hereafter SZ; in English, *Being and Time*) and who had called for a "destruction" of the history of ontology, which he had formally launched in 1929 with *Kant und das Problem der Metaphysik* (in English, *Kant and the Problem of Metaphysics*).[12] Heidegger's recent and short-lived excursion into academic administration and matters political had just ended with his resignation from the rectorship of the university (spring, 1934), and the following fall Rahner registered in Heidegger's classes. Rahner preserved until his death a list of the lecture courses and seminars he took from the man who forty years later he would call his one and only teacher:[13]

Winter semester, 1934–35:
    Lecture course: Hölderlins Hymnen ("Der Rhein" und "Germanien")
    Seminar, upper level: Hegel, *Phänomenologie des Geistes*
Summer semester, 1935:
    Lecture course: Einführung in die Metaphysik
    Seminar, upper level: Hegel, *Phänomenologie des Geistes*
Winter semester, 1935–36:
    Lecture course: Grundfragen der Metaphysik
    Seminar, middle level: Leibnizens Weltbegriff und der Deutsche Idealismus
Summer semester, 1936:
    Lecture course: Schelling, *Über das Wesen der menschlichen Freiheit*
    Seminar, upper level: Kant, *Kritik der Urteilskraft*.

Various circumstances, some of them connected with the Nazi regime, forced Rahner to write his doctoral dissertation—which became GW—under Martin Honecker rather than, as he would have preferred, under

Heidegger. Honecker found the work unacceptable because he felt that Rahner had incorrectly interpreted Aquinas' metaphysics of cognition according to modern philosophy in general and Heidegger's philosophy in particular. Rahner did not receive the Ph.D. He left Freiburg in the summer of 1936 and eventually took a degree in theology at Innsbruck. He published his would-be doctoral dissertation in 1939 and followed it two years later with *Hörer des Wortes.* In between he published an article in French translation (the German is now lost) on Heidegger: "Introduction au concept de philosophie existentiale chez Heidegger."[14]

The question of how much Heidegger influenced GW is complicated and not easily answered. In the book itself Rahner writes:

> The limited scope of this work does not permit an *explicit*, detailed confrontation of modern philosophy from Kant to Heidegger with Thomas, nor did it appeal to me to try to make the relevance of the problems treated in the book more apparent by a few timely indications of such parallels. I hope, then, that those who are familiar with more recent philosophy will take note of these points of contact themselves.[15]

Then, in the 1941 edition of HW, Rahner mentioned Heidegger explicitly once within the text at page 81 and once in the running title at the top of page 80. In the second edition (1963) these references were struck out, and the text was altered considerably. Nonetheless, it is clear that in both of these editions Heidegger's position, as Rahner understood it, was under attack on those pages. Rahner's French article from 1940 is the only relatively full exposition and critique of Heidegger that we have from Rahner, and it is treated in Chapter III below. At this point I may simply indicate that in the late thirties Rahner had a good grasp of SZ and the book on Kant, but that he misunderstood some essential issues in Heidegger, particularly the topics of being and nothingness (*das Sein, das Nichts*), and in part the question of Heidegger's relation to metaphysics. Much more important and interesting are the parallels (perhaps they are borrowings) that I have alluded to above and that are treated in the second part of this essay.

Rahner has frequently asserted—correctly, as far as it goes—that the greatest philosophical influence on GW was the work of Father Maréchal. "I owe my most basic, decisive, philosophical direction, insofar as it comes from someone else, to the Belgian philosopher and Jesuit, Joseph Maréchal. His philosophy already moved beyond the traditional neo-Scholasticism. I brought that direction from Maréchal to my studies with Heidegger, and it was not superceded by him."[16] Of Heidegger Rahner says that "it is not specific doctrines that I have taken from

[him], but rather a style of thinking and of investigating which has proved most valuable."[17] The reference here is to the retrieval of the "unsaid" from Aquinas' text. But beyond this matter of approach there is in fact, as this essay will show, a striking convergence between GW and Heidegger's SZ. Much of the overall thrust of GW is shaped by Heidegger, as well as key issues such as abstraction and conversion to the phantasm. This similarity of some of the major strategies of GW and the work of Heidegger may have been due in large measure to Rahner's awareness that what Heidegger and Aquinas share in common—in very different ways—is Aristotle.

The present study is in two parts. The first part traces the foundations of GW in the works of Immanuel Kant, Pierre Rousselot, Joseph Maréchal, and Martin Heidegger (Chapters I to III). The second part investigates GW itself as a foundation for metaphysics (Chapters IV to VIII). In both parts of the study my concern is not historical or expository but critical; that is, I seek to ascertain, expound, and evaluate the philosophical issues that underlie Rahner's work and, insofar as it influences Rahner, the works of those he drew upon. These issues are chiefly two— in Rahner's terms, the nature of human subjectivity and the nature of subjectivity's transcendental correlate—in short, man and being. And since man's nature *is* his transcendence to being, this study is about Rahner's "transcendentalism": its sources, its internal structure, and its adequacy as a philosophical position.

In Rahner as much as in Heidegger, the two issues of man and being come down in fact to one: the nature of *movement*, not as an ontic phenomenon (e.g., locomotion) but as the ontological structure of entities, of man in particular, and ultimately of being itself. This ontological motion is the reality (*esse, das Sein*) that something has when it is not perfectly and fully in reality, the relative presence that something has while it is still absent from fulfilled actuality. Using Heidegger's terminology, we may call ontological movement "presence-with-absence" or simply "pres-ab-sence." By such a formula I am attempting to preserve the connection between Rahner's Scholastic reading of movement as *actus imperfectus* or *tendere in actum* or *actus existentis in potentia* and Heidegger's lexicon of presence and absence.

Moreover, in both Rahner and Heidegger we can distinguish an earlier and a later discussion of pres-ab-sence. In their earlier periods (for Heidegger, SZ; for Rahner, GW) both men discuss movement in terms of the essence of *man*, whereas in their later periods (in Rahner, for example, in his theological writings) they discuss the movement of "being itself." The early Heidegger calls the movement of man's essence "temporality" (*Zeitlichkeit*), whereas Rahner calls it the self-unifying unity of agent and possible intellect in cogitative sense. The later Heidegger calls the movement of "being itself" *Ereignis* (roughly "the enabling/ impropriating event"), the process whereby the finite realm of intelligibility is opened up in conjunction with man's finite transcendence. The later Rahner speaks, instead, of the movement of the ever receding absolute future—God—which draws man onward through the world. The earlier and later positions of both Heidegger and Rahner each form an internal unity. In Heidegger, the movement of man's transcendence is "the same" (*to auto*) as the movement of "being itself." In Rahner, man moves through the world only because his movement is wrapped in that of the present but receding God. Of course, it is quite another question whether the topic of *Ereignis* in Heidegger (the unexplainable eruption of the world of sense in conjunction with man's movement) has anything essential to do with the topic of theological anthropology in Rahner (man's orientation to the self-communicating God of revelation).

The difference between these two interpretations of movement seems immense. Nonetheless, I shall pose it as a thesis that movement in the general, formal sense of "ontological becoming" is the touchstone for discussing the relationship between Rahner and Heidegger. In order to distinguish this ontological movement from ontic movement, I shall use the Greek word *kinēsis* (or the adjective "kinetic") to name this ontological pres-ab-sence. In this book we shall focus mainly but not exclusively on *kinēsis* in the early Rahner and the early Heidegger, i.e., movement as the structure of man's essence.

The Scholastic term that Rahner uses to describe what he calls the nature of human subjectivity could be misleading: *reditio completa in seipsum*, the complete return to the self. This phrase seems to say that man is a self-contained monadic subject, entirely present to himself over against the world. However, as we shall see in Chapter VII, the word "complete" (*completa*) is an open and heuristic term that here simply designates the *degree* of self-presence that belongs to man—in fact a degree of self-presence that always comports a *twofold element of absence.* Man is "absent" from any supposed monadic self insofar as he is (1) present to the world in sensibility and thus always "eccentric," outside a supposed Cartesian ego, and (2) transcendent towards being as the ground of entities. What the phrase "complete return to the self" means in man's case is this: man returns to his self-transcending state of self-absence (his reach towards God) every time he knows a worldly being. That is, he is present to the world by being relatively absent from it. In Heidegger's terms we could say: he finds himself thrown (cf. *Befindlichkeit*) in among entities only because he projects the being of entities. This bivalence is man's *kinēsis*, his presence to the world and to himself on the basis of his relative absence from wordly entities. Rahner discusses this *kinēsis* in terms of (1) agent intellect as the power of abstraction, and (2) possible intellect as the power of conversion to the phantasm or of sensibility as presence to the world.

In GW, the hermeneutics of this bivalence opens the space for a transcendental metaphysics. If man's cognitive activity (and therefore his nature) is intrinsically kinetic, then so too the science of metaphysics is essentially kinetic—as Blondel put it, "the progressive science of our itinerary towards being."[18] This science simply spells out what man himself already is: a movement towards, an anticipation (never a grasp) of, the elusive ground of the real. Metaphysics is thus the index of man's finitude rather than an intuition of being as being; it is a confirmation of his kinetic, asymptotic weakness rather than a pledge of angelic purity and stasis in an afterlife. For Rahner as much as for Heidegger, in this matter of man's relation to the ground (or groundlessness) of things, *Alles ist Weg*, everything is a question of movement.[19]

It is precisely the centrality of the phenomenon of movement that allows Rahner, following Rousselot, Maréchal, and Heidegger, to overcome Kant's inadequate notion of subjectivity and his exclusion of a legitimate metaphysics from the realm of *logos* in its speculative exercise. Chapter I below sketches out the problematic and the problem of subjectivity and metaphysics as posed by Kant's *Critique of Pure Reason*. The problem for Rahner was Kant's strict limitation of theoretical reason, in its proper employment, to the categorical synthesis of sense data before the transcendental unity of apperception, and therefore the supposed impossibility of metaphysics on the basis of such a form of subjectivity. The problem, broadly speaking, is that the possibility of man's openness to the ground—or groundlessness—of reality (and for Rahner, man's openness to a possible revelation) is shifted from the theoretical to the practical reason. The question that confronts Rahner and anyone who would engage the question of metaphysics at the point of the modern transcendental turn to man is that of an adequate conception of subjectivity, and Chapter I delineates the issue of subjectivity within the framework of transcendental method.

Chapter II shows how Pierre Rousselot and Joseph Maréchal, in different but complementary ways, argued that man has an unthematic and anticipatory, but nonetheless real, awareness of the noumenal dimension of being-as-such by virtue of his finite human dynamism rather than via any intellectual intuition. Both Rousselot and Maréchal ground their work in a pre-critical reading of the nature of God as perfect self-presence, the coincidence of knowing and being in perfect self-intuition. This pre-critical interpretation, based on Thomas Aquinas, establishes the primacy of intuition—and therefore self-unity, immanence, and interiority—in the cognitional process. This insight lies at the heart of that stream within neo-Scholasticism which has come to be known as "transcendental Thomism" and of which Rahner's GW is a basic text.[20] The title of Rousselot's major work, *The Intellectualism of St. Thomas*, really means: "The Intuitionism of St. Thomas," and its chief argument, which Maréchal transposes into a transcendental mode, is that affirmation in human cognition is a dynamic substitute for the immediacy of pure intuition in angels and ultimately in God. That is, man by nature is an intuition *manquée*, a tendency towards pure and perfect actuality (Aquinas writes: "our intellect in knowing stretches into infinity"), and man knows an individual entity by introducing it, as a partial end, into his own finality or movement towards unlimited being. Man is thus himself an analogical (*pros ti*) reference to God: he is a metaphysician (one who knows entities in their being) because in some way he is a theologian (one who is projected towards God in every act of knowledge). In this interpretation, metaphysics is possible on the basis of a theoretical intellect focused on sensible entities, once one has understood the dynamic and not just the formal-synthetic nature of speculative reason.

Chapter III spells out what it was in Heidegger's early work that Rahner found usable for his own GW. Although Heidegger focuses on man's pre-predicate performances whereas Rahner takes up predicative knowledge, both men share in common the conviction that the primary issue in human *logos* is man's projective *kinēsis*. Rahner has brilliantly, if unthematically, uncovered the fact that the Aristotelian roots of the two co-equal moments of Dasein's opening of the realm of sense, namely, existentiality and facticity, are to be found, with the requisite "retrieve," in *nous poiētikos* and *nous pathētikos*. Transformed into modalities of movement and rescued from the Rube Goldberg mechanisms of medieval Scholasticism, this bivalence of active and possible intellect is the fundamental structure whereby man knows "anything-that-is" in terms of its "is-ness," its reality or being. However, if Rahner goes that far with Heidegger, in GW he stops short of reading being itself in terms of *kinēsis* and thus confines himself to the traditional interpretation of being as stable presentness ("beingness") and ultimately as the self-presence of God to himself.

Chapter IV probes the origins of Rahner's notion of being as self-presence (*Bei-sich-sein*) in the Aristotelian-Thomistic tradition in particular and in the "ousiological" tradition in general, and it argues that Rahner's transcendental starting point and his analogical procedure in the search for the meaning of being still remain encased in traditional metaphysics as ontotheology. Chapter V provides an overview of

Rahner's methodology and teleology in GW, while Chapters VI and VII—the center of the present essay—study man's cognitional bivalence under the rubrics of active intellect (abstraction) and possible intellect (conversion to sensibility). Chapter VIII shows how Rahner establishes the possibility and limits of metaphysics on the basis of man's worldly spirituality, and it argues that Heidegger's strategy of "overcoming" the metaphysics of stable presentness is approximated but finally missed by Rahner.

My treatment of GW rearranges the material of that volume for the sake of greater comprehension. The following diagram illustrates that rearrangement.

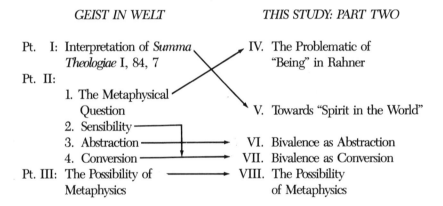

The major change is the treatment of the question of sensibility not before abstraction but rather with the material on conversion to the phantasm. It differs, in that regard and others, from a number of recent treatments of Rahner's philosophical thought.[21]

The present essay has certain internal limitations. It does not treat Rahner's *Hörer des Wortes*—his philosophy of religion—but only draws on that work insofar as it illuminates or extends the issue of cognition treated in GW. Of the two editions of GW, I use only the first, published in 1939, although I give the corresponding pagination in the second edition. The reason for this choice consists in the fact that Professor Johannes B. Metz, who supervised the second edition, made some changes in the text. Even though these changes have Rahner's approval, I prefer to cite the edition that comes directly from Rahner's hands. In the footnotes the references to GW give (1) the pagination in the first edition, (2) the pagination in William Dych's English translation, *Spirit in the*

World—which was made from the second edition—and then (3) corresponding pagination in the second German edition made by Professor Metz. To take as an example the first footnote in Chapter I below: GW 4/15 (30) refers to *Geist in Welt*, page 4 of the first German edition, which is found on page 15 of the English translation and on page 30 of the second German edition. References to *Hörer des Wortes* follow the same pattern. For example: HW 63/49 (67) refers to *Hörer des Wortes*, page 63 of the first German edition, which is found on p. 49 of the English translation and on p. 67 of the second German edition. When I cite from the English translations of Rahner's works, I frequently amend those translations without giving notice. Moreover, when several citations are made within a single paragraph, the references are often collected in a footnote later in the paragraph or at the end of the paragraph in order not to interrupt the reader.

One of the major arguments of the present essay is that the highest principle of reality in Thomistic philosophy—what Aquinas called *esse* and what Rahner calls *das Sein* (both usually translated as: being)—remains caught within the parameters of metaphysics. In order to stress that this *esse entium* or *das Sein des Seienden* (the being of beings) names the realness *of beings*, I shall, beginning in Chapter IV, translate Aquinas' *esse* and Rahner's *das Sein* as "beingness" or "being-ness." When referring to the specific and proper sense that Heidegger gives to *das Sein*, I shall use inverted commas: "being." The issue is explained in Chapter IV, A.1 and further in Chapter VIII, B.1. Moreover, in order to translate the Greek *to on*, the Latin *ens*, or the German *das Seiende*, I use both "entity" and "entities" and phrases like "a being," "the being," "the beings."

Finally, throughout this essay the words "man," "he," and "his" are intended as meaning "man/woman," "he/she," and "his/hers."

Geist in Welt is not an easy work to read. In studying some pages of it (for example, the self-contained treatise on causality that appears in Rahner's chapter on conversion to the phantasm) the reader frequently has a feeling analogous to riding a bicycle through sand dunes. But for all its difficulty it remains a brilliant treatise. While the following study is hardly adequate to Rahner's book, whatever merits it has are the fruit of the guidance and encouragement given me by Professors Ewert H. Cousins and Joseph Donceel, S.J., of Fordham University, who supervised my first trek through Rahner many years ago. The dedication of this book to them does not indicate that they agree with all its contents. It does say that they helped me to see, with regard to Rahner, the truth of something that Pierre Rousselot once wrote: "When a person enters seriously into a book on philosophy, the question is not whether the study will demand a lot of work, but whether that work will be repaid proportionately."[22]

Notes

1. Karl Rahner *Geist in Welt. Zur Metaphysik der endlichen Erkenntnis bei Thomas von Aquin*, first ed. (Innsbruck: Rauch, 1939). I use this first edition of Rahner's work, not the second edition expanded and reworked by Johannes B. Metz (Munich: Kösel, 1957). English translation by William Dych, S.J., *Spirit in the World* (New York: Herder and Herder, 1968). In the footnotes the references to *Geist in Welt* (hereafter: GW) give (1) the pagination in the first German edition, then (2) the pagination in William Dych's translation, which is made from the second edition, and then (3) the pagination in the second German edition. The reason for this is explained at the end of this Introduction. Rahner's theological essays are collected, among other places, in his *Schriften zur Theologie* (Einsiedeln/Zurich/Cologne: 1954 ff.). English translation by Cornelius Ernst et al., *Theological Investigations*, 15 vols. (Baltimore: Helicon, 1961 ff.). For bibliographical information on Rahner, see Roman Bleistein, ed., *Bibliographie Karl Rahner, 1924–1969* (Freiburg: Herder and Herder, 1969), and *Bibliographie Karl Rahner, 1969–1974* (Freiburg: Herder and Herder, 1974). Also Raul Imhof and Heinrich Treziak, eds., "Bibliographie Karl Rahner, 1974–1979," in *Wagnis Theologie*, ed. Herbert Vorgrimler (Freiburg: Herder and Herder, 1979), pp. 579-97, and Albert Raffelt, ed., "Karl Rahner: Bibliographie der Sekundärliteratur, 1948–1978," *ibid.*, pp. 598-622.
2. Dom Patrick Granfield, "An Interview: Karl Rahner, Theologian at Work," *The American Ecclesiastical Review*, XV, 3/4 (October, 1965), p. 220.
3. Rahner *Theological Investigations*, vol. 1, trans. Cornelius Ernst, p. 7.
4. Rahner, GW, xii/lii (14)
5. From Rahner's article "Anthropologie (theologische)," in *Lexikon für Theologie und Kirche* by K. Rahner and J. Höfer, 2nd ed. (Freiburg: Herder 1957 ff.); here: vol. I (1957), p. 621. The text appears in a slightly abbreviated form in *Sacramentum Mundi: An Encyclopedia of Theology*, ed. Karl Rahner, Juan Alfaro et al. (New York: Herder and Herder 1968 ff.), vol. III (1969), p. 367. On the "turn to the subject" see Karl Rahner *Theological Investigations*, vol. IV (1966), p. 324. Plato, *Meno*, 96 E: "We must then at all cost turn our attention to ourselves...."
6. Rahner, GW, 294/405 (405), for "the free spirit...destiny of the earth." GW, 295/407 (405 f.), for "all thought...sense intuition."

7. Karl Rahner, *Hörer des Wortes*, first ed. (Munich: Kösel, 1941). Hereafter: HW. I use this first edition of Rahner's work and not the second edition reworked by Johannes B. Metz (Munich: Kösel, 1963). The English translation by Michael Richards is unfortunately often incorrect (*Hearers of the Word* [New York: Herder and Herder, 1969]). In the footnotes the references to *Hörer des Wortes* (HW) give (1) the pagination in the first German edition, then (2) the pagination in the English translation, which is made from the second edition, and then (3) the pagination in the second German edition.

8. Karl Rahner, "Theology and Anthropology," in *The Word in History*, ed. T. Patrick Burke (New York: Sheed and Ward 1966), pp. 1, 2, and 14.

9. For biographical information on Rahner, see Herbert Vorgrimler, *Karl Rahner: His Life, Thought and Works*, trans. Edward Quinn (New York: 1966); Karl Rahner, *Erinnerungen im Gespräch mit Meinhold Krauss* (Freiburg: Herder, 1984); also the articles in note 2 above and note 10 below.

10. Karl Rahner, "Living into Mystery: Karl Rahner's Reflections at Seventy-five," ed. Leo J. O'Donovan, *America*, 140 (March 10, 1979), 178.

11. See Chapter II, note 70, below.

12. Martin Heidegger, *Sein und Zeit*, first ed. (Tübingen: Max Niemeyer, 1927); latest edition within Heidegger's *Gesamtausgabe* (Collected Edition) (Frankfurt: Vittorio Klostermann, 1977); English translation by John Macquarrie and Edward Robinson, *Being and Time* (New York: Harper and Row, 1962). Martin Heidegger, *Kant und das Problem der Metaphysik*, first ed. (Bonn: Cohen, 1929); fourth, expanded ed. (Frankfurt: Vittorio Klostermann, 1974); English translation by James S. Churchill, *Kant and the Problem of Metaphysics* (Bloomington, Ind.: Indiana University Press, 1962).

13. Rahner communicated this list of courses to the author in an interview in September, 1976. All the lecture courses have since been published: *Hölderlins Hymen "Germanien" und "Der Rhein,"* ed. Susanne Ziegler, *Gesamtausgabe*, II, 39 (Frankfurt: Vittorio Klostermann, 1980); *Einführung in die Metaphysik* (Tübingen: Max Niemeyer, 1953, 1966³); in English, *Introduction to Metaphysics*, trans. Ralph Manheim (New Haven, Conn.: Yale University Press, 1959); the course "Grundfragen der Metaphysik" is published as *Die Frage nach dem Ding: Zu Kants Lehre von den transzendentalen Grundsätzen* (Tübingen: Max Niemeyer, 1962); in English, *What is a Thing?*, trans. W. B. Barton and Vera Deutsch (Chicago: Regnery/Gateway, 1967); *Schellings Abhandlung "Über das Wesen der menschlichen Freiheit" (1809)*, ed. Hildegard Feick (Tübingen: Max Niemeyer, 1971); in English, *Schelling's Treatise on the Essence of Human Freedom*, trans. Joan Stambaugh (Athens, Oh.: Ohio University Press, 1985).

14. Karl Rahner in *Recherches de sciences religieuses*, XXX (1940), 152–71; English trans., "The Concept of Existential Philosophy in Heidegger," trans. Andrew Tallon, *Philosophy Today*, XIII (1969), 126-37.

15. Rahner, GW xiii/1ii (14). The references to Heidegger in Rahner's later, theological writings are few and unilluminating: *Schriften zur Theologie*, III, 95; IV, 278, n.; VIII, 67 and 177; IX, 310; X, 25 and 29; XII, 599; XIII, 143.
16. Rahner, "Living into Mystery" (see note 10 above), p. 177.
17. Granfield, "An Interview" (see note 2 above), p. 220.
18. Blondel cited in Frederick J.D. Scott, "Maurice Blondel and Pierre Rousselot," *New Scholasticism*, XXVI (1962), 345.
19. For "Alles ist Weg" see Martin Heidegger, *Unterwegs zur Sprache* (Pfullingen: Günther Neske, 1954), p. 198; English trans., by Peter D. Hertz, *On the Way to Language* (New York: Harper and Row, 1971), p. 92. Also *Vorträge und Aufsätze*, vol. II (Pfullingen: Günther Neske, 1967³), p. 59.
20. On transcendental Thomism, see Chapter II, note 2.
21. See Vincent P. Branick, *An Ontology of Understanding: Karl Rahner's Metaphysics of Knowledge in the Context of Modern German Hermeneutics* (St. Louis: Marianist Communications Center, 1974); Anne Carr, *The Theological Method of Karl Rahner* (Missoula, Montana: Scholars Press, 1977), pp. 59-123; Peter Eicher, *Die anthropologische Wende: Karl Rahners philosophische Weg von Wesen des Menschen zur personalen Existenz* (Freiburg, Switzerland: Universitätsverlag, 1970); Andrew Tallon, *Personal Becoming: Karl Rahner's Christian Anthropology*, revised edition (Milwaukee, Wisconsin: Marquette University Press, 1982), first edition published in the journal *The Thomist*, 43, 1 (January, 1979); Friedemann Greiner, *Die Menschlichkeit der Offenbarung: Die transzendentale Grundlegung der Theologie bei Karl Rahner* (Munich: Chr. Kaiser Verlag, 1978), pp. 7-136.
22. Pierre Rousselot, "L'Espirit de saint Thomas d'après un livre récent," *Etudes*, CXXVIII (1911), 625, note 1.

PART ONE

The Philosophical Foundations of Spirit in the World

CHAPTER I
Kant: Method and Metaphysics

As much as GW is a work in philosophy—and I shall treat it as such in this book—it is aimed at a theological goal that stands on the other side of its treatment of cognition: an interpretation of man as open to a possible engagement with the self-communicating God of Christian faith. Thus, what Rahner says about Aquinas' philosophy applies ultimately to his own: "In this context [i.e., the *Summa Theologiae*] the 'soul' as the essential ground of man is considered ultimately only insofar as it is the place for a *theological* event, insofar as it can be addressed by a revelation."[1]

What is at stake in GW, as in any other metaphysics, is the nature of human spirit and in particular the extent of man's openness to the ground—or groundlessness—of reality. That is why Rahner's foundations for philosophy begin at the point where the metaphysics of man took a modern turn: Kant's *Kritik der reinen Vernunft (Critique of Pure Reason:* hereafter KRV). Rahner constantly emphasizes that metaphysics gives no "new" knowledge but only the reflexive elaboration of the implicit, unthematic knowledge that man already has of himself. Therefore, if Rahner hopes to establish that man is open to the possibility of revelation (its actuality could not be known from philosophy), he must first demonstrate that man's unifying center already transcends to the ontological dimension where being and truth are one. But this is precisely what KRV denies to human subjectivity. Rahner's options, in effect, were either to by-pass the Kantian problematic of transcendental subjectivity (and so to risk putting himself outside the pale of modern thought) or to attempt to "overcome Kant through Kant." This he chose to do, with a good deal of assistance from Joseph Maréchal and Martin Heidegger.

The overriding concern of KRV is that the questions of God and the soul—the basic issues of the noumenal order—be resolved with certitude rather than by the random groping among concepts which characterized "dogmatic philosophy." And the model according to which Kant sought to reform metaphysics was the mathematical method of classical science as exemplified in Newton's physics. The initial step towards resolving the questions of God and the soul according to this scientific exigency was to show the intrinsic limitation of speculative reason: its matter is confined to the data given by the senses, and its form, in *a priori* synthetic judgments, comes from the categories of the understanding. The question behind KRV, therefore, is: What form of subjectivity is operative when man has necessary and universal—that is, true—knowledge of an object? Kant, of course, confines that subjectivity to the formal functions of synthesis and denies it any legitimate openness to the ontological realm of the in-itself-ness of objects. The question of the noumenal order, and hence ultimately the issue of man's openness to God, gets steered in the direction of the practical reason.

It is not our task to detail the consequences of that posture for the question of human access to a possible revelation. It is enough, for our understanding of Rahner, that we note the discrepancy between that understanding of human subjectivity on the one hand and the Catholic tradition that Rahner champions on the other. The First Vatican Council (1870) unambiguously asserted that the human intellect is able to demonstrate the existence of God, and this position, with its implicit defense of the integrity of intellection as a faculty of the ontological, underlies the whole of Rahner's metaphysics of knowledge.[2] The interesting point, of course, is just how Rahner works out that thesis.

The present chapter makes no pretense of interpreting KRV either as a whole or in great depth. My purpose in this chapter is simply to set the stage for Rahner. And since Rahner learned his Kant from Maréchal and Heidegger, I shall draw on those two commentators as much as possible in order to set the stage for Rahner's own work. The chapter has two divisions: (A) a brief overview of the problematic of metaphysics in KRV, and (B) transcendental method, its theory and practice, in that same work. The first division sketches the occasion and nature of Kant's "Copernican Revolution"—the impossibility of scientific metaphysics within pure speculative reason and the consequent necessity of transposing the "special metaphysical" questions to the domain of practical reason. The limited scope of the chapter dictates some compression here, and as an artificial device for organizing and summarizing the problematic of metaphysics, I shall simply gloss the first sentence of KRV. The second division of the chapter discusses transcendental method: first of all, its origins in classical physics and, more remotely, in medieval theology: secondly, its application to some problems in the Transcendental Analytic; and finally, its formal structure as a methodological technique.

A. THE PROBLEM OF METAPHYSICS

Good pedagogue that he was, Kant began KRV by telling the reader in one sentence what the following eight hundred pages were about.

Human reason has this particular fate in one species of its knowledge: it is burdened by questions which it cannot ignore, since they are proposed to it by the very nature of reason itself, yet which it cannot answer, since they transcend every power of human reason (A vii).

Those problematic questions, of course, are the metaphysical ones about God and the soul, and by the last page of the book Kant all but promises us that we may soon—by the end of the century, in fact— "secure for human reason complete satisfaction in regard to that which it has all along so eagerly occupied itself, though heretofore in vain" (A 856/B 884). There is a lot of ground covered between the statement of the problem on the first page and its promised solution on the last, and in the interests of a bird's-eye view of the terrain, I divide the first sentence into three component parts and comment on each in turn.

1. "Human Reason": The Scientific Exigency

Kant begins not with *"die Vernunft"* ("reason") but with *"die menschliche Vernunft"* ("human reason"). Was it merely a question of stylistics that moved him to say "human" reason? No, we see the adjective repeated at the end of the sentence, as if to reinforce the point. What is its significance? Heidegger notes the importance of the fact that KRV begins with human and not divine reason: only a human, that is, a finite, reason can ask the questions which spur the work on. Metaphysics is an index of finitude.

An omnipotent being need not ask, "What am I able to do?", i.e., "What am I not able to do?" Not only does such a being have no need to ask a question; it is contrary to its nature to be able to ask it. . . . Whoever asks, "What am I able to do?" betrays thereby his own finitude.[3]

The title of the work already tells us that when Kant says "human reason," he means *pure* reason, i.e., reason before it acquires its objects— not as chronologically prior but as the condition for the possibility of objects at all. KRV is about knowledge that posits itself and mediates its objects to itself: the modern subject. The word "pure," therefore, means not only "empty of objects" but more fundamentally, "related to objects in general" (cf. A 845/B 873), without taking into account the particular objects that *de facto* may be given. By human reason in the sentence cited, Kant means one "which contains the principles whereby we know anything absolutely *a priori*" (A 11/B 24; cf. B x).

Moreover, pure or *a priori* reason is *transcendental* reason. Kant uses the word "transcendental" in at least two senses.[4] On the one hand we may speak of the transcendental *subject*, insofar as it is the prior condition of the possibility of objective knowledge. On the other hand, we may speak of transcendental *knowledge*, the reflexive awareness that the knowing subject has of itself as the *a priori* determination of the object to be known. As an instance of the first, Kant will speak of the "transcendental unity of apperception," whereas it is the second usage he has in mind when he writes his classical formula: "I entitle *transcendental* all knowledge which is occupied not so much with objects as with the mode of our knowledge of objects insofar as the mode of knowledge is to be possible *a priori*" (B 25; cf. A 56f./B 80f.). Heidegger neatly encompasses both meanings of the term, i.e., man's precursory relation to object in general and his reflective awareness of that relation:

> The transcendental is what concerns transcendence. Viewed transcendentally, thought is considered in its passing over to the object. Transcendental reflection is not directed upon objects themselves nor upon thought as the mere representation of the subject-predicate relationship [as in traditional logic], but upon the passing over [*Übersteig*] and the relation to the object—as *this relation*.[5]

But human reason is not only pure, prior, transcendental reason: insofar as it can know *a priori*, it can be *scientific* reason. In Kant as much as in Aristotle, science is knowledge through the necessary *aition*, through the ground or reason or explanation that is responsible for the object as object. Insofar as the *aition* allows the thing to be what it is, it metaphysically precedes, or is prior to, its *explanandum*. In that sense, *aition* is "essence," i.e., "what enables the thing to be what it is." And necessary, certain (scientific) knowledge is *a priori* cognition which relates to the object in terms of its prior ground or essence. "The priority of the *a priori* concerns the essence.... The *a priori* is the title for the essence of things."[6] To be sure, Kant is not operating within the Aristotelian framework. Yet he shares in common with the above analysis the conviction that what constitutes reason as scientific is its prior relation to its objects. "If reason is to be a factor in these sciences [e.g., mathematics and physics], something in them must be known *a priori*" (B ix).

The issue of scientific reason brings us to the heart of Kant's Copernican Revolution. If reason is to become scientific, the prevailing notion of knowledge as a "copy" of objects must be radically reversed. Were the representations that make up our knowledge mere "photos" of objects "out there," reason could in no way anticipate objects; that is, it could not establish anything *a priori* in relation to them by means of pure concepts. In order to lay the groundwork for a scientific reason, Kant must initiate a revolution in the metaphysical conception of reason, comparable to the upheavals in thought which had previously brought mathematics and physics to the state of real sciences.

> Hitherto it has been assumed that all our knowledge must conform to objects. But all attempts to extend our knowledge of objects by establishing something in regard to them *a priori* by means of concepts have, on this assumption, ended in failure (B xvi).

However, the example of scientific reason in both mathematics and physics provides a new model for thinking. In mathematics from the very beginning (Kant cites the example of the demonstration of the properties of the isosceles triangle), there took place a revolution in thought which recognized the precursory, anticipatory—that is to say, *a priori*—nature of scientific thinking. "If he [the mathemetician] is to know anything with *a priori* certainty, he must not ascribe to the figure [of the triangle] anything save what necessarily follows from what he himself has set in accord with his concept." (B xii). And sometime later in the sixteenth century, physicists like Galileo

> learned that reason has insight only into that which it produces after a plan of its own, and that it must not allow itself to be kept, as it were, in nature's leading-strings, but must itself show the way with principles of judgment based upon fixed laws, constraining nature to give answer to questions of reason's own determining (B xiii).

The nature of scientific reason as anticipatory or prior is clear: reason "must adopt as its guide [in investigating nature] that which it has itself put into nature" (B xiv).

This exemplary progress of mathematics and physics towards scientific status prompts Kant to ask whether philosophy itself should not attempt "to alter the procedure which has hitherto prevailed in metaphysics, by completely revolutionizing it in accordance with the example set by the geometers and physicists. . ." (B xxii).[7] "We must make trial whether we may not have more success in the tasks of metaphysics, if we suppose that objects must conform to our knowledge" (B xvi). This is the clear path to *a priori* and scientific knowledge, for:

understanding has rules which I must presuppose as being in me prior to objects being given to me, and therefore as *a priori*. They find expression in *a priori* concepts to which all objects of experience necessarily conform and with which they must agree (B xvii f.).

The alternative would exclude metaphysical reason from science.

> If intuition must conform to the constitution of objects, I do not see how we could know anything of the latter *a priori;* but if the object (as the object of the senses) must conform to the constitution of our faculty of intuition, I have no difficulty in conceiving such a possibility (B xvii).

In fine, a scientific reason must be an *a priori* reason—but that requires a revolution in the conception of thought. Out with the copytheory of knowledge, and in with a "new method of thought, namely, that we can know *a priori* of things only what we ourselves put into them" (B xviii). To return to the words we have been glossing: the phrase *"die menschliche Vernunft"* announces the *Copernican Revolution*, which, according to Kant, "forms indeed the main purpose of this critique of pure speculative reason" (B xxii).

2. "Questions It Cannot Answer": The Scope of Speculative Reason

The "species of its knowledge" in which human reason finds itself "burdened" is, of course, speculative knowledge, and there Kant points to the three questions of God, immortality, and freedom. These questions come from that area of metaphysics which had come to be called "special metaphysics" and which fell first into dogmatism and then into skepticism, and which finally had become a battleground (A ix and B xv). Because it is "the common fate of human reason to complete its speculative structures as speedily as may be, and only afterwards to inquire whether the foundations are reliable" (A 5/B 9), these questions will remain a burden and find no solution until reason turns back upon itself to reestimate the materials that go into the building of the edifice (Transcendental Doctrine of Elements) and then project an adequate building plan for the structure (Transcendental Doctrine of Method; System of Pure Reason).

The three questions, Kant says, are not occasional ones that strike only philosophers. They are issues "in which everyone necessarily has an interest" (A 840 n.), and their solution is the "ultimate aim to which the speculation of reason in its transcendental employment is directed" (A 798/B 826). "Indeed, we prefer to run every risk of error rather than desist from such urgent inquiries, on the ground of their dubious character, or from disdain and indifference" (A 3/B 7). Kant, in fact, frequently speaks of reason as being *impelled* by its own nature to raise and resolve these ultimate questions of freedom, immortality, and the existence of God (B 22; A 797/B 825).

> ...Metaphysics actually exists, if not as a science, yet still as natural disposition *(metaphysica naturalis)*. For human reason...proceeds impetuously, driven on by an inward need, to question.... Thus in all men, as soon as their reason has become ripe for speculation, there has always existed and will always continue to exist some kind of metaphysics (B 21).

Among the three issues, that of freedom is the first and foremost, "the keystone of the whole architecture of the system of pure reason and even of speculative reason" for "through the concept of freedom, the ideas of God and immortality gain objective necessity and legitimacy and indeed subjective necessity (as a need of pure reason)."[8]

By stating that the solution of these questions cannot be had in speculative reason ("one species of its knowledge"), Kant summarizes in one stroke the whole import of the Transcendental Logic. In its legitimate employment, human speculative reason is limited to its logical use in relation to sense experience: "...we must never venture with speculative reason beyond the limits of experience" (B xxiv). But then there is the paradox "that we can never transcend the limits of possible experience, though that is precisely what this science is concerned above all else to achieve" (B xix). KRV thus has both a negative and a positive result: the limitation of pure speculative reason to sense experience, and the clearing of the way for eventual answers obtained through practical reason. We take up the first result now.

The three "special metaphysical" questions concern the noumenal order, but theoretical reason is limited, in it scientific role, to the phenomenal. The argument may be formalized as follows. (1) Kant, we said, is concerned to establish metaphysical reason as scientific reason, that is, a reason which knows *a priori*. (2) But reason knows *a priori* only what it has constituted or, from the other perspective, only what conforms to or "copies" reason, and not *vice versa*. Here what was said about human, i.e., finite, reason comes into prominence. An infinite, divine reason constitutes the "objects" of its knowledge wholly, insofar as they depend on that reason for their very existence. On the other hand, human reason as finite is a receptive reason.[9] It does not constitute the thing in itself (the noumenal nature of the entity in question) but only one aspect of the thing: its objectivity as an appearance to the human knower. (3) But an object appears to be a knowing power only through intuition, and for man as finite reason, that entails a receptive, *sense* intuition. Since sense does not exhaust the thing in itself, human reason can have prior or scientific knowledge not of the thing in its in-itself-ness but only of the thing insofar as man can relate to it: only as phenomenon.

Another way to establish the same point is to clarify the meaning of "knowledge" as contrasted with mere "thought." Kant writes: "To *know* an object I must be able to prove its possibility [cf. *aition*: that which possibilizes], either from its actuality as attested by experience, or *a priori* by means of reason" (B xxvi n.). Kant, of course, is concerned with the latter. But to prove the possibility (the ground or "essence") of something *a priori* is precisely to "put" that possibility "into" the thing, for "we can know *a priori* of things only what we ourselves put into them [*hineinlegen*]" (B xviii). Now, man cannot ground things as they are in themselves, for that would be to create them. All he can know of beings is that of them which he determines or constitutes: beings as they appear to him.

> [Human] knowledge has to do only with appearances and must leave the thing in itself as indeed real *per se*, but as not known by us (B xx).

> We have no concepts of understanding, and consequently no elements for the knowledge of things, save insofar as intuition can be given corresponding to these concepts; and . . . we can therefore have no knowledge of any object as thing in itself, but only insofar as it is an object of sensible intuition, that is, an appearance (B xxv f.).

But why must we hold that the thing in itself is real? Kant's not unproblematic answer is: because otherwise we would "be landed in the absurd conclusion that there can be appearance without anything that appears" (B xxvi f.). Without going into the problems attendant upon Kant's theory of the thing in itself or the solutions to which it gave rise in German Idealism and neo-Kantianism, we may simply note Kant's position that, whereas human reason can only *know* (prove the possibility of) appearances, it can *think* the thing in itself, so long as it observes the law of non-contradiction (cf. B xxvi, n.).

In short, because the human intellect is at once finite and *a priori* or constitutive, it is limited, as regards scientific knowledge, to appearances alone. With that, the general thrust of the Transcendental Analytic is announced (". . . all this is proved in the analytic part of the critique," B xxvi). Likewise we see that, insofar as metaphysics wants to be the science of the noumenal order,[10] there can be no metaphysics in the legitimate sense within the domain of pure speculative reason. Yet the paradox remains that the transcendence of possible experience is precisely what man, as *metaphysica naturalis*, seeks to achieve. Must reason set aside the three questions which impel and burden it but which it cannot answer?

3. "Questions It Cannot Ignore": The Shift to Practical Reason

The problems of freedom, immortality, and the existence of God cannot be answered by speculative reason since they transcend its critically delimited powers, yet they cannot be brushed aside, since they arise from the natural metaphysics inscribed in man as man. These "three cardinal propositions are not in any way necessary for *knowledge*, and yet are strongly recommended by our reason" (A 799/B 827). What, then, is the source of man's drive to transcend experience and reach these issues? "Is this endeavour the outcome merely of the speculative interests of reason? Must we not regard it as having its source exclusively in the practical interests of reason?" (A 797/B 825).[11]

Because the categories of pure speculative reason have a legitimate employment only in terms of the matter of sense experience, any attempt to use them in relation to the noumenal order will only end in the transcendental illusions studied in the Transcendental Dialectic. But insofar as KRV, in its negative function, points up this deficiency in speculative reason, it has the positive function of opening the way to the legitimate and correct resolution of the three questions by pure practical reason. Kant finds it necessary "to deny *knowledge* in order to make room for *faith*" (B xxx), for the "importance [of the three cardinal propositions], properly regarded, must concern only the *practical*" (A 800/B 828).

> So far, therefore, as our Critique limits speculative reason, it is indeed *negative;* but since it thereby removes an obstacle which stands in the way of the employment of practical reason, nay threatens to destroy it, it has in reality a *positive* and very important use. At least this is so as soon as we are convinced that there is an absolutely necessary *practical* employment of pure reason— the *moral*—in which it inevitably goes beyond the limits of sensibility (B xxv).

It is not our task to follow the solution Kant presents in the *Critique of Practical Reason*, nor to note the influence of this attempted solution on the Idealism of Fichte or even on Maréchal's effort to "overcome Kant through Kant." Our purpose in this chapter is merely to set the stage for Rahner, and the central point at stake in that regard is the Transcendental Analytic's delimination of the legitimate function of theoretical reason. And within that arena, the somewhat unthematic issue is transcendental method, not primarily as a formal technique for establishing explicit philosophical positions but more deeply as the structure and function of transcendental subjectivity as it pursues (cf. Aristotle's *methodos*) its realm of proper objects.[12]

B. THE PROBLEM OF METHOD

The Copernican Revolution is what KRV is about, and as such the treatise is an effort to establish a new "method" on the basis of which general metaphysics can be erected anew and the questions of special metaphysics resolved. "It is a treatise on the method, not a system of the science itself" (B xxii).

The new method which emerges in KRV is not an isolated event in the history of Western philosophy but the climax of a long tradition of the "turn to the subject." Therefore, in what follows we seek to show its origins in the classical physics of the modern period and in certain elements of earlier philosophy. Then we shall watch the method at work in the Transcendental Analytic, and finally we shall sketch out its formal structure. In the section that immediately follows we shall draw on Heidegger's reflections on "mathematical method."

1. The Method of Modern Science

The main purpose of KRV, Kant asserts, is "to alter the procedure which has hitherto prevailed in metaphysics, by completely revolutionizing it in accordance with the example set by the geometers and physicists" (B xxii). Kant does not speak of science in general but of the modern science exemplified by Galileo's experiments and Newton's treatises. He does not have in mind, therefore, Aristotle's conception of science as worked out in the *Posterior Analytics* and applied, for example, in the *Physics*. And yet, as we have seen, something in common remains. What then is it that makes science specifically "modern"? And how does the method of that kind of science indicate a revolutionary new emphasis on the knowing subject?

There can be no doubt that modern science is distinct from its ancient and medieval predecessors and that the sixteenth and seventeenth centuries made great progress in a new direction. But the problem lies in discerning precisely what makes for the distinction and the progress, and here we must be careful not to fall into popular (perhaps ultimately positivist) readings of the difference. Does the modernity of science lie in the fact that it deals with data rather than with general propositions?

Or that it experiments rather than philosophizing? Or that it measures and calculates rather than seeking "causes"? But Galileo's greatness, as well as that of all the major scientists of the modern period, consists in the fact that he did philosophize and did know that without hypotheses there are no facts. Medieval and modern scientists together were both experimenters *and* philosophers in their science; indeed, the medieval scientist may have been more empirical than the modern insofar as he did not rely as much on mathematical formulae, even if he did work with measurement and number.

I have suggested that the popular interpretation of the distinction between ancient and modern science is "positivist" because it seems to presume that scientific facts somehow simply lie "out there" in the world and need simply to be collected into some kind of order—without the aid of philosophical presuppositions—for there to be science. But Heidegger argues at length that the greatness of the sixteenth and seventeenth century scientists consisted precisely in the philosophizing that undergirded their work. "They understood that there are no mere facts, but that a fact is only what it is in the light of the fundamental conception [of a science] and always depends upon how far that conception reaches."[13]

Scientific knowledge (or any knowledge for that matter) is never a brute encounter between two "things," the scientist and the datum. Knowledge for a human being requires mediation whereby the data are structured in a intelligible framework "prior" to the sense encounter (not chronologically, of course), for if the data are to be *known*, they must have some common ground with the intellect, i.e., must conform to some exigency of human knowing. There must be an *a priori* possibility of encounter with the data, an affinity between intellect and the knowable, an intelligible horizon or "world" within which data are humanly encounterable by the knowing power. There are no "mere facts" that the positivist may blindly collect—if only because he has already decided which "facts" are to be collected. There are, rather, data implicitly or explicitly interpreted within an intelligible framework which establishes them as facts of such and such a kind and which allows the knower to "see" and to understand them.

Heidegger continues: "Both Galileo and his opponents saw the same 'fact.' But they interpreted the same fact differently and made the same happening visible to themselves in different ways."[14] Descartes says as much in the Fourth Rule of his *Rules for the Direction of the Mind:* "Necessaria est Methodus ad rerum veritatem investigandam." Here Descartes is not making the somewhat bland assertion that every science needs a formal technique. Rather, as Heidegger points out, Descartes is claiming that "the procedure, i.e., how in general we are to pursue things *(methodos)*, decides in advance what truth we shall seek out in things."[15] The positivist error consists in not recognizing that natural science in the modern era is shot through with philosophical presuppositions, and necessarily so. "There is no presuppositionless science, because the essence of science consists in such presupposing, in such prejudgments about the object."[16]

Therefore, the essence of modern science as distinct from the ancient cannot be found in experimentation or in the abolition of philosophical presuppositions as guides for research. Nor can it reside in the discovery of new and more accurate tools for calculating and measuring. In what, then, does the distinction between the two periods of science consist? Modern science works on two fronts, on the one hand there is the work of observation, measurement, collection of information, graphing of it and generation of formulae to express it. On the other hand there is the "pre-understanding" that governs *how* the scientist will collect the data and *what* data will be "visible" for the act of collection. Galileo, for example, operated with the pre-understanding that nature would fit Euclidean geometry, a presupposition that we do not necessarily entertain today. Kant himself recognizes both areas of work when he writes of modern physics:

> Reason, holding in one hand its principles, according to which alone concordant appearances can be admitted as equivalent to laws, and in the other the experiment which it has devised, must approach nature in order to be taught by it (B xiii).

We note the priority of the pre-understanding over the experiment: Kant says the latter is devised "in conformity with these principles" of the pre-understanding.

Now, it is precisely a radical shift in the pre-understanding of the possible objects of knowledge that constitutes the momentous shift from medieval to modern science. In *Being and Time* Heidegger notes:

> Scientific research accomplishes, roughly and naively, the demarcation and initial fixing of the areas of its subject-matter. The basic structures of any such area have already been worked out after a fashion in our pre-scientific ways of experiencing and interpreting that domain of being in which the area of subject matter is itself confined. [. . .] The real "movement" of the sciences takes place when their basic concepts undergo a more or less radical revision which is transparent to itself. The level which a science has reached is determined by how far it is *capable* of a crisis in its basic concepts.[17]

If we can discern the new pre-conception that made a datum be a scientific fact for modern science, that is, the new set of presuppositions in terms of which the modern scientist projected the intelligible framework of possible encounter with data, we shall catch a glimpse of what prompted Kant to initiate a revolution in the idea of philosophical reason.

Heidegger calls the pre-understanding of modern science "mathematical method," and he uses the term not exactly in Descartes' sense and certainly not to indicate that modern science uses higher arithmetic. Although the *science* of mathematics is basic to modern science, the import of that kind of mathematics is only in terms of its function in experimentation, not in terms of the pre-conception which guides the experiment. Mathematical *method*, however, characterizes the pre-conception. We may begin to discern the essential function of that method in a phrase from Galileo's description of his experiment with free fall. "Mobile super planum horizontale projectum *mente concipio* omni secluso impedimento. . . ."[18] The emphasized words are the clue. Galileo says that he *conceives in his mind* a moving object on a horizontal plane from which every obstacle has been removed. Of course it is in his mind. There are and can be no such planes without obstacle in reality, where there will always be friction. The experimenter's mind, therefore, runs ahead of all physical data to project an intelligible framework that will govern his experiment. It is this anticipatory or *a priori* character of thought that characterizes the meaning of "mathematical method."

Heidegger analyzes how the term "mathematical" is derived from the Greek. The verb *manthanō* means "I learn," *mathēsis* is the act of learning (or secondarily, the doctrine to be learned), and *ta mathēmata* are those things which can be learned and taught. Heidegger translates *mathēsis* as "taking cognizance" *(zur Kenntnis nehmen)*, and he asks what kind of "taking" this might be. When we learn or "take cognizance" of something—say, learning how to drive a car—we already know, in some way or other, *what* the car is (we hardly learn that by practicing at the wheel); yet, in learning how to drive, we do gain some new knowledge. We appropriate the car as our own; we learn what we *already* know but now in a explicitated, differentiated, and mediated way. Thus: *"Ta mathēmata*, the mathematical, is that 'about' things which we really already know. Therefore we do not first get it out of things, but, in a certain way, we already bring it with us." *Mathēsis*, therefore, as the act of "taking into knowledge," or learning, "is an extremely peculiar kind of taking, a taking where he who takes takes only what he actually already has."[19]

We can see how the question of numbers (mathematics in the usual sense) is a special and particularly clear instance of the broader meaning of *mathēsis*. If we find three things before us, the number "three" is what we already necessarily know in order to be able to recognize *(man-thanein)* these things as "three" things. The number three is not the three objects but rather, as Heidegger says, "that evident aspect of things [*jenes Offenbare an den Dingen*] within which we are always already moving and according to which we experience them as things at all and as such things."[20] The mathematical method as a process of learning (as contrasted with that which is learned) is thus the "fundamental position which we take towards things and by which we take up things as already given to us and as they should be given." In its barest form mathematical method—not a technique but a structural characteristic of man—is the anticipation-of-what-can-be-anticipated. It is the precursory projection of the realm of that which is *a priori* in relation to objects.

It is clear that Galileo's *"mente concipio"* is such a projection. Prior to any encounter with data, the scientist projects (consciously anticipates) an intelligible framework that will give meaning or intelligibility to the data. He states a law about nature and accepts the data only in terms of that law. He does not haphazardly collect stuff lying about, but "runs ahead" of the data with his axioms and theorems. In projecting a hypothesis, he builds, as it were, a foundation (-thesis) under (hypo-) the data, constructs the model to which the data must conform if they are to be accepted in the experiment. Kant says as much in his description of reason in modern physics. When reason seeks to learn from nature

> it must not do so in the character of a pupil who listens to everything that the teacher chooses to say, but of an appointed judge who compels the witnesses to answer questions which he has himself formulated. Even physics, there-fore, owes the beneficent revolution in its point of view entirely to the happy thought, that while reason must seek in nature, not fictitiously ascribe to it, whatever (as not being knowable through reason's own resources) has to be learnt from nature if it is to be learnt at all, it must adopt as its guide, in so seeking, that which it has itself put into nature (B xiii f.).

By way of conclusion we may note the following characteristics of the mathematical method operative in classical physics. (1) It is an act of the thinking subject (cf. *mente concipio*) which transcends things by precursorily projecting a horizon in which the datum may show itself. (2) Insofar as the project thereby establishes, prior to the data, a pre-determined criterion for recognizing and evaluating the data, it is axio-matical (cf. the Greek *axiō*, "I evaluate"). The axioms of modern science function as the fundamental pre-conceptions or evaluations in terms of which the data are recognized. (3) As such, the projection is an anticipation of the ground or "essence" of the objects to be known, their conditions of possibility. (4) The precursory projection is that on the basis of which things can appear to a knower at all as objects for a knowing subject.

Hidden at the base of all modern science is the act of the subject who projects a horizon or world within which meaning can happen. The new method of modern science thus marks a decisive "turn to the subject." But if one looks more closely at mathematical method from certain perspectives of medieval philosophy, one might note a formal homology with certain elements of the medieval description of God's creative relation to the world. There too we find an "anticipation" of beings on the part of God's creative act which "projects" the world. God's prerogative is precisely and in a preeminent sense that of the *a priori*, in comparison with which the remainder of reality is *a posteriori*. The roots of the mathematical method whereby Kant revolutionized metaphysics may go deeper than classical physics.

2. Knowledge and *A Priori* Determination

This section is already on the way towards observing the practical function of transcendental method in KRV. But we pause for a moment to compare the method of KRV with a certain understanding of the normative state of knowledge in God as read by some medieval thinkers. Apart from occasional and very important references to divine knowledge in KRV, Kant does not make this issue an explicit concern of his own. Yet, Heidegger argues convincingly that the model of divine knowledge functions as a basic negative norm (albeit an implicit one) in KRV.

We begin again with Kant's assertion that "we can know *a priori* of things only what we ourselves put into them" (B xviii), and we recall the claim that for Kant as little as for modern science is knowledge ever a raw encounter between knower and known. This issue is the arena of encounterability between the mind, which cannot become an mere object, and the object, which must assume the characteristics of mind if it is to be knowable. It is the intelligence that sets the standard for the encounter and the norm of the correlativity or affinity that holds between it and its object. In order to know, the human mind must have—or better, *be*—a precursory reference to the domain of encounterability. Therefore, it must be prior to the object that is to be known. This does not mean that the human mind constitutes the knowable object in existence, but only that, upon the condition of sensible reception of the data, it constitutes *a priori* the conditions for the encounterability of the knowable object.

This position parallels the medieval discussion of the formal object of knowing powers: *Quidquid recipitur, recipitur secundum modum recipientis* (Whatever is received, is received according to the mode of the receiver). To relate this in terms that bring us closer to Kant, we may say that the spontaneity of the human knower is found in the prior projection of the horizon of possible encounter between knowing subject and knowable object. This prior projection "transcends" the data and thus is "transcendental." When Kant says that we have *a priori* knowledge only of what we contribute to things, he is implicitly asserting that knowledge is the prerogative of "act," of spontaneity rather than of receptivity, of activity rather than of passivity. In short, knowledge determines rather than copies.[21] Man is a knower to the extent that he determines the object-as-knowable. If we recall that in KRV Kant is always dealing with necessary, universal, scientific knowledge after the pattern of classical physics, we may indeed say that "*a priori* knowledge" is a tautology. Knowledge as scientific is measured by the antecedent presence of the object "in" the faculties of the subject. Or conversely, it is measured by the antecedent presence of the subject "in" (i.e., its determination of) the object to be known.

What is revolutionary about this Kantian position is that Kant is speaking specifically of *human* reason as an *a priori* determination of objects. In the phrase "to know is to determine *a priori*" a medieval philosopher could easily recognize the characteristics of divine cognition as creative. But Kant speaks of man's knowledge in these terms. Is it possible that Kant's determination of knowledge stands in the long tradition that reaches back at least to the medieval conception of God's cognition as constitutive of the objects he knows? Is there a hidden theological basis to trancendental method?

In its general ontology of cognition, mainstream medieval Scholasticism held that the normative principle of knowledge is God. (See the following chapter.) For God, to know the other is to create the other; or conversely, to be an "object" of God's knowledge is to be known—creatively—into existence. We may think of St. Augustine's words: "It is not the case that God knows all creatures, both spiritual and corporeal, because they exist, but rather that they exist because he knows them." Or John Scotus Erigena's, "Where beings are known, there they are; indeed they are nothing more than their being known"—by God, of course. Or Aquinas' "They [i.e., natural things] cannot exist except by reason of the divine intellect which keeps bringing them into being."[22]

Within Aquinas' thought, truth is the proper term of the intellect, and to know is to know the true. But the ultimate basis for the truth of the creature is its relation to the divine creative intellect. "Truth is primarily in a thing because of its relation to the divine intellect..., because it is related to the divine intellect as to its cause." These texts could be multiplied.[23] We have no difficulty in recognizing here the position that God's knowledge of the creature is prior and constitutive insofar as it grounds the creature in its very truth, existence, and objective reality.

Now, in KRV—that is, in the Copernican Revolution—Kant effects a radical shift in the definition of the finitude of the finite human being. In the general lines of medieval philosophy, the finitude of creatures consisted in the fact that they were not their own ground but were related to a grounding ground external and prior to them. Founded on its created relation to God (Aquinas: *"creatio est quaedem relatio ad Deum cum novitate essendi"*[24]), the creature had its meaning because it was finite, i.e., referred to the divine idea which was its creative ground or condition of possibility. In KRV, however, the finitude of beings is founded not on the reference to divine intellection but on the reference of beings to the human, sensibly receptive intellect. And the grounding ground for finite beings in their knowability is not creation but the *a priori* constitutive powers of the human intellect. This is not to say that Kant would deny creation or the finitude that is correlative with it, for his phenomena are always limited by the thing-in-itself, the ontological "inseity" ("in-itself-ness") of the entity. The *Ding-an-sich* is defined ultimately by its relation to the creative intellect. (In Maréchal's terms, KRV thus represents a "precisive" rather than an absolute epoché of the noumenal order.) Nonetheless, the revolutionary quality of KRV in this regard is clear. The work no longer moves in the Leibnizian framework that Kant accepted prior to 1776, where God's constitutive creative idea (the "adequate notion") was the prior factor operative in man's knowledge of objects. Rather KRV limits itself to the specifically human *a priori* factor and deals only with objects as appearances. In so doing, Kant preserves the formal character of knowing as *a priori* determination.[25]

The above is concerned with the act of knowing in its first moment of being directed upon the object. Transcendental method, however, is a reflexive mode of knowing wherein, in the second order, the degree and kind of the subject's constitution of the object is thematized. Transcendental method specifically disengages the determining activity of the subject from the constituted object and recognizes the subject's determining presence in the object. This reflexive moment shows that, if the truth (objective reality) of the thing is determined by its relation to a constituting intellect, then the object as known is nothing other than the object as constituted, and the subject's degree of objective knowledge is in direct proportion to the antecedent presence of the object in the subject's knowing powers. Since knowledge is the prerogative of act, the centrality of finitude again comes to the fore. Infinite knowledge is infinitely spontaneous; it is the act of relating to . . . , which suffers no reciprocal being-related-unto. Human knowledge, on the other hand, is only finitely spontaneous and therefore only partially constitutive of the object. Thus the finitude of the human subject gets defined in KRV in terms of receptivity rather than createdness. The human knower must find his data factually "on hand"; he cannot "produce" the object totally. This receptivity is specified as "sensibility," but this latter does not primarily mean "having sense organs" but rather means being "receptive" or "non-creative."[26]

The goal of transcendental method is to penetrate to the very constitution of the known object by the knowing subject, to reveal the genesis of objectivity out of subjectivity, to show the very "becoming-objective" of the object. By uncovering the active contribution of the subject to the known object, transcendental reflection breaks the "naive viewpoint" or "natural attitude" which looks upon known objects as somehow subsisting "out there" apart from human activity.[27]

Transcendental method as a technique has two distinct but complementary moments. First, there is the reduction of the object to the subject's constitutive activites (the reductive or regressive phase of the technique), i.e., the movement from the object as posterior, to the faculties of the subject as prior. Secondly, there is the exhibition of the very possibility of the objectivity of the object from out of and on condition of the subject's determining powers (the deductive or progressive phase). We shall return to this later. But for just a moment we may wonder whether these two moments are present, analogously, in the *Summa Theologiae:* the *quinque viae* as the reduction of the creature to the creatively constitutive powers of God, and the treatise on creation (S.T. I, q. 27) as the "deductive" phase, the exhibition of God's creative power as the condition of the possibility of the creature. Be that as it may, what is at least shared in common in this regard by both KRV and a work like the *Summa* is the fact that in neither case is the "method" a proof, and in both cases it is circular. The same holds of Leibniz's *via inventionis* and *via demonstrationis*. In *analogous* ways (and we are insisting on no more than that), all three cases evidence a reduction of finite things to their possibility in the positing, constitutive powers of an *a priori* determining intellect. Just as the *Summa* does not, strictly speaking, "prove" that God exists or that he creates, so neither does KRV "prove" that objects must conform to human knowing. Rather, Kant *assumes* the apriority of knowing and shows what, on that assumption, must be the case. There is a kind of circularity not totally unlike that of *mathēsis* (coming to know explicitly what one already knows implicitly). The subject is defined as that which determines the objectivity of the known object; the object is defined in terms of its constitution by the subject; and KRV shows what follows from those assumptions. The circularity, of course, is not the vicious circularity of a *petitio principii* unless *principium* be taken in its most fundamental sense as the essence or origin of something. In that case, the circularity of the method is the same circularity characteristic of all human activity as metaphysical: a reaching out to (a *petitio* of) the ground (or groundlessness) of whatever is in question.[28]

3. Knowledge and Unification in Consciousness

In the final analysis, transcendental method is nothing other than the proper reflexive functioning of trancendental subjectivity. Transcendental method is (1) a technique with a formal structure, (2) for the purpose of revealing transcendental subjectivity, (3) and in fact a technique carried out by the very subjectivity that it reveals. As we shall see in later chapters, transcendental method properly interpreted becomes "hermeneutics" or "self-interpretation" (in the sense of the German *Auslegung*, "laying out in the open," rather than the German *Interpretation*[29]). In the previous section we pointed out that such self-interpretation reveals that "to be an object" means "to be before an intellect which is the ground of its truth" (to radically adapt a phrase: *ens et verum convertuntur*).[30] In the present section we move directly into some themes of Kant's Transcendental Analytic in order to show that "to be an object" means "to be before a unified and unifying consciousness" (*ens et unum convertuntur*). For man to know an object is for him to say in effect "*I* think this"; hence, being-an-object means that the thing participates in the formal unity of consciousness as an "I think. . . ." As in the previous section, so too here we shall read Kant against the background of some general issues in the medieval understanding of divine knowledge. We take up three topics: (a) the normative principle of objective unity in consciousness, by reference to divine creative knowledge as unification of the "object"; (b) human synthetic unity as transcendental apperception; and (c) the necessity and use of the categories. Again, our treatment of these issues in KRV is schematic and entirely at the service of setting the stage for Rahner. It is guided by those interpreters through whose eyes Rahner read Kant.

The Divine Norm of Knowledge. To say (as Thomism does) that God, as the norm of the knowledge of the other, knows an object by creatively grounding it in himself, is to say as well that the known object is unified in itself before the self-identical consciousness of God. In Scholastic philosophy, creative knowledge makes a thing be this *one* thing and knows the object in its simple entirety in one single glance. To judge by this normative condition, we would have to say that objectivity is measured by the degree of unifying power in the consciousness of the knower. If to know is to determine *a priori*, and if to know is likewise to unify the known, then to know is to determine *a priori* the unity of the known before consciousness. We may look at the same issue from the side of the object. If to be a creature is to be one thing before a divinely creative, determining intellect, then the degree of the unity of the object in the act of knowing is directly proportionate to the degree of the knower's unifying power. If we bring both perspectives together, we can establish a general, analogical definition of knowledge according to Scholastic principles: to know is to be conscious of a unified object in a unifying ego. God's unity of consciousness (his "I think") creatively unifies the object entirely and all at once by creating or totally constituting the thing. Man's unity of consciousness (his "I think")—as finite/non-creative and yet still constitutive—requires that data be first given to him before he can bring that data to unity in a known objectivity. Man's consciousness is thus a unifying unity rather than an "already-having-unified" unity. In contrast with divine knowing, which unifies *totum simul*, man is always "bringing something *into* unity." His knowledge is a synthetic unity.[31]

In Leibniz's terms, God's creative idea, as the "adequate notion" of a thing, knows the necessary unity of the S with all its Ps, and it knows this all at once, insofar as God brings the creature into being. But in human knowing, the act of judgment is the necessary substitute for the all-at-once-ness of creative unifying. Man knows only by com-posing (*synthesis*) and simultaneously taking-apart (*dia-airesis*) this P and this S. Whereas in God the very "I think" immediately supplies the manifold as united (and all of this *ex nihilo*), in human receptive, non-creative knowing the manifold must be given as *to be united*. In fact, man cannot have self-consciousness at all except insofar as he synthesizes a sensibly given manifold. Kant writes:

> An understanding which through its self-consciousness could supply to itself the manifold of intuition—an understanding, that is to say, through whose representation the objects of the representation should at the same time exist—would not require, for the unity of consciousness, a special act of synthesis of the manifold. For the human understanding, however, which thinks only and does not [intellectually] intuit, that act is necessary (B 138 f.).

Furthermore, it is clear that because knowledge (and hence the unify-ing of the known object) is the prerogative of act or spontaneity, unity cannot be accomplished within sense knowledge, but rather only by the understanding. Again Kant:

> The combination (*conjunctio*) of a manifold in general can never come to us through the senses, and cannot, therefore, be already contained in the pure form of sensible intuition. For it is an act of spontaneity of the faculty of rep-resentation... (B 129 f.).

In what way is that the case?

Unification in Transcendental Apperception. In every synthesis of the manifold of sense there must be an antecedent norm of unity which gov-erns the act of bringing-into-unity; otherwise we might have a random collection but no synthesis in the proper sense. Kant writes: "But the concept of combination includes, besides the concept of the manifold and of its synthesis, also the concept of the unity of the manifold" (B 130). Heidegger explains:

> This act of reflective unification is possible only if it is itself guided by a pre-cursory reference to a unity in the light of which all unification becomes pos-sible. The act of representation, quite apart from whatever concept arises from its action, is already the precursory act of representation of a unity which as such guides and directs the work of unification.[32]

Since the synthesis in question is one of knowing, the governing unity (the *unum* in terms of which one unifies) is the unity of self-consciousness, the "I think," for if a knower cannot say "*I* think this," the object is certainly not known.

> It must be possible for the "I think" to accompany all my representations; for otherwise something would be represented *in me* which could not be thought at all, and that is equivalent to saying that the representation would be im-possible or at least would be nothing *to me* (B 131 f., emphasis added).

The meaning of the "in me" is that the data is passively received in the senses, whereas the "to me" refers to the object as brought to synthetic unity before self-consciousness. In God, as creative knower, there is no distinction between the "in" and the "to," for he does not sensibly receive the being but spontaneously creates it in its unity. In man there is such a distinction and hence a need to bring the manifold to unity. The synthe-sis of understanding, guided by the unity of self-consciousness, is what mediates the "in me" and the "to me."

In man, moreover, the "I think" can be spoken only insofar as it is directed upon a given manifold. Man has no self-consciousness without synthesis of the manifold, no perception of the self which is not likewise synthetic perception of the other. His unity of self-consciousness is thus always and only an *apperception*, a self-perception along with, or in the act of being directed to (*ad, ap-*), the object to be known. Man is conscious of his identity only when he has a manifold that he can call his, that is, only when he can say that the whole multiplicity of data belongs to one representation of an object on the part of the subject.

> But this amounts to saying that I am conscious of myself as a need for synthesis of representations—to be entitled the original synthetic unity of apperception—under which all representations that are given to me must stand, but under which they have also first to be brought by means of a synthesis (B 135 f.).

Kant states that this principle of the need for synthetic unity of apperception is an analytic principle. The following polysyllogistic reconstruction of his argument lays out the analytic nature of the principle of apperception. To know is to say "I think this," hence to call the data "mine." But for data to be mine, they must fulfill all the conditions whereby they can indeed be mine. Those conditions come down to one: the data must stand before an identical self-consciousness, an "I think." But the manifold of data is always just that: a multiplicity. Therefore, the manifold must be united before and by a unified self-consciousness which accomplishes its own unity in the very unifying of the manifold. Thus, the very definition of human self-consciousness contains the principle of synthetic apperception, and the principle stated above is analytic.

> Although this proposition makes synthetic unity a condition of all thought, it is. . .itself analytic. For it says no more than that all *my* representations in any given intuition must be subject to that condition under which alone I can ascribe them to the identical self as *my* representations, and so can comprehend them as synthetically combined in one apperception through the general expression "I think" (B 138).

> As *my* representations (even if I am not conscious of them as such) they must conform to the condition under which alone they *can* stand together in one universal self-consciousness, because otherwise they would not all without exception belong to me (B 132 f.).

So far we have considered the unity of apperception only as synthesis. It remains to be seen why that synthetic unity requires the use of categories, and why categories are the condition for the objectivity of the object to be known; that is, why the unity of apperception is a transcendental unity which antecedently renders that objectivity possible.

The Necessity and Use of the Categories. If the synthetic unity of apperception is itself already a concept of unity, why does it require a set of diverse categories in order to bring the manifold before self-consciousness?[33] We proceed in three steps.

First of all, *sense* intuition necessarily mediates the data and the unity of apperception. In all knowing it is intuition which presents the data, and in human knowing it is receptive intuition which does so.

> In whatever manner and by whatever means a mode of knowledge may relate to objects, *intuition* is that through which it is in immediate relation to them. . . . But intuition takes place only insofar as the object is given to us. This again is only possible, to man at least, insofar as the mind is affected in a certain way [i.e., sensibly] (A 19/B 33; cf. A 35/B 51).

If there were no mediation of the unity of apperception and the datum itself—if, that is, there were no sense knowledge—the unity of consciousness would be creative of the object. On the other hand, if in receptive or non-creative knowledge the unity of apperception were somehow *itself* the immediate relation to the data, it would be the unity of sense and not of understanding. But in human knowing there must be both a mediated relation to the data (for the unity of apperception is not the unity of sense) and a sensible, i.e., receptive, relation to the data (for human knowing is not creative). Therefore, sense intuition necessarily mediates the data and the unity of apperception.

Secondly, sense intuition must comprise the form of *time* as well as that of space. If the form of sense intuition were only space (i.e., homogenous quantity), the sensed object would be experienced only in one undiversified way (roughly put, as "out there"). Hence there could be no diversity in the relation of the unity of apperception and the data, and as a result there would be only one mode of unification possible before the unity of apperception. One concept (one act of synthesizing) would apply to all objects. But we know that we work with a diversity of concepts, each concept being a way in which self-consciousness is aware of the unity of objects. For example, we experience the data not merely as present in one homogenous space but as present in a simple "now" or over a series of "nows" with a "before" and "after," and this temporality provides the possibility of the sensibilization or schematization of the categories. Thus, over and above our experience of space we have a mode of sense intuition that perceives the given as temporal, and sense intuition must comprise the form of time (the succession of the "now sequence") as well as that of space.

Thirdly, the relation of apperception to sense must therefore itself be diversified: there must be a *plurality of categories*. For each way that an object can be given in sense there must be a way for the unity of apperception to unify the manifold of that object if it is to be known at all as a unified thing. This is merely to say that we judge about objects in a variety of modes or that the judgment, as the synthesis whereby the manifold is brought before the unity of apperception, can be performed in a number of ways (cf. Aristotle's *to on legetai pollachōs*). But the categories are the rules of unity that govern the synthetic unifying of judgment. Therefore, there must be a variety of categories as rules for the unity of self-consciousness.

With that, the essential lines of the trancendental deduction in the second edition of KRV have been sketched out. If we accept that the manifold, in order to become an object of knowledge, must be synthesized before self-consciousness, and if we further agree that the act of so synthesizing is the logical form of judgment, then we will accept that the categories, as the rules of the judgment, are the conditions under which all data must stand or to which data must conform in order to be an object for the human subject. As Kant states it programmatically in his Preface:

> The understanding has rules which I must presuppose as being in me prior to the objects being given to me, and therefore as *a priori*. They find expression in *a priori* concepts to which all objects of experience necessarily conform, and with which they must agree (B xvii f.).

This brings us to the heart of KRV and therefore to the battleground on which Rahner will raise the standard of the possibility of some kind of metaphysics within the *speculative* or theoretical function of human reason: knowledge of the being of entities—inclusive of the highest entity—within an intellection that is necessarily confined to sense experience ("spirit *in the world*"). To do that, Rahner will have to both accept and revise the Kantian understanding of transcendental method as the functioning of transcendental subjectivity. His revision—let us say "retrieval"—is the subject of later chapters. For now we turn to the formal structure of transcendental method as a technique of thought in Kant.

4. Transcendental Method in KRV

Kant's *claim* to have worked out a "method peculiar to transcendental philosophy" different from "all *dogmatic* methods, whether borrowed from the mathematician or specially invented" (A 737 f./B 765 f.) is clear, but a search through the Transcendental Doctrine of Method, where we would expect to find it elaborated, is ultimately disappointing. The methodology which governs KRV (we prescind from the "analytic" method of the *Prolegomena*) can only be teased out of its actual performance in the Transcendental Aesthetic and Transcendental Analytic. And even there it is fraught with problems as regards both its operation and its very claim to validity as a method. All we can hope to do is to reconstruct it formally and somewhat ideally from its concrete employment. The first task is to lay out the claims that the method makes about itself. Later we may raise questions about their legitimacy as claims.[34]

Unlike traditional empiricism, which, resolutely adhering to the factuality of experience, moved inductively from facts as experienced to generalizations and hypotheses based on those facts, Kant's method seeks the essential nature of factual experience by attempting to argue demonstratively (not inductively) from experience to its necessary conditions of possibility. This constitutes the method's *reductive phase*, which claims to operate according to the exigencies of logical presupposition. In this phase, Kant, although not unproblematically, contributes his most fundamental and original insights to the issue of method. And since the technique is not a free-floating, formal construction but rather grows out of Kant's material insights into the nature of transcendental subjectivity, here is where we expect to find the core of the Copernican Revolution. If this phase of the method reaches its term in establishing the apriority of the formal elements of all experience, the *deductive phase* reverses the movement and argues from the *a priori* forms to the validity of the truths which they supposedly ground. Prior to both of these phases we may speak of a third (i.e., first) phase: the initial analysis of the structure of experience at all. As a whole, then, the trancendental method begins with experience, arises to its *a priori* presuppositions, and then descends to *a priori* truths.

The second and third moments of the method—the regressive-reductive and the progressive-deductive—operate together in both the Aesthetic and the Analytic. In the Aesthetic, the reductive phase is capsulized in the Metaphysical Exposition of the concepts of space and time (A 22/B 37 and A 30/B 46), while the deductive phase is found in the Trancendental Exposition of the same concepts (cf. B 40 f. and 48 f.). In the Analytic, the reductive phase is found generally in the Analytic of Concepts, and the deductive phase in the Analytic of Principles. (Note: The deductive phase of the transcendental *method*, which is found in the Analytic of Principles, is not to be confused with the trancendental deduction of the pure concepts of understanding, which corresponds to the *reductive* phase of the method and is found in the Analytic of Concepts.[35])

However, these divisions are not always clear and distinct in KRV. In the Transcendental Analytic, for example, the Analytic of Principles (corresponding to the third or deductive phase of the method) in fact only prolongs the reductive methodology at work in the Analytic of Concepts (the second phase of the method), as we shall see in a moment. Likewise, in the Transcendental Aesthetic the term "Metaphysical Exposition" is hardly geared to revealing clearly its function as a transcendental deduction (reductive phase of the method) of the forms of space and time. Kant recognizes this problem when he writes retrospectively: "We have already, *by means of a transcendental deduction*, traced the concepts of space and time to their sources. . ." (A 87/B 119 f., emphasis added). And where do we find the first phase of the method, i.e., the preliminary analysis of the structure of experience? It must be culled from sentences in the Introduction and in the Transcendental Aesthetic. In this whole matter, confusion is well-nigh inevitable, and any sorting out of the steps in the transcendental method in KRV remains an idealization. Kant clearly was pioneering rather than polishing transcendental method. Nonetheless, within those limitations, we may sketch out the ideal three phases of the method.

The Preliminary Analysis of Experience.[36] KRV wants to begin at a point that is both *de facto* uncontested and *de jure* uncontestable: experience, taken not as the raw data of sense impressions but in the full sense of the product of sense and understanding acting cooperatively. Within that arena Kant first makes the distinction between matter and form and then further divides form into sensuous and categorial. The preliminary analysis of the structure and ingredients of experience thus yields material and formal elements: (1) Material: the discrete sense qualities, (2) Formal, sensuous: the forms of sense intuition, space and time, and (3) Formal, categorial: the pure concepts of the understanding, the relational or categorial elements of experience.

> In the transcendental aesthetic we shall, therefore, first *isolate* sensibility, by taking away from it everything which the understanding thinks through its concepts [= (3) above]. . . . Secondly, we shall separate off from it everything which belongs to sensation [= (1)] so that nothing may remain save pure in-

tuition [= (2)]. . . . In the course of this investigation it will be found that there are two pure forms of sensible intuition. . . namely, space and time (A 22/B 36).

The distinction of matter and form appropriates outright the traditional understanding of the formal as that which is structural, determinative, and relational—the principle of unity—and the material as that which gets determined and structured by its subsumption under form—the principle of multiplicity. "That in the appearance which corresponds to sensation I term its *matter;* but that which so determines the manifold of appearance that it allows of being ordered in certain relations I term the form of appearance" (A 20/B 34). The material element is given apart from the subject's activity, although not entirely passively, and the formal elements are the subject's active and determining contributions.

This *de facto* analysis, which investigates experience directly and reads off its three moments, makes no claim to *a priori* groundedness at this point. It does represent an improvement over, for example, the Humean empirical analysis of experience, insofar as it discerns, beyond the atomic impressions, experience's structural and relational elements. However, this *de facto* analysis is only preliminary and neither complete nor adequate. At this point in the method, for example, no basis is given for the division of the formal element of experience into the sensuous and the material. Moreover, there is no adequate analysis of sensuous matter, and indeed the method will concentrate entirely on the formal elements and have nothing to contribute to a philosophy of the sensible as such apart from the forms of intuition. The point of this phase is simply to establish *that* there is a formal element in experience.

The Regression from Experience to its Conditions of Possibility.[37] The Introduction to the second edition of KRV opens by saying: "There can be no doubt that all our knowledge begins with experience. . . . [But] it does not follow that it all arises out of experience" (B 1). If the first phase of the method discovered that there are indeed formal elements in knowledge, the second (reductive or regressive) phase is devoted to establishing that these elements are *a priori* and adhere in the subject. The argument is presuppositional and moves from experience to its necessary conditions of possibility; that is, it seeks to show that experience as previously analyzed is possible only if the formal features found *in* experience are prior conditions *of* experience. It is a separate question whether the argument is purely logical and demonstrative, as Kant claims, or whether in fact it is psychological as well. In any case, basic to the argument is the presupposition which Kant shares with the tradition, namely, that the formal elements, as unifying and universalizing, are the prerogative of an entity that is in act, i.e., spontaneous. Kant adapts the position to say that the formal elements in experience cannot be merely given but must be contributed by the subject. From the discernment of the logical apriority and necessity of the formal elements, he moves to a subjective or idealistic location of apriority "in the mind" (cf. A 20/B 34).

In the Transcendental Analytic the reductive phase is found in the Metaphysical Expositions, and here we need not delay. The ideal structure of the argument for the apriority of space may be formalized as follows.

(1) Those elements of experience without which experience is impossible are necessary. (2) Now space is an element of perceptual experience without which such experience is impossible. Hence (3) space is necessary. But (4) necessity is an infallible criterion of the *a priori*. Therefore (5) space is an *a priori* form of the mind.[38]

The difficulties which remain unsolved in the Metaphysical Exposition are well known.[39] Our purpose is simply to underline the claims and the formal movement of the transcendental argument on the basis of the rule that "we cannot represent to ourselves anything as combined in the object which we have not ourselves previously [i.e., *a priori*] combined" (B 130). At the level of sense knowledge we discover a unified manifold, present to consciousness. The unified manifold thus bespeaks both a unified multiplicity and a formal unifier (preliminary analysis of experience). Since by definition the unifying element cannot be from the multiplicity itself, we reach the first level of *a priori* constitution, the unifying forms of intuition (pure forms of sensibility) in which the first synthesis of the object appears.

But the ultimate condition of synthesis must come from the understanding, that is, from self-consciousness working through the pure concepts as rules of unity. Thus in the Transcendental Analytic the regressive-reductive moment of the method is devoted to the deduction of the categories, again on the basis of the structural analysis of experience given above. The first step is the metaphysical deduction of the categories, a supposedly exhaustive inventory of all the rules of synthesis, derived from the forms of judgment as the clue or *Leitfaden* for the discovery of all pure concepts of understanding (A 67/B 92 et seq.). The goal of this moment of the deduction is to show that these categories and no others are exhaustive of the realm of categorical thinking in pure reason. As Kant writes: "Now I maintain that the categories, above cited, are nothing but the conditions of thought in a possible experience, just as space and time are the conditions of intuition for the same experience" (A 111).

Kant's claim to have deduced the complete and closed body of categories on the basis of his Table of Judgments is open to serious question. What is beyond dispute, however, is why he chose to arrive at the categories in this way. In Greek, *kata-agoreuein* means to accuse someone in the open court (*agora*) of being the one who did this or that. A *katēgoria* thus became the naming of what something *is*. As a philosophical term, a category is a representation of the essence or being of things, and it sustains the ordinary worldly discourse which gets developed into assertions or judgments, *logoi*. Thus the assertion or *logos* can serve as the clue for the discovery of the underlying categories. So too, the categories as the determinations of the being or essence of things (and this is metaphysics in one stream of the tradition) are, when thematized as a science, logic (knowledge of *logos*) and, specifically in Kant, transcendental logic. Kant's metaphysical deduction of the categories within the Transcendental Logic is thus no more a question of epistemology than is Hegel's *Science of Logic*. Both are metaphysical efforts within a transcendental framework.[40]

The second and more important step in this reductive phase of the method is the (objective) transcendental deduction of the categories. The goal is the demonstration of how the pure concepts relate *a priori* to objects and thus render experience possible.

> The objective validity of the categories as *a priori* concepts rests, therefore, on the fact that, so far as the form of thought is concerned, through them alone does experience become possible. They relate of necessity and *a priori* to objects of experience, for the reason that only by means of them can any object whatsoever of experience be thought (A 93/B 126).

We can see from this text the implicit syllogism. Experience as analyzed above is characterized by objectivity. But the necessary condition of that objectivity is the categorial. Therefore, on the basis of the principle that concepts which yield the objective ground of the possibility of experience are for this very reason necessary (A 94/B 126), the categories are necessary and *a priori*. How may one show that experience is impossible without categories? Professor Wood remarks: "The elimination [of the categories] can only be performed... imaginatively by a thought experiment.... De-categorize experience and it dissolves into a mere phantasmagoria of sense qualities haphazardly distributed over the spatiotemporal field like pigments carelessly daubed on a canvas."[41] Is such a thought-experiment a demonstrative proof? Not really, for whereas we might be able to legitimize the generalization that all experience is categorial, the claim that the categories are *a priori* "in the mind" is more in the order of a hypothesis than a logically necessary demonstration. On the other hand, this state of affairs may not undermine the transcendental argument but only reveal its necessarily circular character.

The Progression from Presuppositions to Valid Knowledge.[42] If the second phase of the method sought to show that the formal elements of experience are *a priori*, this last phase seeks to validate *a priori* knowledge by making the inference from the categories to the truths they ground. At stake, then, is the validity of the synthetic *a priori* judgments that make use of and are constituted by the pure categories. In the Transcendental Aesthetic this "deductive" phase of the method is carried out in the Transcendental Expositions of space and time.

> I understand by a transcendental exposition the explanation of a concept [here read: a form of intuition] as a principle from which the possibility of ...*a priori* synthetic knowledge can be understood (B 40).

At stake in the Transcendental Exposition is the validation of the truths of mathematics on the presupposition that space and time are *a priori* forms. In the Transcendental Analytic, and specifically in the Analytic of Principles, the purpose is to validate the fundamental propositions of the natural sciences on the basis of the apriority of the pure concepts of the understanding. The reductive phase had shown only that categories (globally) are universally and necessarily valid for actual and possible experience. However, the deductive phase now seeks to show that the synthetic *a priori* propositions that articulate the various categories and apply them to experience are themselves valid. The move is from *a priori* categories to *a priori* true knowledge. But, as Professor Wood points out, Kant's "proofs" in the System of all Principles of Pure Understanding "are, for the most part, deductions of the individual categories rather than proofs of the correlative synthetic *a priori* principles, and accordingly they illustrate the second and not the third step in the transcendental procedure."[43] It may be that Kant gives us not an inference from the category to the truth it grounds so much as a propositional articulation of the universal and necessary applicability of the concept already transcendentally deduced in the prior phase.

This fact shows the difficulty of isolating precisely where the second phase of the method ends and the first phase begins. Contrary to Professor Wood's schematization of the method, which we have followed up to this point, it is possible that the "deductive" phase of the method is already operative in the transcendental deduction of the categories and in the transcendental exposition of the forms of intuition. Kant himself seems to hint at this possibility when he writes, concerning the *whole* of the Transcendental Aesthetic: "We have already, by means of a transcendental deduction, traced the concepts of space and time to their sources, and have explained and determined their *a priori* objective validity" (A 87/B 119 f.). Does not the question of "objective validity" include that of the knowledge grounded by the concepts? In that case, the purpose of the reductive phase in the Analytic would be to show that we do in fact use categories (Metaphysical Deduction), whereas the deductive phase would show that we cannot *not* use categories, i.e., that they are—both as categories and in their form as principles—the *a priori* ground for the objectivity of objects-for-the-subject. This seems to be Kant's meaning of "deduction" when he writes at the beginning of the second chapter of the Analytic of Concepts:

> Jurists, when speaking of rights and claims, distinguish in a legal action the question of right (*quid juris*) from the question of fact (*quid facti*); and they demand that both be proved. Proof of the former, which has to state the right or the legal claim, they entitle the *deduction* (A 84/B 116).

If we apply this to Kant's own deduction of the legitimacy of the categories discovered in the metaphysical deduction (*quaestio facti*), then the deductive phase of the method (*quaestio juris*) would cover both the second chapter of the Analytic of Concepts ("Transcendental Deduction") and the second chapter of the Analytic of Principles ("Principles of Pure Understanding").

The question is complicated and points again to the fact that Kant uses and applies the method without ever bothering to stop and thematize it for itself. No small part of the problem may lie in the hurried conditions in which Kant put the entire work together.

More important are the questions about the legitimacy of the claims that Kant makes for the method. And since the method as a technique is but the expression of Kant's positions on transcendental subjectivity, the problem becomes that of the adequacy of his concept of the subject. The question that haunts Kant's transcendentalism, as well as positions like Husserl's which draw upon him, is whether it succeeds in overcoming psychologism. At stake is not the vulgar psychologism which would reduce all truth to the relativism of individual egos but rather what, following Husserl, we might call "transcendental psychologism." The problem forces us back to Kant's very starting point in "experience." We may grant Kant the propriety of taking, as the original datum of his transcendental analysis, objects "in consciousness," prescinding from their representing any ontological in-itself-ness. But how can he abstract from their adherence in a psychological subject? And then is not his Transcendental Logic simply the logic of a transcendental psyche? This would explain the ease with which Kant moves from his analyses of the logical necessity of formal ingredients to his position on the ideality of the *a priori* forms "in the mind." It would also explain why his arguments, which claim to be purely logical and demonstrative, in fact rely on psychological argumentation (especially in the Aesthetic), and necessarily so. But rather than fundamentally solving the transcendental problematic, this whole stance (which Husserl himself adopted more and more after his *Logical Investigations*) only sharpens the question of whether modern subjectivity can lay claim to philosophical groundedness and ultimacy.

One very radical alternative is that proposed by Professor Wood, namely, that "the whole transcendental paraphernalia" be abandoned and that the salvageable insights be "expressed in the language of present-day psychology and epistemology."[44] A second and more philosophical alternative was that pursued by German Idealism. It consisted in elevating subjectivity beyond the realm of the finite subject-object relation and taking it in the direction of the absolute point of unity, the original ground or *telos* of history. But if Hegel thereby regained for speculative knowledge the thing-in-itself that Kant had denied to it, he did so at the expense of sublating finite subjectivity into infinite subjectivity in a form of consciousness that became "adequate to a history which, having unfolded all of its potentialities, essentially has completed its course."[45] This is what Rahner (correctly or not) calls "the mad and secret dream of equality with God."[46] Perhaps this dream was already prepared for by St. Augustine's notion of the human being as a *mens secreta* that, in faith, knows itself to be privy, through illumination and grace, to the divine mind. Much later that Augustinian notion was continued (much transformed) in the Leibnizian notion of the world as a rational system and in Leibniz's invitation to the philosopher, as a secularized *mens secreta*, to analyze "backwards" (*via inventionis*) to God's creative, causative idea (the "adequate notion"), from which vantage point all the properties of the notion could supposedly be deduced (*via demonstrationis*). And even though the Leibnizian adequate notion no longer serves in Kant as the ground for deducing scientific knowledge in the world of nature, we may see elements of continuity with Leibniz in Kant's insistence on the necessity of the regulative function of the ideas of pure speculative reason.

What presses to the fore, then, is the question that, even though it seems to arise out of the modern "turn to the subject" in Descartes and Kant, in fact reaches back far behind them: the question of how to arrive at an adequate understanding of the reality of what Kant calls "subjectivity" and what the tradition has always concerned itself with, whether thematically or not, under such titles as *nous, logos, mens, intellectus, ego, Vernunft, Geist, Existenz, Dasein.* Could it be (we recall the first words of KRV) that the issue at stake in all these titles is human finitude? That certainly was the issue for Rahner, as it was for his teacher, Martin Heidegger. And yet as we saw, Kant insists that, for all man's finitude, he is nonetheless impelled towards the question of God. If metaphysics is the index of finitude, finitude is the demand for metaphysics. These three issues—man, metaphysics, and God—motivated the thinkers who, on this side of the transcendental revolution, mediated the transcendental problematic to Rahner. It is to these thinkers that we now turn.

Notes

1. Rahner, GW 4/15 (30). On Heidegger's own early self-characterization as a theologian, see Karl Löwith, *Heidegger: Denker in dürftiger Zeit,* 3rd ed. (Göttingen: Vandenhoeck und Ruprecht, 1965), p. 145.
2. See Karl Rahner, *Theological Investigations,* trans. Cornelius Ernst et al., 16 vols. (Baltimore: Helicon, 1961ff), I [1961]. 82 ff.
3. Martin Heidegger, *Kant and the Problem of Metaphysics,* trans. James S. Churchill (Bloomington, Ind.: Indiana University Press, 1962), p. 223. See also pp. 27-39.
4. Joseph Maréchal, S.J., *Le point de départ de la métaphysique,* 2nd & 3rd eds. 5 vols. (Paris: Descleé, de Brower and Brussels: L'Edition Universelle, 1943-1949), III [1949], 113-16.
5. Martin Heidegger, *What is a Thing?,* trans. W. B. Barton, Jr., and Vera Deutsch (Chicago: Regnery-Gateway, 1967), p. 176.
6. Heidegger, *What is a Thing?,* p. 165-66.
7. For the similar situation in Maréchal, see E. Dirven, *De la forme à l'acte: Essai sur le thomisme de Joseph Maréchal* (Paris and Bruges: Desclée de Brouwer, 1965), pp. 54-55.
8. Immanuel Kant, *Critique of Practical Reason,* trans. Lewis Beck White (New York: Bobbs-Merrill, 1956), pp. 3 and 4.
9. Heidegger, *Kant and the Problem of Metaphysics,* pp. 35-39 (divine reason) and 27-34 (receptive reason).
10. On metaphysics as the science of the noumenal, see Maréchal, *Le point de départ,* III, 306, n. 1.

11. On the question of Rousseau's influence on Kant's shift to the practical reason, see Hermann-J. de Vleeschauwer, *The Development of Kantian Thought: The History of a Doctrine*, trans. A.R.C. Duncan (London: Nelson, 1962), p. 39.
12. On Fichte, see Maréchal, *Le point de départ*, IV [1947]. On *methodos* in Aristotle, see *Physics*, G 200 b 12 ff., and Martin Heidegger, "On the Being and Conception of *Physis* in Aristotle's *Physics*, B, 1," trans. Thomas Sheehan, *Man and World*, 9 (1976), 246.
13. Heidegger, *What is a Thing?*, p. 67.
14. Ibid., p. 90.
15. Ibid., p. 102.
16. Ibid., p. 180.
17. Martin Heidegger, *Being and Time*, trans. John Macquarrie and Edward Robinson (New York: Harper and Row, 1962), p. 29.
18. Heidegger, *What is a Thing?*, p. 91. For the present discussion of mathematical method, see pp. 69-98.
19. Heidegger, *What is a Thing?*, pp. 74 and 73.
20. Ibid., p. 75.
21. On knowledge as *a priori* determination, see Maréchal, *Le point de départ*, V [1949], 53.
22. St. Augustine, *De Trinitate*, XV, 13 (P.L. 42, 1076); cf. VI, 10 (P.L. 42, 931). John Scotus Erigena in *Selections from Medieval Philosophers*, ed. Richard McKeon (New York: Scribners' Sons, 1929), p. 120. (Cf. his "What is there astonishing if the idea of things which the human mind possesses . . . be understood as the substance of the very things of which it is the idea— that is, in the likeness of the divine mind in which the idea of the whole created universe is the substance of that whole," [Ibid., p. 118.].)
23. The above citation is from *De Veritate* I, 4. Cf. S.T., I, 14, 10, c. ("The knowledge of God is the cause of things," etc.); *De Veritate*, I, 2 ("things are measured by the divine intellect in which are all created things"); S.T., I, 16, 5, c. ("things are true insofar as they express the likeness of the species in the divine mind").
24. *De Potentia Dei*, III, 3.
25. On the notion of "finitude" in medieval philosophy and in KRV, see Martin Heidegger, *The Essence of Reasons*, trans. Terrence Malik (Evanston: Northwestern University Press, 1969), p. 63. On phenomena as limited by the thing-in-itself, see Paul Ricoeur, "Sur la phénomenologie," *Esprit*, 21 (1953), 821-23, and "Kant et Husserl," *Kant-Studien*, 46 (1954-1955), 44-47. On Maréchal's position on the "precisive" epoché, see his *Le point de départ*, V, [1949], 158. On KRV and the shift from divine to human apriority, see *Le point de départ*, IV, 35 ff.
26. On the derivation of sense organs from the receptivity of human knowledge, see Heidegger, *Kant and the Problem of Metaphysics*, p. 31; and Rahner, GW 250/344 (345).
27. On the genesis of objectivity, see Maréchal, *Le point de départ*, III, 111 ff.

On breaking the naive viewpoint, see Ricoeur, "Kant et Husserl," pp. 47-49.

28. On "petitio principii," see Heidegger, "On the Being and Conception of *Physis*," pp. 225-26.

29. The difference between the two words is spelled out in the translators' note to Heidegger, *Being and Time*, p. 19, n. 3.

30. Cf. Pierre Rousselot, *L'Intellectualisme de saint Thomas*, 2nd. ed. (Paris: Beauchesne, 1924), pp. 11-12; English trans., *The Intellectualism of St. Thomas*, by James E. O'Malony (New York: Sheed and Ward, 1935), p. 25.

31. See Heidegger, *Kant and the Problem of Metaphysics*, p. 84.

32. Ibid., p. 57.

33. Cf. Maréchal, *Le point de départ*, II, 161-68.

34. For the following I am largely indebted to Ledger Wood's classic essay, "The Transcendental Method," in *The Heritage of Kant*, ed. George Tapley and David F. Bowers (New York: Russell and Russell, 1962), pp. 3-35. See also Johannes B. Lotz, "Die transzendentale Methode in Kants *Kritik der reinen Vernunft*," in *Kant und die Scholastik heute*, ed. Johannes B. Lotz (Pullach/Munich: Berchmanskolleg, 1955), pp. 35-108; Kenneth Baker, "Rahner: The Transcendental Method," *Continuum*, II (1964), 51-59; Joseph Maréchal, *Le point de départ*, V, 51-66, in English: Maréchal, *A Maréchal Reader*, ed. and trans. Joseph Donceel (New York: Herder and Herder, 1970), pp. 71-86; Otto Muck, "The Logical Structure of the Transcendental Method," *International Philosophical Quarterly*, 9 (1969), 342-62. For "analytic" method, see Immanuel Kant, *Prolegomena to Any Future Metaphysics*, trans. Paul Carus, revised, Lewis Beck White (New York: Liberal Arts Press, 1951), pp. 11, 22-23, 26, 30, and Wood, pp. 31-35. The relation of transcendental method to transcendental Thomism is studied in Otto Muck, *The Transcendental Method*, trans. William D. Seidensticker (New York: Herder and Herder, 1968).

35. I here follow Professor Wood's analysis; but for criticism of this approach, see below.

36. Wood, "The Transcendental Method," pp. 4-10. Cf. Maréchal on Kant's starting point: *Le point de départ*, III, 109.

37. Wood, "The Transcendental Method," pp. 10-25.

38. Ibid., p. 12.

39. Ibid, pp. 12-18.

40. On "category" and *kata-agoreuein*, see Heidegger, "On the Being and Conception of *Physis*," p. 232. On Hegel's logic as metaphysics, see Hegel, *Science of Logic*, trans. W.H. Johnston and L.G. Struthers, 2 vols. (London: George Allen & Unwin, New York: Macmillan, 1929) I, Preface to the First Edition and Introduction, pp. 33-37 and 53-70.

41. Wood, "The Transcendental Method," p. 22.

42. Ibid., pp. 26-31.

43. Ibid., p. 29.

44. Ibid., p. 35.

45. Nicholas Lobkowicz, *Theory and Practice* (Notre Dame, Ind.: Notre Dame

University Press, 1967), p. 159. See as well Emerich Coreth, "Zu Fichtes Denkentwicklung: Ein problemgeschichtlicher Durchblick," *Bijdragen* 20 (1959), 229-41; "Vom Ich zum absoluten Sein: Zur Entwicklung der Gotteslehre Fichtes," *Zeitschrift für katholische Theologie*, 79 (1957), 257-303; and "Dialectic of Performance and Concept," *Spirit as Inquiry: Studies in Honor of Bernard Lonergan*, ed. Frederich E. Crowe, *Continuum* (1964), 447-54. Maréchal treats Fichte and German Idealism in his fragmentary *Le point de départ*, IV.

46. Karl Rahner, "The Concept of Existential Philosophy in Heidegger," trans. Andrew Tallon, *Philosophy Today*, 13 (1969), p. 136.

CHAPTER II

Rousselot and Maréchal: Transcendental Thomism

In the Preface to GW Rahner writes: "If Pierre Rousselot and Joseph Maréchal are mentioned more than others, this should emphasize that I feel the work particularly indebted to the spirit of their interpretation of Thomas." And later he wrote of Maréchal alone that his works "are without doubt the best explanation of Kant according to the spirit of St. Thomas."[1] Pierre Rousselot (1878-1915) and Joseph Maréchal (1878-1944), both Jesuit priests, stand at the head of that current within neo-Scholasticism that has come to be known as "transcendental Thomism," in the mainstream of which we find Rahner's own philosophical efforts. Both of them, that is, undertook a "retrieval" of St. Thomas (a reinterpretation of certain possibilities in his thought) in terms of the modern problematic of the "turn to the subject." Although this confrontation between Kant and Aquinas is more thematic and elaborate in Maréchal, it is already at work in the truncated philosophy of his predecessor, Rousselot.[2]

It is to the credit of both Rousselot and Maréchal, that they faced the critical problematic squarely, engaged it at the crucial point of difference between St. Thomas and Kant—the question of the noumenon—and worked through the problem from a position on subjectivity that surpassed Kant without surrendering his legitimate insights. As in part with German Idealism, so too with Rousselot and Maréchal the task was to restore to speculative reason a positive metaphysical function that was not simply regulative, but without claiming for human knowing any intuition beyond the sensible. From a new reading of the human subject Rousselot and Maréchal sought to show that a second-order speculative affirmation of God and the soul could properly be grounded in the implicit first-order affirmation of absolute reality performed within every judgment about the world.

Therefore, balancing and guiding Rousselot and Maréchal's vigorous engagement with Kant's *formalistic* critique of the subject was an equally intense advancement of the traditional theme of the *dynamism* of subjectivity. While Maréchal enriched this thematic by his studies of Fichte, Rousselot found its roots in St. Augustine's *Fecisti nos ad te* and in Plato's *Symposium* (the soul as *eros* for ultimate reality). Rousselot, for example, writes: "The desire for God is the dynamic and active element of knowledge: man understands things only insofar as he desires God."[3] This interior movement of the soul towards absolute reality is the basis of Rousselot's (and later Maréchal's) attempt to build an "interiorized Scholasticism" that would reground Thomas' objectivist metaphysics on a transcendental base.

But just as their reading of subjectivity is much richer than Kant's, so too is the historical scope of their transcendental turn much broader. In fact, it reaches back to the origins of the philosophical tradition. Rousselot, for example, not only speaks of "the intimate relation that holds between the Thomisitic theory of knowledge and that of St. Augustine," but also remarks: "It is the Aristotelian concept of the immanence of knowledge which forms the link between the two systems."[4] The reference is to Aristotle's doctrine of God as the self-coincidence of thinking and thought (*Metaphysics* L, 9), the point where "to be" and "to think" are the same (cf. Parmenides, Fragment 3). Here—and not in any critical exigency born of dogmatism and skepticism—is where transcendental Thomism locates the essential reason for the "turn to the subject."

Basic to Rousselot and Maréchal's encounter with Kant, Aquinas, and the tradition was reassertion of the necessary unity of the "two moments" of the science of metaphysics. From Aristotle through Suarez First Philosophy was seen as a unified science of beings as beings (ontology) and of the highest instance of being (theology)—in a word, ontotheology. Classical modern philosophy broke that unity down into two distinct sciences: general metaphysics and special metaphysics. But Rousselot and Maréchal restore the earlier position. Why must ontotheology be one science? Because it is the thematization of the one movement of knowledge that is man, a movement whereby man knows anything in being (ontology) only because he necessarily anticipates knowledge of God (theology). The separation of ontology from theology takes place when the tradition no longer grounds man's knowledge of particular beings in his anticipation of universal and ultimate reality but substitutes something else for that basis: subjectivity, knowledge of nature, etc. With the "critical" reassertion of man's absolute transcendence, ontology and natural theology can no longer be two sciences alongside each other, not even two moments in affinity within one science. They are in fact seen as identical: man is a metaphysician (*panta pōs, capax entis*) only because he is already implicitly a theologian (*theos pōs, capax Dei*). In short, the problematic of the unity of the thematic science of metaphysics is reduced to the question of the unity of the movement of human spirit, which is directed to being because it is directed to the divine.

To divide the present chapter between these two thinkers is inevitably to invite repetition, for Maréchal resumes many of the themes which Rousselot, some years before, had discovered in St. Thomas. Yet, despite the overlap, it is worthwhile treating each man individually. Rousselot is more the pioneer who opens up a new land, while Maréchal is more the colonist who settles the territory. Rousselot resembles the artist, working under pressure, who throws off insights like sparks, while Maréchal is the laborious systematizer who works out the ideas in detail and tests them against the whole of Thomas' theory of knowledge. Rahner is indebted to both men in different ways: to Maréchal, the painstaking author of five volumes on the historical and theoretical development of the problem of knowledge, and to Rousselot, the "existentialist" who saw that all philosophical problems "are posed for man by his very nature and depend on the wider, the more concrete problem of his existence."[5] Investigating each man separately will prefigure for us two sides of Rahner's own work—the systematic and the existential—while a study of both of them is the background for measuring the indebtedness and novelty of GW.

A. ROUSSELOT: THE DYNAMISM OF HUMAN SPIRIT

Pierre Rousselot enjoyed a brief but brilliant career before his tragic death as a soldier in World War I. In the seven years between his doctorate at the Sorbonne and his death in the trenches at Éparges he taught systematic theology at the Institut Catholique in Paris for four years and produced an impressive series of books and articles. We shall leave his specifically theological writings aside in order to focus on the theory of knowledge and metaphysics found in his *L'Intellectualisme de Saint Thomas* and in the philosophical articles.[6]

1. The Approach to Aquinas

Although Rousselot's formal Jesuit education was devoted to the study of Thomism, his broad and intense reading opened him to virtually all the contemporary trends in philosophy. He was well versed in Hegel, especially the *Science of Logic*, and had read the British proponents of neo-Hegelianism. He knew and deeply respected Kant, but had little use for the typical neo-Kantianism (abolition of the thing-in-itself; assertion of the mind's autonomy in forming the phenomenon; construction of philosophy as the groundwork for the sciences) which had come to dominate late nineteenth century France through the generation of professors trained by Renouvier and Lachelier. He excoriated it as "that bastard ontology which is supposed to result from a general systematization of the sciences and be indefinitely revisable as it follows their progress."[7] He frequently cited Blondel (whose work he greatly admired), Bergson, Le Roy, and even Newman (whose psychology he appreciated more than his philosophy or theology), and he was conversant with the French spiritualists, Ollé-Laprune, and many others. But the point is that in Rousselot's writings all of these philosophers, and perhaps even Aquinas himself, underwent transformation to the degree that they were incorporated into Rousselot's own thesis on intellectualism.

Aquinas as well? If we leave apart for a moment the content of Rousselot's reading of St. Thomas, the manner of his approach to the Angelic Doctor—his method in the broadest terms—was radically unique for the times. We have called this method a "retrieval," in anticipation of the approach to historical texts which Rahner will borrow from Heidegger (see Chapter V, A.2, below). The title aside, the same approach is at work in Rousselot, and we may reconstruct it from some of his critical remarks on a work by Sertillanges.

To respect a text, Rousselot notes in his essay,[8] is to correct it, perfect it, perhaps even "to modify. . . profoundly the physiognomy of the system one is explaining." The point is never just to describe but to reconstruct as well, never to be "a simple photographer" but to "clarify" in the sense of "providing a more complete and definite satisfaction" than the work itself does, and thus necessarily to "pose. . . problems beyond those which the master himself posed." He protests against those Thomists who seem "to insinuate that everything has already been said by St. Thomas, for without a doubt that is the best way to discredit Thomism." One must go beyond the ideas explicit in the system in order to engage its underlying "spirit," its "original character," the "unifying plan of the whole," so that one can then "show what meaning these Thomistic theses might have for men trained in the mentality of modern philosophy." We can see the outline of the approach: penetration through the surface of a text or system (the "said") in order to find its living potential (often "unsaid") for contemporary thought; then actualization of that possibility through questions and orientations which may never have occurred to the original author. Not to do that much is not to have philosophized. At best it is to have presented history.

Rousselot calls his own retrieval of St. Thomas an "interiorized Scholasticism," which will transform Aquinas as radically as Aquinas had transformed Aristotle, and yet, for all that, will remain in continuity with the spirit of Thomas' thought. Over the door of this transformed Scholasticism he places a motto from Marcus Aurelius (he could as well have chosen St. Augustine's *Rede intus*): "Look within yourself. Within lies the source of good, which is ever able to spring up anew, if you know how to dig for it." Metaphysics is to rejoin the critique of knowledge at the interior point of man's infinity of potentiality, his ascent to God in every act of cognition.[9]

But what evidence justifies this turn within? It is the experience of the "permanent obscurity in the object," correlative to the "intrinsic and substantial non-being of the subject" as "a progressive being," a "spirit, incomplete and tending towards subsistent and supreme truth." "This," he says, "is what a metaphysics of St. Thomas calls the critique of knowledge."

> We take it that whoever does not see potency in and by act is not *prepared* for absolute metaphysical knowledge. We take it that being holds absolutely only from the viewpoint of God. Only that vision which sees beings in terms of their ascent, their mounting up towards God, leaves no obscurity in potency but absorbs, resolves, "liquidates" it entirely into act. Thus conceptual intelligence, which receives being as a mixture of potency and act precisely because it is not itself entirely in act, is not an instrument for bringing being completely into the light. Nonetheless, this recognition of our limits, of a certain infinite potentiality in us (corresponding to which there is always a knot of darkness in the conceived object), is far from confining our intellectual ambitions to the "metaphysics of the sensible." Rather it shows the powerful, ever-present necessity of affirming God and the legitimacy of the ideas we form of spiritual realities.[10]

That is, whereas the object of our conceptual knowledge appears to us as ultimately irreducible to and impenetrable by our spirit, nonetheless "intelligence in its natural movement invincibly presumes that the object *is* penetrable and reducible." Thus:

> The fact that our knowledge does not presently penetrate the object comes from the provisional and "in-between" character of this movement itself. The soul affirms itself as pure spirit in potency by the very fact that it affirms that being holds. In reasoning about potentiality in general (i.e., *essentiality*, which in every finite being differs from actuality) in the same way that we reason about material potentiality, we see that the affirmation of God is implied in each of our acts of intelligence even more intimately than is the affirmation of ourselves. Thus, it is not only exterior reality, the "thing-in-itself," which shows itself to be unstable and which calls for God. Rather, the soul's own spontaneous movement presupposes him.[11]

In these two citations we see the major themes that structure Rousselot's thought: the primacy of act over potency in cognition and metaphysics; the critique of conceptual intelligence; the positive function of
representational knowledge as an implicit affirmation of the soul and of
God; the interior "proof" for God as complementary to the exterior one.

But where is this "within," this Aurelian *endon* or Augustinian *inte-*
rioritas? Does Rousselot invite us to retreat to some monastery of the
mind, to back into a Cartesian closet and shut the door against the body
and the world? Can we really turn around and look inside ourselves
(intro-spect) to see the long ego pulling the levers of the cognition machine? No, Rousselot says that in Aristotle as much as in Kant "the soul is
not conscious of itself except by being conscious of a corporeal object,"[12]
and the task of interiorization is that of capturing the soul in its involvement in, its synthetic apperception of, the world. All the language of
"turning within" is potentially misleading and, to the degree it suggests
a *volte-face* from the world, should probably be dropped. The meaning
of the "within" lies entirely in the other direction. The point is to find
the soul *within the world* and at the heart of material beings. His "interiorized Scholasticism" is simply the awareness that "the science of the
soul is at the heart of the science of things."[13] To turn within is to find
oneself thrown outside into active affinity with things. The inner movement of the soul happens only in and on the world.

We shall now spell out some of the major themes of Rousselot's reading of St. Thomas, beginning *da capo* with the normative state of intellectual knowledge.

2. Cognition and Perfection

With Rousselot's *L'Intellectualisme de saint Thomas* we are really
present at the creation of the basic insights of transcendental Thomism.
Not that Rousselot forges those insights from nothing; rather, he redis-
covers them, latent or explicit, in Thomas's own thought. Nor does he
put these ideas into direct confrontation with Kant the way Maréchal
will later do. Rather, he points to the wider context for the transcendental turn in the history of the philosophical tradition. Thus he argues for
the turn to the subject not from the critical exigencies of Kant's Copernican Revolution but from the normative state of knowledge in the highest
being. This broader contextualization of the subjective turn is also the
basis for surpassing Kant's formalistic limitation of theoretical knowledge within the metaphysical project. Because of the centrality of these
issues, we back up for a moment to reflect on some of the basic presuppositions of traditional metaphysics and theory of knowledge.

Two fundamental metaphors recur in Western philosophy from the dawn of thought in the pre-Socratics down to Nietzsche and Heidegger: the tension between darkness and light, and that between movement and repose. These metaphors speak of what classical Greek philosophy knew as the relation between the *ateles* and the *teleion*, between that which is not yet in *telos* and that which is. The *telos* is the state of something that is fully present-in-reality as what and how it is; the *a-teles* is something claimed and appropriated by, and therefore in movement towards, the *telos*. When Aristotle wanted to name the state of presence-in-reality, he coined the word *entelecheia*, the very having of oneself (cf. *echein*) in *telos (en telei)*. In place of *telos* he equally uses *ergon*, not "work" in the sense of the activity or the product of labor, but "full present appearance." Thus *en-tel-echeia* is the same as *en-erg-eia*. The Latins translated *teleion* as *perfectum*, that which is "thoroughly done or achieved" *(per-factum)*. But the *facere* points not to making or doing in the ordinary sense but rather to the Greek *poiein, poiēsis*, which Plato defined as a bringing from non-being (non-presence) into being (present reality) (cf. *Symposium* 205 a). Behind the word *poiēsis* in Greek thought we frequently find the metaphor of light (cf. *De Anima*, G, 5, 430 a 16f.): *poiein* is "to bring something to light" in the sense of rendering it *teleion*, present in reality. To bring something to light is likewise to reduce its imperfect state of movement to the perfect repose of beingness. *Genesis heneka ousias*, becoming is for the sake of being; *proteron to teleion tou atelous*, the perfect has primacy over the imperfect; *proteron energeia dynameōs*, being in *ergon* has primacy over being on the way to *ergon*.[14]

Here is the basis for the traditional position, echoed above by Rousselot, that potency is to be read in terms of act, for *"secundum quod aliquid est perfectum, secundum hoc est in actu"* (S.T., I, 4, 1, c.). According to the metaphors we noted above, philosophy is a meditation on the nature of light or repose (the perfect as perfect) and on the emergence from dark to light or the reduction of movement to repose. In traditional thought there is no possibility of considering darkness or becoming for their own sake. *Motus non habet rationem termini.* "A being tends toward something; there is no such thing as tending to tend. An absolute dynamism is impossible."[15] If we say "the imperfect *as* imperfect" that always means for the tradition: as-unto-perfection. The viewpoint of philosophy is always reality as *teleion*, and all else is judged therefrom. "We could say that all of metaphysics simply answers this question: *Granted that there is being*, what must we affirm? what else must have being?"[16]

The tension of perfect/imperfect can equally be expressed as that between the *proteron* and the *hysteron* (the *a priori* and the *a posteriori*).

Aristotle speaks of the *proteron tēi physei*, what is prior in being (cf. *Physics* A, 1, 184 a 16ff.), and even more strikingly of *to ti ēn einai*, what it "was" to be something (cf. *Meta.* E, 1, 1025 b 29). The latter phrase stands in for the missing perfect form of *einai*, and it indicates what being is "prior" to any reception or modification, i.e., what it already (perfectly) is, in comparison with which everything else is derived and secondary. The prior measures and appropriates the posterior, not diachronically or serially but in terms of levels of reality.

What the metaphors of light and repose contribute to these analyses is the understanding of the original Greek vision within which philosophy moves: reality is transparency and perfect self-presence, clarity and stability. Because "to be" means to be translucent (first of all to oneself), then to the degree of one's own self-clarity, all else is clear. Perfect self-coincidence (luminosity, repose) is therefore the perfect state of knowing: it is *nous*, immediate self-presence, both the state of being luminous to oneself and the cause of luminosity in others. Anaxagoras gave expression to this in his *pantōn nous kratei*, "Nous empowers everything" (Fragment 12:18), and Aristotle saw this power, when it operates in man, as either divine or "the most divine element in us" (*Nic. Ethics*, K, 7, 1177 a 16). In God, where there is no obscurity (*mē hylēn echei*), *nous* and *nooumenon* are one and the same (*to auto kai mia* [*Meta.* L, 9, 1075 a 5]). In man, where obscurity and clarity are mixed, *nous* (Latin, *intellectus*) is bound up with *dianoia* (Latin, *ratio*) and therefore with the imperfection of having to move through *(dia)* things in discursive progress towards clarity. If man's faculty of intuition, his "intellectualism," makes him like God and the separated substances, his rational, discursive faculties measure his distance from them. *Rationale est differentia animalis, et Deo non convenit nec angelis* (*I Sent.*, d. 25, q. 1, a. 1, ad 4): rationality is a quality of the genus "animal" and befits not God and angels but those spirits which know conceptually and discursively.

Between the perfect and the imperfect, the prior and the posterior, lies the *chōrismos*, the metaphysical "gap" bridged by *methexis*, the appropriation of the imperfect by the perfect. And human knowing, even if it finds itself on this side of the gap, is intrinsically a *krisis* or *krinein*, a "critical" measuring of the distance by already anticipating the end. Critical knowledge in its full sense is not cognition in which the knowing faculty measures its own limitations without knowing reality as it is, but rather that knowledge which, as moving intrinsically towards perfection, measures itself and all reality against the fullness of the real. This is the basis for Rousselot's response to those who claimed that his theory of knowledge was not critical enough: "In order to be sure to presuppose nothing, there is no other means than to presuppose everything."[17] To isolate a part of reality (the *cogito*, perhaps, or phenomenal knowledge) is inevitably to have taken a position on the meaning of all reality as such. The truly critical stance, then, is to see the whole and to know one's place within it (*krinein*: to measure and judge the lower against the higher[18]). And one can see the whole because by nature one already anticipates it: becoming is for the sake of being.

Rousselot sees this Greek vision, centered on what he calls "illuminative clarity" and "transparency," both preserved and elevated in the Christian experience of reality.[19] If he calls his reading of St. Thomas an "ontological Platonism," it is because he sees in Aquinas "the least 'geocentric' and the most 'noocentric' synthesis that ever was." For, "the primary fact which conditions and dominates the whole intellectualism of St. Thomas [is] the living and personal existence of absolute Spirit." Indeed: "Spirit is first, and all being is for spirit," and "the true finality of nature is its knowing and knowable origin; the beings 'willed for their own sake' are 'subsistent intelligibles.' " Thus the "first principle of Scholasticism" is that "the perfectly intelligible is living spirit." In Christianity, reality is personalized in a way that it could not be in the Greeks. The noumenal realm of Plato is transformed into a realm of pure persons: God and the angels.[20]

> The spirit of Christianity consists in placing at the summit of everything not an Idea but a spiritual person. . . . Even this assertion supposes a contrast between Idea and spiritual person which St. Thomas does not admit. The fundamental principle of his intellectualist metaphysics is precisely that every spiritual person is an Idea, that there is a perfect identity between Idea and spiritual reality. "Knowing in act" and "knowable in act" are for him two convertible notions. The true Ideas, the true "noumena". . . are the "subsisting Intelligibles."[21]

For Rousselot, Aquinas' theory of being is not only dominated by his theory of knowledge, but the latter, far from being a consequence of the former, is the principle from which the metaphysics follows as a corollary. "The strong and quiet confidence in reason, which is one of the most obvious characteristics of Thomistic philosophy, presupposes a certain conception of the relation of being and spirit," which, whether it be formulated or remain latent, is logically antecedent to everything Thomas has to say thematically about ontology and theology.[22] For Rousselot that relation is initially expressed in the thesis that being is in accord with itself (*l'être est d'accord avec lui-même*), which in fact coincides with another thesis: being is in accord with spirit (*l'être est d'accord avec l'esprit*), but "not in an extrinsically preestablished harmony" but insofar as they are naturally complementary because ultimately identical.[23] In the last analysis ontology and theology are identical because being and God are identical. "What is the meaning of being? What does being demand and postulate? St. Thomas answers: the existence of God. That is the cause of being as being."[24] And that is why reality cannot be defined in any terms which prescind from knowledge. If being is knowable, it is because it participates in the very nature of knowing as such. On every other hypothesis, knowability and being cannot be brought together except extrinsically. And if they are united only extrinsically, nothing *a priori* can be established about things. For Rousselot the ultimate roots of the transcendental apriority of knowledge lie in the coincidence of knowing and being in God.

This doctrine of radical intellectualism (i.e., *nous*, not *dianoia; intellectus*, not *ratio*) establishes what knowing as such is by revealing its normative state. The proper measure for knowing cannot be the conceptual, representational, discursive knowledge which we call reason and which issues in science *(epistēmē, scientia)*. The Thomistic critique of knowledge in that sense joins the Bergsonian critique of reification (Rousselot: *solidification et morecelage*[25]) which emphasizes the represented form and synthetic affirmation as paradigmatic for knowing. For Thomas, the *prōton pseudos* of rationalism is to equate discursive reason with intellect as such.

> Every critique of knowledge finds its final explanation in the theory of divine intellection. We measure the decreasing perfections of intuition, concept, judgment, and discursive knowledge by their . . . distance from God's unique simplicity. A being is the more intelligent as its consciousness is more totalizing, and the less intelligent as its perceptions are more multiple. . . . Doubtlessly, our power to synthesize and generalize, which makes us the lowest of intellectual beings, renders us capable of creating groupings of ideas (sciences, systems, symbolic poems) which try to approach the pure idea without ever attaining its intensity and clarity. But these substitutes are poor satisfactions. Christian life seems to have developed in St. Thomas an enthusiasm for intelligence with a correlative disdain for discursive human reasoning.[26]

The norm for knowledge, therefore, is unity with oneself in transparent identity. Intellection is not dispersion, a *spargi ad multa* (of. *Opusc.* 28, ch. 1), but interiority, immateriality, and self-presence.[27] For Aquinas, "The supreme and perfect degree of life is that according to intellection, for the intellect is reflected upon itself and can know itself" (S.C.G., 4, 11). Thus:

> Human intelligence can know itself, but the principle of its knowledge comes from without, since it knows nothing without a sensible image. The intellec-

tual life of angels is more perfect, for there the intellect knows itself by itself without going outside at all. Yet, theirs is not the supreme perfection, for their idea, which is interior to them, is nonetheless not their substance: being and knowing are not identical in them. Therefore, the ultimate perfection of life belongs to God in whom to know is to be and in whom the idea (understanding by "idea" that which the intellect conceives in itself of the known object) is the divine essence itself *(ibid.)*.

The heart of Thomas' doctrine, therefore, is the simplicity of the divine intellect which knows all things by its very being (cf. S.T., I, 55, 3) and thus is "at one and the same time perfect immanence and perfect extensiveness penetrating to the depths of things."[28] "Thus St. Thomas' doctrine can never be founded on the initial disjunction and logical conjunction of the *cogito* and the *sum* but on the recognition that the *cognosco* and the *est* mutually envelope and penetrate each other."[29]

The immanence and interiority of perfect knowledge also sets the norm for knowing things other than oneself. Exteriorization or possession of the other is in direct proportion to self-possession, and the norm of knowing the other is not objectivity in the sense of distance from the known, but subjectivity in the sense of *a priori* determination of the known. All talk of "having" an object is inadequate; rather, the point is to *be* the other.[30] The act of knowing another "is the more perfect to the degree that it more fully attains the other as such, that is, in the intimacy, totality, and *unity* of its being, and it is the more imperfect the more it leaves the other untouched *(Ens et unum convertuntur)*."[31] Intellect is fundamentally a return to oneself *(reditio in seipsum)* or self-presence, and the more one finds the other within one's own being, the more one knows it. God the creator knows beings in their being by knowing his own being and thus sets the norm of immanence for knowledge of the other. Rousselot calls this "knowledge by embrace" *(étreinte[32])*. And by a diminution of perfect self-presence, angels know others by intuition of their (the angels') own form and thus know things in terms of form, whereas man, as composed of matter and form, knows things by composition and division of form and supposit. What is common to all three levels is that knowledge is *per connaturalitatem* or *per modum naturae*, that is, by the knower's level of being or self-presence, which is the level of his self-knowledge.[33]

These remarks on the primacy of personal self-coincidence in knowing and being touch the foundations of the enterprise of transcendental Thomism. They are the grounds on which Rousselot, and later Maréchal, confidently proceed when they turn to the human subject and attempt to establish critically the scope of the dynamism of subjectivity in knowing.

3. Cognition and Kinēsis

Rousselot repeats time and again the basic thesis of his intellectualist reading of St. Thomas. If we grant Aquinas his doctrines of the primacy of contemplation and the absolute value of the act of *intellectus*, then:

> We have the master idea which brings everything into unity and joins philosophy and theology into an indissoluble synthesis. It can be formulated as follows: for St. Thomas *intelligence is essentially the sense of the real, but it is so only because it is the sense of the divine.*[34]

> Intelligence is the faculty of *being* in general only because it is the faculty of *infinite being.*[35]

> We have said in effect that spirit is defined by the possibility of incorporating, so to speak, the absolute (by intuitive vision). The consequence of this is spirit's power to attain even the contingent in a definite and irreformable way. Spirit is *theos pōs* before being *panta pōs.*[36]

> The soul is in symphony with being as such because ultimately it is *capax Dei.* Man understands things only insofar as he desires God.[37]

The whole thrust of his critique of knowledge, therefore, "converges entirely on the affirmation to the infinite, pure, divine Idea. One must possess that in order to gain oneself."[38] Indeed, "to be spirit means to be able to be deified" *(esse spiritus est deificari posse).*[39]

But between the human soul and the divine paradigm of intuitive being and knowing there is a middle term which serves as a limit-idea and closer model for the movement of human knowing: the angels. Angelic knowledge functions in Rousselot's works less for its own sake (i.e., as an angelology) than for the purpose of defining the *telos* of human knowledge. For human beings, he says boldly, "the natural end is to realize in themselves the power of spirit, to arrive at the maximum of consciousness, to become monads reflecting everything *(ut in ea describatur totus ordo universi).*"[40] "One would like to act as an angel, i.e., possess oneself intellectually at one swoop. And this is the true end, at least the ideal end," because "to possess being intellectually is to possess oneself fully" and "the first condition for having the intuition of being is to have an intuition of oneself."[41]

Angels, he says, "these models of the intellectual process in its ideal state," function as guiding limit-ideas for human cognition, for not only do they prevent us from identifying intellectual knowledge as such with discursive reasoning and suppress the opposition between being and idea, but they show man what he is to become and therefore why and how he knows.[42] "One can rightly say that the unknown and most loved end, whose discovery accounts for all our mental dynamism, is the subsistent noumenon which we [potentially] are and will become."[43] The angelic hypothesis shows that the goal of knowledge is oneness with the known (ens et unum convertuntur) and that, short of this, man must work with imitative substitutes.

> Pascal says, "The more one is spirit, the more one sees...the originals." Whoever is entirely spirit is entirely an affinity with beings, entirely a noumenal affinity. The whole of reality is "sympathetic" with him, all of its qualities are "connatural" to him.... Pure spirit, St. Thomas says, knows the individual in its very singularity; in turn, the human soul abstracts the idea of the quiddity.[44]

In fact, however, "the angelic act is refused us. Man does not have full consciousness of himself." We are "the spirit whose synthesis is never made (while the angel, being a discrete succession of intuitive plenitudes, is the spirit whose synthesis is given)." Man's proper but not adequate faculty is reason rather than intuition, he is "the series of a noumenon" rather than noumenal being itself.[45] And according to the principle Quod non potest fieri per unum, aliqualiter saltem fiat per plura, he imitates pure intuition by his abstractive, conceptual affirmations and by such natural substitutes as art, history, science, and symbols.[46] His reasonings are to pure intuition "as time is to eternity and as the circumference of a circle is to its center."[47]

As a mediating term between man and God, angelic knowledge shows man the meaning of his kinetic cognition, indeed, of the very temporality of his being. Capax Dei, man is also capax sui, a "capacity for conscious transparence and luminous enjoyment of the self."[48] We now take up, therefore, the nature of human dynamism and the elements of the knowing that is connatural to it.

The Kinetic Nature of Man. The formulae, often poetic, abound. Man "does not fill up his essence," he is "a spirit imperfectly spiritual, who desires to possess himself," "an innate desire...to equal and gain his nature." His essence "is to be an inclination towards infinite being insofar as this is the good, the supreme truth, of intelligent beings." His knowledge is all motus and per modum amoris. "Insofar as the soul is not freed from its material potentiality, insofar as it has not equaled its nature, there is an anxiety which moves the soul in its depths: it is the desire for the self...." "To stop is to deny ourselves.... It is in the 'passage' beyond that we conquer more being, and only by passing beyond can we remain equal to ourselves."[49]

... Our existence has scarcely begun: *nondum apparuit quid erimus*. Let us not treat as a finished being the embryo which we are: *initium aliquod creaturae*. My reality is not what I am at this second, what I was ten years ago, or what I shall be in six days. It is the very series of all the positions of this mobile being which I am....[50]

... The only sufficient reason, the only interior impetus of our whole mental life, that which gives meaning to each of our conceptions, is the love for this ideal goal: the soul's intuition of itself....[51]

The critique of knowledge, then, becomes "the progressive science of our itinerary towards being" (Blondel),[52] and the first step in that is to apply the tension between the *teleion* and the *atelēs*, the perfect and the imperfect, to man's own being. If Aristotle introduced into philosophy the schema of act and potency, Aquinas deepened it by distinguishing degrees of potency. In God, essence and existence coincide: he is pure act, separated *esse*. In angels, existence is received, but as pure subsistant forms they know no distention between nature and supposit and therefore know all particular instances (all S's) through a simple intuition of the universal (the P). In man, not only are essence and existence distinct, but nature and supposit as well: no man exhausts manhood *(Socrates non est sua natura)*. This twofold distention (supposit as potential to nature; essence as potential to existence) is the reason why man must know through concepts (he knows S only through P) and affirmation (he knows S-and-P only by *judging* them to *be*).

At the instant when man's interior distention would cease, his representative distention, that of his concept, would cease as well. Man would *envisage* his essence, his substantial self, he would live his soul, his entire soul; and in the same instant he would know exterior being by a sympathetic intuition. All material *apathy* would evaporate into spiritual *sympathy*. No longer having a *remainder* to be reduced within itself, the soul would no longer be impeded from penetrating its objects. In short, the very root of conceptual distention and abstraction... is the imperfection of our spiritual nature. The reason why man does not bring his object completely to light is that he himself is not completely brought to light.[53]

But the positive side of the picture is found in the nature of this imperfection *as* imperfect, i.e., on the way to perfection. All potency is for act, all becoming is for being, man's kinetic nature as such is a being-appropriated by the term of his movement. God's perfect state of being draws the soul on (Aristotle's *kinei hōs erōmenon*, [*Meta.*, L, 7, 1072 b 4]). And reciprocally the soul, appropriated by "the drawing of this Love and the voice of this Calling,"[54] that is, in its desire for itself and for

God, generates conceptual knowledge and the affirmation of being. Notice that this movement happens only in and on the world; there is no knowledge of self or God except in apperceptive synthesis. Man's movement thus becomes the crux of the movement of the whole cosmos towards God.

> One could say that creatures, such as they are, are nothing but inclinations towards the divine essence. . . . But corporeal beings can be led back or (to use the ancient term) "reduced" to God only by the mediation of humanity. On the other hand, spiritual creatures, whose nature is defined by their appetite for the known God, are somehow pure inclinations towards the first truth and are like "transcendental relations" to God. Their end is divine contemplation and their divine potentiality is regulated entirely by the drawing power of this end.[55]

Man's very nature as kinetic is a *pros ti*, a transcendental referral to the divine, and in carrying out the "analogical relation" which he himself is, he brings the whole world back to God. The scope of movement is as broad as its term is simple, and at the midpoint we find "this anxiety," this "palpitating infinity" called man. All things are for man, and man is for God. As we see later, these are the two themes which Rahner will interpret as the possible and the agent intellect.[56]

The Kinetic Nature of Knowledge. How does man's knowledge imitate the angel's and strive towards God? Where do we find that knowledge growing out of the movement of man's being? Rousselot offers two complementary approaches. The one is found throughout all his philosophical publications and consists in an analysis of the structure and teleology of predicative knowledge. The other and by far more striking approach appears only in one essay published almost fifty years after his death and consists in a hermeneutics of pre-predicative cognition *in actu exercito*. This second approach is all the more extraordinary for the fact that it anticipates many of the elements of Heidegger's later treatment of "being-in-the-world," and both of these, in fact, are rooted in Aristotle's studies of everyday life in such terms as *empeiria, pathos, phronēsis*, and the like. Whereas the study of predicative experience centers around the topics of abstraction, conceptualization, and judgment, Rousselot's hermeneutics of pre-predicative experience seeks to capture what he calls "the primitive transparency of 'life' " in its moment of sympathetic unity with its world. We take up this approach first.

Rousselot begins with two phenomenological descriptions, one of a man directly observed, the other of a child known through a poem.

Go to your window and look out into the garden behind your house. Your neighbor is at his window and looks out at it from his side. It's the hour of full sun, and the beautiful acacia in the garden, its leaves green and tender, its flowers white, stands out under the lovely blue Parisian sky. The man at his window looks at the acacia—or rather, no, not at the acacia. He just looks. To some he might seem stupid, others would find him intelligent; in any case, he just looks. He's not terribly absorbed, and when his young daughter enters the room all of a sudden to announce a visitor, he doesn't reawaken as if from a distraction. And there, it's over. He leaves the window and goes back to work.[57]

The second description follows Victor Hugo's poem "La Rose de l'Infante":

She is so small. Her nursemaid watches over her.
She holds a rose in her hand and looks.
What does she look at? She doesn't know. The water,
A bowl which conceals the willow and the birch,
What she has before her, a swan with white wings,
The lapping ripples under the singing boughs. . . .

Rousselot continues:

The poem should plunge you, all at once and with the instantaneous clarity of an intuition, into all the color and flesh of an afternoon of your childhood. You hardly dare to call the experience *psychological*, and yet it is at the very heart of life: the confused presence—no, more simply, the *known* presence of the white apron that guards you, the pails and the shovels, your hands covered with damp sticky sand, the flow of life. . . . Don't let yourself believe that only children and primitives know such states. No, they are the daily bread of mental life.[58]

What is common to both these related experiences is our inability at first glance to isolate "facts" of conceptual cognition and even less so of sensation. Rather, these experiences deal with a prior state, of which conceptualization and sensation taken for themselves are only extracts and abstracts. This state of consciousness "really has no name in any language; the word 'life,' which is the least inappropriate, is too large for it." However, although perhaps unnamable, it can be described.

Fundamentally, it consists in living. . . . We must understand that it never stops, that it persists underneath "intellectual conception". . . . This state which, for reasons of facility, we represented as delimited in time and as occupying all of consciousness, corresponds in all human intellection to the atemporal moment of *perception* as distinct from the moment of *conception*. [Even though those two are finally inseparable], if we just consider the moment of perception, then essence and *esse*, realness and suchness, are here mixed together indissolubly and are perceived together; here affirmation adds nothing to perception, and the distinction of the real and the possible has not yet arisen.[59]

What Rousselot is groping for is an understanding of a lived state of cognition that is not just sensation *(aisthēsis)* nor yet judgment *(logos)*, but what Aristotle called *empeiria* and Heidegger called *Sich-Auskennen*, know-how or lived knowledge in its human form of "immediacy." By the two descriptions, Rousselot writes, "we only wanted to reexperience the apparent *stupor*, the indifference, the lack of distinction from things. . . . This stupor is an intense life."

We don't seem to find either reflection or negation. Sensation and intellection are so well mixed here that they are not distinct. Nature and supposit, body and soul, *real and possible*, subject and object—I do not say all these *realities* but all these *oppositions*—have disappeared. . . . The so-called stupor is, by vital identity, a vigorous affirmation. . . . The first, natural, irresistable tendency, prior to any deceptions, is to *affirm* everything.[60]

In this primitive transparency of "life," Rousselot finds the human experience of imitating the simplicity of angelic knowledge. This is *cognitio per modem naturae* in its anticipation of the unity that draws on human knowledge; and conceptual knowledge has its validity precisely because of its continuity with this pre-predicative cognition. "Even if from below [such cognition] seems to continue the instinctive knowledge of animals, it also offers, if we look above, an image of the knowledge of pure spirits, always essential, concrete, and sympathetic."[61]

If Rousselot's first approach to human knowledge emphasizes the *goal* of cognitional movement, the second and better known approach stresses its character as *in via*. If the former analysis captured human knowledge in its unity, the latter begins with man's distance from himself.

If it is true that "our intellect renders abstract everything that it touches," the reason is that man himself is abstract.[62] The word "abstract" is here meant in the sense of the Greek *chōrizein* and *dia-hairein*, to separate and take apart. It points to a defect in being or knowing, not to the perfection denoted by "separate substances." The latter are a matter of simplicity, the former refers to fragmentation and multiplicity. And yet, like all imperfection, it points the way towards overcoming its own deficiency. Abstraction is man's therapy as well as his disease. In his knowing, man takes apart (*diairesis*) the nature and supposit that are united in the thing, he separates out the one as P and the other as S, and provisionally renounces knowing the supposit except through its general characteristics. At the same time he necessarily refers the P to the S, affirms their union even if he cannot intuit their unity, declares that P fits S even if, in relation to the supposit, the universal is broader and points beyond to a "remainder."

> To posit this real synthesis of subject and nature is to affirm that being is found in the individual itself. It is to announce that a new glance at the "remainder" will make being show up again, that the "remainder" can always be translated into the terms of the soul. . . . The real individual being will never be exhausted, and yet the soul. . . affirms its sympathy or connaturality with all of being as strongly as if it hoped to exhaust the real by this route. The strength of conceptual knowledge lies in its complete confidence that reason is made to assimilate things. The essential weakness of the concept lies in the irrepressible persistence of a remainder.[63]

Human abstraction and affirmation are thus "efforts on the part of an intelligence bound up with sense to find a substitute for pure ideas," an "unconscious imitation of the intuitive mode of knowledge," an "artiface on the part of man to impart to material things, by a purification of sensible data, the appearance of spiritual realities."[64] To "pronounce on the remainder" is to declare (one doesn't see) that there is a point where nature and supposit coincide (pure spirit) and whence all supposits are seen perfectly in their nature. In each conceptualization of S in terms of P we anticipate a spirit that can totally penetrate and totally bring to light the intelligibility of that S. "To conceive being is to dream of spirit."[65] But further, to affirm that S-and-P together *is*, is to anticipate (again, one doesn't see) that being itself holds at a point where there is no remainder at all, a point where all potency (not just of supposit with regard to nature) is dissolved into pure act and where all things are known in their very being. Beyond just uniting nature and supposit in a mental synthesis, we also affirm that the union holds "in being." But to say that there is "some being" is to imply than being *itself* is.

> We can reason about the synthesis of essence and existence which is expressed in the judgment "Being exists" in the same way we did about the synthesis of nature and subject which is expressed in the judgment "It is a being." To affirm the synthesis of essence and existence, of which we have no intuition, is to implicitly affirm that there is a point of view whence the one is seen in the other. . . . To say "This is" is to say "Whoever would see all being would see this here." To form this synthesis is therefore the same as to presuppose, to

presume, to dream of absolute creative truth. Every act of intellection not only supposes that reality is intelligible, i.e., can be brought to light, but also that reality is somewhere understood, somewhere completely brought to light. Therefore it presupposes God.[66]

The concept of remainder at both levels (intelligibility and being) and the correlative notion of man's movement towards the resolution of all remainders show at once the weakness and the strength of conceptual knowledge. The truth of the concept lies in its role as an indicator of a "more" (or, from the viewpoint of simplicity, a "less"): "it is a sketch of the true intuition, i.e., a semblance of it and an effort towards it." It is a "means for a future intuition," "not an end but only the image of the end." Man's potential and partial knowledge of being implies the actual fullness of being, it "implies then a progress, and to consider my conception by isolating it not only from what sustains it but even from what will follow it, is to lie to oneself, to truncate the experience of oneself which alone grounds certitude."[67]

If God knows by his very being, if the angel knows by its pure form, then man knows by his intrinsic distention, his essential movement, which is what Rousselot finally means by "the abstract idea of being." Man's being, as imperfect and kinetic, can never be understood "in itself," can never be cut off from the *telos* toward which it thrusts. To define man is to have gone beyond him, to have surpassed any of his moments, to have already included the rest and fullness which he anticipates. Thus Rousselot can and must say both of the following sentences: "It is proper to the spirit in search of itself, the soul still absent from itself, to light its path with the abstract idea of being." And: "*Being*, the formal object of the intellect, is the perfume which totally draws and guides the soul in its search for subsistent intelligibles, i.e., itself and God."[68]

What abides from any reading of Rousselot is a double sense of the existential power of his intuitions, and the clarity they lend to the whole body of traditional philosophy. In few other thinkers were the man and the philosopher so much in harmony. If his tragic death at thirty-seven cut short a rich life full of more promise than he could redeem, it also left a legacy which others expanded and enriched in turn. Although it remained for these later thinkers to systematize his insights, the basic intuition which guided his thought was already the destruction of all systems: *Ipsum magis.* "Move beyond to the more. . . ." The legacy of Rousselot is the awareness that only man is the issue and yet that man exceeds himself. "*L'être soi*, being oneself, must judge in the final count"[69]—but to be oneself is to point into the distance.

B. MARÉCHAL: THOMISM AND CRITICAL PHILOSOPHY

Joseph Maréchal gained his fame as the author of the monumental work *The Starting Point of Metaphysics*, subtitled *On the Historical and Theoretical Development of the Problem of Knowledge*. Four of the five volumes appeared in the mid-twenties, including the third volume on Kant and the famous *Cahier V*, "Thomism in Confrontation with Critical Philosophy." The fragmentary fourth volume, centered on Fichte, was published posthumously. In this division we concentrate on *Cahier V* because of its direct and major influence on Rahner.[70]

The crux of that work is Maréchal's interpretation of the knowing subject's movement beyond all conceptual forms to the fullness of pure act as the condition of the possibility of the objectivity of the contents of consciousness. In terms of this dynamism, which, like Rousselot before him, he grounds in Aquinas, Maréchal confronts Kant and surpasses the formalism of *a priori* knowledge in KRV. The stages in our treatment are four: the nature of knowing in its normative state; the function of affirmation in human knowledge; dynamism and finality in human knowledge; and the transposition of Thomism into critical terms.

In what follows I shall proceed mainly by laying out the general lines of Maréchal's ontology and epistemology—by explicating it, almost in thesis form, rather than by arguing for or against it. The reason for this procedure lies, quite simply, in the fact that I am not interested in presenting Maréchal for his own sake or in arguing for or against his own philosophy. Maréchal enters the present essay only insofar as he prepares the way for Rahner's own re-interpretation of Aquinas.

1. Divine Knowledge: The Normative State

The centrality of the *teleion* in Aristotle becomes in Aquinas the centrality of *esse* in the domain of reality and of simplicity in the domain of knowing. "Nothing has actuality except insofar as it is; therefore *esse* itself is the actuality of all things" (S.T. I, 4, 1, ad 3). But *esse* begins to reveal its secrets adequately only when seen in the light of its fullness as the divine *ipsum esse subsistens;* and it is significant that the first designation that Aquinas gives of the "manner of God's existence" is simplicity (cf. S.T. I, 3). By a gradual reduction St. Thomas shows that God is not composed of matter and form, that he is the same as his essence or nature, and finally that he is not only his own essence but also his own act of being.

> *Esse* is the actuality of all form or nature.... It is necessary, therefore, that *esse* itself be compared to an essence which is distinct from it as act to po-

tency. Therefore, since in God there is nothing potential. . ., it follows that in him essence is not distinct from his own act of being. Therefore, his essense is his own *esse*. [S.T., I, 3, 4, c]. In God there is no difference between "being" and "what he is," *esse et quod est* [I, 50, 2, ad 3].

All the operative attributes of God, beginning with his knowledge (S.T., I, 14), follow from his simplicity and pertain "to the unity of the divine essence" (S.T., I, 26, Introduction). Thus: "His act of being is his act of understanding" (I, 14, 5, c.). The ruling principle in knowledge, therefore, is identity. In the first formulation of his doctrine, Maréchal wrote that "all knowledge is exercised according to some kind of identity between subject and object. . . ."[71]

In *Cahier V* Maréchal takes up the issue of knowledge by self-identity in his crucial chapter "The General Ontology of Knowledge." He comments on Aquinas' question, "Whether God understands himself" (S.T., I, 14, 2) by noting St. Thomas' response to the first objection.[72] It would seem, Thomas says, that God does not know himself, for to know one's essence means to "return completely" to it. But this is impossible for God because he never leaves his essence. Therefore, God does not know himself (obj. 1). Aquinas answers that self-knowledge is an immanent act and that the object or term of the operation must therefore be in the operator. Thus, the actuality of the operation is in direct proportion to its immanence, and an intelligence that is perfectly in act must necessarily be perfectly identical with what is actually known. Only if there is some trace of potentiality in the knower or the known would there be a necessary *informatio ab extra*, a receptivity or a "going outside" (*exitus*). But God is pure act and has no potentiality, his intellect and its object are in this case the same: God understands himself through himself.

What then has become of the objection? Aquinas has redefined and clarified its terms and accepted it into his own argument:

> In response to the first objection it can be said that "to return to one's own essence" means nothing else than for a thing to subsist in itself. For insofar as a form perfects matter by giving it being, it is in a certain way poured out [*effunditur*] over it. But insofar as a form has being in itself, it returns to itself. . . .
>
> Knowing powers that subsist in themselves know themselves. And for this reason it is said in *De causis* that "one who knows his essence returns to his essence." But it preeminently belongs to God to subsist in himself. Therefore, according to this way of speaking, God is the one who preeminently returns to his essence and knows himself (ibid., ad 1).

Here again we are at the heart of transcendental Thomism and of its insight into what Rahner will later define as *Bei-sich-sein*, being-with-oneself. Perfect being is *subsistere in seipso* or *redire in seipsum*, and this is equivalent to perfect self-knowledge. The core of Aquinas' system is the existence of absolute spirit, a personal, self-possessed, self-reflective spirit who defines being and for whom all being is.

God, therefore, sets the model for all knowing; cognition is by identity, immanence, and immateriality. Maréchal writes:

> The knower coinciding with that which is known, the subject with the object *in the identity of an act*, such is the whole metaphysical secret of knowledge as such. Knowledge is the prerogative of *act*, of act which is self-luminous because it is not separated from itself. All opaqueness comes from potency which divides act from itself. Therefore, God, the pure act, must know himself perfectly.[74]

This thesis abolishes the tyranny of "objectivity" as the norm for the necessity and universality of knowledge. If self-intuition is the supreme model of knowledge, then "the more [an intelligence] is in act through the subjective determination of its very nature, the less it needs an intelligible object distinct from itself." Again, we go back to the divine self-knowledge and, according to Maréchal, find subject and object identified in the luminous oneness of pure act. The degree to which the known object necessarily belongs to the subjectivity of the subject determines the necessity and thus the certitude of knowledge.

> In man, that which keeps the *species* or the *propria passio facultatis* (the phenomenon as subjective determination [i.e., mental representation]) from being the primary object of knowledge is not its *subjectivity* but its fundamental relativity, the fact that it belongs to the subject in a merely accidental and contingent way.[75]

It is important to note that Maréchal is not just making the bland assertion that the intellect *in actu secundo* remains identical with itself, nor is he declaring that knowledge is by unification with the known. Rather, he is asserting that knowledge is by identity and immanence, by unity, not union, by interiority, not confrontation of knower with known. "There can be no doubt about the thought of St. Thomas: there is knowledge exactly to the extent of the ontological immanence of an object in a subject."[76] In the prototypical instance of divine knowledge we see the norm that will hold true on all lower levels of intellection: knowledge occurs only to the degree that self-consciousness holds. And self-consciousness is proportionate to the actuality of the subject, its *esse*. Consciousness happens where being is. "Consciousness is the self-presence of act to itself. It is present wherever act emerges out of potency, i.e., wherever an activity takes place which is, wholly or partially, its own term."[77] In the earliest drafts for *The Starting Point of Metaphysics* Maréchal wrote: "Thus the mode and perfection of cognition follows the mode and perfection of the object's *immanence* in the subject."[78]

A corollary of knowledge by identity and immanence is knowledge by immateriality. What distinguishes spirit from matter in Aristotle and Aquinas is the fact that spirit is open to all reality whereas matter is closed in upon itself. Thus spirit is essentially characterized by knowing, i.e., natural suitability to possess not only its own form but those of others as well (cf. S.T., I, 14, 1, c.). But Aquinas argues that *coarctatio formae est per materiam:* matter is what restricts form (ibid.); that is, to the degree that a knower is not fully in act his ability to possess other forms is inhibited. "Therefore, the immateriality of anything is the reason why it can be cognitive, and the mode of cognition is in proportion to the mode of immateriality" (ibid.). Maréchal comments:

> The formal immanence of the object, required for knowledge, is made impossible by the "materiality" of the subject, while the latter's "immateriality," that is, the fact that it enjoys the prerogatives of the form as such, makes this immanence possible, so that the degree of immateriality is exactly the degree of the cognitive power.[79]

What precisely is this "immateriality"? As we shall see in Chapter IV, C.2 below, it is not primarily "corporeality" but "deficiency in being," which is manifested in "exteriority" or lack of self-coincidence. For now we must be satisfied with Maréchal's negative description of it.

> . . . The degree of immateriality—that is, of remoteness from the lowest principle of potency, matter—defines the degree of knowledge in any being whatsoever. For matter is a principle of concretion and passivity, a chain bound to the "here and now," whereas knowledge requires a certain universality, or at least a greater plasticity of the subject, and a wider field of its virtual powers.[80]

Thus, immateriality, knowing power, and knowability all go together, "so much so that a *pure form* would be a pure idea."[81] And they are ultimately reducible to modes of *esse* (see Ch. IV, A.4). The degree of *esse* is in direct proportion to the degree of immateriality and is likewise the measure of what Aquinas calls the "return to the self" which is the paradigm of all knowledge.

What we have said so far deals largely with the knower's pole of knowledge. Although in God, where knower and known are one, such a formulation does not hold, we still must consider how God knows things other than himself and thus sets the norm for all "objective" knowledge.

What is the ground of the knowability of the known object when that object is other than God? Maréchal says that the condition of knowability at any level come down to one: the object's degree of *esse*. The texts in Aquinas abound: "Each thing has as much knowability as it has *esse*." "A thing is knowable to the degree it is in act." "The *ratio* of truth is founded in *esse*, not in quiddity."[82] God knows everything in terms of *esse* because, since he is perfect actuality, only *esse* is proportionate to his intellect *(cognitio est per modum naturae)*. The reason why God can know beings other than himself is that they participate in his own act of being. For God to know is to look at himself: "God sees other things not as they are in themselves but as they are in God himself, because his essence contains the likeness of things other than himself" (S.T., I, 14, 5, c.). This likeness is the divine idea of the creature, inseparable from God's essence and therefore inseparable from his act of being. And if God's knowledge of others is to be the norm of all inferior levels of cognition, then according to St. Thomas identity, immanence, and immateriality—that is, being—will set the norm for man's way of knowing.

2. Human Knowledge: Apriority and Affirmation

According to Aquinas, in God knowability and knowing power are one same and simple act of subsistent being. But what of man, who is not only a living distention of essence and existence, but of supposit and nature as well? The conditions remain analogously the same—identity, immanence, and immateriality—but the level of immateriality, and hence the power for immanence and identity, is according to the decreased perfection of the act of being. In angels, while there is no composition of matter and form, there is the reception of *esse* and hence no perfectly subsisting act of being. To the degree that they have an element of potency in their metaphysical structure, they lack perfect immanence in the act of knowledge and must receive their intelligible species from without, from God. Unlike God, their known object is not the product of their knowledge, and yet it still is immanent.[83]

In the case of man, there is a further decrease in immateriality and immanence in accordance with his greater degree of potentiality. Because of his necessary bond with matter, he must receive the objects of his knowledge through the senses. Yet passive reception of the data is not the whole story of human cognition, not even its fundamental element. As in God and angels, so too in man the *reditio in seipsum* remains the

norm of the knowing power. To the degree that man is spirit and immateriality, his being and knowing are the same.

In God it is precisely because he creates beings that those beings are
knowable. The apriority of the subject over the object measures the degree of knowability of objects. Even at the human level that norm still
holds, but in an analogous way. The apriority of man—his ability to introduce the object into his own act of being—determines the objectivity
of the datum to be known. Interiority and subjectivity remain the measure of being, just as being is the measure of objectivity. The greater the
subjectivity of the subject, the greater the objectivity of the object. A
posteriori reception of the data from without, far from being the guarantee of objectivity, in fact indicates deficient knowledge and therefore
reduced possession of the other. In man's receptive knowledge, which
must always move from potency to act in order to know, objectivity is in
proportion to man's *a priori* ability to subsume the other into his own act
of being. Maréchal writes:

> In short, an object is known only to the extent that, through a series of cau-
> salities..., it is subsumed by the natural form of an active power, in the
> unity of an immanent operation.[84]

In man's finite and imperfect cognition, the known object does not depend on man for its being, hence it is not perfectly immanent in consciousness. If knowledge is by identity and interiority, if there is
knowledge exactly to the extent of the ontological immanence of an object in a subject, then, except in the case of the ego, the immanence of
the object in knowledge can only be accidental and not essential. The
object becomes present in consciousness by means of an ontological substitute, the "species" (or "representation") which is the specifying form
of human knowledge.

But because the species must be objectified if the object is to be
known in itself, we come to the question of the relation between man's
relative apriority and his proper act of affirmation. The point is to explain the objective validity of the contents of man's consciousness.

We have said that the passivity and receptivity of the senses cannot of
themselves explain objectivity, but that man's objective knowledge must
somehow participate in the *norm* of all knowledge of the other: the apriority of divine knowing. Human objectivity, Maréchal argues, must
somehow be grounded in an *apriority* vis-à-vis the species. "Once we
have condemned pure empiricism, the question for us is no longer to
find out whether or not there is an intellectual *a priori*, but what exactly

this *a priori* is and how it does not exclude but rather demands the concurrence of exterior objects."[85]

The apriority of human knowledge is not to be located in innate ideas, not even virtual ones, but will be found to consist in *"exigencies for intelligible content, universal exigencies defined* as much by the nature of intelligence as by its necessary coordination with sensibility."[86] Maréchal continues:

> The *a priori* which is exercised in intellection consists, therefore, according to us, in the natural and permanent contribution brought to bear by intelligence on the formation of the immanent object or the "mental word." The immaterial faculty confers its own "act" of intelligibility on the material object which is intelligible only "in potency."[87]

Moreover, the source of man's apriority is finally traceable to his participation in divine intellection. Drawing on his theology Maréchal claims that:

> Finite intelligence bears *in its nature*, by the fact of its having been created, a deficient but inalienable participation in the first truth. This participation may be either the *natural possession of intelligible contents* (essential intuition, inborn *species*, in the pure angelic intelligences) or only a privative possession, an *exigency of intelligible contents* (active-passive intellectual power in man).[88]

For Aquinas and Maréchal, the agent intellect is precisely this participation in first truth, this "natural motion of the first truth."[89] Agent intellect is what allows for the reconcilation of the essential passivity of human knowing and for its equally essential spontaneity. Were there no agent (active) intellect, knowing would be the mere passive reception of material phantasms into the intellect and so would merely be "sense on a second level."[90] But if there is to be intellectual knowledge—that is, active and *a priori* determination of the passively received data—then there must be in man a faculty constantly in act which can therefore reduce the intellect from potential to actual knowledge. This faculty, the source of man's cognitional apriority and spontaneity, always in act and in need of no extraneous actualization, is the agent intellect.[91]

We now look at this same issue from the viewpoint of *affirmation*. The principle whereby God knows the other is "the internal perfection and creative initiative of the divine thought itself."[92] In man, however, affirmation is the substitute for both God's creativity and the angel's intuition. Whereas God's creativity makes the being of the thing be immediately present to himself in a relation of total constitutiveness, man's affirmation establishes a mediate and co-constitutive relation to the known object. "... The objective function of the affirmation, as a substitute for intellectual intuition, is *necessary in every non-intuitive knowledge*."[93] Maréchal establishes this principle in three steps.

In the first place, "The object of *affirmation* is not commensurate with the object of *conceptual* representation."[94] One must distinguish between the *id quod* (the signified or the objectively affirmed) and the *id quo* (the mode of representation, that according to which the *id quod* is understood). When, for example, man apprehends spiritual essences analogically, the *id quod* surpasses the *id quo*: the way in which we express our meaning is not adequate to that which we mean. In effect, we can mean more than we can represent, and the power of objectification extends in us beyond our power of formally representing in concepts. Our power of affirming is not restricted to the objects that we can represent according to their proper form.[95]

Secondly, "*Affirmation* covers objects in the exact measure of their actuality."[96] The principle at work here is: the actuality (*esse*) of a thing is the measure of its intelligibility. We can see, therefore, gradations in the intelligibility of objects according to how they are related to different degrees of actuality on the side of the knowing. All beings are affirmable to the degree that they participate in act; and to the degree that an object is *immanent* in the actuality of knowing, to that degree it is real. But Maréchal points out that, according to Aquinas, to affirm any lesser degree means that one thereby implicity affirms the maximum (cf. S.T., I, 2, 3: the *quarta via*). Hence:

> There is no doubt that, in the thought of St. Thomas, affirmation only covers an object according to a *definite measure* of act or of *esse*, that is (since the affirmation of the degree as degree logically implies the affirmation of the *maximum*), affirmation implicitly refers this object to the pure and full act of being.[97]

Finally, "*Affirmation* is a dynamic substitute for intellectual *intuition*."[98] If an object is known to the degree that it is interior to the subject, and if knowledge is an immanent activity, the principles for the objective or subjective value of knowledge must be found *within the subject*. Now, when it is a question of divine knowledge, all the determinations of objects are found in God himself. In knowing himself, God knows everything about everything. "In God alone, consequently, known objects have their full interiority, the interiority of the effect in its adequate cause."[99] However, as we move to lower forms of knowledge, the object ceases to be known in and by the essence of the knower. Receptivity and potency in some way or other enter the picture, and the degree of interiority decreases in proportion to the lack of subjectivity. In angelic knowledge we discover, instead of pure act, a "potency always in act."[100] Angels know intuitively, i.e., have innately (although given by God) and *a priori* (although not creatively) all the constitutive principles of their knowledge of the other, both form and content. However, since they lack creative intuition, angelic intellects do not have the same comprehensiveness as does God's. In human knowledge, finally, we discover neither a pure act nor a potency always in act, but a being that is intermittently in potency and act (cf. S.T., I, 50, 1, ad 2). To say that man moves from potency to act in cognition is to say implicitly that he has an internal potency to do so, i.e., that he is *somehow already* in act. Man preserves in himself something of the interiority of God and the angels, not in the form of creative intuition or innate ideas, but in the form of a "*transcendental mode* of unity calling for some matter to which it may apply."[101] Thus man has only a "privative" possession of being, such that he must assimilate other beings by sensation in order to pass from potential to actual knowledge. However:

> It is evident that none of the material data deriving from the "thing in itself" *equals* the "potency" of the intellect. It is true that their accumulation *tends* to fill the abyss which separates the intellectual power from the fully saturating cognitive act. Since this "potency" possesses the whole objective capacity of being, its full actuation, by means of material data, looks like an inaccessible *limit*. . . which means that the transcendental unity, innate to our intelligence as a functional disposition, will never be totally objectivated in our concepts.[102]

What then allows us to objectify our concepts? What lets us refer them to the absolute horizon of reality as if they "occurred, each in its respective place, within a totalizing intellectual intuition"?[103] The answer that Maréchal gives is: the affirmation. Because the particular determinations of the concept do not exhaust the capacity of the intellect to affirm the unity of reality, the intellect is constantly in movement beyond its concepts, and this *excessus* is a tendency towards nothing less than the fullness of being, God. By projecting the form on the plane of absolute being, the intellect sets it up as an object. Affirmation is thus the mode of objectification for a non-intuitive intelligence.

In short: The affirmation covers the object in proportion to its reality: man can affirm only the real. But the affirmation of a limited degree of reality implies co-affirmation of full reality. Therefore human affirmation refers any given object to the horizon of absolute being/reality. Affirmation is thus a "dynamic substitute" for intellectual intuition. It is man's way of objectifying the contents of consciousness, of knowing the other as other.

3. Human Knowledge: Dynamism and Objectivity by Finality

Maréchal's argument for objectivity from the intellect's tendency towards absolute being/reality is a complex and carefully nuanced chain of reasoning spread over one hundred and fifty pages and four chapters of *Cahier V.* Our interest in the argument is circumscribed by the fact that Rahner's GW, aided by insights drawn from Heidegger, follows a different though analogous path to the same conclusion. We limit ourselves, therefore, to the major features of Maréchal's demonstration and thus avoid questions which, important and interesting in themselves, are finally moot from the viewpoint of Rahner.

At the beginning of *Cahier V* Maréchal states that the single purpose of the volume is to show "the possibility of the metaphysical affirmation" which is expressed in the principle, "Whatever is, is."[104] Modern philosophy, he says, accepts this principle only as an analytic statement of identity or non-contradiction, with its application limited to logic, whereas classical metaphysics understands it as a synthetic principle which refers the content of consciousness to absolute being. For Maréchal himself, it is both analytic and synthetic.

> While it is the prime foundation of analytic judgments, it is at the same time the *a priori* synthesis *par excellence*, the synthesis which has precedence over all others because it becomes identified with the very life of the intellect, the faculty of being.[105]

This first principle states the essential need of man to know things within the horizon of necessity, i.e., in relation to the ultimate order of being/reality.

If it is the case that the contents of consciousness as such cannot be, properly speaking, the object of human knowledge, that is so not because the species is subjective (for immanence is the *a priori* condition for the possibility of knowledge) but because the species is related to our intellect only relatively, accidentally, contingently. For Aquinas it is the case that, in God's knowledge, things are known as they are because of their essential and necessary relation to the divine creative intellect. Man, however, does not constitute beings in their very existence; therefore beings are related to his intellect only accidentally, even if really. For the species to become objective, i.e., for man to know the object as it is in itself, that species must be referred somehow to the order of necessary being. The first principle about being must somehow be affirmed of these contents of consciousness.

> . . . The subjective datum (or species) can turn into an object of thought only by submitting itself to the first principle, that is, by assuming a necessary relation to the absolute form of being.[106]

Of itself the datum of consciousness does not express its necessary existence in extramental reality. "If the contingent datum reaches the luminous region of consciousness under the universal and necessary attributes of an object, it is because the first principle has grasped and frozen it in identity with itself" in such a way that we can affirm, "this is."[107]

Thought enacts itself within the dimension of being. Since we cannot deny objective truth (to deny it is to affirm it: argument from retorsion), and since pure non-being is unthinkable, the only object of thought, the only term of the intellect, is being/reality. "The necessity of affirming being is identical with the very necessity of thought."[108] The order of phenomena (as Kant understands that) cannot be the final order for man. The species or content of consciousness is only *id quo cognoscitur objectum*, not the *id quod* of knowledge.

How is the species to be referred to the absolute order of being? Maréchal's strategy is to show that the *ens rationis* (the species as content of consciousness) is objectified, i.e., becomes the means whereby an *ens reale* is known, precisely insofar as it comes to participate in man's own act. And since man's act is imperfect (a being-unto-act), the species will be objectified only by being inserted into man's dynamism—inserted as a partial end within a movement reaching to the ultimate end of absolute and limitless reality. Maréchal states this in the form of a thesis:

> For a non-intuitive intelligence, which receives formal determinations (species) from outside, these immanent determinations will have the immediate value of *objects* only if the very mode of their immanence to the subject *opposes* them to the subject. . . .[109]

To unfold this thesis we shall consider the two fundamental elements of Maréchal's deduction of the ontological affirmation: first, the dynamism and finality of the intellect, and secondly, the insertion of the species into that dynamism.

The Dynamism and Finality of the Intellect. Dynamism or movement is the hallmark of imperfection, and it has its measure of being or reality only insofar as it is appropriated by the *telos*, the fulfilling end, that draws it towards, and lets it partake in, some measure of perfection. Motion is always measured from the end, and thus, as on the way to the end, it partakes in a deficient way in the perfection of the *telos*. This is the meaning of Aristotle's designation of motion as *energeia* (or *entelecheia*) *ateles*. We are not to understand motion (*kinēsis*) merely as ontic, physical motion (change of place, state, etc.) but as the very being of imperfect things. Ontologically considered, movement is potentially-for-being (*tendere in actum*, cf. *In VII Phys.* lec. 10). It "touches upon" being without exhausting it. In a fundamental sense it is "contingency," which Maréchal says "implies *of itself* a thoroughgoing indetermination vis-à-vis being, a lack of achievement of internal conditions of possibility."[110]

It is such an ontological dynamism that characterizes man's being and his intellect. Although his form is spiritual (*rediens in seipsum*) and not just a form-of-matter, man experiences himself as a distention between form and supposit and between essence and existence.

> Let us remember that the form as such is nothing but the immediate limitation of *esse*, the limitation of *act* as such. In virtue of the principle of the infinite virtuality of the act, the distance between the formal limitation and the absolute fullness of *esse*, between the degree and the maximum, must determine, in the finite form or essence, the range of an inner drive, of an urge toward infinite self-transcendence.[111]

Because man is in potency to act (i.e., because he is *esse quodammodo*) and because, on the other hand, knowledge is only by act, man must necessarily pass from potency to act if he is to know. He must reduce a potentially intelligible datum to actual intelligibility. But that means that his knowledge is always in motion. "When our intellect knows an object, it is moved from potency to act. Thus the objective form [*forma objectiva*] of our intellect is the form of motion (in the broad sense) and is proportioned to some ultimate end."[112] To be sure, man knows only because he shares in the apriority of God's first truth by means of his active intellect. But this intellect "always in act" is always in motion towards the first truth.

> This intrusion of finality into an essentially logical function reveals the imperfection of the human intellect. If it were perfect, the intellect would exhaust the intelligibility of every object. Because it is imperfect, it remains "in potency" vis-à-vis all objects, even those which it already partially possesses. But to say "potency" in a real subject is to say, in an ontological sense, "tendency" and "appetite." The imperfect intellect "tends" to the truth as to an end (S.T., I, 16, 1, c.): it possesses the partially true only in the very aspira-

tion for the totally true. Or in other words, the imperfect intellect is not totally in act, is not pure luminous consciousness. The successive flashes of
knowledge are struck on the dark ground of an infinite desire.[113]

But although man is finite insofar as he is in ontological motion, the
range of his dynamism is potentially (or "materially") infinite. It can always grow, it is never satisfied with any single object nor put to rest by
an endless series of objects. It can always ask beyond the particular
given, can always intend and signify more than the whole series of
givens. "The objective form of the potential intellect is intrinsically unlimited, both as possible intellect (*quo est omnia fieri*) and as agent intellect (*quo est omnia facere*)."[114] The intellect in man is *panta pōs*,
quodammodo omnia. Its adequate object is always more than what it
knows according to the proper mode of its intellection. To be sure, material quiddities are the only things that man can *represent*, but he *affirms*
objects insofar as they are in being (*esse*). The realm of being-in-itself is
not to be shunted off towards the regulative musings of pure speculative
reason nor dangled at the end of the postulates of pure practical reason.
It is found, *as anticipated*, in the very stretching of man's affirmation
beyond what his conceptualizing function can grasp. Maréchal cites
Aquinas: "Our intellect, in knowing, stretches into infinity. This is
shown by the fact that whatever finite quality may be presented, our intellect can think of a greater one." And not only think it, but, by the process of *negatio, remotio*, and *excessus*, affirm it.

Where can we halt this dynamism, this stretch toward full reality?
Every limit we impose on it can always prompt the question of what lies
beyond the limit, and thus we surpass the boundary. The only limit (cf.
peras: that which holds something in its *perfection*) to man's range of
knowledge is being, and the only "goal" towards which it cannot reach
is non-being. As wide as being extends, so wide does the intellect expand. "The ultimate objective end of our intellect is the infinite."[115]

> The very law of the intellect's imperfect exercise obliges us to admit, at the
> origin of this active finality, a first principle whose impelling power cannot
> be less than that of pure *esse*. And it is also this *esse*, pure actuality, the abso-
> lute as wholly "in itself," which the intellect wishes to embrace in an imme-
> diate intuition.[116]

> The adequate subjective end of our intellectual dynamism—perfect happi-
> ness, the possession of the perfect good—consists in a saturating "assimila-
> tion" of the form of *being*, in other words, in the possession of God.[117]

With this we are at the core of the problematic of finality in Maréchal's theory of affirmation. The ultimate condition of the possibility of

knowledge is founded "in the last analysis on the unconditional apriority of act—creative act which 'moves [us] by being desirable': *kinei hōs erōmenon*. Every creature, in effect, has a nostalgia for the perfect actuality from which it has emanated. . . ."[118]

We note that Maréchal here speaks of God as the *subjective* end of our desire. Is that the last word, or is God also the *objective* end of human finality, as Maréchal also asserts? And if so, how?

As a first step in answering this question Maréchal notes that it is at least possible that this end be really attainable.

> To posit any intellectual act whatsoever in virtue of the natural tendency toward the subjective ultimate end of the intellect is tantamount to implicitly or explicitly willing this end, hence to adopting it *as at least possible*. Strictly speaking one may intend an end without being certain of reaching it, even with the certitude of never reaching it. But it would be contradictory to strive towards an end which one considers *absolutely and in every respect unattainable*.[119]

Now, what about the objective reality of that possible end? Maréchal answers that, whereas in the case of finite ends, man can desire an object that only *may* exist, the case is wholly other with God:

> But when this object is God, when the objective end is satisfied with the being which is *necessary by itself* (the pure act), which has no other mode of reality than absolute existence, the dialectical exigency implied by the desire assumes a new scope, not merely on account of the natural desire, but on account of the nature of the desire's *object*. To affirm of God that he is possible is the same as to affirm that he exists, since his existence is the condition of every possibility.[120]

Here we reach one of those moot points that we mentioned at the beginning of this section. To trace down the implications of Maréchal's position that affirming the possibility of God is the same as affirming his existence and to place his position into dialogue with the tradition of the ontological argument, would be interesting and perhaps fruitful in itself but would not bear directly on Rahner's very different approach to human dynamism. Let it suffice for now that we retain the main point (movement towards God as the condition of the possibility of objective knowledge) and table the other point (that demonstrating the possibility of God is equivalent to demonstrating his existence). What is clear is that man's "con-tingent" contact with God is *anticipatory*, not achieved: "Only at the *end* could the question of 'being' be stated in its fullness—and perhaps be resolved."[121]

The Insertion of the Species into the Finalism of the Intellect. The gain thus far is that man is an ontological dynamism that can have for its end only the fullness of being. If he were only a material being, that is, one whose form was only the form-of-matter, the goal of his dynamism would be only the perfection of his form, for the distention at the heart of his dynamism would be only the disproportion between the perfection of form *per se* and the imperfection of the form as restricted to this particular matter. But man's form is immaterial and hence able to know, able to assimilate forms other than itself insofar as they are other, without losing his own form in the process. In short, man can transcend himself.

> But for the immaterial form, which is already perfect as a natural form, there is only one way of self-transcending and of striving for the perfection of being: the "objective" way, through intentional enrichment, through assimilation of intelligibles. Hence, on its higher level, human finality no longer intends the acquisition of "natural" but of intelligible perfections.[122]

Such intelligible perfections are called the "species," which at this point we may define heuristically as that whereby the data are ontologically assimilated to the knowing subject.

But the imperfection of the human intellect requires that, besides the immanence of the datum (or better, precisely *in* this immanence), there must be the element of otherness or opposition. The question is: In what relationship between knower and known is the known seen precisely as opposed to the subject (hence, seen as an object) while at the same time being immanent to the subject?

Maréchal answers: Precisely insofar as the datum is assimilated into the subject's *tendency to its end* (i.e., into its very being), it is known as opposed to the subject. Five steps lead to this conclusion.

(1) Man can know an object only insofar as it is in being and somehow correlative to man's own mode of being, hence, only insofar as it is caught up in man's own dynamic tendency toward full reality. (2) But that means that man can know a being only in terms of *his own finality.* "There is no knowledge of a finite object that is not accompanied, at least implicitly, by a consequent finality. Whatever is desired, is desired in virtue of the ultimate end."[123] (3) But because the goal of man's finality is always more than the particular known object, that object cannot satisfy man's appetite for knowing. It can be known only as a partial, subordinate end. "The assimilation occurs under the initial and permanent influence of a wider end, with respect to which the assimilated form is grasped and held as a *subordinate end.*"[124] (4) But precisely inso-

far as the finite object is known as a *partial* end, it shares the character of the final end of the movement:

> But once they are posited, subordinate ends possess exactly the same necessity as the higher, superordinated ends on which they depend.[125]

> Thus the reception of the impressed species in the possible intellect takes on the necessary meaning of a partial anticipation of the final intuitive possession. In other words, the reception of the species must share in that which, for the intellective subject, constitutes the attractive value of the intuition of being.[126]

(5) Thus the conclusion: "In a discursive intelligence, the assimilated form is opposed to the subject and acquires an 'in itself' insofar as it constitutes, for the subject, a *dynamic value*, a *moment of an active becoming*."[127] The species is seen as an end (albeit partial) and as a participation in the final end of being. It is therefore known (a) as opposed to the subject and (b) as referred to the absolute order of necessity, the order of being. The species is objectified.

Excursus: Dynamism and the Possibility of a Supernatural End. At the heart of his deduction of the ontological affirmation Maréchal inserts a brief, twelve-page reflection on the relation between the final end of intellectual becoming and the possibility of a supernatural end for man. Insofar as this contribution had a marked influence on the Rahner of HW and later works (even perhaps the theological "hidden clef" of GW), it deserves at least a brief mention at this point.

Maréchal begins his treatment by noting the general principle:

> The ultimate *end* of intellectual becoming can be read in the natural *form* (formal object) of this "becoming," and it has been shown in our concept of "transcendental being" (*ens qua tale*). Since the formal object of a tendency is the measure of the amplitude of the end whither this tendency keeps striving, we know that the ultimate and satiating end of the intellect must be a reality possessing no limiting determination, that is, a transcendent object, a *subsisting infinite*.[128]

Aquinas holds that human acts are specified by their intended ends and that every object of human willing is willed in virtue of the ultimate end. Man's ultimate end is beatitude or happiness—which for man cannot consist in any created thing, since *universal* good cannot be found in creatures. "Man's happiness consists, therefore, in God alone" (S.T., I-II, 2, 8, c.).

Maréchal asks what is the intellectual fullness that defines the objective term (*finis cujus*) of human activity, and he argues that it must be contemplation of God—not the general or confused knowledge that all men have of God, nor knowledge by way of demonstration (which is analogical and imperfect) nor the knowledge had through faith (since faith is the most imperfect kind of intellectual knowledge).

> Only one kind of knowledge would leave us nothing more to desire in the intellectual order: the *intuitive knowledge of absolute being*. Thus St. Thomas concludes with a perfectly justified boldness: "There cannot be ultimate and perfect beatitude except in the vision of the divine essence" (S.T., I-II, 3, 8, c; cf. S.C.G., III, 50 ff.).[129]

For such an intuitive knowledge of God's essence it is necessary that God communicate himself actively to the soul and that he become an intelligible form of it, that is, that he be both *quod videtur* and *quo videtur*. That is to say that over and above nature, man requires a divine initiative, a supernatural grace, if he is to be able to intuit the divine essence.

This, of course, poses a problem to the whole method that Maréchal has been using in *Cahier V.*

> We should not forget that our inquiry about the ultimate end has been conducted from the critical point of view. If we really hoped to discover in this way the unshakable foundation of an epistemology, it is not rather embarrassing to discover that our absolute ultimate end depends on the free bestowal of a supernatural grace?[130]

Maréchal's answer to that question is his unique contribution to the debate about the supernatural in Catholic philosophy and theology. It is clear, he says, that the full satisfaction of our higher faculties cannot be had in the purely natural order. Yet from that evidence we cannot conclude to the existence of a supernatural end, for that can be known only through supernatural revelation. All that we are sure of, from the argument so far, is the *negative* possibility of a supernatural end. "The fact that we desire an end is not an evident sign of its real possibility."[131] Yet Aquinas does not condemn man to fideism; he does not say that there is total ignorance in man about the existence of a supernatural end, even without revelation. From our very faculties and their dynamic striving we can deduce "*the absolute* (positive) *possibility* of this beatitude, that is, the *existence of the remote objective causes which render its realization possible.*"[132]

The crux of this proposition is the Scholastic axiom that a natural desire cannot be absurd, "which means that the natural finality—the fundamental law of becoming—reveals at least the *possibility in se* of an

end toward which it strives."[133] Given the earlier position that man's dynamism is toward a being that cannot be impossible in itself, Maréchal
proposes a hypothesis that bears citing in full.

> . . . If the first causes of the motion are, at least in part, *free agents*, they may
> create, in the subject who is in motion, an initial orientation whose full de-
> velopment remains subordinated to a new free intervention coming from
> them. In this event it is not certain that the subject in motion, whatever may
> be its natural [as contrasted with elicited] "desire," will be able to reach its
> ultimate end. Reaching this absolutely ultimate end would belong only to
> the domain of remote *possibilities*. The only thing which would be certain is
> *the existence of all the factors required for this possibility.*[134]

Thus Maréchal has not overstepped critical boundaries in his philosophical doctrine on man's ultimate end. He holds with St. Thomas that the
intuition of God's essence does indeed exceed natural powers, yet he
cannot deny the objective (i.e., absolute) *possibility* of man's reaching
that end, given the nature of human striving.

> But this objective, even remote, possibility implies two necessary conditions:
> *the existence of an absolute being*, which is capable of communicating itself,
> and the *capability of our intelligence* for receiving this communication.[135]

These are close to the conclusions that Rahner will reach in HW on the
question of the possibility of revelation.

4. The Transcendental Transposition

The first five hundred pages of *Cahier V* go under the title "The Theory of Knowledge Within the Framework of Thomistic Metaphysics,"
that is, they constitute what Maréchal calls a "metaphysical" rather
than a "transcendental" critique of cognition. In carrying this out, however, Maréchal constantly highlights elements of the Thomistic theory of
knowledge that invite a *rapprochement* with Kantianism, such as the
apriority of knowing faculties expressed in their formal object. But if the
limitations of Kant's position are to be shown up and surpassed from
within the very methodology of Kant, a further and very radical step
must be taken: Maréchal must translate the entire metaphysics of
knowledge into a transcendental framework. This is the topic of the last
seventy pages of the work: "The Thomist Critique of Knowledge Trans-
posed into the Transcendental Mode."[136] Again the question of "moot
points" emerges from the perspective of Rahner's work, and our treatment here will emphasize only the main features of Maréchal's critical

transposition, especially the question of how the transcendental method works in the effort to reach the transcendent level.

The very title of *Cahier V* indicates the goal of the work: "Thomism in Confrontation with Critical Philosophy." Maréchal's purpose is to confront the metaphysics of knowledge, which has already been elaborated, with Kant's transcendental critique of the faculty of knowing and in so doing to overcome the inherent relativity and phenomenalism of KRV. In the earliest redaction of that fifth volume (1917), Maréchal had already summarized his criticism of the Kantian "ontological epoché":

> Proceeding from a viewpoint that is peculiar to the whole modern critique, i.e., from the viewpoint of "appearance," we feel that this starting point must be validated and that we must establish that "objective appearance" can be determined only in relation to an absolute. The viewpoint of pure appearance is obviously artificial and full of contradiction.[137]

Cahier V begins with a comparison of "the two ways of critique," the metaphysical critique of the object and the transcendental critique of the subject's knowing faculties. The cornerstone of traditional metaphysics, we have seen, is the principle of identity interpreted as a synthetic and ontological principle, which Maréchal insists affirms the absolute reality of the object.[138] When traditional metaphysics say "This thing is," it means that the object of thought belongs within the horizon of absolute being/reality. However, when Kant says "This thing is," he means that the content of consciousness is an object-for-me, that is, a phenomenal reality. Basic to this restrictive affirmation, Maréchal says, is Kant's employment of the transcendental method wherein objects are referred to *a priori* faculties as matter is referred to form.

> If the analysis of Kant is exact, to know *objectively*, i.e., to become conscious of something as an object, therefore consists in determining *a priori*, according to increasingly general formal conditions, a material content imposed from without on our sensibility.[139]

Maréchal suggests that, if we are to employ transcendental method in a manner suitable to contemporary requirements, we must bracket Kant's presumption of the universal and necessary character of mathematics and Newtonian scientific principles.

> If, therefore, one wishes to institute a critique which does not presuppose, before any inquiry, the universal and necessary character of certain categories of synthetic judgments, one will have to demonstrate, more directly than

by appeal to the pure sciences, the intervention of *a priori* conditions in the very constitution of the object.[140]

Cahier IV shows how Kant often approximates a more dynamic and less formalistic conception of knowledge,[141] and it is this dynamic tendency that Maréchal himself seeks to work out. Kant indeed knew that the object is present to consciousness dynamically (in his *Reflexionen* he wrote: *Intelligere ist ein Thun*[142]), but he failed to follow out this insight to its full consequence. Given this failure, Kant came to see the categories as static forms rather than as *performances* of the subject in a dynamic function of synthesis. But if the *a priori* subject is essentially an activity, and if the contents of consciousness are indeed "in" that subject (and in a sense *are* the subject), then what Kant's transcendental reduction should have discovered is the subject's *activity* immanent in the constituted object.

The subject of KRV is a functional reality, the locus of the totality of *a priori* determinations. Moreover, the "faculties" do not designate for Kant some kind of abstract, detached labels in the object but partial groups of *a priori* determinations *of* the object. Once again these definitions lack a base and even become unintelligible if the formal apriority in the object is not understood in an active, dynamic sense.[143]

Shining through this "active" formulation of the transcendental reduction is Maréchal's conviction that, according to the normative state of constitutive knowledge in God, perfect objectivity is the result of perfect (creative) activity. Objectivity (true knowledge of the other as it is) is in direct proportion to the apriority of the knowing subject. Thus Maréchal can affirm that the goal of the transcendental reduction is "to rediscover *the active part of the subject in the immanent object.*"[144] In Scholastic language one could say that the subject's *a priori* contribution to the known object is not merely the act of imposing inert formal conditions on the material element, but is "the active investment of a knowable material with the *internal finality*, the 'natural becoming' of the subject."[145] In the final analysis the subject's potency for being, his movement towards his ontological *telos*, is the metaphysical *a priori* that Maréchal hopes to uncover by a transcendental reduction.

It is the role of the transcendental deduction to go back over the ground covered by the transcendental reduction in order to show that only on the condition of the *a priori* that was discovered in the reduction can the contents of consciousness be established as objective knowledge.

If man is a movement from potency to act, and if the contents of consciousness (*intellectum in actu*) are identical with the knowing subject
(*intellectus in actu*) in one and the same act, then the known object
would have to be given to us in reflection "not as a 'dead thing' but as
'passing from potency to act,' as a phase in a 'movement' or 'becoming'
of the intellect," and the transcendental deduction would demonstrate
that "the immanent object is revealed to reflection as the exercise of an
activity and not as an inert form."[146]

> In brief, the presupposition of the transcendental method of analysis seems
> to be this: that our objective concepts are given to us in reflection as the ac-
> tive determinations of an assimilated material, as the passage from an objec-
> tive potency of determination to actual determinations, in a word, as the
> immanent "movement" of a knowing faculty insofar as it is knowing.[147]

If Kant did not go this far, Maréchal says, it was because he was
caught between two tendencies of his thought. On the one hand he did
affirm the dynamic element in human knowledge (for example, he frequently compares human knowing with, and measures it by, the standard of God's spontaneity), yet on the other hand he fell victim to the
static understanding of knowledge that he inherited from Descartes and
Wolff. As a consequence he adhered to a rigid view of form, and he read
the transcendental unity of apperception not as an *act* of synthesis but as
"an abstract index of unity."[148] From this follows the restrictive formalism of Kant's critique of cognition. Were Kant to have followed the first
or dynamic tendency, his analysis of the genesis of the object as object
would have revealed the subject's *a priori* role as consisting in an active
power of unifying, and from this vantage point he could have conceiv-
ably gone on to an ontological affirmation by way of the finality of the
intellect.[149]

Maréchal's reinterpretation of the transcendental method stands at
the heart of his transposition of the Thomist theory of knowledge into
critical terms. The actual carrying out of the program in the last pages
of *Cahier V* is of less interest from the viewpoint of Rahner. In a series of
thirteen theses spread over some forty pages, Maréchal shows how,
while prescinding from the distinctions between the phenomenal and
the noumenal and between the logical and the ontological, that is, by
beginning on "neutral terrain," one can show the ontological affirmation to be constitutive of the objectivity of the contents of consciousness.
Beginning with those contents of consciousness, Maréchal shows that
the static and categorial concretive synthesis (the union of concepts
without objectively referring them to the real order of being) must be

surpassed by an objective synthesis or affirmation that is both dynamic and transcategorial. From there, by an analysis of the intrinsic finality of intellect and the assimilation of data as moments in that finality, he shows the speculative necessity of an ontological affirmation of noumenal reality.

> The intellectual assimilation of the data, inseparably joined to their introduction into the absolute order of finality, is nothing but the affirmation, the "transcendental act" or the "objective form" of the judgment. Therefore, the affirmation has a metaphysical value.[150]

Since we have already covered this matter from another viewpoint (see Section 3 on the insertion of the species into the finality of the intellect), we may omit further discussion of it here. The important thing to note is that on the basis of the transcendental method Maréchal claims to have opened up the necessity of an implicit affirmation of God in every act of true judgment and thus to have established the possibility of a thematic metaphysics by way of analogy (*negatio, remotio, excessus*). The crux of the transcendental transposition has been Maréchal's move from form to act within a critical framework.

After Rousselot, reading Maréchal is a different kind of philosophical experience. Something gained, something lost. The poetry is gone, the existential excitement is toned down, but the insights have matured and are systematically grounded in the full sweep of Aquinas's theory of knowledge. Not the least factor in the shift of tone was the mindless ecclesiastical censorship that forced Maréchal to rewrite his work time and again over a period of sixteen months before it could be published with an *imprimatur*. As a result *Cahier V* is bulky and repetitious. Everyone, Maréchal said, wanted to "contribute his stone to the monument." Nonetheless, even if a bit clumsy, the monument stands.

Although Rahner was to follow different paths in his own theory of knowledge, the influence of Maréchal, like that of Rousselot, helped to determine much of GW, especially in the following areas. First and above all, there is the thesis that knowledge is—in analogical degrees, of course—a matter of identity. The normative state of knowledge in God shows that subject and object are one in the act of knowing and that being and knowing are, in the final analysis, the same. This is the position that Rahner will thematize under the heading of "being/reality as *Bei-sich-sein.*" Secondly and as a corollary, there is the thesis that the non-identity of being and knowing in the act of knowledge—that is, the distance between subject and object—is a sign of imperfection and can adequately be explained only in ontological terms, namely, as a lack of self-presence. This is what Rahner will work out in his notion of prime matter as *Beim-andern-sein*. Thirdly, affirmation is read as a dynamic substitute, in human discursive cognition, for the intellectual intuition operative in different ways in God and the angels. As a dynamic substitute, affirmation will be interpreted in terms of man's ontological movement towards absolute being and as covering the whole range of being, from prime matter to pure act. Fourthly, affirmation will be seen to have as its constitutive (and not merely regulative) function the implicit affirmation of the fullness of being. God is presumed (and thus somehow known) in every act of knowledge. Fifthly, the presence of the fullness of being to man in the act of knowledge will be seen as given always under the aegis of man's dynamism, his potentiality for being—what Rahner, following Heidegger, will discuss as the "questioning" and "anticipation" (*Vorgriff*) of being.

Clearly, the crucial problem at stake is that of movement. And perhaps in no other thinker of this century has the issue of *kinēsis* received such a radical and thoroughgoing analysis as in Martin Heidegger. After Rahner's studies of Rousselot and Maréchal at Pullach (Munich), it was almost the next logical step for Rahner to go to Freiburg to study under the man who was interpreting human existence and even being itself in terms of the kinetic tension of presence and absence.

Notes

1. Rahner, GW v/xlvii (9) (Rousselot and Maréchal). Karl Rahner, "Aquinas: The Nature of Truth," *Continuum* II (1964), 68 (Maréchal alone). See D. Patrick Granfield, "An Interview: Karl Rahner, Theologian at Work," *American Ecclesiastical Review*, 153 (1965), 217-30, esp. 221.
2. On transcendental Thomism: Joseph Donceel, "A Thomistic Misapprehension?" *Thought*, 32 (1957), 189-98; "On Transcendental Thomism," *Continuum* 7 (1969), 164-68; and "Trancendental Thomism," *Monist*, 58 (1974), 67-85. Edward Mackinnon, "The Transcendental Turn: Necessary but not Sufficient," *Continuum* 6 (1968), 225-31. Bernard A.M. Nachbar, "Is it Thomism?" *Continuum* 6 (1968), 332-35; Leslie Dewart, "On Transcendental Thomism," *Continuum* 6 (1968), 389-401; and "A response to J. Donceel," *Continuum* 7 (1969), 453-62. A survey of transcendental Thomism is given in Helen James John, *The Thomist Spectrum* (New York: Fordham University Press, 1966); and George van Riet, *Thomistic Epistemology*, trans. Gabriel Franks (St. Louis and London: Herder and

Herder, 1963), vol. I. The relation between transcendental method and transcendental Thomism is studied in Otto Muck, *The Transcendental Method*, trans. William D. Seidensticker (New York: Herder and Herder, 1968).

3. Pierre Rousselot, "Amour spirituel" (see n. 6 below), p. 229. Italicized in the original.

4. Pierre Rousselot *L'Intellectualisme de saint Thomas*, 2nd. ed. (Paris: Beauchesne, 1924), p. 77; *The Intellectualism of St. Thomas*, trans. James E. O'Malony (New York: Sheed and Ward, 1935), p. 84 f. Hereafter the work is abbreviated *L'Intellectualisme* followed by the French and then the English page numbers.

5. Pierre Rousselot, "L'Esprit de saint Thomas" (see following note), p. 623.

6. For a biographical sketch of Rousselot, see Leonce de Grandmaison, "Pierre Rousselot" in Rousselot, *L'Intellectualisme*, pp.[v]-[xi]. A bibliography of his works is found in *Mémorial Pierre Rousselot, S.J., 1878-1915: Recherches de science religieuse*, 53 (July-Sept. 1965), 340-42. That entire issue of *RSR*, pp. 337-544, is devoted to Rousselot. I use the following works of Rousselot:

   1. *L'Intellectualisme* (see n. 4 above).
   2. "Amour spirituel et synthèse aperceptive," *Revue de Philosophie*, 17 (1910), 225-40.
   3. "L'Etre et l'Esprit," *Revue de Philosophie*, 17 (1910), 561-74. (This is a continuation of the previous article.)
   4. "Métaphysique thomiste et critique de la connaissance," *Revue Néoscolastique de Louvain*, 17 (1910), 476-509.
   5. "Intellectualisme," *Dictionnaire Apologétique de la Foi Catholique*, II (1914), 580-91.
   6. "Théorie des concepts par l'unité fonctionnelle suivant les principes de saint Thomas. Synthèse aperceptive et connaissance d'amour vécue," *Archives de Philosophie*, 23 (1960), 573-607.
   7. "L'Esprit de saint Thomas d'après un livre récent," *Etudes*, 128 (1911), 614-29.

7. Rousselot, "L'Esprit de saint Thomas," p. 615.

8. This paragraph is drawn from "L'Esprit de saint Thomas," pp. 621-25, except for "Métaphysique thomiste," p. 478 (insinuate...discredit).

9. Rousselot, "Métaphysique thomiste," p. 509 (interiorized Scholasticism, Marcus Aurelius); also "L'Esprit de saint Thomas," p. 623 f. (interiorized Thomism; metaphysics and critique of knowledge).

10. Rousselot, "L'Esprit de saint Thomas," p. 623 f. For "progressive being," p. 622.

11. Ibid., p. 624.

12. Rousselot, "Théorie des concepts," p. 590.

13. Rousselot, "Métaphysique thomiste," p. 509.

14. Cf. Aristotle: *De Partibus Animalium*, A, 640 a 18 (*genesis heneka ousias*); *Topics*, Z, 139 b 20 (*hē genesis agogē eis ousian*); *Physics*, TH, 9, 265 a 23 (*proteron to teleion*); *Metaphysics*, TH, 9, 1049 b 5 (*proteron energeia*

dynameōs); also Rousselot, *L'Intellectualisme*, p. 226/219 and Heidegger, *What is a Thing?*, p. 84.

15. Rousselot, *L'Intellectualisme*, p. 53/44.
16. Rousselot, "Métaphysique thomiste," p. 501.
17. Ibid., p. 507, n. 1. Cf. "The originality of St. Thomas' intellectualism consists precisely in the fact that his rigorous critique of human cognition is joined to his unshakeable confidence in its results, insofar as human cognition participates in *intellectus*" (Cited in Jules Lebreton, "Rousselot [Pierre]" *Dictionnaire de Théologie*, XIV [1939], col. 134).
18. See Martin Heidegger, "On the Being and Conception of *Physis*," *Man and World*, 9 (1976), 241.
19. Rousselot, *L'Intellectualisme*, p. 20/32; "Théorie des concepts," p. 581; "Amour spirituel," p. 232.
20. Rousselot, *L'Intellectualisme*, p. 24/36 (Platonism, noocentric), p. 9/22 (absolute Spirit), p. 22/34 (Spirit first, subsistent intelligibles). "Amour spirituel," p. 225 (first principle of Scholasticism).
21. Rousselot, *L'Intellectualisme*, p. x/8.
22. Rousselot, "L'Esprit de saint Thomas," p. 618.
23. Ibid., p. 620.
24. Ibid., p. 616.
25. Rousselot, "Métaphysique thomiste," p. 476. On the necessity of the "blemish" of "solidification," *L'Intellectualisme*, p. vi/10. For Rousselot's ratification of Blondel's critique of representative thought, "Métaphysique thomiste," p. 502, n. 1.
26. Rousselot, *L'Intellectualisme*, p. 228f./223. Cf. ibid., p. 25f./37 (the role of angelic knowledge in preventing the "idolatry of the enunciable").
27. Rousselot, *L'Intellectualisme*, p. 3/17, p. 11/24, etc.
28. Ibid., p. 19/31.
29. Rousselot, "L'Esprit de saint Thomas," p. 620.
30. Rousselot, *L'Intellectualisme*, p. 77/84. Cf. p. 90/96 f. (seizing being itself).
31. Ibid., p. 11f./25. Cf. p. 17/29.
32. Rousselot, "Théorie des concepts," p. 601; "Métaphysique thomiste," p. 484.
33. On the levels of knowledge, Rousselot, "Métaphysique thomiste," pp. 482-89. On knowledge by connaturality, ibid, p. 487, n. 4; "Théorie des concepts," pp. 591-96 and 606. Text translated in Frederick J.D. Scott, "Maurice Blondel and Pierre Rousselot," *New Scholasticism*, 36 (1962) 350, "L'Etre et l'Esprit," p. 562 and 569.
34. Rousselot, *L'Intellectualisme*, p. v/2 f.
35. Ibid., p. 38/49.
36. Ibid., p. 62/71.
37. Rousselot, "Métaphysique thomiste," p. 504. Cf. "Amour spirituel," p. 229.
38. Rousselot, *L'Intellectualisme*, p. 226/220.
39. Cited in Pierre Tiberghien, "A propos d'un texte du Père Rousselot," *Mélanges de Science Religieuse*, 10 (1953), 104.

40. Rousselot, *L'Intellectualisme*, p. 45/54. Angelic knowledge plays a similar role in Rahner: GW 19f./36f. (50 f.). On angels as monads, see GW 249/343 (344) and "Aquinas: The Nature of Truth," *Continuum*, 2 (1964), 61.

41. The first two quotations are cited in Scott, "Blondel and Rousselot" (see n.33 above), p. 338; the last, Rousselot, "Métaphysique thomiste," p. 490; cf. ibid., p. 495: "*La condition pour étreindre ou envisager l'être même corporel, c'est d'étreindre ou d'envisager l'esprit.*"

42. Rousselot, *L'Intellectualisme*, p. 24/36.

43. Rousselot, "Amour spirituel," p. 232.

44. Rousselot, "L'Etre et l'Esprit," p. 569. Cf. *L'Intellectualisme*, p. 18/30.

45. Cited in Scott, "Blondel and Rousselot" (see n. 33 above), p. 338 (angelic refused us), p. 339 (synthesis never made), and p. 341 (series of noumenon).

46. See Rousselot, *L'Intellectualisme*, p. xvii/13.

47. St. Thomas Aquinas, *In Librum Boëtii De Trinitate Expositio*, Lect. II, q. II, a. 1, ad tertiam: "Unde dicit Boëtius in IV *de Consol.* [prosa 6], quod similiter se habet ratio ad intellectum, sicut tempus ad aeternitatem et circulus ad centrum." In St. Thomas Aquinas, *Opuscula Theologica*, ed. M. Calcaterra (Rome: Marietti, 1954), II, 382. Cf. Rousselot, *L'Intellectualisme*, p. 57/56.

48. Rousselot, "Amour spirituel," p. 232.

49. Ibid., p. 233 (does not fill); "L'Etre et L'Esprit," p. 566 (imperfectly spiritual), "Métaphysique thomiste," p. 488 (innate); "Amour spirituel," p. 229 (inclination); "Théorie des concepts," p. 604 (motus, amoris); "Amour spirituel," p. 233 (anxiety); Rousselot in Scott, p. 339 (to stop is to deny).

50. Cited in Scott, p. 340 f.

51. Rousselot, "Théorie des concepts," p. 605.

52. Cited in Scott, "Blondel and Rousselot," p. 345.

53. Rousselot, "Métaphysique thomiste," p. 488.

54. T.S. Eliot, "Little Gidding," V in *The Complete Poems and Plays of T.S. Eliot* (London: Faber and Faber, 1969), p. 197.

55. Rousselot, "Amour spirituel," p. 230.

56. On *pros ti*, cf. Rousselot, "Théorie des concepts," p. 605. On the meaning of "palpitating," *L'Intellectualisme*, [ix f.]: Introduction by Grandmaison.

57. Rousselot, "Théorie des concepts," p. 576.

58. Ibid., p. 576-77.

59. Ibid., p. 577.

60. Ibid., p. 578. On *empeiria*, see *Meta*, A, 1, 981 a 1-30.

61. Ibid., p. 592-93.

62. Rousselot, "Métaphysique thomiste," p. 485.

63. Ibid., p. 489.

64. Rousselot, *L'Intellectualisme*, p. xii/9.

65. Rousselot, "Métaphysique thomiste," p. 497.

66. Ibid., p. 498-99.

67. Cited in Scott "Blondel and Rousselot," p. 352 (sketch, semblance), p. 339

(image of end; implies a progress); "Théorie des concepts," p. 602 (future intuition).

68. Rousselot, "L'Etre et l'Esprit," p. 564 (all italics in original) and 574.

69. Cited in Scott, "Blondel and Rousselot," p. 340.

70. The title of all five volumes of Maréchal's magnum opus is *Le point de départ de la métaphysique: Leçons sur le développement historique et théorique du probleme de la connaissance* (Paris: Desclée de Brouwer; and Brussels: L'Edition Universelle). The individual volumes are:

Cahier I: *De l'antiquité à la fin du Moyen Age: La critique ancienne,* 3rd ed., 1943. (Originally published, 1922).

Cahier II: *Le conflit du rationalisme et de l'empirisme dans la philosophie moderne avant Kant,* 3rd ed., 1944 (original, 1923).

Cahier III: *La critique de Kant,* 3rd ed., 1944 (original, 1923).

Cahier IV: *Le système idealiste chez Kant et les postkantiens,* 1st ed., 1947.

Cahier V: *Le thomisme devant la philosophie critique,* 2nd ed., 1949 (originally published, 1926).

Brief excerpts from the first three volumes and almost half of the fifth volume are found in English in Joseph Maréchal, *A Maréchal Reader,* ed. and trans. Joseph Donceel (New York: Herder and Herder, 1970). References to *Le point de départ* give the volume (*Cahier*) and page of the French, followed by the corresponding page in *A Maréchal Reader* when the passage has been translated there. Bibliographies of Maréchal's works can be found in *Mélanges Maréchal,* 2 vols. (Paris: Desclée de Brouwer; and Brussels: L'Edition Universelle, 1950), I: *Oeuvres,* pp. 47-71, and in E. Dirven, *De la forme à l'acte: Essai sur le thomisme de Joseph Maréchal, S.J.* (Paris-Bruges, Desclée de Brouwer, 1965), pp. 289-94.

71. "Omnis cognitio exercetur secundum aliquam identitatem subjecti et objecti..." (*Première formule d'une doctrine complètement formée dans mon esprit,* in *Mélanges Maréchal,* I, 299). This brief document (pp. 299-303) stems from 1920 and represents Maréchal's first formulation of his critical Thomistic viewpoint.

72. Maréchal, *Cahier V,* 110 ff./98 ff.

73. Here too is the root of Bernard Lonergan's designation of God as *Ipsum Intelligere.* See his *Verbum: Word and Idea in Aquinas,* ed. David B. Burrell (Notre Dame, Ind.: Notre Dame University Press, 1967), p. 190 f.

74. Maréchal, *Cahier V,* 110/103.

75. Ibid., 102/97, for this and the previous citation.

76. Ibid., 117/109.

77. Ibid., 112/104.

78. "Modus, igitur, et perfectio cognitionis sequuntur modum et perfectionem *immanentiae* objecti in subjecto" (*Première formule,* p. 300).

79. Maréchal, *Cahier V,* 119/110.

80. Ibid., 327.

81. Ibid., 191, n. 1.

82. Respectively: S.C.G., I, 72; S.T., I, 12, 1, c. (cf. S.T., I, 5, 2, c.); *I Sent.*, 19, 5, 1, ad 7 (cf. *De Ver.* 1, 3, sed contra).
83. Maréchal, *Cahier V,* 348 f.
84. Ibid., 121/111.
85. Ibid., 22
86. Ibid., 23.
87. Ibid., 23 f.
88. Ibid., 108/101.
89. Ibid., 24.
90. Ibid., 187.
91. Ibid., 187/194.
92. Ibid., 107/101.
93. Ibid., 355/160.
94. Ibid., 320.
95. Ibid., 519.
96. Ibid., 321.
97. Ibid., 338.
98. Ibid., 321.
99. Ibid., 347/156.
100. Ibid., 349.
101. Ibid., 354/159.
102. Ibid.
103. Ibid., 355-160.
104. Ibid., 13.
105. Ibid., 431, in the *first* edition, cited in Van Riet, *Thomistic Epistemology* (see n. 1 above), p. 269.
106. Maréchal, *Cahier V,* 95/94.
107. Ibid., 94/93.
108. Ibid., 97/95. Italicized in the original.
109. Ibid., 458/189 f.
110. Ibid., 337.
111. Maréchal, "On Intellectual Dynamism," *Maréchal Reader,* p. 247.
112. "Intellectus noster, dum objecta cognoscit, movetur de potentia ad actum. Ergo forma objectiva nostri intellectus est forma motus (latiori sensu) et proportionatur alicui fini ultimo" (*Première formule,* p. 301).
113. Maréchal, *Cahier V,* 26.
114. "Forma objectiva potentiae intellectivae est per se illimitata, spectatis tum intellectu possibili (quo est omnia fieri) tum intellectu agente (quo est omnia facere)" (*Première formule,* p. 301).
115. "Sequitur finem ultimum objectivum intellectus nostri esse infinitum" (*Première formule,* p. 301).
116. Maréchal, "On Intellectual Dynamism," *Maréchal Reader,* p. 248.
117. Maréchal, *Cahier V,* 448/184.
118. Ibid., 155.
119. Ibid., 448f./185.

120. Ibid., 449f./185.
121. Cited in Van Riet, *Thomistic Epistemology* (see n. 2 above), p. 268 f.
122. Maréchal, "On Intellectual Dynamism," *Maréchal Reader*, p. 247.
123. "Nulla est cognitio objecti finiti, quam non comitetur, saltem implicite, finalitas consequens; quidquid enim appetitur appetitur in virtute finis ultimi" (*Première formule*, p. 301).
124. Maréchal, *Cahier V*, 459/190.
125. Ibid.
126. Maréchal, "On Intellectual Dynamism," *Maréchal Reader*, p. 248.
127. Maréchal, *Cahier V*, 444/181.
128. Ibid., 412/172.
129. Ibid., 417.
130. Ibid., 419/172.
131. Ibid., 420/173.
132. Ibid., 421/173 f.
133. Ibid., 421/174.
134. Ibid., 422/174.
135. Ibid., 424/175.
136. Ibid., 505-68/217-31.
137. Cited in Otto Muck, *The Transcendental Method*, trans. William D. Seidensticker (New York: Herder and Herder, 1968), p. 43 f.
138. Maréchal, *Cahier V*, 49 and 51.
139. Ibid., 53.
140. Ibid., 54.
141. Maréchal, *Cahier IV*, 112-37.
142. Cited in *Recherches de Science Religieuse*, 53 (1965), 409.
143. Maréchal, *Cahier V*, 58.
144. Ibid.
145. Ibid., 59.
146. Ibid., 61.
147. Ibid., 63.
148. Ibid., 65.
149. Thus Maréchal formulates his own task vis-à-vis Kant, "to establish *a priori*. . .that for *every* non-intuitive intelligence the means and the only means of representing the contents of consciousness as *objects* is their strictly metaphysical affirmation, that is, their well determined, at least implicit, relation to a transcendent reality, so that a rejection of such an affirmation would amount to a denial of the very possibility of objective thought" (*Cahier V*, 318/154; see also V, 65 f).
150. Maréchal, *Cahier V*, 553/223.

CHAPTER III

Heidegger: A Rahnerian Reading

When Karl Rahner began his philosophical studies at the University of Freiburg in the fall of 1934, his favorite teacher, Martin Heidegger, was already underway toward what would later be called "the turn" (*die Kehre*) in his thinking.[1] The book that made Heidegger's reputation in 1927, *Sein und Zeit* (hereafter SZ), had set for itself a threefold goal: first, the analysis of the existential movement (or "temporality") that constitutes man's transcendence; second, the elaboration of the kinetic (or "time-determined") structure of all modes of the being of things; and third, the "destruction" of the tradition of Western metaphysics in order to reveal the kinetic-temporal source of its categories of being. However, in 1927 only the "first half" of SZ was published (in fact, the "second half" was never to appear), and this "first half" fulfilled only the first of these three goals: the analysis of the existential movement or temporality of human transcendence (or Dasein). The promised "turn" in philosophical thinking about being was to occur in the unpublished second area of analysis, which was to demonstrate that the "meaning of being" is "time."

The promised "turn," or as Heidegger had earlier called it, the "transformation" (*Umwandlung*) in Western thinking, was not to be a change in the aim that Heidegger had stated in SZ. Rather, the turn was to fulfill that aim in a new realization of what it is that constitutes the essence of the being of entities (*das Wesen des Seins*). Heidegger would show that being is not the static and objective "presentness" of entities in reality but rather the dynamic "disclosure" of entities within the lived world of man's concerns. Moreover, Heidegger would show

(1) that this kinetic disclosure of entities *conceals itself* precisely while it *discloses entities;* and
(2) that this self-concealing disclosure of entities happens only in

conjunction with *human transcendence*, the "term" of which is nothing other than the disclosedness of entities.

There is, of course, a circularity to this "being": human transcendence moves beyond entities, unto the ontological disclosedness-of entities that in fact originally prompts human transcendence. Heidegger would eventually call this circle by the name *Ereignis*. We may paraphrase *Ereignis* roughly as the "event" whereby everything is "impropriated" or "comes into its own": man is brought into his transcendence, entities come into appearance, and the disclosure-process remains concealed.

According to Heidegger, the archaic or pre–Socratic Greek thinkers already had an intimation of *some elements* of this threefold process. At least they knew about the kinetic disclosure-of-entities (*alētheia*). It can be argued that they even had a penumbral, not totally thematic, awareness of the self-concealing nature of *alētheia (lēthē)*. It is harder to make the case that they knew about the essence of human being as transcendence to (and evoked by) the self-concealing disclosure-of-entities. At any rate, Heidegger's own retrieval of the unsaid subtext in various pre-Socratic fragments—a task he was already involved in when Rahner came to study with him—sought to reveal the full tri-dimensionality of the process of "being."[2]

Heidegger's strategy was that of unpacking the structure of *kinēsis* both within man's essence as transcendence and within the process of disclosure. In classical Greek thought *kinēsis* is movement as the ontological reality (the being) of whatever is in movement, that is, of a thing that does not fully appear (is not completely present) and yet in fact does appear in its incompleteness. Therefore, the kinetic-ontological presence of a moving entity is always fraught with absentiality: a "not yet" and a "no longer," a coming into and a going from presence.

Such relative absentiality is precisely what lets the entity *be* a moving entity. In the case of man, his relative absentiality is his living into possibilities: this not-yet-ness is constitutive of whatever momentary being or presence he has. Moreover, as we shall see below, man's kinetic pres-absence cooperates in opening up the realm of the accessibility or sense of entities, the "clearing" in which entities become available. In Heidegger's phenomenological interpretation of the history of philosophy, this realm of the accessibility-of-entities is what the tradition has called the being-of-entities (the *ousia* of *to on*, the *esse* of *entia*, the *Sein* of *das Seiende*).

For the early Heidegger, the kinetic nature of man is what determines the kinetic nature of being in all its modes, insofar as the kinetic nature of man (transcendence or ekstasis) projects the field of pres-ab-sentiality that is the being of entities. Heidegger summarizes the general lines of his earlier kinetic strategy as follows:

> We ourselves are the source of the idea of being. But this source must be understood as the *transcendence* of ekstatic Dasein. Only on the basis of transcendence does there take place the articulation of the various modes of being. A difficult and ultimate problem is to define the idea of being-in-general. Because the understanding of being belongs to transcending Dasein, the idea of being can be drawn from the subject.[3]

If these words indicate the earlier formulation of Heidegger's problematic (where human transcendence *projects* the realm of the being-of-entities), by the early Thirties Heidegger had begun reformulating his problematic in terms of the full tri-dimensionality we mentioned above, where it is the intrinsic self-concealing of the disclosive process that *evokes* man's transcendence and thus allows for the meaningful appearance of entities.

Above, in the Introduction, we saw how Rahner invites the reader of GW to seek out that book's connections with the early Heidegger and other modern philosophers. A clue to how Rahner himself understood the early Heidegger is found in Rahner's French article, published in 1940, "Introduction au concept de philosophie existentiale chez Heidegger."[4] When one considers the difficulty of Heidegger's thought, this short essay is almost a gem of lucidity and good sense. In places where the article in fact is wrong in its interpretation, Rahner is cautious and tentative in his presentation and leaves room for further development and clarification on Heidegger's part. The present chapter analyzes that article in terms of *Rahner's* understanding of Heidegger and leaves for Chapter VIII a more comprehensive reading of Heidegger on his own terms.

The most important sections of the article treat of (1) three "formal" aspects of Heidegger's work: the metaphysical question, its transcendental form, and the need for a fundamental ontology; (2) a commentary on SZ; (3) the question of nothingness and atheism in Heidegger; (4) the possibility of ethics on the basis of SZ; and (5) the possibility of using Heidegger's thought for Christian philosophy. The fourth topic is underdeveloped, and we leave it aside. Here we treat the first two topics and the last topic, leaving the third topic to Chapter VI. Our remarks are divided according to what Rahner calls the "form" and the "content" of Heidegger's thought: (A) his "transcendental" approach to the question of metaphysics—with some preliminary remarks on Heidegger's development—and then (B) the content of SZ as Rahner interprets it.

A. METAPHYSICS IN TRANSCENDENTAL FORM: FUNDAMENTAL ONTOLOGY

1. The Genesis of "Being and Time"[5]

The philosophical development of Martin Heidegger (1889–1976) grew out of Scholasticism. Indeed, in a 1915 biographical note written for the philosophy faculty at Freiburg, he called himself an Aristotelian Thomist. However, between 1913 and 1917 Heidegger developed some fundamental reservations about his earlier position. Among those reservations were the following.

First, he felt a strong attraction to what, in a broad sense, we may call *Lebensphilosophie*. While a seminarian studying for the Catholic priesthood (1909–1911) he had "secretly" read Blondel's *L'Action* and found therein the dynamic and existential matrix that he would much later thematize as "being-in-the-world." (The work continued to earn his praise as late as 1950.) Later and more importantly, thinkers like Simmel, Bergson, Kierkegaard, and Nietzsche exercised considerable influence on the young scholar.

A second reservation lay in Heidegger's interest in the neo-Kantian value philosophy of Heinrich Rickert, then at Freiburg. Rickert's distinction between history and nature on the basis of individualizing vs. generalizing thought was, for all its primitiveness, basic to the young thinker at that time; and some forty years later he remarked that in those pre-war years when experimental psychology was attempting to become the one and only philosophy, "the value-philosophy school was an essential and decisive support for what was known as philosophy in the great tradition."[6] In that regard, Heidegger read with great interest the works of the young Emil Lask.

A third reservation lay in the area of German Idealism. During his first two years at Freiburg University (1909–1911) Heidegger came under the influence of Carl Braig, a Catholic theologian of the Tübingen school, and from his books and courses as well as from private conversations Heidegger learned of the internal restrictions of Scholasticism and the possibilities inherent in German Idealism, particularly Schelling and Hegel.

A fourth reservation, and a decisive one, began to take shape during World War I: Lutheranism. Heidegger reports that even during his seminary years, he was "particularly agitated over the question of the relation between the Word of Sacred Scripture and theological-speculative thinking."[7] Although he was still known as a Catholic philosopher at Freiburg, nonetheless by 1917, according to a letter of Husserl's, he "had already freed himself from dogmatic Catholicism, and soon afterwards he drew all the conclusions and cut himself off, clearly, energetically, and yet tactfully, from the sure and easy career of a 'philosopher of the Catholic worldview.' "[8] In fact, Husserl speaks of Heidegger's "migration over to the ground of Protestantism,"[9] a not unrelated impetus for which may have been his marriage in the spring of 1917 to a Protestant, Fräulein Elfride Petri.

A fifth reservation was born of his discovery of phenomenology. Although he began reading Husserl's *Logical Investigations* in 1909, his purpose was to find a possible solution to the Scholastic problem of the analogical unity of being, awakened in him by his earlier reading of Brentano's dissertation on that question. However, Husserl's transcendental turn to subjectivity in the later *Ideas* (1913) seems to have dampened Heidegger's enthusiasm for the new philosophy. Nonetheless, with Husserl's arrival in Freiburg in April, 1916, Heidegger came more and more under his spell. In a letter of early October, 1917, Husserl could report that Heidegger was no longer satisfied with Rickert's neo-Kantianism and that "he now seeks to come to grips with phenomenological philosophy from within. And it seems to me that he is doing this seriously and with thoroughness."[10]

Despite this creative turmoil and even though, by 1919, it would be difficult to call Heidegger either an Aristotelian or a Thomist, his sights after the war were still set on the same question of the analogical unity of being which had first aroused his philosophical interests. In 1913, at the end of his doctoral dissertation he had spoken of the need of "articulating the whole region of 'being' in its various modes of reality."[11] This statement thematized the question that had dawned on him in 1907 when at the age of seventeen he had read Brentano's *On the Several Senses of Being in Aristotle* (1862).[12] That straightforward, 220-page treatise examined the meaning of the Greek participle *on* (which has the verbal sense of "to-be-in-being" as well as the substantive sense of "that-which-is-in-being") and found it to be a homonym whose analogous meanings Aristotle ordered according to a fourfold distinction: being as accidental, being as true, being as potential and actual, and being according to the schema of the categories. Heidegger repeatedly characterized the work as "my first guide through Greek philosophy in my secondary school days," as "the 'rod and staff' of my first awkward attempts to penetrate into philosophy," and as "the first philosophical text through which I worked my way again and again from 1907 on."[13] More important than the book was the question it raised for Heidegger but could not answer: If that-which-is-in-being *(das Seiende)* has several meanings, what does "being itself" *(das Sein)* mean in its unity? From this question, rooted in Aristotle and not in Husserl, the road leads—

with some wavering, as Heidegger says—to the publication of SZ.

If one studies Heidegger's courses prior to the writing of SZ, especially those at Freiburg from 1919 through May of 1923, and even those at Marburg from the fall of 1923 through the drafting of SZ in its final form (spring, 1926), one finds little enough said about the question of the unified meaning of being. Everything seems concentrated on the elaboration of an existential analysis of human facticity within an adapted phenomenological method of investigation. To be sure, Heidegger's focus was clearly on *alētheia*, the disclosure or givenness of whatever is given, and here we see a glimmer of what was to come fully to light as the question of the meaning of being. Even though *alētheia* (and not consciousness) was the issue, Heidegger approached the problem from within a phenomenological framework: how does *alētheia*, that is, the domain of the accessibility or sense of entities, get opened up in human existence? In this regard, Heidegger's question seems to be posed in a transcendental phenomenological framework. In order to know what the givenness (or being) of entities might mean, one must first investigate the performances of "subjectivity" by which the realm of the givenness (or *alētheia*) of entities is constituted.

But for Heidegger it was no longer a transcendental ego, as in Husserl, that was doing the constituting. As early as June of 1919 Heidegger had declared openly in front of Husserl that the "primordial Ur-ego" was the *historical* ego and that the Husserlian pure transcendental ego was a derived and secondary actuation of the self.[14] This "historical ego" was an initial name for what Heidegger would soon call factical life or "existence" (Dasein), not a substance or an ego at all but man's movement beyond himself, a *kinēsis* appropriated by its ever receding and unreachable term. As claimed and pulled out by this term, factical life "transcends itself"—that is, it is fundamentally "transcendental"—and is thrown into or "fallen" among the things of its practical concern. The kinetic structure of (1) exceeding oneself by being drawn out towards the receding *telos* and thus of (2) having things meaningfully present, is the fundamental *temporality* of human being.

The first or "excess" dimension points to the two temporal moments of "future" and "past," now phenomenologically interpreted as "becoming" what one "already" (or essentially) is, that is, reappropriating "futurally" one's already operative condition of being appropriated unto the unreachable *telos* of one's movement. The second or "access" dimension points to the temporal moment of the "present," now phenomenologically interpreted as "making meaningfully present" the things of one's practical concern. This kinetic temporality, in turn, is "disclosive," that is, it opens up the arena of sense within which things become mean-

ingfully present. It is the happening of *alētheia*. But disclosure/*alētheia*
is Heidegger's phenomenological way of reading what the tradition
called "being" *(esse)*, no longer as some objective in-itself-ness of things
detached from the performances of "subjectivity," but rather as the
*meaningful appearance of things in their whatness and howness on the
basis of man's movement or temporality.* Therefore, in the hands of the
young Heidegger "ontology" became "transcendental phenomenology":
The understanding of being was to be worked out by a concrete investigation of man's temporal transcendence. And if being, phenomenologically interpreted, happens in conjunction with man's temporal
movement, then the unified meaning of being would itself be kinetic
and temporal: the meaning of being would be "time."

These are the reasons that underlie Heidegger's silence about the
question of being between 1919 and 1926 and his concentration on
working out the structure of human movement and its correlative disclo-
siveness. He begins with an analysis of the world of lived, factical meaning (lecture course, 1919-1920, "Grundprobleme der Phänomenologie"),
develops an existential doctrine of temporality from early Christian
sources (1920-1921, "Einleitung in die Phänomenologie der Religion"),
works out the structures of everyday disclosure of meaningfulness in
Aristotle (the two courses, 1921-1922), and draws the whole thing together in a primitive sketch of SZ (1923: "Ontologie: Hermeneutik der
Faktizität"). When he moves to Marburg he already has the basic features of the existential analytic worked out and presents them a year
later, July 25, 1924, in a brief lecture called "The Concept of Time"
(Der Begriff der Zeit) and elaborates them at length in a course called
Geschichte des Zeitbegriffes (summer, 1925), which is a first draft of SZ.
In that course he outlines the connection between the existential analytic and "The Question of Being in General and of History and Nature
in Particular." Human movement, i.e., existential temporality, opens the
horizon of present, meaningful givenness in which man has *access* to beings, only because that same movement or temporality *exceeds* or transcends beings in the direction of the self-concealed (or ever recessive)
term of man's movement. Meaning on the basis of movement, disclosure
possibilized by temporality, the appearance (or being) of entities happening because of man's self-absence—this is the formula for raising
and answering the question of the meaning of being in a "transcendental phenomenological" mode.

Although SZ as we know it only treats one half of the formula (movement, temporality, self-absence), it is clear what the other, unpublished
half promised to do: show that the recessive term, which claims and appropriates man's movement into self-absence by being *itself* recessive

and absent, is primordially responsible for rendering present the beings of man's world. In other words, being itself in its fundamental "unity" —and not just the being of man—is movement, a tension of presence-by-absence, which in Greek might be called *energeia atelēs*. Its moment of privative "absence" (self-concealment) is its ever-recessiveness which "already" claims man's factical self-absence ("past") and calls him to accept and "become" that facticity ("future"). Correlatively, its moment of "presence" is inscribed in man's presence to, his "rendering present" of, the things of his world. There can be no talk of being (primordial movement) except in correlation with man (existential movement), and all such talk *(logos)* is geared to showing how beings *(onta)* appear *(phainesthai)* as what and how they *are*. The phenomenology of movement would thus constitute the "foundations" of a new ontology.

2. The Question of Metaphysics

The history of interpretations of SZ has frequently been a history of misinterpretations. There are many reasons for this fact. In the first place, the dedication of the volume to Husserl, which expressed a personal and professional indebtedness that reached back at least ten years, led many to read the work as an extension of the Husserlian project of a transcendental phenomenology. Oskar Becker, for example, read it as continuing in the line of Husserl, but with the substitution of "transcendental *existence*" (Dasein) for the transcendental ego; and Heidegger himself, for whatever motives, gave some credence to this interpretation in his famous letter to Husserl, October 22, 1927. Dasein, he wrote, "contains it itself the possibility of transcendental constitution" and "the existence-structure of Dasein makes possible the transcendental constitution of everything positive." It was already clear, however, that Heidegger's shift from the transcendental ego to the issues of temporality, truth, and facticity had drawn the line between him and Husserl: "What is the mode of being of this absolute ego [in Husserl]—in what sense is it the *same* as the particular factual 'I' and in what sense is it *not* the same?"[15]

Secondly, because of the book's debts to Kierkegaard and Jaspers and above all because the only published part of it dealt with human existence as transcendence, SZ came to be known as "existential" philosophy. Sartre's use of the book for his own *Being and Nothingness* helped to promote that idea. Moreover, in other circles it was read as a foundation for nihilism, decisionism, and/or Nazism. Some have even chosen to read it against itself as a crypto-Kantian foundation for the sciences.[16] Not to mention what theologians, Protestant and Catholic, have made of it, or what certain Anglo-American thinkers have chosen to find in it.

For Rahner, however, SZ continues and radicalizes the question of the meaning of being: "Metaphysics is what Heidegger is about, what he means to do.... Metaphysics and nothing else is his purpose."[17] And metaphysics means "ontotheology" (Rahner borrows the word from Heidegger), "the inquiry about being as such and in its totality, . . . being as such under its most general and most total aspect."

> By "most general" is meant, ultimately, the simple fact of being, *esse*, characteristic of every *ens;* by "most total" is meant *esse* again, as the unifying aspect under which every possible object can be grasped, summed up, and related to its unique and ultimate explanation. Thus metaphysics, insofar as it studies being as such, is *ontology;* and insofar as it searches for the universal basis of being, it is *theology*—if we grant that *theos*, God, is the name one would wish to give this universal ground of being. And this is why since Plato and Aristotle metaphysics in its unity was always ontotheology, if we may, following Heidegger, hazard this term.[18]

As far as the general formulation goes, Rahner is certainly correct. Heidegger is concerned with being *as such* and not with the being *of man* as an end in itself. "What Heidegger says about man is always first and foremost subordinated to the universal question of being."[19] But when Rahner specifies the formulation, he begins to run into some trouble as regards Heidegger's understanding of himself. In the first place, Rahner writes: If, under all its various changes, metaphysics has always been ontotheological,

> it is thus, formally as ontotheology, that Heidegger has taken it up; it is this Western thought which is his inheritance; it is the task of these thinkers [from Thales to Hegel] that he has made his own. Metaphysics and nothing else is his purpose, and thus he recognizes, properly speaking, only one question: What is being as such and in its totality?"[20]

Some remarks are in order here, and in making them I have no desire to criticize Rahner for not commanding an understanding of Heidegger which only later years could yield. My purpose is simply to understand what "kind" of Heidegger Rahner felt he could use in GW. And from the paragraph above, it is clear that Rahner felt that Heidegger could be aligned with those masters of traditional philosophy who devoted themselves to the meaning and structure of the being of entities, insofar as that being is common to all entities and, as God, is the ultimate principle and cause of all entities. Rahner will grant (see the next section) that Heidegger bases his inquiry into being on a new "foundation"—man as transcendence rather than as rational animal—but even on that basis it would seem that, according to Rahner, Heidegger was out to build a doctrine of the common and ultimate meaning of being.

Does this hold for Heidegger? Yes and no. It may well be that Rahner invokes the ontotheological structure of traditional metaphysics and connects Heidegger to it simply in order dissociate SZ from purely existentialist interpretations. And if that is the case, then we may applaud Rahner's remarks as correct and even precocious. (Heidegger himself waited until 1946 to declare at large that his thought was not "existentialist."[21]) But the issue is more complicated than that. Briefly stated (see Chapters IV and VIII for further treatment), "being as such" in the traditional sense is not at all Heidegger's central concern. Being, in Rahner's acceptance of the term, is the ontological state or condition of entities insofar as they are present-in-reality. This is what Aquinas called *esse* and what, analogously, Plato called *eidos* and Aristotle called *energeia*. For all the differences between these designations (*esse*: the act of to be; *eidos* and *energeia*: the form or essence of to be), they share in common the fact that they characterize *entities* in their thatness and/or whatness. In general, therefore, whether in terms of act or essence or form, these traditional designations tell about the *being-ness* of entities, and Heidegger labels the tradition globally just that: a historically evolving and many-sided doctrine of the beingness (*Seiendheit*) of entities (*Seiendes*), with the two structural moments of beingness-as-universal (ontology) and beingness-as-ultimate (theology).

But as he understands himself, Heidegger's own question is different. He seeks not the beingness of entities, but the *condition of the possibility* of beingness, specifically, that which renders possible the fact that there "is" beingness at all and that man can comprehend it. This question is one step back from the beingness of entities in its common and ultimate features. Over his professional career Heidegger gave this "prior" inquiry three different titles: the question about the temporal-kinetic *meaning* of beingness; or about the *event-of-appearing* of beingness at all; or about the disclosive *place* in which beingness shows up. Unfortunately Heidegger's own lexicon does not always reveal this crucial distinction between beingness and its prior *Sinn* or *Erschlossenheit* or *Lichtung*: he often uses the word "being" (*das Sein*) for both the tradition's beingness and his own "condition *for* beingness." In the end, in order to avoid the confusion, he dropped the term *das Sein* or used various substitutes for it (the archaic *Seyn* or the artificial S͟e͟i͟n͟, and so on). But in any case, very little of Heidegger can be understood—and we may question how much Rahner understood—if the difference between these two issues is not made clear from the outset.

Heidegger does not exclude beingness (e.g., the *esse* of *entia*, the *einai* of *onta*) from consideration, but he seeks to incorporate it into the arena which lets it happen at all. Throughout the tradition he finds that, despite the various and, relatively speaking, revolutionary transformations that the idea of beingness undergoes, it always connotes presence-in-reality: presentness. Not in a chronological sense, of course. The beingness of Napoleon is not *now* a matter of presence-in-reality the way it was in 1815, and yet it is no less a matter of beingness because it lies in the past. But the term "presence-in-reality" does raise the question of just what this "reality" might be, presence "in which" makes something to be. The contribution of transcendental philosophy in all its forms is that it calls attention to the often hidden and unthematic role of *man* in this issue, the one who raises the question about presence-in-reality. Reality is somehow correlative to human perception in the broadest sense (Parmenides, fragment 3, *noein* and *einai* are *to auto*, "the same" or "together"). Beingness has something to do with the presentness of a thing in and to an actual or possible "awareness" on the part of man, whether that awareness be practical, theoretical, aesthetic, or whatever. That is, the traditional problematic of an entity's *ousia* or presence-in-reality is, properly speaking, a matter of *meaningful* presence, accessibility to and for human beings.

Heidegger's question, therefore is: What allows for the chiaroscuro domain of meaningful presence (of entities), within which we can say that "something is"? Any answers that simply point to the is-ness of things (their state-of-being, their beingness) or that point further to an ultimate instance of is-ness (God) do not resolve the question, which asks how it is that there is is-ness at all and how man can know entities *in terms of* is-ness. The only way to answer that question is to turn back to the place where the question about meaning emerges: the questioner himself. But even then, the final term of this second-order reflective inquiry will not be, as it is in metaphysics, the common and ultimate structure of is-ness (beingness) but rather will be the possibilizing condition of any "happening" of is-ness at all in the domain of human existence. In fact, Heidegger's hunch is that just such a relocation of the beingness-of-entities within the arena that makes it possible will radically transform traditional ontotheology.

It seems that Rahner both did and did not understand this whole state of affairs in his 1940 article and per force in his earlier work, GW. He did see the need for a transcendental turn within metaphysics, one that goes back not to a formal Kantian synthetic unity of apperception, but more deeply, to the very essence of man as *transcendence*, that is, as an understanding of the beingness of entities. It seems, however that he did *not* understand Heidegger's radical refocusing of the question on the conditions of is-ness rather than on is-ness itself. While the next chapter takes up this claim in some detail, we may now note that Rahner here reads Heidegger's *das Sein* as equivalent to *Seiendheit*, and specifically to that mode of beingness which Aquinas thematized for the first time as *esse*. In terms of GW and our particular question about what "kind" of Heidegger Rahner found usable for that work, the crux is this: Rahner believes that Heidegger's topic is *esse* and that, although Heidegger himself hesitates, Rahner can show on the basis of an analysis of human transcendence (Dasein) that the final meaning of *esse* is God as pure and absolute *esse*. If Rahner uses Heidegger in order to extort an existential transcendental turn out of Aquinas, he uses Aquinas to extort an affirmation of God out of Heidegger.

But there is more, and at this point we can only mention it. There is a *special* misunderstanding within this section of Rahner's article which in fact might rescue Rahner from the *general* misunderstanding with which we have charged him. Rahner articulates Heidegger's overarching issue in the form of two questions, the second of which purports to be a quotation from the end of Heidegger's *Was ist Metaphysik?:* "What is being as such and in its totality? Why is there being rather than pure nothingness?" This reading is very curious. In the first place, from what Rahner had just said it is clear that "being" in both these sentences means Aquinas' *esse*, which Rahner takes as the equivalent of Heidegger's *das Sein*. This is what we call his general misunderstanding. But secondly, Rahner *misquotes* the sentence from Heidegger's *Was ist Metaphysik?*. Heidegger's German text reads: "*Warum ist überhaupt Seiendes und nicht vielmehr Nichts?*", a translation of Leibniz's "*Pourquoy il y a plustôt quelque chose que rien?*" Rahner's French article renders this: "*Pourquoi y a-t-il de l'être au lieu du pur néant?*"[22]

This "specific" misunderstanding, as we have called it, has three moments to it. (a) Heidegger asks, "Why are there *entities* or *beings* (*entia, onta*) rather than the Nothing?" If we emphasize the first half of the question, we note that Rahner misreads the question as: "Why is there *esse* (*das Sein*) . . . ?" (b) By "Nothing," Heidegger emphatically does not mean "pure nothingness," a *nihil absolutum et negativum*. He means what we have called "the condition for beingness," which, from the traditional perspective that sees beingness as exhausting the range of the ontological question, looks like nothingness, but which in fact, as experienced in dread, is the most "real" and "positive" of everything, much more "in being" than all entities in their presence-in-reality. Rahner, however, both in this essay and in HW, misunderstands *das Nichts* as empty, meaningless "nothingness" and charges Heidegger with the possibility of propounding a nihilistic atheism. (c) The third moment of misunderstanding ties together the previous two—and perhaps constitutes a "creative" misunderstanding whereby in fact Rahner grasps Heidegger's meaning and "rescues" himself from a general charge of distorting Heidegger's position. As Rahner reads the sentence, it asks: "What is the condition for the possibility of the fact that there is *esse* (beingness) at all rather than pure nothingness?" On a benign interpretation, that reading of Heidegger's sentence says the very thing that Heidegger's overall topic is about: What accounts for the fact that man can experience things in their meaningful presence-in-reality? Continuing the benign interpretation, we would read Rahner's "rather than pure nothingness" to mean: "rather than the lack of any experience of things in their presence-in-reality." Thus far the rescue-job: Rahner and Heidegger would agree that the so-called metaphysical issue is really the phenomenological issue of what lets beings show up in their beingness. Rahner and Heidegger would even agree partway on the answer to the question, insofar as both of them insist on investigating the essential *movement* of man, manifest in how he knows and/or acts: a transcendence beyond beings, one which, appropriated by its ever recessive term, makes possible the meaningful presence of beings. Or as Rahner, freely citing Heidegger, puts it: Unless we first let ourselves *be* grasped, we shall not be able to grasp in turn. But then comes the parting of the ways. Heidegger sees man's movement as grasped or appropriated by an unknowable "recess" which cannot be spoken of in terms of beingness but which is the reason why there is beingness at all, whereas Rahner reads the appropriating recessive term as pure beingness, absolute *esse*, which (he claims) all men can know and do call "God."

We shall return often to this point—it is the major question of this essay. For now we retain the essentials. Rahner claims that Heidegger is carrying out a transcendental inquiry into the universal and ultimate structure of *esse*. Heidegger claims that he is trying to "locate" *esse* and all other forms of beingness within a larger horizon. Rahner will hold that a transcendental turn to the existential structures of human being can reawaken metaphysics in general and the affirmation of God in particular, i.e., "reground" them on a modernly acceptable "foundation." Heidegger claims that to follow out man's existential movement into its appropriation by the self-withdrawing, self-hiding mystery (*Geheimnis*) will not ground any ontology or theology, in fact will lead to an "abyss" (*Abgrund*) which, beyond pessimism and optimism, is the inexhaustible origin of meaningful presence. Rahner, as we shall see below, claims that one can and indeed must—even if only implicitly—know this "mystery" as the divine. Heidegger will answer with a measured skepticism.

3. The Transcendental Exigency

The second formal characteristic of Heidegger's thought, Rahner writes, is its transcendental approach. "For Heidegger this metaphysical study of being as such and under its most general aspect assumes a *transcendental* form. In other words, he poses the metaphysical problem as modern philosophy since Descartes has posed it, and as Kant in particular formulated and elaborated it."[23] These references to Descartes and Kant are only marginally correct. Heidegger does not return to a "subject," as we have seen, but to the movement of self-transcendence inscribed in the very heart of human existence. Rahner clarifies this matter by spelling out both the general or formal meaning of transcendental method and its material application to the question of the meaning of being.

A transcendental question, Rahner says, "asks for the *a priori* conditions that make knowledge of an object possible." Rather than attempting to approach the object head-on, as it were, in forgetfulness of one's own constitution of it, the transcendental thinker "turns back to reflect upon himself and examines in himself, as subject, what the conditions are which permit him to make this object his own." The word "object," of course, is used in the most general sense of "issue-for-thought" (*Sache*), and "subject" is merely a heuristic devise for "the essence of thinking" and will later be specified as Dasein. To return to the self is not to bracket out all understanding of the issue-for-thought, for "a certain provisional knowledge of the object is always presupposed"; and the conditions of possibility which one seeks are not experiential and ontic but "those revealed by an *a priori* deduction, thus conditions necessary for the apprehension of every object that can come under a finite human knowledge."

Rahner's formulation of the transcendental approach is markedly Kantian and, to that degree, not well suited to Heidegger. Heidegger prefers to formulate the methodology of his early work in a way that is closer to the general lines of Husserlian phenomenology.[24] First, a transcendental "reduction," not from things to the consciousness which constitutes them as objects, but from things as meaningful in everyday comportment to things *in their mode of meaningful givenness*, i.e., to their beingness, read phenomenologically. Secondly, a phenomenological "construction" of the realm of meaningful givenness in terms of the tension between presence and absence in human movement. (Strictly speaking, there is no "transcendental deduction" in SZ.) What, then, may we retain from Rahner's characterization of the transcendental approach in SZ? Only this much: that the only way into the metaphysical problematic is through an investigation of the one who raises that problematic; and specifically, that one must seek out the essential structures of man's self-transcendence whereby the issue-for-thought becomes accessible for human involvement and discourse. Rahner clarifies all this in his second step, the application of the general transcendental procedure to the question of the meaning of being.

To apply the transcendental procedure to the fundamental metaphysical question about being means "to establish the *a priori* conditions under which man can raise that question. Precisely *what [kind of] entity is man himself* as the one who asks about being as such and without restriction?" And why must we investigate man in order to get at being?

> The reason for this special procedure is that being is simply not an "object" in the ordinary sense of the word, not an object among others, not a fact alongside other facts. It is not something added on to the rest, not something that can be isolated from the whole and obtained in a pure state, as it were. As the *a priori* and necessary universal propositions show, the notion of being *pre-exists, underlying* every individual cognition. There is no way, therefore, of defining it by appealing to such and such a characteristic of some particular being; we have to go all the way back to that initial notion that the human mind possesses of it. In other words, we must return to man himself: the inquiring subject becomes the subject of the inquiry.[25]

Again, Rahner's formulation is Kantian rather than phenomenological (cf. "necessary universal propositions"), but the sense is salvageable. Being is pre-understood as that which allows knowledge of or action upon the things of man's world. Being is not an entity but the possibilizing condition of the appearance of entities as what and how they are, the "medium" of understandability within which man has human access to them. As such a medium, being is bound up in some way with human "mediation," and the goal is to seek out the essential or *a priori* structures of that performance whereby man allows this medium to be. We know that in general this structure is man's facticity as "already" (i.e., *a priori*) appropriated into movement and thus that the essential "performance" that allows the medium to be is human temporality. All notions of "the subject" are heuristic and provisional: The "subjectivity" of man is his ontological *kinēsis*, what Heidegger calls *Bewegtheit* or "being-moved." And the discussion of being as an "object" has yielded to an understanding of it as the givenness or presence-in-reality of things, which happens in conjunction with man's projectedness beyond things towards the ever-receding term of his own movement.

But what Rahner does not say in his formulation of transcendental method is as important as what he does say, and here again we return to the discussion of the previous section. Heidegger is after the "how" of the happening of all modes of being (or beingness), from which "how" he could define the analogically unified sense of all the various ways beingness is given in human understanding. If the fundamental performance whereby beingness happens is the absentiality intrinsic to movement, then absence is the possibilizing condition of presence-in-reality, and the basic meaning of beingness is presence-by-absence, pres-absence. It is not at all clear that Rahner sees what Heidegger is after in his "transcendental" approach, and therefore Rahner will end up by defining the meaning of beingness as perfect self-presence (God). Or perhaps Rahner did understand Heidegger and consciously rejected his problematic. That is, perhaps he learned the starting-point of the transcendental question from Heidegger, but found unacceptable Heidegger's refusal to follow that question into what Rahner takes to be its unavoidable source, the infinite and absolute instance of presentness which the Christian philosopher calls God. In that case Rahner might admit a great debt to his former teacher, and yet would have to say: *magis amica veritas*.

In my opinion, it was a bit of both. Because Rahner, before encountering Heidegger, had already formulated his own problematic as the Scholastic issue of beingness (*esse*) in its general and its highest form, and because he already "knew"—or at least held on faith—that the ultimate instance of reality was God as pure self-presence, he could not accept, or perhaps even fully understand, Heidegger's position on the phenomenological "ultimacy" of atelic movement. Heidegger might say that, whereas one can *argue* to the *possibility* of the self-coincidence of the term of movement, one cannot phenomenologically *experience* it in its self-presence but can only experience one's own striving for such an asymptotic point. Rahner argues that to have anticipated the term by experiencing one's own movement is already to have "pre-grasped" perfect self-coincidence and that, by an analogical argument, one can demonstrate the existence of that point and legitimately call it God.

The real issue in transcendental method is the *content* of the transcendence which that method discloses, that is, the scope of man's movement. Does human transcendence consciously, even if only unthematically, reach the very being of God? Or does it land in a cloud of unknowing?

4. Dasein and Fundamental Ontology

After metaphysics and transcendental method, Rahner lists a third formal characteristic of Heidegger's thought: the elaboration of a fundamental ontology. Rahner develops the point negatively (Heidegger's critique of traditional *logos*) and positively (the understanding of man as transcendence or Dasein).

Granted that Heidegger wants to arrive at the "*meaning* of beingness" and that the way to that goal is an inquiry into the nature of the questioner of beingness, Heidegger separates himself from the entire tradition of metaphysics that has always considered beingness as (in Rahner's words) "that which is referred to thought, to *logos*, to reason" and that correlatively has defined man in terms of *ratio* and *logos*. The tradition has thus always perceived beingness only in the light of *logos* (cf. onto-*logy*, theo*logy*), whether in classical Greece or Christian philosophy or in modern thought. Not so the pre-Socratics, for whom *nous* and *logos* "still kept a value much closer to the original than for Plato and Aristotle." Heidegger, therefore, seeks to go back behind the common starting point of the tradition—"the *logical* grasp of being by thought"—to a pre-logical having-to-do (*Umgehen*) with entities, and thereby to break the circle of man-as-*logos* and beingness-as-logical. This rupture with the tradition is an effort "to resurrect the gigantomachy of a transcendental question about being, without conceiving it beforehand as onto-*logy*."[26]

Positively, Rahner says, the program is that of a "fundamental ontology" or analytic of man as the "bearer of relations with being" in his existential, concrete facticity.

> Dasein designates in Heidegger not some "being-present-there," the "existing" of fact, in the trite sense of the word, not therefore something affirmable of everything that surrounds us. It is rather . . . the human being himself, each one of us, characterized by the fact that essentially he can ask the question about being, that his is *the connatural transcendence which orients him toward all being*.[27]

"Fundamental ontology," therefore, is not limited to the published parts of SZ, which are only an existential analytic of Dasein, but includes as well the unpublished third division of Part One of that work, i.e., the elaboration of the kinetic time-character of being on the basis of man's own kinetic temporality. Fundamental ontology, in other words, is not an existential anthropology for its own sake but spans the correlation between man's movement and the movement that is being. Fundamental ontology answers the question of the nature of man "while still relating it to the question of being in general."[28]

Rahner's understanding of the negative and positive aspects of fundamental ontology accords with the early Heidegger's own. We might add, however, that Heidegger does not repudiate the notion of *logos* but

deepens it—even in such masters of the tradition as Aristotle— by interpreting its underlying kinetic structure. Heidegger's 1925-1926 course on
logos in Aristotle showed that, before *logos* means judgment or reason, it
designates a binding together of otherwise separate elements into a
unity of sense. Such a synthesis or relating presupposes a concomitant
keeping-separate of what is related. And again, this composition-
division or *synthesis-diaresis* rests on the primordial presence-and-
absence of man himself. Man can be present to the things of the world
(and thus synthesize their elements into unities of sense) only because he
transcends, or is relatively absent from, those things. He has meaningful
access to entities because he *exceeds* them towards the ever-recessive
term of his movement. The tension between access and excess, or
equally between actual presentness and privative absence, is what
Heidegger takes as man's essential kinetic temporality. Thus, the meaning of *logos* is time, and fundamental ontology is basically a "phenomenological 'chronology' " *(phänomenologische Chronologie).*[29]
    What influence did this fundamental ontology exercise on GW? In his
own metaphysics of cognition Rahner begins with and remains with
predicative knowledge rather than taking up the pre-predicative having-
to-do with the world that we find in SZ. But for all that, Rahner's focus
is analogous to Heidegger's. For both thinkers, the issue common to
predicative assertion *(logos)* and pre-predicative having-to-do *(praxis)* is
movement. While Heidegger will investigate the ordinary, everyday performances of movement and from that will conclude to the pres-ab-
sential structure of human existence, Rahner will thematize the
movement of agent intellect towards full meaning and from that will
conclude that man is a striving for the akinetic term of pure perfect beingness (God). The general definition that Rahner gives of fundamental
ontology ("the analytic of man as bearer of relations with being") is
broad enough to encompass the starting points of both Heidegger's and
Rahner's efforts, even if their conclusions are radically different. But the
divergence, I believe, is not due to the fact that Heidegger begins with
pre-predicative experience and Rahner begins with predicative knowledge. As Chapter VI will show, even on the basis of an analysis of predication one can end up with an "open" *kinēsis* (Heidegger) rather than
with the affirmation of God as pure act of beingness (Rahner). Indeed,
it is even questionable whether what Rahner calls *excessus* or *Vorgriff*
should be translated as a "pre-grasp" of God, when in fact it is only an
anticipation of or movement towards an ever-recessive term. The difference between SZ and GW may lie rather in the fact that Rahner already
"knows" from a different *kind* of experience (faith) what the end of
man's striving is, and thus the difference in *levels* of natural experience

(pre-predicative versus predicative) do not account for Rahner's divergence from Heidegger. Even if GW had begun and remained with pre-predicative experience (HW began there but quickly moved to an analysis of judgment), it is a safe bet that the outcome would have been the same. And on the other hand, in the spring of 1950, perhaps recalling his early reading of Blondel, Heidegger told Henry Duméry that he thought a personalist theodicy was conceivable on the basis of Heidegger's own work so long as anthropomorphisms were rigorously and critically avoided.[30] If Heidegger himself did not carry one out (although in the Twenties he did project writing one in conjunction with Romano Guardini), it may be because of the strict limits he felt were imposed upon philosophy *as philosophy*.[31]

In discussing the three formal aspects of Heidegger's thought as outlined by Rahner, we see one and the same problematic coming to the fore: being-and-movement. The remarks on metaphysics prompted the question of whether the topic of Heidegger's thought is being-as-beingness and ultimately as self-coincident presentness. Discussion of the transcendental exigency raised the issue of the scope of man's movement, correlative as it is with being, and thus the issue of what kind of being is available for human experience. Finally, the question of "fundamental ontology" has led us to ask what kind of ontology is to be "founded": one which already "knows" (by faith) that the meaning of being is the self-coincident God? Or one which finds only that beingness happens in conjunction with man's appropriation by an unknown and ever-recessive dimension? To sort out Rahner's answer to this unified set of questions we shall have to turn to his interpretation of the contents of SZ. At this point Rahner concludes his treatment of the *formal principle* which governs Heidegger's work (note the Kantian formulation in the final phrase):

> We may define it as follows: existential philosophy in Heidegger's sense is the transcendental investigation of what man is insofar as he raises the question of being, an investigation that rejects the initial traditional stance in this matter—exclusively intellectual—and that is undertaken with the intention of providing an answer to the question of being in general: fundamental ontology, as the basis of all metaphysics that will henceforth be able to make any claim of being scientific.[32]

B. A READING OF *BEING AND TIME*

SZ is projected in two parts, each composed of three divisions, but as published, it got no further than Part One, Division Two. All of Part Two was to be devoted to the so-called destruction of the history of ontology, i.e., the uncovering of the hidden theme of temporality in Kant, Descartes, and Aristotle. Part One, Divisions One and Two (hereafter: SZ I.1 and I.2) were given over to an analysis of Dasein as kinetic temporality, while the crowning Division Three (SZ I.3) was to work out the time-character of being itself in its analogical unity.[33]

1. The Preliminary Analysis of Dasein

Rahner properly understands that the governing issue of the whole existential analytic of Dasein is *Erschlossenheit*, i.e., the realm of disclosure, inscribed in man's movement, within which entities appear in their modes of beingness. Rahner calls this *Erschlossenheit* " 'openness' (transcendence) to being in general." (He also calls it "existential consciousness," but it is clear that he means Dasein and no kind of *Bewusstsein*.)[34] He notes that the purpose of the preliminary analysis of Dasein in SZ I.1 is to lay out "Dasein as a phenomenon" with particular attention to the "general formal structures" of being-in-the-world, these in turn being united in the definition of Dasein as care (*Sorge*).

Rahner begins: Dasein is no closed subject that would have to find his way out to an external world, but is "always already 'outside himself' in the things of the world." This exteriority is not a matter of purely local presence among things nor is it even the sum total of his *a posteriori* relations to things. Being-in-the-world, rather, means that

> man is from the very first open to the totality of the world, and the totality of the world is, albeit under an empty form, given to him right from the outset. In order to be present to himself, he must externalize himself, must make room in himself for the totality of the world: this is how he is man, how he is Dasein.[35]

Within this framework man's primordial attitude is not theoretical and contemplative but practical: he establishes "*useful* relations . . . with things for the needs of his own existence, and theoretical knowledge about things is but a deficient mode of these natural and original relations." Likewise, Dasein primarily experiences entities not "as being situated-there-before-us [*Vorhandenes*] but as a material-placed-at-the-disposal of man [*Zuhandenes*], consecrated to his practical service."[36]

Rahner passes over Heidegger's discussion of the worldhood (*Weltlichkeit*) of the world, i.e., how human purposes in concrete activities free entities for their mode of givenness, and instead engages Heidegger's crucial fifth chapter on the existential structures of being-in-the-world: *Verstehen* (understanding), *Befindlichkeit* (situatedness or disposition), and *Verfallenheit* (fallenness). (We note at this point that Rahner avoids the error of many commentators who see the third existential component as *Rede* [speech]).[37]

Verstehen or existential understanding is not a theoretical cognitive state but "man's way of comprehending himself, of grasping and restructuring his own ability at existing."[38] It is a matter of "knowing one's way around" (cf. Aristotle's *empeiria*) in one's own existence by taking risks, trying out possibilities, working out projects. Thus it has a fundamental character of being ahead of oneself in the direction of the possible, of living into the future. "Everything man does is but an anticipation of his 'later,' of what-is-to-come, his future. . . . He is always 'ahead-of-himself,' preceding himself, so to speak, in his restless stretching forward. Heidegger calls this stretching-ahead-of-self-toward-the-future *Verstehen* or understanding. . . ." The first structural moment of being-in-the-world is man's movement as a being-towards, a becoming.

Befindlichkeit or existential situatedness does not simply point to concrete moods which locate us in an emotional situation, but rather indicates the structural possibility of those moods. It is Heidegger's term for a phenomenologically interpreted "corporeality" whereby man is "always already caught up and engaged in the world in such and such a direction." If Heidegger spells out this structure in the dramatic term *Geworfenheit* (thrownness) or by reference to *Faktizität* (de-facto-ness), he is in no way anticipating later existentialist visions of man thrown onto the refuse-heap of absurdity and abandoned to his own despair, but simply indicating that every projection of the possible, every understanding of oneself as a becoming, has a situated starting point and an ineluctable relation to things, and that man cannot overcome this *a priori* "passivity" of his location amidst entities. Rahner writes: "He can take command of his future only by first accepting the starting position that he has not given himself, that has indeed been imposed on him: this precise place in the world." If existential understanding revealed man's movement as a becoming or being-towards, existential situatedness discloses that same movement as already somehow determined by man's milieu. If understanding intimates man's futurity, situatedness reveals *not* the "past and by-gone" but man's "alreadiness," his need to work out his futurity in and upon the entities of his world. The crucial point (it emerges in SZ I.2) is to discover what it is to which man is most basically "already" determined. The preliminary analysis of situatedness and understanding deals with concrete everyday projects and determinations; the conclusive analysis will relate these two structures to man's own existence.

Verfallenheit or fallenness is not, properly speaking, the third formal structure of being-in-the-world (but even less so is *Rede*, "speech"). Rather it is the *everyday* way that man relates to things: He forgets about the existential performances which render them present and instead simply goes about his business in a meaningful world of practical concerns. Fallenness has nothing to do with slipping from some imagined secular state of grace. Rather, it is Heidegger's parallel term for what Husserl called the "natural attitude." If we formalize the third structural moment of being-in-the-world, it is simply "being-present-to-things." In its "natural" rather than fully self-aware mode this being-present focuses on the *things* as if they were given apart from any human mediation, and more often than not it becomes a kind of "practical enslavement" to things and a forgetfulness of their location within a humanly effected context. Properly speaking, man's situated becoming, his *befindliches Verstehen*, is what opens up the primordial realm of *logos* within which he can become present to things. Situation and becoming are two sides of the one coin of human *excess* (movement as being *beyond* onself in a *determined* way), while presence-to-things is the resultant *access* that man has to particular objects of his attention. The three structural moments thus reduce to two: access by excess, or presence to particular things by being already beyond the particular in the direction of the ever unclosed whole.

Heidegger draws these three (or better, two) moments together in his definition of being-in-the-world as care (*Sorge*). Heidegger's classical formulation (being *ahead* of oneself while being *already* situated, such that one is *present* to particular beings) is admirably captured in Rahner's paraphrase: "Dasein, man, is always preceding himself as he proceeds in the world, he must always reckon with his factual place in the world, and he cannot forego mixing with particular things of the world." The definition of care already prefigures the next step in the analysis, where the ontological meaning of man's kinetic structure is read as temporality.

2. Dasein and Temporality

In general, the second phase of Heidegger's analysis of human existence is threefold: clarification of the *term* of man's becoming (death), elucidation of *how* man is called to accept that term (conscience and resolve), and spelling out the authentic *meaning* of man's movement (temporality).

The first point is to determine, as Rahner puts it, "the proper term of the movement which draws Dasein on beyond and ahead of himself in his virtual becoming." That term is death as man's absolute and exclusive possibility, at once certain and undetermined. And yet "death" does not mean some future end-point, something that would be "the last in a series, but meanwhile totally foreign to man." Rather, it is the ever-

present possibility of man's own impossibility, his on-going condition of
finitude towards which he is always related in what Heidegger calls
man's continual being-at-the-point-of-death (thus I render *Sein zum
Tode*, "being-towards-death"). "Only there [i.e., at this present point,
not in some end-state] in fact does man reach his fullness, only there is
his disposition of his existence effective, total, definitive, and unforfeit-
able."[39] Yet one may avoid seeing the inevitable by distractions, occupa-
tions, the need to make it through the day. But all such conscious or
unconscious evasion only confirms the ineluctability of that which one
tries to avoid.

The inner call that our finitude sends us, the attendant awareness,
whether in dread or peace, of our ontological fragility, and the possible
decision to face the inevitable and accept our dying—all these are matters of seeing and becoming what we already properly are. The possibility of seeing and accepting what Rahner calls our "authentic and proper
term" reveals that the ontological structure of care is temporality. By
"temporality" Heidegger does not mean chronology, of course, or mere
location within a time structured by a linear past, present, and future.
Temporality is fundamentally the human movement within which
things become meaningful—an existential rather than a naturalistic
movement. In a brief formula, proper temporality means *becoming*
what we *already* are, in such a way that things become meaningfully
present.

The italicized words above show Heidegger's transposition of the
chronological "future—past—present" into human terms. What are we
"already" determined towards? This question asks not about the by-
gone past, but about the nature of our essential (cf. *wesentliche*) "alreadiness" (*Gewesenheit*). Answer: We are already and always appropriated unto our dying, we are at the point of death. What then are we
to "become"? The question asks not about some chronological futurity,
some goal of movement "up ahead," but about the ever-present yet ever-
receding drawing power of our movement. Again the answer is: one's
dying. Becoming what we already are means stretching ahead of ourselves and yet always finding ourselves as what we properly and essentially are. It discloses us as an open space within which things show up
for us and are meaningfully present, indeed in a new and fresh way insofar as they stand out against the background of our finitude. Rahner
writes: "We must not imagine three successive moments in a uniform
thread of time in which Dasein somehow unfolds himself piece by piece.
This temporality is very much intrinsic to him, *identical* with him. He it
is who constitutes time in the first place."[40] Dasein "generates" (*zeitigt*)
his temporal existence—but not out of himself as a subject. Rather, time

and existence are generated (*zeitigt sich*) in him by the fact that, beyond his own powers, he is appropriated by an ever-recessive term over which he does not dispose.

3. The Time-Character of Being as Such

Whether one appropriates it or overlooks it, one's kinetic temporality opens up the "clearing" or realm of concrete accessibility (or "intelligibility") within which things appear or are given as what and how they are. In that sense, temporality "gives" the modes of givenness of things. But the "givenness of things" is Heidegger's phenomenological way of saying the "beingness of entities." Therefore, temporality is the one element which unifies the various modes of the givenness of entities. Whereas Aristotle had seen the *hen pros hon*, the one nature towards which all instances of being are referred, as the self-coincident and unmoved God as term of all movement, Heidegger finds the analogical unity of all modes of givenness in movement itself, in the very condition of a dynamic *pros ti*. Although the unpublished crowning section of SZ was to work this out concretely (SZ I.3), all of SZ as published is focused on human temporality. As Rahner writes: "So far Heidegger has treated only *Dasein und Zeit*, not *Sein und Zeit*."[41] Rahner, however, goes on to hazard some personal conjectures about two possible directions that Heidegger might take in an eventual publication of SZ I.3.

In *Was ist Metaphysik?*, Rahner notes, Heidegger delved further into the experience of dread (*Angst*) where "Dasein has a presentiment of what his ultimate virtuality is: nothingness, as already involved in nothingness."[42] This experience is not exhausted in an existentialist self-referral; rather, it is for the sake of the revelation of entities. To have access to things, man must exceed them, and "this constant anticipation of nothingness makes him go beyond every particular object; in other words, it constitutes his transcendence." And since this self-exceeding opens the realm of being, then "transcendence *toward nothingness* thus becomes the express condition, first and last, in order that an entity may appear for Dasein *in the light of being*."

On the basis of *this* reading of nothingness (Heidegger's own interpretation is, as we noted, quite different), Rahner draws out one possible line—for him, the probable one—that SZ I.3 might follow in elaborating the time-character of being itself.

> We must conclude, therefore, that this transcendence . . . only goes beyond the diverse entities to end up in nothingness, that every particular entity is necessarily finite, participating in nothingness, and that "pure being is identical with pure nothingness." The more man goes beyond particular entities,

the more he grasps not, as Western philosophy from the Greeks to Hegel has taught, the Infinite, but nothingness. The *No* is prior to the *Yes*. The problem of an absolute entity, infinitely perfect—the problem of God—far from admitting of a sure positive answer, cannot even be asked. The hypothesis of a pure entity, positively higher as such than all finitude, can find no foothold in such an ontology.[43]

But this is only one possibility, and Rahner opens the door to yet another. He notes that in Heidegger's *Vom Wesen des Grundes* (1929) and in a 1932 article authorized by Heidegger himself, it was noted (in Rahner's words) that "this necessary finitude of being deals with only the *human concept* of being: SZ in no way defines whether being (*esse*) is in itself finite or infinite." Rahner, however, has his doubts. Given the fact that Heidegger interprets Dasein in terms of temporality, death, and nothingness, Rahner says, "it seems consequently that this 'existential analytic' of Dasein' ought to have as a logical, even necessary, sequel not an ontology but an *ontochrony* (the expression comes from Heidegger himself), that is, a science showing that the meaning of all being as such, and the meaning of being as absolute, is nothingness."[44]

We shall take up in its proper place (Chapter VI) the matter of Rahner's misunderstanding of *das Nichts* in the early Heidegger. At this point we may simply observe how much of Heidegger is perceived by Rahner as unusable for GW. Despite his openness to further clarification from Heidegger, Rahner seems to read SZ as directed towards atheism. "If, as some are afraid is the case, radical atheism is the last word of this anthropology, then finitude and nothingness must be the last word of its coming ontology." He goes so far as to refer to the daimonic ("the secret temptation that by nature we bear within us something that makes us prefer darkness to light") and to Nazism ("the mystery of cruelty which today dons apocalyptic garb") in referring to this possibility. At the same time Rahner intimates his own *transformation* of Heidegger in GW. If (we expect Rahner to say *per impossibile*) Heidegger's path were to lead to a religious solution and "at the final stage of this analytic the first *a priori* of human transcendence should reveal itself as the infinity of the absolute" (as in GW), then SZ would be a propaideutic to a Christian natural theology and ultimately to faith. If SZ I.3 were to reveal God at the end of man's movement, then

to jar man loose from the pure idea and to cast him into his own existence and into history, as Heidegger is doing, would be to prepare him, to make him attentive in advance to the existential, historical fact of a divine revelation. It would be to open him to "the God of Abraham, Isaac, and Jacob," to the "Word of Life, seen, heard, touched" by human hands, "Jesus of Nazareth". . . .[45]

How much influence does Heidegger exercise on GW? Obviously the matter is complicated. And the complication gets a further twist by the fact that, although Rahner misreads certain basic issues in Heidegger's thought, he ends up reproposing many of those issues without being aware of the fact.

It is clear that Rahner consciously appropriates Heidegger's turn to human existence as the questioner of being, even if he begins on the predicative rather than the pre-predicative level of that existence. It is less clear, but nonetheless a fact, that Rahner draws upon Heidegger's *Verstehen* and *Befindlichkeit* for his own interpretation of active and possible intellect in Aquinas. These matters will be spelled out in the following chapters, along with the extent to which Rahner drew upon Heidegger's *Kant und das Problem der Metaphysik* in the central sections of GW. It is also clear that a common formal structure runs through both men's treatment of movement and meaning: excess (Heidegger: *geworfener Entwurf*; Rahner: active and possible intellect) renders possible access to entities. What seems to separate Heidegger and Rahner is the question of the scope of man's transcendence and therefore the knowability or not of the term of that movement. Heidegger will be able to go only so far as man's appropriation by an unknowable recess (*lēthē*), whereas Rahner will see man claimed by the mystery of God. But both thinkers share in common a certain spirit of philosophizing that Rahner captures in some sentences from the opening days of Heidegger's course "Die Grundbegriffe der Metaphysik (Der Weltbegriff)" of 1929-1930. Rahner was not present and therefore cites from a student summary of the lectures, but the text is worth giving in full.

The philosophers of the University will never understand these words of Novalis: Philosophy (and all philosophy is metaphysics) is properly speaking a *nostalgia*. It is not a discipline that one learns. The sciences are only servants with respect to it, but art and religion are its sisters. Not to know what nostalgia is, is not to know how to philosophize. Philosophizing is possible only because, and if, we do not feel at home anywhere, because an "all" somehow calls to us, because we are ceaselessly driven straight toward being in its most total and essential, because we are at home nowhere but *on the way toward the total and the essential*. We are men without a country, and it is restlessness itself, a dynamic restlessness, that makes us have to philosophize. And this restlessness is our limitation, a limitation to us who are finitude itself. And we have no right to go to sleep, to sooth ourselves with some illusion of totality and contented infinity. We must not simply carry it around inside, but whet it, and when at last we are no longer just limited but completely isolated, then at last we will draw a bit nearer to the essential, then we will no longer feel like stirring ourselves up or playing the important and civilized ones. Then at last we will be capable of being "gripped." In making ourselves able to be "gripped," in handing ourselves over to the real, nostalgia makes men of us. This is our indispensible disposition: not to let oneself be grasped is for oneself not to be able to grasp. How empty and vain, when faced with the ultimate questions, is all our speculative subtlety—a grasp we have tried and practised—if it is not animated and sustained first of all by this being-grasped which we undergo in our depths.[46]

Notes

1. The first mention of the word *die Kehre* apparently occurs in Heidegger's 1928 lecture course published as Martin Heidegger, *Metaphysische Anfangsgründe der Logik im Ausgang von Leibniz*, ed. Klaus Held, *Gesamtausgabe*, II, 26 (Frankfurt: Vittorio Klostermann, 1978), p. 201, English translation by Michael Heim, *The Metaphysical Foundations of Logic* (Bloomington, Indiana: Indiana University Press, 1984), p. 158. There Heidegger speaks of what we call above in the text the elaboration of the kinetic structure of being, and he says: "This temporal analysis is likewise the *turn [Kehre]* in which ontology itself returns to the metaphysical ontics in which it always implicitly remains" (my translation).

2. See Thomas Sheehan, "Heidegger's Philosophy of 'Mind,' " in G. Flóisdad, editor, *Contemporary Philosophy: A New Survey* (The Hague: Martinus Nijhoff, 1983), IV, 287-318.

3. Martin Heidegger, "From the Last Marburg Lecture Course," translation (here slightly revised) by John Macquarrie in *The Future of Our Religious Past*, James M. Robinson, ed. (New York: Harper and Row, 1971), p. 321.

4. Rahner, *Recherches de Sciences Religieuses*, 30 (1940), 152-71; in English, "The Concept of Existential Philosophy in Heidegger," trans. Andrew Tallon, *Philosophy Today*, 13 (1969), 126-37. Hereafter: "Existential Philosophy."

5. See Thomas Sheehan, "Heidegger's Early Years: Fragments for a Philosophical Biography," in *Heidegger, the Man and the Thinker*, ed. T. Sheehan (Chicago: Precedent, 1981), pp. 3-19.

6. Heidegger made this remark during a discussion in the pro-seminar of Professor Spoerri in Zürich, Nov. 6, 1951.

7. Martin Heidegger, *Unterwegs zur Sprache* (Pfullingen: Günther Neske, 1959), p. 96; *On the Way to Language*, trans. Peter Hertz (New York: Harper and Row, 1971, p. 9 f.

8. Edmund Husserl's letter to Paul Natorp, 11 February 1920, Husserl Ar-

chives, Leuven, R I Natorp 11.II.20. Cited with the kind permission of the Director of the Archives, Professor Samuel IJsseling.

9. Husserl's letter to Rudolf Otto, 5 March 1919, published in an imperfect transcription in Hans-Walter Schütte, *Religion und Christendom in der Theologie Rudolf Ottos* (Berlin: de Gruyter, 1969), pp. 139-42. English translation in *Heidegger: The Man and the Thinker* (see note 5 above), pp. 23-6, following the transcription in the Leuven Archives, R I Otto 5.III.19.

10. Husserl's letter to Natorp, 8 October 1917, cited, with permission, from the Leuven Archives: R I Natorp 8.X.17.

11. Martin Heidegger, *Die Lehre vom Urteil im Psychologismus. Ein kritisch-positiver Beitrag zur Logik* (Leibniz: Johann Ambrosius Barth, 1914), p. 108; also in Martin Heidegger, *Frühe Schriften*, ed. Friedrich-Wilhelm von Herrmann, *Gesamtausgabe*, I, 1 (Frankfurt: Vittorio Klostermann, 1978), p. 186 (1972 edition, p. 128).

12. Franz Brentano, *Von der mannigfachen Bedeutung des Seienden nach Aristoteles* (Freiburg: Herder, 1862; reprinted: Darmstadt: Wissenschaftliche Buchgesellschaft, 1960); *On the Several Senses of Being in Aristotle*, trans. Rolf George (Berkeley: University of California Press, 1975).

13. Heidegger, *On the Way to Language*, p. 7; *On "Time and Being,"* trans. Joan Stambaugh (New York: Harper and Row, 1972), p. 74; "Preface" to William J. Richardson, *Heidegger: Through Phenomenology to Thought* (The Hague: Martinus Nijhoff, 1963), p. x.

14. See the letter of Walter to Pfänder, Husserl Archives, Leuven, R III Walter 20.VI.19.

15. Martin Heidegger, "The Idea of Phenomenology, With a Letter to Edmund Husserl (1927)," trans. Thomas Sheehan, *Listening*, 12 (1977), pp. 119-20.

16. See Hans Seigfried, "Descriptive Phenomenology and Constructivism," *Philosophy and Phenomenological Research*, 37 (1976), 248-61. The article attempts to reduce phenomenology to neo-Kantian transcendental method.

17. Rahner, "Existential Philosophy" (see n. 4 above), p. 128.

18. Ibid.

19. Ibid., p. 129. Italicized in the original.

20. Ibid., p. 128.

21. Heidegger, "Brief über den 'Humanismus,' " *Wegmarken*, ed., Friedrich-Wilhelm von Herrmann, *Gesamtausgabe*, I, 9 (Frankfurt: Vittorio Klostermann, 1976), p. 329 (1967 ed., p. 160); "Letter on Humanism," trans. Frank A. Capuzzi and J. Glenn Gray in *Martin Heidegger: Basic Writings*, ed. David Farrell Krell (New York: Harper and Row, 1977), p. 208. An earlier statement was made to a smaller circle: *Bulletin de la Société française de Philosophie*, 37 (1937), p. 193.

22. Rahner, "Existential Philosophy," p. 128; in the French, p. 156. Heidegger's text is in *Wegmarken*, p. 122, Leibniz's text is from "Principes de la Nature et de la Grace, fondés en raison," no. 7, in G.W. Leibniz, *Die philosophischen Schriften von Gottfried Wilhelm Leibniz*, ed. C.J. Gerhardt, vol. 6 (Hildesheim: Georg Olms, 1961 [reprinted unchanged from the 1885 edition]), p. 602.

23. Rahner, "Existential Philosophy," p. 129, for all citations in this and the following paragraph.

24. On phenomenological method in Heidegger, see his *Die Grundprobleme der Phänomenologie*, ed. Friedrich-Wilhelm von Herrmann, *Gesamtausgabe*, II, 24 (Frankfurt: Vittorio Klostermann, 1975), pp. 26-32; English translation by Albert Hofstadter, *The Basic Problems of Phenomenology* (Bloomington, Ind.: Indiana University Press, 1982), pp. 19-23; and "The Idea of Phenomenology," pp. 112-17.

25. Rahner, "Existential Philosophy," p. 129-30.

26. Ibid., p. 130.

27. Ibid., p. 131.

28. Ibid., p. 130.

29. Heidegger, *Logik: Die Frage nach der Wahrheit*, ed. Walter Biemel, *Gesamtausgabe*, II, 21 (Frankfurt: Vittorio Klostermann, 1976), p. 127-63 (*logos*) and p. 199 (*Chronologie*).

30. Henry Duméry, "Blondel et la philosophie contemporaine (Etude critique)," *Etudes blondéliennes* (Paris), 1952, fascicule 2, p. 92, n.l.

31. Heidegger, "Brief über den 'Humanismus,' " *Wegmarken*, p. 352 (1972 ed., p. 182), in English, p. 230. See also Johannes B. Lotz, "Was von Heideggers Denken ins künftige Philosophieren einzubringen ist," in *Martin Heidegger, Fragen an sein Werk: Ein Symposium*, ed. Jürgen Busche et al. (Stuttgart: Philipp Reclam, 1977), pp. 28-32. The information about Heidegger and Guardini comes from a personal communication from Josef Pieper, 1963.

32. Rahner, "Existential Philosophy," p. 131.

33. Heidegger, *Sein und Zeit*, ed. Friedrich-Wilhelm von Herrmann, *Gesamtausgabe*, I, 2 (Frankfurt: Vittorio Klostermann, 1977); *Being and Time*, trans. John Macquarrie and Edward Robinson (New York, Harper and Row, 1962). Abbreviated SZ, with German and English pages. The German pages are always those of the first edition of SZ.

34. Rahner, "Existential Philosophy," p. 131.

35. Ibid., p. 132.

36. Ibid.

37. Heidegger himself is ambivalent about the component structural elements of disclosedness (*Erschlossenheit*): (1) Sometimes he lists them as four: *Befindlichkeit, Verstehen, Rede,* and *Verfallen*; see SZ 269/314, 270/315, 335/384f. (2) Sometimes he lists them as three, i.e., without *Verfallen*: SZ 180/224, 220/263, and 295f./342. (3) Sometimes he lists them as three, i.e., without *Rede*: SZ 349/400, 335/385 (*das verfallend, gestimmte Verstehen* etc.), 349/400. (4) Sometimes he lists them as two, i.e., *Befindlichkeit* and *Verstehen*, both of these determined by *Rede*: SZ 133/171f., 260/304.

The apparent solution is this: *Erschlossenheit* or *Da* as a whole is *logos* or *Rede* (cf. SZ 349/401: *Rede, d.h. Dasein*). Its moments are *Befindlichkeit/ Schon-in-sein, Verstehen/Vorweg-sein,* and *Sein-bei,* which in its everyday mode is *Verfallen.*

The source of the currency of the *Befindlichkeit-Verstehen-Rede* interpretation in the secondary literature is Alphonse de Waelhens, *La philosophie de Martin Heidegger* (Louvain: Institut Supérieur de Philosophie, 1942), p. 790 et seq. It is carried over in Thomas Langan, *The Meaning of Heidegger: A Critical Study of an Existentialist Phenomenology* (New York: Columbia University Press, 1959), pp. 23 and 41-51. Richardson, in *Heidegger* (see note 13, above), uses the fourfold schema, pp. 59-71, as does Albert Chapelle, *L'Ontologie phénoménologique de Heidegger* (Paris-Brussels: Éditions Universities, 1962), p. 58 f. For a correct reading of the schema, see Karl Jaspers, *Notizien zu Martin Heidegger,* ed. Hans Saner (Munich-Zurich: Piper, 1978), pp. 26-27.

38. All quotations in the remainder of this paragraph are from Rahner, "Existential Philosophy," pp. 132-33.

39. Rahner, "Existential Philosophy," p. 133 f.

40. Ibid., p. 134.

41. Ibid.

42. Ibid., p. 135.

43. Ibid.

44. Ibid., p. 135 f.

45. Ibid., p. 137.

46. Rahner's citation is a collection of discrete sentences from Heidegger's lecture of Monday, October 28, 1929, in the lecture course "Die Grundbegriffe der Metaphysik: Der Weltbegriff," WS 1929/30. It has been edited by Friedrich-Wilhelm von Herrmann as *Die Grundbegriffe der Metaphysik: Welt—Endlichkeit—Einsamkeit, (Gesamtausgabe* II, 29/30) (Frankfurt: Vittorio Klostermann, 1983). Rahner's citation is a very free borrowing from the material on pp. 7-10.

PART TWO

Spirit in the World and Philosophical Foundations

CHAPTER IV

The Problematic of Being in Rahner

Rahner's GW can be designated as an effort to construct "philosophical foundations" in two senses. In the first and primary sense the work is "foundational" insofar as it seeks to be a "fundamental ontology," that is, an investigation into the possibility and limits of a general metaphysics on the basis of an interpretation of the nature of man. In the second and derived sense the work is "foundational" insofar as it lays the groundwork for further regional investigations (for example, into the possibility of human reception of divine revelation: HW) as well as for Rahner's entire project of transcendental theology.

We are concerned with GW as "philosophical foundations" only in the first sense. We seek to understand how and with what consequences Rahner tries to construct a theory of the meaning of being-as-being from out of a hermeneutics of man as the questioner (and therefore interrogative knower) of the very to-be-ness of beings. Throughout this second part of our study we shall be putting Rahner into dialogue with another—often similar and finally divergent—attempt at elaborating a "fundamental ontology," that of Martin Heidegger. The goal is not to force Rahner into a Heideggerian mold, but to find the points of contact and the differences between the two thinkers, and to note the Heideggerian issues that Rahner borrowed, and those that he refused, in the writing of GW. The major difference between these two thinkers will be Rahner's search for the ultimate ground of entities and Heidegger's retrieval of the groundlessness of the "being"-process.

The remaining five chapters are divided as follows. Chapters IV and V introduce GW by presenting the major problematic and method of that work as well as an overview of Rahner's philosophical project. Chapters VI and VII analyze the contents of GW in terms of the unity-in-bivalence that is man: agent intellect and possible intellect or, equally, abstraction and conversion to sensibility. Chapter VIII con-

In order to understand Rahner and to bring him into dialogue with Heidegger we must first decide whether the two men even share the same topic of thought. Both claim to be after "the meaning of being" *(der Sinn von Sein);* both insist that being is analogical and not univocal; both root their understanding of being in the philosophical tradition while at the same time "retrieving" what allegedly lies unsaid in that tradition; both assert that philosophy is only the thematization of what man already essentially is. Yet for all such similarities we must say from the outset that Rahner and Heidegger are not focused on the same topic. The remainder of this study is devoted to substantiating that claim.

In the present chapter we shall take up three topics: (A) an initial sketch of the problematic of being in Rahner, (B) a determination of the starting point of metaphysics in Rahner, and (C) an interpretation of the meaning of *esse* as the self-presence of beings.

A. PRELIMINARY DETERMINATIONS OF BEING IN RAHNER

Our first effort must be to locate the traditional problematic of being. This entails a review of the problematic of being in Greek and medieval philosophy and, inevitably, a certain amount of linguistic archeology.

The word "being" is ambivalent in both ordinary and philosophical usage, and in keeping with this ambivalence Rahner, like Heidegger, uses two German words for it, *das Sein* and *das Seiende.* The first word is a substantized form of the infinitive of the German verb "to be," *sein,* and it corresponds in form to the Greek *to einai,* the Latin *esse,* the Italian *l'essere,* and so on. The second word is a neologism and, outside of philosophical parlance, not good German. *Das Seiende* combines the definite article with the present participle of the German verb "to be." It corresponds in form to the Greek *to on,* the Latin *ens,* the Italian *l'ente,* and so on. In general *das Sein* expresses the act or state or condition of being, whereas *das Seiende* expresses *that which* has such an act or state or condition of being. The problem, as everyone knows, is more complicated than this, and Rahner himself compounds the problem by frequently using *das Sein* as interchangeable with *das Seiende.* Such usage is not in error but rather accords with the ontological perspective crucial and proper to metaphysics. However, it will expose Rahner's work, along with all metaphysics, to Heidegger's charge of the "forgottenness of being."

To sort out these issues and to discover Rahner's specific understanding of the meaning of "being," we begin with a preliminary clarification of the problematic of being in traditional metaphysics and in Rahner. These considerations are preliminary because we here take up only Rahner's *formal* designation of being as being-actual *(Wirklichsein)* while reserving until later in this chapter the material designation of being as self-presence *(Bei-sich-sein)*. What is immediately at stake is the question whether the Thomistic reading of being as *esse* transcends the most general ontological perspective of traditional metaphysics, or whether it is only one moment—even if a revolutionary one—*within* metaphysics.

1. The Problem of Being and Beingness

The uniqueness of a properly philosophical question lies in its search for *essence*. A philosophical inquiry usually claims to look "beyond" the accidental and individual dimensions of things in order to ask about the "nature" of those entities. With Socrates and Plato the philosophical question emerges in the West as the dialectical search, for instance, beyond virtues to virtue-ness (the *Meno*) or beyond pious acts to the essence of "piety" (the *Euthyphro*). In general terms, the philosophical question asks about the "X-ness" of X, and we designate this "-ness" dimension as the *nature* of X or (if we may use the word broadly and prescind for now from the distinction of "essence-and-existence") as the *essence* of X.

But the highest form of philosophy—what Aristotle calls "first philosophy"—asks not about the essence of particular regions of things (the X-ness of all Xs, the Y-ness of all Ys) but rather about the "is-ness" of all that is. As contrasted with particular sciences, which investigate delimited sets of things, first philosophy encompasses everything that is, and inquires into it from the most universal viewpoint, that of its "being." The question, "What is a being—any being, every being—insofar as it is at all?" is the question of beings as being *(to on hēi on)*, the very same question which moves all Western philosophy regardless of how it answers or refuses to answer it.

Aristotle, who poses this question in Book G of the *Metaphysics*, specifies it further in Book Z: "The ever-puzzling question that has always been asked and is still being asked today and ever will be asked—namely, What is a being?—comes down to the question, What is beingness?" (Z, 1, 1028 b 2f.). This word "beingness" translates the Greek *ousia* and places us at the center of a problematic that we can begin to understand only by reflecting on the Greek words underlying the English "being" and the German *Sein/Seiendes*.

The Greek verb "to be" (*einai*) declines the masculine, feminine, and neuter of its present participle as, respectively, *ōn*, *ousa*, and *on*. To form the word "a being" or "the being," Greek combines the definite article with the neuter present participle: *to on*, parallel to the Latin *ens*, the Italian *l'ente*, and the German *das Seiende*. *To on* can express *one* thing which is in being, or equally *all* that is in being (sometimes expressed by the plural *ta onta*). We may translate *to on* into English as "the being" or "a being" or simply as "beings" when it refers to particular things which are. Or, in an unavoidable ambivalence, we may say just "being" when *to on* refers to all that is.

The primary philosophical question, "What is any being as being?" *(ti to on hēi on;)* comes down to the question, "What is the beingness or is-ness of anything that is?" *(tis hē ousia;)*. This noun *ousia* is constructed from the feminine of the same present participle of the Greek verb for "to be": *ousa→ousia*. The usual translations of it as "essence" or "substance" are very problematic, and they immeasurably complicate and prejudice the question Aristotle was posing. For example, Scholastic translations (i.e., interpretations) of *ousia* as "essence" tend to read this word in contradistinction to "existence" and thereby to deny that Aristotle had a philosophical insight into the priority of existence over essence. On this basis Thomists declare that Aquinas' thematization of *esse* as the existential act of being steps beyond the ontological framework of Greek metaphysics. But, as I hope to show below, the translation of *ousia* as "essence" is not a neutral and innocent act, and in fact it allows Scholasticism to beg the very question it should ask. To preclude such a step at the beginning, I will let the English "beingness" stand for the Greek *ousia*—a bland and inelegant rendering, to be sure, but one whose virtue consists precisely in the fact that it says so little and thus leaves the philosophical issue more open. Not only that, but it also preserves in English the connection between *ousia* and *to on* (beingness, beings). If we choose, not unproblematically, to render *to on* by "the real" or "whatever is real," *ousia* could become "reality," but even this terminology, which may well be better than "essence," carries over into the Greek experience elements which at least for now are better left aside. Therefore, let the question of First Philosophy, "What is any being insofar as it is in being?" come down to the question, "What is the beingness of any being?" On that basis let us explore the thesis that the issue of the beingness of beings controls the metaphysics of Aquinas and Rahner as much as that of Aristotle.[1]

2. Beingness as *Energia* in Aristotle

Ousia was a common Greek term before Plato and Aristotle brought it into the province of philosophy. It simply meant property or possessions, goods or wealth, perhaps in the form of livestock, land, or a worker's tools—in short, something present at hand to be used. The German language can translate it either as *die Habe*, one's holdings, what one has, or *das Anwesen*, present possessions. The latter especially preserves the resonance of "presence," and points to the connection between *ousia* and *parousia*.

In Plato's and Aristotle's specifically philosophical use of the term, *ousia* retains some of the connotations of that ordinary usage. In Plato *ousia* means the stability of things, the ever-present and intransient aspect which perdures throughout change. Its connotations are identity, unchangeability, and permanent presence, as we can see from Socrates' question in the *Phaedo* (78 d), which expects an affirmative answer: "Is the very beingness of to be (*ousia autē tou einai*) always in the same manner and in the same way...?" With the cautions mentioned above, one can see that *ousia* means the "reality" of things, so long as one remembers that, in the Parmenidean framework which Plato appropriated, reality means permanence in self-identity. For Plato, of course, the realm of *ousia* is the world of Forms as the really real, the permanently present.

Aristotle carries over these connotations of stability, permanence, and presence into his use of *ousia*, while at the same time he gives the word a meaning fundamentally different from Plato's. Aristotle too wants to know the stability and permanent reality, the beingness of beings, but at issue in his world are concrete singular things, the *tode ti* ("this thing here"). Rather than relegating concrete beings to the status of less-than-being (*mē on*) in contrast to the Forms as real being (*ontōs on*), Aristotle asks what it is *in* the *tode ti* which makes it have beingness and be real. It would be simplistic and misleading to interpret Aristotle as bringing the world of Forms, and therefore of *ousia*, from heaven down to earth and embedding it within individual things as "energies" or "powers."[2] Surely Aristotle first had to have conceived of concrete beings as real before he could supposedly "bring down" Plato's Forms to earth; and to think of individuals as real beings, he certainly first had to have a different notion of beingness itself. Unless we are to reduce Aristotle's philosophical contribution to a simple inversion of Plato, we must try to understand how he revolutionized metaphysics by conceiving the individual as the first instance of reality. In this way we may see how the question of First Philosophy became, in Aristotle's unique way of thinking, the question of beingness.

Aristotle says that "being" (*to on*) has a variety of meanings with one analogically common referent, and he provides two basic lists of the multiple meanings of being, a broad fourfold one (cf. *Meta.*, E, 2) and, within that, a more limited tenfold list of the categories. According to the broad list, "being" can mean being accidental, being true or false, being according to the schemata of the ten categories, and being potential and actual. With the exception of Heidegger, the search for the common analogical referent (the *hen kai mia physis*, G, 2, 1003 a 33) has traditionally been carried out within the tenfold list of the schemata of categories. Thus the category of *ousia* is the prime instance to which the other nine categories refer, for one can speak of being-this-way-or-that only in terms of a concrete something, an *ousia* or reality, which bears those modes in itself. Thus, if we exclude on the one hand accidental, and on the other hand generic or universal features, the fundamental meaning of *to on* is *ousia* as concrete present reality. "*Ousia*, in the predominant and primary and most definite way it is said, is that which is neither predicated of some *hypokeimenon* nor present in a *hypokeimenon* but rather is, for example, this individual man, this individual horse" (*Cat.* 5, 2 a ll ff.). *Ousia*, reality, is first of all the *hypokeimenon*, something which lies there present, hence something of which we may predicate accidental ways of being such as quantity, quality, and so forth.

Moreover, within *ousia* thus understood there is a further order of reference towards the primary instance of *ousia* in which being will be present in the most normative way. Within sensible *ousiai* Aristotle finds that not matter but form accounts for the definiteness and reality which are characteristics of being itself. Form is the leading instance of reality, and the divine beings as pure forms or separate immaterial realities are final and pure being. As divine and eternal, these realities formally account for all the other beings, all of which strive to imitate the actual permanence of the separate *ousiai*. The question, "What is it in a *tode ti* that makes it an *ousia*?" gets answered in terms of form (*morphē*) and by reference to separate, pure form.

Thus in Aristotle *ousia* means both the concrete individual reality and that which, "in" that concrete thing, is truly real: its intelligible form.[3] The English word "reality" allows of this twofold meaning. It can refer both to a concrete individual or state-of-affairs ("A united Vietnam is now a reality") and to that which allows a concrete individual to be and be understood as real ("What is the reality of contemporary capitalism?"), i.e., both to that which is and to its is-ness or state-of-being, its beingness. The ambivalence is not accidental. *To on* always means a being-*in*-its-beingness, and *ousia* always connotes the beingness-*of*-a-being. And in passing we may note (we take this up below) that when Rahner "confuses" *das Sein* and *das Seiende*, he is acting in accordance with this positive insight which is the major gain of metaphysics.

But the task now is to specify what we mean by saying that for Aristotle beingness ultimately is *energeia;* and at this point the problem of how to translate Aristotle's key terms becomes most acute. Specifically we must question (and doubt) whether *actus* or "act" is at all an adequate translation of *energeia* and ultimately whether Thomas Aquinas' interpretation and incorporation of Aristotle into Christian metaphysics is the preservation of the genuine fundamental constituent of Aristotle's thinking and at the same time its progressive development.[4]

With Aristotle we find ourselves in a universe that is both concrete and dynamic, and both characteristics find expression in his word *energeia.* With Aristotle we may well apprehend that a concrete *ousia* is present by its actions, by what it does. Seen as the origin of its actions, an *ousia* is called a *physis,* a "nature," or more exactly, a *physei on,* a being that is present through an internal and intrinsic source of change. Moreover, we may distinguish, first, the particular actions, operations, and changes which the being occasions in itself and others (in Latin, *actus secundus*) and, secondly and of more importance here, the primary "act" or "doing" which the thing itself *is (actus primus).* In this interpretation—which is the usual Scholastic one—since a being acts and does, it is itself an act or a doing. If a thing is all that it does to itself and others, then most fundamentally such a being is "act," and "to be" signifies the exercising of an act. Indeed, "*Energeia* means the thing's very act of being present [*hyparchein*]" (*Meta.* Theta, 6, 1048 a 31).

But it is one thing to say that "being" means a "subsisting doing," even the very doing of being-present-at-all, and quite another thing to identify the content of that doing. And bound up with this question is the problem of whether "acting" and "doing" are even proper ways of rendering *energeia.* The very use of such language (*agere, actus*) points to a later and different universe of discourse from Aristotle's. Can such a linguistic transition be made innocently by simply consulting, let us say, a Boethian dictionary, when that dictionary itself comes from the later and different world of discourse? For some interpreters, "Aristotelianism is first and foremost a language. . . . There was therefore no reason why theologians should not have successfully extended the use of Aristotelianism to the definition of the truths of faith."[5] Other interpreters, however, will insist that Aristotle's language be read much more carefully on its own terms before one presumes outright that Latin translations preserve Greek meanings. Let us, then, first try to discern what kind of "doing" (if we use the word at all) *energeia* might be in Aristotle's thought before we go on to the radically new reading of that "doing" in Aquinas' creationist metaphysics.

Ousia, we have said, carries over into philosophy such meanings as "stability" and "presence," and it comes to mean something like the "staying power" of beings. Aristotle echoes these resonances of stability when, for example, he speaks of *ta onta* (beings) as *synestōta* and *synistamena* (*Physics*, B, 1, 192 b 13 and 193 a 36). These participial forms come from the verb *histēmi*, "I stand" or "I make to stand." We take it that *to on* is something which "stands on its own" and in that sense "endures" thanks to the staying power of its beingness. So too the nouns *hypostasis* and *hypokeimenon* ("that which stands there or lies there") point in the direction of something which "holds forth on its own." As such, a being holds itself in its limits (*peras*), shows itself for what it is (*eidos*), and so comes to its fulfillment (*telos*). As stable, delimited, and appearing as itself, a being "fulfills itself" as a "work," in the specifically Greek sense of *ergon*. This word does not mean the end-product of a making, nor the act of making, but rather that which has come forth in stable, self-contained self-manifestation, that which stands out in evidence as what it is. *En ergōi einai* (to be in work) means the same as *en eidei einai* (to be in evidence) and *en telei einai* (to be fulfilled as itself). Aristotle captures these meanings in the words which express the core of his thought: *energeia* and *entelecheia*. The staying power or beingness of a being is that whereby the being "has itself" in its *telos* (not "aim," "purpose," or "cessation," but "fulfillment") and is "in *ergon*," in self-manifestation. In this interpretation—which is Heidegger's—Aristotle's Greek world of being is one suffused with luminosity, presence, and appearance, the philosophical reflection of the archaic Greek world which Professor Finley describes as "the brilliant world" characterized by "the show and impression of things" in their "bright particularity."[6] The major features of this world of bright appearance (*alētheia*) are the openness, transparency, and up-front-ness of things, where the very implicitness of this vision constitutes the beauty and enchanting naïveté of the Greek universe.

Even though this vision be implicit, it is *this* implicitness and not another which must be thematized if we are to understand what kind of "doing" characterizes beings for Aristotle. If we were to use these terms at all, we might say that as their "first act" beings "do" their emergence into stable, in-gathered self-manifestation.[7]

3. Beingness as *Esse* in Aquinas

With Thomas Aquinas we enter a thoroughly different universe, no longer the eternal, necessary, and self-sufficient cosmos of Aristotle, but the created, redeemed, and radically finite world of Judeo-Christian faith. And just as the world of lived experience is entirely transformed, so too the philosophical meaning of beingness gets scored in a radically new key. If, as Scholastics maintain, the world of Aristotle enters that of

Aquinas whole, it also becomes wholly different, and the result is nothing less than a revolution.[8] For Aristotle the question of the origin of the world did not arise. *Ousiai* existed in their own right without need of any bestowal of their beingness. The cosmos, moreover, was not *one* in any final sense of the word, insofar as the self-thinking thought was not *the* cause but one of the causes. And while beings in some way depended on pure *energeia* for their measure of beingness, there was no creation and no *eschaton* but an infinite succession of birth and death in imitation of and desire for the pure permanence of God.[9]

Aquinas, however, held two different presuppositions, learned from faith, which were the basis for the rescoring of beingness as "act" (*actus*). One was the radical contingency of the world; the other was the supernatural supremacy of God. In a phrase: faith in creation and creation's God.

Creatio ex nihilo means the absolute production of beings from no other preexisting condition than the free will of the Creator, such that all beings have, as a "gift," that whereby they are at all. On that basis, presumably for the first time, beingness can be read as a radical insurrection against nothingness, what Pierce calls "the object's crowding out of a place for itself in the universe,"[10] the act whereby a thing is placed outside non-being, the event in virtue of which it is established on its own and begins to be. In this creationist vision of reality as perhaps in no other, the world appears as radically and totally contingent: radically contingent insofar as it might never have existed; totally and permanently contingent insofar as it could at any moment cease to exist. No worldly being can be the cause of itself; all must receive existence from without. Existence-at-all becomes understood as the point of impact or first effect of the creative act of God, and yet, as received in the creature, becomes that creature's very own.

This vision allows Aquinas, beyond Aristotle, to distinguish between the mere fact (*factum*) that something exists, i.e., its condition of being *something*, and the very act or actuation (*actus*) of existence as the inner "doing" whereby something is at all.[11] The former is the state into which a being is posited by the act of beingness, whereas the latter is the very act or doing whereby the thing is so posited. It is "existential energy" or "pure existential act."[12] This new understanding, in which beingness (the condition of being in being) is most fundamentally identified with this very act, doubtlessly became possible only through faith in a unique relation of beings to God in which newness of beingness (*novitas essendi*) happens. On that basis the first act of beings is no longer, as it was in Aristotle, their "doing" of emergence into self-manifestation, but the very "doing" of their beingness at all.

Here the word "existence" (Aquinas prefers *esse*) takes on a new meaning. For Aristotle the "ex-" (Greek *exō*) of "existence" meant that something perdures on its own as stable in itself and "in its own place" (*chōriston*) outside of man's mind (cf. *Meta.*, E, 4, 1028 a 1 ff. and K, 8, 1065 a 24).[13] But in Aquinas "existence" means literally the act of "standing outside"—of nothingness.

This creationist doctrine of the radical contingency of worldly beings, however, points first and foremost to the doctrine of a supreme supernatural God. And with that, the understanding of beingness as "act" reaches its highest point.

Let us distinguish three elements in the received belief in the supernatural Creator God: his perfection, his independence, and his presence to creatures, all of which at once require and provide a new notion of beingness as "act."

First, for God to be perfect means that he can suffer no determinations from without, that he can be, through himself, nothing other than his own supreme self, the most noble reality. To deny of God any determination (negation) of his beingness is to affirm that he is nothing other than this beingness, that he is not a being which *has*, i.e., participates in, beingness, but rather is beingness itself. His "essence" (if we chose to use this word of him) is simply: to be.

Secondly, as this pure subsisting act of beingness, God is, beyond all potentiality, pure simplicity existing through himself (*ens a se*). As absolutely simple, a being that is its own beingness and exists in virtue of itself, God differs from and is independent of every other being ("*differt a quolibet alio ente*").[14]

And finally, this understanding of God's beingness indicates his relation to creatures. To understand God as the pure act of beingness is to understand that creatures, to the degree they are at all, participate in that act of beingness. The act of beingness in creatures—at once the proper effect of God and the innermost element in every creature—bespeaks God's operative presence, as agent, in all things. "All creatures are to God as air is to the sun which makes it bright."[15] God as the act of beingness makes creatures to be and preserves them, as radically contingent, in their beingness. Thus, within and because of the dual theme of creation (radical contingency) and the Creator God (perfect, simple/ independent, creative), the understanding of beingness changes: Creatures "do" their beingness because God, who as beingness itself preeminently "does" his beingness, gives creatures that "doing."

But there is yet another nuance that accrues to the "act" of beingness in this creationist metaphysics. The finite or infinite "doing" of beingness entails as well the *causal* "doing" of beingness to others. Beings intrinsically do-unto-others as they do-unto-themselves, they "act upon" inasmuch as they are in act (have beingness), and in so doing produce effects like unto themselves. In the creationist vision, "the actuality of being[ness] is an ontological generosity: *omne ens actu natum est agere aliquid actu existens*: That is to say: 'It is natural, for every being in act, to produce some actually existing being.'"[16] In this world of beingness as act, there is a hierarchy of efficient causes ordered according to the hierarchy of beingness. Indeed, the precedent is set in God as self-subsisting beingness who, as act, is the origin of the Word.[17]

We find ourselves apparently at an infinite remove from Aristotle— and yet something in common remains. For Scholastic philosophers, sensitive to the uniqueness of Aquinas' thematization of *esse* as act, our continued use of "beingness" may seem an offense, if not an outright misunderstanding. And yet this "beingness" is the element of continuity with the tradition that perdures even in Aquinas' revolution within metaphysics. If *ousia*, "beingness," is read here as it usually is by Scholastics, viz., as essence in contradistinction to existence, then there would be a misunderstanding—but on the part of those who so read it. "Beingness," rather, is used here as a heuristicon to designate the highest ontological principle in *any* metaphysics, that is, in any thematic inquiry into what is responsible for beings-as-beings (*on hēi on, ens qua ens*) whether that be essentialist *idea* in Plato, "formal" *energeia* in Aristotle, existential act of *esse* in Aquinas, or will to power and eternal recurrence of the self-same in Nietzsche.

Our use of "beingness" when discussing the very act or actuation that is *esse* is neither a misunderstanding of Aquinas nor an attempt to reduce him to some variation on an essentialist metaphysics. Rather, it is in the service of locating the uniqueness of Aquinas' revolution *within* metaphysics. Likewise, the use of the awkward word "doing" instead of the usual "act" to translate *actus* represents no effort to reduce the unique *actus primus* of to-be-at-all to some quasi-physicalistic and secondary "action" of beings. Rather it is an attempt to point to the unique kind of dynamism, so different from Aristotle's, which permeates Aquinas' metaphysics and finds its expression in the hierarchy of existential efficient causality that reaches from God as self-subsistent act of to be to the lowest instance of to be. While we might perhaps and not unproblematically speak of a "doing of beingness" in Aristotle, it was a matter of beings "doing" their emergence into stable presence and self-manifestation. In Aquinas we may properly speak of a "doing of beingness" as the act of being-at-all and as a "doing unto others." The difference is fundamental, but what these positions share in common is an understanding of actuality (Rahner: *Wirklichkeit*) as being-present-in-being (Rahner: *Anwesenheit*),[18] whether in Aristotle it be the stable presence of in-gathered self-appearance or in Aquinas the very "self"-presence of beings (*per se* in God; bestowed in creatures) and their causing of such ontological presentness in others. In a very real sense, while the answer becomes radically new, the Aristotelian question, "What is beingness?" perdures in Aquinas. The insight that the ultimate meaning of beingness is not "to be in this or that way" but simply "to be" was, in Gilson's words, "in no sense a discovery of being[ness], which, since it is the first principle, is as old as the human mind, but it was a discovery *within* the notion of being[ness]."[19]

And beingness—the unifying heuristicon of metaphysics—always means some form of *presence*. In Aquinas beingness means (1) the very act whereby nothingness is overcome and a being enters stability, subsistence, perdurance and (2) this very stability and perdurance itself: the act and the fact of stable presence. For (again, Gilson): "Not to pass away, but to be for ever and ever, that is what it is to exist."[20]

4. Beingness as Act in Rahner

Rahner at once presumes and deepens the traditional Scholastic reading of beingness as act and actuality, although, if we make a distinction between the very act of beingness (*actus*) and the resultant fact of beingness (*actualitas*), Rahner seems to use *das Sein* generally in the latter sense. This section is only a preliminary determination of how Rahner understands beingness (or better, Aquinas' use of beingness) as act, because Rahner places his proper treatment of beingness within the framework of a transcendental reduction to the subject who knows beingness, whereas Aquinas generally elaborates *esse* within an objectivist metaphysics. As we show later, Rahner ultimately reads the meaning of beingness in terms of the self-presence of beings in knowing and being-known (*Bei-sich-sein*), while Aquinas understands beingness as the act whereby things get on the ontological map at all (*Vorhandensein*). Thus, while Rahner embeds his discussion of the Thomistic *esse* within a discussion of agent intellect and judgment and thereby intends a transcendental understanding of the act of beingness, he in fact presumes therein the Scholastic understanding of beingness. Therefore, in the next section we will have to ask whether Rahner's transcendental turn leads him outside of metaphysics or simply allows him to rearrange matters within that science.

To the degree that Rahner focuses on the emergence of beings into intelligibility (transcendental emphasis) rather than on their beingness at all (objectivist emphasis), he tends to discuss beingness as actuality rather than act, with the nuance of presentness-for-knowing rather than as coming into ontological presence as such. His preferred words for *esse* are *Wirklichkeit* (actuality), *Wirklichsein* (being-actual), or, less frequently, *Realsein* (being-real, as he says, "in the modern sense"). All of these mean "*esse*, or, less subject to misunderstanding, *esse actu*."[21] And all these terms indicate ontological *presentness:* "*Wirklichkeit (Anwesenheit)*."[22] Our task now is to see how (1) Rahner reads this actuality, reality, and presentness as the "in-itself-ness" of things, (2) how he reduces essence to a mode of *esse*, and (3) how he understands the formal and transcategorical universality of beingness.

Beingness as In-itself-ness. In the context of discussing the abstractive liberation of knowable form from matter, as well as their *complexio* in the affirmative synthesis, Rahner reasserts Aquinas' position that the predicate, as the content of the form, expresses knowledge of the objective state of affairs of what is to be known (*das gegenständliche Ansich des Gewussten*[23]). This objective in-itself is what man applies, in the synthesis of judgment, to the thing designated by the subject of the proposition. The question is, What is this in-itself? If judgment attains to reality and not to some essentialist validity of propositions or eternal truth, what in fact does it attain? For Aquinas the answer is self-evident: the very being-actual or being-real of the thing to be known. The reality reached in judgment is not an ideal being-in-itself but the real existence (*reales Existieren*) of the knowable. "For [Aquinas], *esse* as 'to-be-real' [*Wirklichsein*] *is* the only fundamental in-itself, and anything is an in-itself only insofar as and to the extent that it expresses 'to-be-real.' "[24] The judgment is *applicatio ad rem*, attainment of what is really the case, and this *res* is *esse*. "Therefore, to-be-in-itself [*Ansichsein*] and *esse* as to-be-real [*Wirklichsein*] coincide for Thomas," and "the judgment as affirmative synthesis always attains to an in-itself, and this is always *esse*."[25]

Esse and Essence. If beingness means to-be-real as act and state, what does "essence" mean in Thomistic metaphysics, whether objectivist or transcendental? Perhaps it is the very richness of the Scholastic thesaurus for expressing beingness (form, act, etc.) which almost ineluctably leads to the unfortunate quasi-hypostasization of ontological principles into things in themselves. In any case, the Scholastic "essence" qualifies as a good example of such hypostasization. Rahner, however, takes a radical step and reduces essence to a mode of *esse*.

Whatever the reasons, Scholasticism tends to talk about essence as if it were some " 'pattern' that dwells in an ideal in-itself, indifferent of itself to real being," a kind of "thing" with a positive status and content alongside *esse*, something co-created as a reciprocal cause of beings such that one could say, "This essence, man, exists."[26] Elaborate metaphors, such as that of a compressed spring (the act of existing) inside a flexible box (essence),[27] whatever their pedagogical value, tend to undermine the subtle doctrine of *esse* by taking essence as a "possible something" which can receive an act of existence. Even the doctrine of the divine ideas as *rationes* of the imitability of God carries this connotation. It may well be that such language and imagery are Scholastic relics of the Greek notion of essence, not, of course, as something real and separate (Plato) and not exactly as indwelling in particulars (Aristotle), but nonetheless as a "reality" alongside the *real* reality that is the act and state of existing. Even to assert the primacy of existence over essence is but a compromise, a halfway house on the road to reducing essence to a mode of *esse*, insofar as such primacy turns creation into a monstrous marriage of essence and existence rather than seeing it as a true birth of *novitas essendi*.[28]

For Rahner, however, "Thomas knows essences only as the limiting potency of *esse*, as the real ground and expression of the fact that *esse* in the individual 'this' is not given in its unlimited fullness. Beyond that they are nothing."[29] "Essence" articulates the fact that being-real, which in itself is limitless, is in fact contracted in a particular being to a definite degree of the intensity of beingness. Rather than being something which limits or specifies or receives beingness, essences are modes of *esse*, *esse*'s own self-limitation and self-specification to this or that— potencies for and limitations of *esse*, expressions of "the extent to which, in a definite existent, *esse*, the ground of reality for such an existent, can let such an existent really exist."[30] Essences "are only confining limits of the fullness which [absolute] *esse* would have in itself," and "even before the creative mind of God, the quiddity is not an object through some kind of an ideal beingness which would belong to the quiddity itself; rather it is an object only in the sense that the divine intellect apprehends its own creative, existing beingness."[31] For Aquinas, as Rahner reads him, outside of *esse* as being-real there is nothing but nothing.

The Formal and Transcategorical Universality of Beingness. The universality of beingness can be understood in two ways: first, as the formal unity both of individual beings and of all beings of a given genus; and secondly, as the transcategorical unity which overrides all genera and beings. In Rahner's treatment of such universality, the formal unity of beingness is only a step on the way to the affirmation of transcategorical unity.

In any individual being, if it is to be *one* thing, there cannot be a different act of beingness for each determination but only one act as the unity of all determinations. Otherwise, there would have to be yet a further beingness as the formal unifier of all the already existing determinations. What is apprehended in judgmental synthesis is precisely this unified formal beingness in one being. In that sense, beingness is the most formal and simple principle of any existing reality. Beingness can also be considered as formal unity in terms of the universality of all beings of one genus. Abstraction consists in "liberating" the quiddity from a particular subject, in the sense of seeing its universal repeatability in any number of subjects of the same genus. But we have seen that the language of quiddity and essence is better expressed in terms of limiting modalities of *esse*. Therefore, what is liberated and understood in its formal repeatability is really *esse*, unlimited in itself (hence, repeatable) and yet instantiated in this particular subject (hence, the reality of *this* thing which we affirm to exist in this way or that). In abstraction, therefore, a further formal universality of *esse* is seen, not just the unifying formality of one given being, but the intrinsic freedom of beingness to bestow reality as much upon one quiddity as upon another. *Esse* "bears all these possible quiddities in itself as the ground which bestows reality upon them and can produce them from itself."[32]

But if beingness is the intrinsic sustaining ground of all the determinations of a being, and also the universal ground of reality for all genera of beings, then everything becomes real through the very act of to-be-real. As the one unity of all formal and categorical determinations, beingness has a trans-categorical universality. It is "the absolute ground of all possible determinations," "the fullness of all possible determinations absolutely," "the one full ground of all possible objects of knowledge."[33] It is to everything as actuality to potency. Of course, no specific judgment can affirm this fullness as pertaining to the particular being in question. Each judgment, rather, is "a critique of the object, an evaluation of the measure of *esse* which belongs to what is judged."[34] But it is now clear that these particular objects of judgment are not primarily distinguished by their "quidditative" determinations, but rather precisely and primarily by *esse* as the ground of such determinations. For Thomas, "The *esse* of each thing is both proper to it and distinct from the *esse* of any other thing" (*De Pot.*, 7, 3, c.).

Such talk of beingness in its fullness and in its limitation to this or that degree of beingness points ahead to a topic which we take up later in this chapter: the analogical "having" of beingness. No finite being (*ens*) is beingness itself (*esse*) but only a "participation" in beingness. *Esse* thus appears not as a genus, not as something static and univocally definable, but rather as "intrinsically variable. . . , oscillating, as it were, between nothing and infinity."[35] The analogy of beingness will go hand-in-hand with Rahner's precision of the content of the meaning of beingness as self-presence. But before taking that up, we must return to the hypothesis which structures these preliminary remarks: Does the issue of the beingness of beings in fact control the metaphysics of Aquinas and Rahner as much as that of Aristotle? And if so, with what consequences?

5. The Question of Ousiology in Rahner

The difference between the act or actuality of beingness (*das Sein, esse*) and those things which have, exercise, or participate in beingness (*das Seiende, ens*) is sacrosanct in contemporary Thomism, and Rahner clearly expresses this distinction. On the one hand he says that beingness itself is *ipsum esse*—he quotes Aquinas—"the ultimate act which can be participated in by everything" (*actus ultimus qui participabilis est ab omnibus*), itself participating in nothing else: "*das Wirklichsein, das esse oder, noch unmissverständlicher, das esse actu.*"[36] On the other hand, a being (*ein Seiendes*) is "a something in which *das Sein* as such is limited by being a *Sosein.*"[37]

After such a clear distinction, then, it is surprising to find that Rahner frequently confounds *das Sein* and *das Seiende*, and in two directions. First, he tends to hypostasize *das Sein* into a thing in its own right, and secondly, he very often uses *das Sein* when one would expect *das Seiende*. The first usage, which is both common and perhaps unavoidable in Scholastic discourse, may take rise not only from the richness of the Thomistic lexicon for beingness, which we already mentioned, but also from the denomination of God as *ipsum esse subsistens*. But regardless of the reasons (which may in fact be part of the problem), let us simply note some of the many cases in which Rahner either hypostasizes *das Sein* or uses it in place of *das Seiende*. The listing is rough and incomplete, and it serves only one purpose: to raise the question of the internal limitations of the metaphysical project in the *philosophia perennis*.

In discussing the content of the meaning of beingness (see Division C, below) Rahner takes the position that the *esse* of *ens* is the self-presence (reflectedness-upon-itself, hence self-knowing) of a being in its beingness. Clearly, then, *esse = Bei-sich-sein*, and *ens = ein Bei-sich-seiendes*.[38] Knowing is *das Bei-sich-sein des Seienden in seinem Sein*[39] or *das Sein des Seienden bei-sich-selber*.[40] But then we are surprised to find throughout his pages the phrase *das Bei-sich-sein des Seins*.[41] Is this genitive meant as subjective rather than objective? That is, does it express *esse* "as" the self-presence (understood: of beings)? If so, then the problem would dissolve once the reader was forewarned. But to compound the problem, Rahner likewise speaks of the self-presence of a *Sein: das Bei-sich-sein eines Seins*.[42] And he speaks equally—and in the same sense—of the

Erkennbarkeit (knowability) of *das Seiende* and of *das Sein;*[43] of the *Seinsmächtigkeit* (*esse*-intensity) of *das Seiende* and of *das Sein*.[44]

When he speaks of an object which man—surely an *ens*—can know, he writes: *die Objekt eines erkennenden Seins*.[45] When he speaks of an *ens* which is not its own *esse*, he writes: *ein Sein*, which is not the *Sein seiner selbst*.[46] In translating Aquinas' *quo est omnia fieri. . .respectu totius entis universalis*, he writes that the intellect is "the possibility for the reception of *alles Sein*."[47] And in interpreting *quidquid esse potest, intelligi potest*, he says that Aquinas rejects the concept of an unknowable *Sein*.[48] And although he is aware that "one cannot properly say that *esse* is, but rather that through *esse* something is," he does not hesitate to affirm, in the case of God, *die Existenz eines absoluten Seins*.[49] He speaks, moreover, of transcendental *Wesenheit* and later clarifies this as *das Sein und sein Transcendentalien*.[50] And when he talks about the most general question of *Sein* (*allgemeinste Seinsfrage*), he means *diese Frage nach dem Seienden im allgemeinen*.[51]

A particular telling case comes to light when we confront the two editions of *Hörer des Wortes*. In the first edition Rahner speaks of the intensity of *esse* as a function which varies with the degree to which any particular being returns to itself and can be present to itself.[52] At the apex of the analogy of beingness stands God as that being (*jenes Seiende*) which is pure *esse* (*reines Sein*), the being in which the meaning of *esse* is absolutely realized.[53] But in the second edition we find two footnotes, written by Professor Metz but approved by Rahner. First, "*Sein* indeed 'is' not 'something' 'next to' or 'above' *das Seiende*, but rather is *das Seiende* as a relation (hence too an 'ontological difference') to itself. . . ." Indeed: "In this sense, even God should not be thought of simply as *das Sein*, but rather—as we show in what follows—as *das Seiende* of the absolute having-of-*Sein*. . . ."[54] And in a second footnote: "If we here designate God as 'pure *Sein*,' we always mean it in the sense that God is *das Seiende* which absolutely has-*Sein*. . . ."[55]

What does this cumbersome list of texts say? It confronts us with some important difficulties that point to the overarching problematic of the unity and intrinsic limitation of the metaphysical project from Plato through Rahner. To begin with, we must ask whether Rahner's use of *das Sein* when the sensitive reader might have expected *das Seiende* represents a fundamental slip, a forgetting of the crucial distinction between *ens* and *esse*. I think it does not. Rather, it indicates that Rahner's metaphysical problematic, like that of Aquinas and Aristotle, is embedded within the structure of the traditional question, "What is a being as being?" We have already noted that, regardless of the answer given to this question, the heuristicon remains the same: the beingness of beings.

Again we stress that "beingness" refers not to essence as versus existence, nor to any specific content (*idea, energeia, esse, Bei-sich-sein*), but rather to whatever constitutes beings as beings, that is, beingness in the heuristic-generic sense of *ousia* and not in Aristotle's specific usage of that term. On that basis we may speak of Western metaphysics as a whole and in each of its phases as an "ousiology," an attempt to show and justify in speech (*legein, logos*) the ultimate reality or beingness of whatever is (the *ousia* of beings).[56] Although Aquinas' reading of being-ness as the act of *esse* is revolutionary within the tradition, it remains, from the broader viewpoint of the metaphysical question, a palace revolution. It takes place *within* the general framework of metaphysics (transformed, to be sure, into a self-explanation of faith), but it neither intends to nor could shatter the intrinsic limitation of metaphysics *as* metaphysics. This I take to be the sense of Gilson's statement that Aquinas' thematization of *esse* was "in no sense a discovery of the notion of being[ness], which, since it is the first principle, is as old as the hu-man mind, but it was a discovery *within* the notion of being[ness]."[57]

But surely, one objects, the wineskins were broken and had to be re-fashioned to accommodate the new wine of faith. But this is the very point that has to be argued: whether refashioning metaphysics with me-taphysics' own language really constitutes an overcoming of that science or whether it is only (even if momentously so) a renewal, extension, and transformation of metaphysics. And further: Is it an unquestionable premise that metaphysics, even transformed, is the proper place to seek the self-understanding of faith? Granted that Aristotle's ousiology was the best that Aquinas may have had to work with, is it the best that we have at hand for retrieving the unsaid in Aquinas, Aristotle, even in Christian faith itself? But these questions point beyond the limits of our "preliminary clarifications" and can only be taken up at the end. For now, let us return to Rahner.

It is the characteristic of all metaphysical questioning to distinguish, within the ambivalence of "being," between beings and their beingness, however one reads the latter. This distinction is the arena within which we must broach the problematic of Rahner's "confounding" of *das Sein* and *das Seiende*.

It is an exclusively human prerogative to experience what-is-the-case as "being" (*to on, ens, das Seiende*). Strictly speaking, animals do not ex-perience "beings," for if *ens* is what first befalls the intellect, the intellect is also the first and only place where *ens* befalls. And here the ambiva-lence of "being" shows its richness. We never experience a simple "that" but always a that which *is*. To speak tautologically, we always experi-ence beings-in-their-beingness; we know the "thats" of sense experience in an implicit awareness that they really are, that they are "reality." Therefore, any experience of *das Seiende* is likewise an experience of *das Sein*—in their togetherness and distinctness (*synthesis, diairesis*). To express the unity and distinction of beings-in-beingness Heidegger coins the awkward but exact phrase *das Seiendsein*, whereas Rahner often prefers the shortcut of simply saying *das Sein*.[58] This latter usage is not at all an obscuring of the metaphysical difference between beings and that whereby they are, but rather is an expression of their unity-and-distinction. It is not accidental, therefore, that we have spoken about beings *in* their beingness or about the beingness *of* beings: The prepositions express the synthesis-and-diairesis between *ens* and *esse*.

Within this context, the glosses which Rahner approved in the second edition of *Hörer des Wortes* find their justification. If *esse* is the very act of beingness and if God is nothing other than the pure, simple, subsisting act of beingness, then his uniqueness is not obscured by Rahner's insistence that God is the *ens* which absolutely "has *esse*." If the word *habens* exclusively meant "participating in," then Rahner's usage would destroy the very ground on which he stands to make the statement. But he speaks of God as the "absolute having-of-*esse*" (*absolute Seinshabe*), and here the adjective swallows and assimilates the noun-phrase.[59] God is the absolute exercise of the act of *esse*. Just as Aquinas, unlike Avicenna, continued to use the language of "essence" when speaking of God, even while transforming its meaning, so too Rahner continues to say *ens* when he means God as the supreme and independent act of beingness.[60] It is important to keep in mind what Aquinas and Rahner mean to assert within the limitations of human language: that God is the pure, simple, unique, independent apex of reality, that which every person somehow already knows in all knowing and that which all metaphysicians, successfully or not, always intend when they ask about the reality of all that is.

Perhaps existential Thomists will find Rahner unsatisfying in his thematization of the very act of beingness insofar as Rahner prefers the language of actuality (*Wirklichkeit, Wirklichsein*) to that of act—just as Rahner might find existential Thomists unsatisfying to the degree that their metaphysics of the authentic existential act remains objectivistic. Or is the objectivist "act of *esse*" a better way to describe God than Rahner's absolute identity of being and knowing in the pure act of beingness, "*die absolute Identität von Sein und Erkennen in reinem Sein, im schlechthinnigen Sein*"?[61]

Ultimately that is a question for Thomists to decide within the parameters of metaphysics, whether objectivistic or transcendental. But for now, another kind of reflection. The ousiological framework that we have shown to be common to Aristotle, Aquinas, and their commentators presents clearly the crucial metaphysical difference between beings and their beingness. And for all the difference among these metaphysicians, we have claimed that a unifying structure runs through the history of their problematic. At each juncture of that self-transforming tradition we can see both revolution and continuity. The continuity consists in the fact that the question remains the same, indeed, that it is intrinsic to man and implicit in all human comportment: *only man* knows things as being, i.e., in their beingness; and man can *only know* them so. To make this distinction is to be human: man *is* the metaphysical differentiation, whether or not he thematizes this condition in the explicit question about the beingness of beings. But once we understand this unity which pervades all the diversity within metaphysics, we can also begin to see its limitation and thus to raise a new question. Beyond the ousiological-metaphysical distinction between beings and their beingness, what is the *"origin"* of beingness itself seen as distinct from beings?

Early in his career, and specifically during the years when Rahner studied under him, Heidegger called this latter question the matter of the "ontological difference." However, this meta-ousiological difference has generally been read by neo-Thomists as nothing but the metaphysical difference between beings and beingness (with beingness read as *esse*) even though Heidegger kept insisting that this question had been overlooked in the entire ousiological tradition, Thomism included. Thomists, to the contrary, have continued to assert that Aquinas "is perhaps the only representative of that tradition . . . who has made Being the central theme of all his reflection in regard to truth" (Rioux) or that "no thinker of the past has been more clearly aware of the ontological difference than Thomas Aquinas, nobody has more clearly distinguished being (*ens*) and being (*esse*), or interpreted beings more consistently in the light of being" (Coreth). Or in a more circumspect and perhaps more promising position, it is claimed that "Aquinas had a real insight into the *physis*-character of Being" and hence was not entirely oblivious of the ontological difference, but with the nuance that "this insight took place in objective thinking rather than in a phenomenological mode" and hence that Heidegger's claim of *Seinsvergessenheit* in Thomism is limited to a charge that Thomas did not thematize *esse* as *alētheia*, emergence into self-showing.[62]

Or could it be that the metaphysical difference is not at all the ontological difference, and that even Heidegger confused matters to the degree he continued to employ *das Sein*, a word he shares with the tradition, to indicate his heuristicon? Perhaps for this reason—to show that *no* meanings of beingness were ever his topic—Heidegger finally dropped the word *das Sein* from his lexicon, and spoke instead of the "meaning" or "truth" or "place" of beingness.

These questions will occupy us later. But for now we must move from these preliminary clarifications of beingness in Rahner to a closer analysis of his own specific contribution to the ousiological debate. By investigating the unthematic understanding of beingness in everyday life and its thematization in the metaphysical question, we can arrive at Rahner's own understanding of beingness as a being's self-presence.

B. THE STARTING POINT OF THE METAPHYSICAL QUESTION

In this and the following division we take up the issues which Rahner discusses in GW, Part Two, Chapter One, "The Foundations."[63] Rahner's chapter has three subdivisions: I. The Point of Departure for Metaphysics; II. The Unity of Human Knowledge; and III. The Correlation between Knowing and the Known. In the present division, we study the first of those three topics. In the following division we take up the other two from a unified viewpoint: Rahner's transcendental deduction of the analogical meaning of beingness as self-presence.

In the second edition of GW, prepared by Professor Metz, the subdivision entitled, "The Point of Departure" underwent some changes. Three substantial paragraphs, written by Metz and approved by Rahner, were added at the very beginning of the subdivision and were entitled "The Basic Structure of the Metaphysical Question."[64] Here Metz roots the origin of metaphysics in the ineluctability of questioning as such in human existence. For my part, I prefer to follow Rahner's briefer—perhaps clearer—presentation in the first edition of GW. In fact, the formal progression in both editions is not all that diverse, insofar as the three steps in both editions can be articulated as (1) the *problem* of a starting point for the question of beingness; (2) the *solution* to that problem; and (3) the *paradoxical nature* of that solution. In spelling out these steps I will supplement the first edition of GW with material from the first edition of HW, Chapter Three.

1. The Problem of a Starting Point in Metaphysics

The paradoxical nature of all inquiry has been clear to thinkers at least since Meno, when confronted with Socrates' assertion that he did not know what virtue was, asked: "How will you look for it, Socrates, when you don't even know what it is? How will you aim to search for something you don't know at all? And if you should meet up with it, how would you know that this is the thing that you didn't know?" (*Meno*, 80 d). The paradox of all questioning is that it seems at first blush to be sheerly impossible. "A man cannot search for what he knows (since he knows it, there is no need to search for it) and he cannot search for what he doesn't know (since he doesn't know what to look for)" (ibid., 80 e).

The classical answer to this dilemma—from Platonic *anamnēsis* to Rahner's *Vorgriff*—is to point out a condition between knowing and not knowing, a "knowing unknowing" which, as unknowing, gets the question started and which, as partial or implicit knowing, gives the question a direction and recognizes the answer when it shows up. In every inquiry which is a real question and not a futile shot in the dark, there is what Rahner calls the "whence" (*das Woher*), the basis on which the questioner stands, the starting point from which he launches his question, and the principle from which he can expect a valid answer. This "whence" is always some prior, implicit knowledge of what is being asked about. Without it, *any* answer could be *the* answer (there would be no basis for discrimination), and the question would thus lose any claim to being a serious and fruitful inquiry. The questioned issue (*das Gefragte*), therefore, is always somehow known (*bekannt, gewusst*), although not explicitly or adequately known (*erkannt*). And the "whence" is both unquestioned insofar as it is known and yet questionable insofar as it is yet to be explicitly known.

But the metaphysical question about the beingness of all-that-is poses a special problem. It asks about simply everything in terms of its unity, the ultimate and single ground of all beings. Like any question, it must have a known-unknown issue, a "whence" that allows of a real question and that can expect a serious answer. The problem lies in discerning what that starting point might be. Insofar as this question includes everything, it includes itself, both the questioner and his question. But if absolutely everything is questionable, including the very question itself, where do we find any extra-questionable ground on which to stand in asking the question? To ask about everything means to start from "nothing." (Rahner points out that Aquinas too was aware of this problem when he asserted that the "universal doubt about truth" necessarily belongs to metaphysics.[65]) Yet in fact we do ask the question about beingness. Is it a shot in the dark? Or does the very problematic nature of the universality of this question indicate a unique, if paradoxical, solution?

2. The Solution: At the Origins of the Metaphysical Question

Since the universality of the question of beingness includes the questioner himself, both as one entity indifferently present among others (ordinary inclusion) and as the particular one who asks the question (extraordinary inclusion), we are not amiss in seeking a solution to the problem by looking at man the questioner. Rahner's strategy is to move from a consideration of *man's nature as an implicit metaphysics* to a discussion of *explicit metaphysics as transcendental questioning*. The possibility of the thematic science of metaphysics lies in the ineluctability of man's lived, unthematic metaphysical nature.

The same Plato who pointed out the paradox of questioning also pointed to the solution: "Some kind of philosophy"—and here as always, philosophy properly means the questioning knowledge of the beingness of beings—"dwells by nature in man's mind" (*Phaedrus* 279 a). Rahner echoes this: "Necessarily. . . the question of beingness belongs to human existence, for it is co-contained in every proposition that a man thinks or speaks, without which thinking or speaking he would not be able to be human at all."[66] Do we in fact have evidence for these claims?

In every utterance of the words "is" or "being," a man betrays some knowledge, no matter how innocent, of "is-ness" or "beingness." In every judgment, whether thematic or not, a man synthesizes predicate with subject (with a claim to correctness) and refers this synthesis to an objective synthesis in reality, to what he claims is in fact the case. Even if he ignores or refuses to raise the explicit question of what this beingness or reality means, even if he declares reality to be "the absurd," he is caught in the ineluctable human pattern of deciding about reality. Even if he makes *a* being (history, for example, or matter), into reality, he is taking a stand on beingness. This ineluctability constitutes the dignity and the frailty of human being. To be human means, fortunately or not, to have lost the innocence of immediacy. Man is "a weakness at the heart of being" (Merleau-Ponty), a need to mediate, to see things *as* such and so, *in terms of* this or that; an inability to have everything simply and all at once (*totum simul*), hence a fundamentally temporal being; in short, a demand for meaning and thus beingness. Metaphysics is the index of finitude. Because only man needs mediation, only man is a metaphysician. Presumably God neither needs nor does metaphysics, and, *pace* Milton (*Paradise Lost*, II, 555-69), angels in hell have better things to do with their sempiternity. The realm of mediation which happens only in and with man, and which is ultimately rooted in his radical temporality, is the realm of the "as-factor" (X *as* Y) wherein there appears the "is" which points to "is-ness." By nature, man is the *krinein* and *diaphorein*, the making of the metaphysical differentiation, insofar as he is the *thaumazein*, the wondering awareness that things *are* (cf. *Theaetetus* 155 d; *Meta.* A, 2, 882 b 12). And as this prior, implicit, imperfect questioning awareness of beingness, man is meta-physics.

Therefore, the thematic metaphysical question posed in classrooms

and books is not a search for "news from nowhere" but simply "the reflexive elaboration of the ground of all human knowledge, a ground already and always positioned simultaneously in this knowledge from the
outset."[67] If man is intrinsically the movement beyond (*meta*) beings (*ta
physika*) to their beingness (*eis physin*), that is, if he is the concrete and
worldly differentiation of beings and their beingness, then the thematic
discipline called metaphysics is not a flight to heaven but a worldly hermeneutics (*hermēneia, Auslegen*) which merely lays out—i.e., brings to
light, appropriates, and articulates—the knowledge man already has.
Indeed, it is only the conceptually formulated understanding of that
prior understanding which man as man *is*.[68]

    Where then does the metaphysical question find its "whence" or start-
ing point? Nowhere outside the lived question itself (for all is in question), but rather in the inevitability of the implicit performance of that
question in man as knowing but partially knowing, as the wondering
need to know what he already knows. One cannot ask about an entirely
unknown (every *Gefragtes* is somehow a *Bekanntes*); indeed an entirely
unknowable being is impossible (for we can *ask* whether it is knowable).
Therefore, the metaphysical question as thematic *can* start—for it already, as unthematic, *has* started and inevitably so. Man is thrown into
it and cannot climb back out behind it. The beingness that is questioned
is already known even as this known beingness is put into question.

    Just as the explicit question of beingness is only a thematization of
man's nature, so likewise it never leaves this starting point behind (that
would be to leave man's nature behind) but runs its course only by continually probing that nature. The metaphysical question becomes and
remains the transcendental question: "The inquiring subject becomes
the subject of inquiry."[69] Metaphysics is a hermeneutics of the nature of
man as the point whence all philosophy arises and to which it always returns. And necessarily so, if metaphysics is not to remain objectivist and
naïve. Because beingness is not an object in any usual sense, not some
fact that occurs out there apart from man, one cannot "take at look at
it," as Bernard Lonergan used to say. Beingness can be questioned by
man only where it shows up for man, namely, in man's very questioning
of it. In philosophy as in life, "The end of all our exploring/ Will be to
arrive where we started/ And know the place for the first time."[70] More
blandly, but analogously: All general ontology is and necessarily remains metaphysical anthropology.

    But if the initial problem of doing metaphysics has found the arena of
its solution, that very place poses a further paradox.

3. The Paradox of the Transcendental Starting Point

    To ask about everything is, in a sense, to start from "nothing," but we have seen that this "nothing" cannot be an empty void that we may fill at will so as to come up with any answer at all. At the same time as it affirms its own questionability, the starting point imposes a concomitant task and directionality. Here is the paradoxical duality of the starting point: man's free *ability* to question and his ineluctable *need* to question. As the ability to question, man is somehow already with the questioned, he somehow knows what is questioned. As able to ask the question of all-beings-in-their-beingness, he somehow is all-that-is (*quodammodo omnia*). Yet the need to question (for man is thrown into questioning) shows that he is not and does not know the questioned; and as the need to question all-that-is, he somehow is a *tabula rasa*. "The one who must ask is *Sein* [i.e., all-beings-in-their-beingness] because in asking about *Sein* he is already with *Sein; yet he is not it because he is not yet with *Sein* in its totality in such a way that this being-with-*Sein* would be a questionless possession of *Sein* in its totality."[71] In relation to beingness man is both present and absent: pres-ab-sent. Although somehow one with all the real, he cannot grasp it as a whole from any standpoint, cannot master it by his will—for otherwise he would not need to question it. And although needing to question it, he cannot be totally ignorant of or absent from it.

Where is this paradoxical starting point? Where does man stand when he necessarily questions the beingness of all that is? He finds himself thrown into the things of the world (but always related to their beingness, never in some mute confrontation), into his body (but always as his access to beingness, never as sheer animality), and into the spatial and environmental factors that go with world and body (but always as human space and environment). As the ability to question beingness, man is always situated, disposed, ineluctably face-to-face with things; he has an "*a priori* passivity" or encounterability-by-things as his only mode of access to their unifying is-ness.[72] Only in the concrete world of things does he interrogatively know beingness in its unity. But these are terms drawn from Heidegger. In the Thomistic framework, man knows beingness only "at" the phantasm or "by" the imagination. Is there no way around this mediation, some kind of escape to a pure intellectual intuition? If man cannot climb "back" out of worldly questioning, can he escape it by moving "forward" toward an eventual "separation of soul from body"? Aquinas might seem to hold out that possibility when he affirms that knowledge "at" the phantasm is the only knowledge man can have "in the present state of life, in which he is united with receptive corporeality" (S.T., I, 84, 7, *respondeo*). However, Rahner insists that union with corporeality "is the *only* 'state' that Thomas knows anything about, in which man who asks about beingness exists."[73]

But if the scope of the imagination is the realm of space and time, how can man, always and inevitably faced to the world, know beingness itself? What is more, in analysing sensibility Rahner will show that man not only is *in* the world but, as sensibility, *is* the world, and is entirely "delivered over to the powers of this earth."[74] The paradox looms: Man has no extra-worldly access to beingness, and yet he can question (and thus somehow know) beingness in its unifying totality. Or could the phrase "conversion to the phantasm" mean that man first "looks away" from the world to some pure realm of spiritual being and then "turns back" to the phantasm to put together intellectually intuited beingness with worldly things, like a Platonic escapee who nonetheless must return to the cave? But Rahner, with Aquinas, insists that the "conversion" to the phantasm means a constant *turnedness* to the phantasm with no looking-over-one's-shoulder allowed.

And at the same time he will assert that metaphysics "transcends everything spatial and temporal, encompasses all *Sein* as such, and reaches the absolute and the absolutely necessary. . . ."[75] The paradox can be stated (with Kant in mind): Granted *that* some kind of metaphysics is a fact in man's very nature, how is metaphysics possible—and what *kind* of metaphysics is possible—on the basis of the imagination? "How is human knowledge to transcend its own boundary, namely, that of the imagination which is its only intuition, without a direct view beyond the imagination, without an intellectual intuition?"[76]

If metaphysics means intellectual intuition, then no metaphysics is possible for the human nature caught in the paradox which Rahner has outlined, a nature which is "thrown" into beings at the same time as it is "projected" into their beingness: man as a "thrown project." But if some kind of metaphysics happens naturally in man, then it is a metaphysics that must remain anchored in this "thrown project." Rahner calls it a metaphysics of "spirit" (projected-unto-beingness) "in the world" (thrown into the beingness of *worldly* beings), or equally, a metaphysics of abstraction-of-*esse* (spirit, project, agent intellect) in conversion to the phantasm (in-the-world, thrownness, possible intellect). There are not two poles here, not even two moments, but a substantially unified human being exercising one act of knowledge. Yet the limits of language seem to force us to think of a both/and, with the danger that the unique unity that is man as worldly spirit or thrown project will split into some variation on Platonic dualism. Therefore, I choose to speak of the "unified bivalence" that is human nature, and I shall formulate Rahner's paradox as the possibility of metaphysics on the basis of this bivalence.[77]

But our task in this chapter is to delineate how Rahner understands the meaning of beingness. Up to this point we have only localized the general question of beingness in the tradition and investigated its origins as a transcendental question which explicates man's ordinary knowing-unknowing of beingness at the paradoxical point of his inevitable worldliness. But all of this is prologue to watching the worldly transcendental metaphysical question unfold into Rahner's specific insight into the meaning of beingness as self-presence.

C. BEINGNESS AS THE ANALOGICAL SELF-PRESENCE OF BEINGS

Rahner's thesis that what makes beings be beings is their degree of self-presence (*Sein ist das Bei-sich-sein des Seienden*) can easily be misunderstood. At the heart of possible misunderstanding is the ousiological problematic we have already studied: Beingness is always and only the act or state *of beings*, really distinct from beings and yet inseparable from them. Rahner's tendency towards a hypostasizing language can abet the misunderstanding to the degree that he speaks of the "self-presence *of beingness*," as if, over and above the presence of beings to themselves (even of God to himself), there was yet another order in which beingness, somehow detached from any instantiation, turned back upon itself. What Aristotle said of Plato's Forms applies here: this would be a needless reduplication that explains nothing. If God is, properly speaking, the *ens* of absolute beingness, he too must be said to be the perfectly simple *entity*, and only in that sense "beingness in absolute self-presence." In other words, the preposition in the phrase "the self-presence *of* beingness" (*das Bei-sich-sein des Seins*) indicates a subjective genitive which requires a further objective genitive to complete the phrase. Fully and properly, then, not "the self-presence *of* beingness," but "beingness *as* the self-presence *of* beings." If we overlook this subtle but crucial distinction, Rahner's transcendental deduction of the sameness of beingness and knowing would become of itself an *a priori* proof for the existence of God. As we shall see in a moment, this is not the case.

The insight that beingness and knowing are "the same" did not first dawn with Rahner. Not only did Rousselot and Maréchal each claim it in their own way, not only is it at the heart of Heidegger's reflections on "impropriation" (*Ereignis*), but in fact it is the birth certificate of Western philosophy, sealed with Parmenides' dictum that *noein* and *einai* are *to auto*, that is, somehow belong together. The question is: How and why do beingness and knowing go together? Rahner's brief presentation of the case in GW, even with Metz's additions, does not show all its cards, and the implicit intermediate steps in his deduction must be teased out. That analysis will then refer us immediately to the overriding question of the analogy of beingness.

1. The Togetherness of Beingness and Knowing

We may distinguish three steps in Rahner's transcendental deduction of this proposition, the first of which we have already taken: Questioning implies, indeed requires, prior imperfect knowledge of the questioned. The second step (Rahner calls it the "doorway," *Eingangstör*, to the proper thesis[78]) interprets knowability and beingness as intrinsically proportioned to each other. Thirdly—and here misunderstandings can arise—he shows that beingness and knowing are "the same" in origin. Since we have already dealt with step one, we may immediately take up steps two and three.

All beings are able to be questioned. This thesis is demonstrated by one's own experience: I do ask, "What is the unified and fundamental meaning of everything?" Beings, therefore, are somehow knowable as what, that, and how they are. Aquinas puts it succinctly: "Whatever can be, can be known" (C.G. II, 98); every being is *verum*. Intelligibility is a transcendental (in the Scholastic sense of trans-categorical) property of every being insofar as it is; hence, it is a transcendental property of beingness. If to-be-at-all means to be able to be questioned and thus, to some degree, known, then any claim of metaphysical irrationalism is thereby excluded from the Thomistic universe, whether it be the claim that some area of beings (perhaps "life" or "becoming") is inaccessible to knowing, or the assertion that at some point knowers have no more *logos*, no more access to beings-in-their-beingness. To say this much is not to assert that all beings are fully known, but only that, to the degree that they can be questioned, they can be, and in fact already are, known in some way (*quodammodo*).

If every being is ordered to a possible knowing, then intelligibility does not befall beings from without; it is not an extrinsic relatedness between beings and knowing which, because it is an addition, would be subsequent and therefore accidental to beings, a mere "*de facto*" that might or might not happen in an individual case. Rather, knowability is natural, intrinsic, and essential to beings. A being's beingness is its questionability (it invites and demands an interrogative stance) and therefore its knowability, but not as some separable condition that floats off, self-sufficient unto itself. Knowability is the ability *of beings* to be known. To be at all is to be able to be known. From the side of knowing, this means that cognition is not a "bumping up against things," not an intentional stretch out towards things that are intrinsically separate and different from the knower, not a *contactus intellectus ad rem*. Rather, Aquinas' many statements about the sameness of the intellect and what it knows affirm precisely this transcendental correlation or intrinsic proportionality of beingness and knowability. This is likewise the one topic that concerns Heidegger from start to finish.[79]

But if beingness and knowability are intrinsically proportioned, what is the norm which measures the relation? If it cannot be accidental and *a posteriori*, what is the reciprocally limiting *a priori* relation that obtains between them? Truly separate things do not bring themselves together (Aquinas: *non enim plura secundum se uniantur*); so, if beings and knowing powers are correlative, they must be gathered up by something intrinsic to each and common to both. The problem, we have said, is as old as Parmenides' *to auto* (fragment 3), which is echoed in Aquinas' talk of *proportio*.[80] But what is this "sameness"? When Aquinas asserts that the intellect and the intelligible are not only proportioned but "of a single origin" (*unius generis*), and when Rahner describes that sameness as "unity," the reader could be mislead into thinking that this is an *a priori* assertion of the existence of a perfect self-coincidence of beingness and self-knowledge, a *noēsis noēseōs*: God. Not so, even if the assertion can and, for Aquinas and Rahner, must be mediated in that direction. It seems that Rahner makes an unwarranted leap from proportionality to self-coincidence when, having just cited the text on *unius generis*, he continues quite simply: "Thus beingness and knowing exist in an original unity."[81] However, we cannot emphasize enough: The "unity" here means "intrinsic togetherness" and leaves open the question of whether this togetherness points towards a possible perfect simplicity. The task remains that of checking out the birth certificate (cf. *genus, genos*) of these two which might be one. But it must be said that Rahner's text aids and abets us in wrongly supposing that the job has already been done.

What valid conclusion can be deduced transcendentally—that is, in terms of the condition of its possibility—from the fact of an intrinsic proportionality between beingness and knowability? Only that *somehow*, in a way yet to be determined, beings and knowing powers do not just accidentally collide while going their own separate ways. But Rahner will say more: that beingness is the unity of self-knowing and self-knownness in an entity. Knowing, for Rahner, is beingness as the being-present-to-itself of beings, and this self-presence is the beingness of beings. Or again, for a being to be is for it to know itself and be known in an original unity. This thesis appears to be a major leap, and the cautious reader is not impressed by the barrage of Thomistic texts that Rahner assembles to buttress the thesis. It would be one thing if Rahner were establishing his point merely from texts in the history of philosophy. But he claims to be carrying out a transcendental deduction which any thinker could repeat without appeal to Aquinas' positions.

Two questions overlap and must be separated out. First, if this thesis results from a transcendental deduction, what are the intermediate steps which Rahner passes over in arriving at it? And secondly, what is the content and force of the conclusion? Is it that a self-thinking thought exists? or something more modest?

First, how does Rahner move from the proposition that beingness is knowability (to be a being is to be able to be known by some knowing) to the thesis that beingness is *self*-knowing and *self*-knownness in "unity"? It seems to me that Rahner does not show all his cards—and yet he operates by no slight of hand. Let us lay out the cards one by one.

The basic presupposition is that to be means to resist fragmentation and to achieve some relative degree of self-unification or simplicity: Beingness and unity are convertible. Another presupposition is that to know is a perfection, a mode of ontological actuality, and therefore likewise a resistance to fragmentation and an achievement of some degree of simplicity: To know is not a *spargi ad multa*. But to be (relatively) simple is to coincide (relatively) with oneself. But self-coincidence is self-presence. But self-presence—here Rahner draws upon *the* presupposition of Western metaphysics—is a matter of luminosity or transparency, in a word, self-knowledge. The light-metaphor of the West, as Rahner reads it, is not primarily a matter of *lumen ab extra* but *ab intra*: self-clarity as the precondition of lending clarity to others. Therefore, to be is, to some degree, to know oneself, to be known by oneself. We note that the progression does not go from know*ability* to self-knowing, but rather from (1) beingness as relative simplicity and (2) knowing as a form of beingness and simplicity, to (3) self-knownness.

But what necessary conclusion can we draw from the deduction? Only this much: *To the degree a being is* it knows itself and is known by itself in a relative unity. In other words, far from having discovered the zenith of self-coincidence, we are immediately thrown into the question of the *analogical degree* of beingness as self-presence. Even if a being of perfect self-presence could be mediately drawn out as a necessary conclusion, that would happen only after further investigation, through experience, of the beings man can know in his performance as thrown project, spirit in the world.

To state this otherwise, the "unity" of which Rahner speaks indicates a problem, not a solution. His transcendental deduction deposits us right back on the ground occupied by the problematic word *to auto* in Parmenides. Everything is somehow knowable, but what does that entail? For Aristotle it entailed the self-thinking thought; for Aquinas and Rahner it entails *ipsum esse subsistens qua intelligens*. But insofar as these men are philosophers, these are conclusions, not premises. Rahner does not begin with a univocal concept of beingness and only later work down to the question of analogy.[82] He does distinguish a material insight (beingness is self-presence) from a formal insight (beingness is held analogically), but the material insight coincides with the formal and at this stage leaves open the question of a possible perfect self-coincidence. In one sense, the ground on which Rahner's problematic stands at this point is shared with Heidegger. They both ask, under the aegis of Parmenides' dictum, what the analogically unified condition of the beingness (however that be read) of beings is. But they *ask* it without yet having a full answer. And we may wonder whether any "answer" would undo the asking, or whether the asking, the interrogative knowing-unknowing, will not always remain correlative to a self-unifying which as far as philosophy can know, remains ever asymptotic.

2. The Analogical Character of Self-Presence

In the material insight that the beingness of beings is their self-presence, self-presence is not something in addition to beingness but *is* the very meaning of beingness. This knownness is "truth" in a sense more fundamental than the adequation of intellect and thing in correct judgment; truth is convertible with beingness. However, if beingness is self-presence, "then it seems that there could be no being which would not from the outset be knowing and being-known in identity,"[83] that is, in perfect self-coincidence. This objection is answered with the formal thesis that the intensity of self-knownness (of togetherness of knowing and known) varies with the intensity of beingness. Self-presence is a "variable function" (*gleitende Funktion*), "oscillating, as it were, between nothing and infinity."[84] Aquinas, who Rahner claims had the material insight into beingness as self-presence, prefers to formulate his understanding formally: "To the degree that something is a being, it is knowable" (*In VII Meta.*, 1, i, n. 1034). That is, each thing is knowable insofar as it is in act (*In II Meta.*, 1, i, n. 280). Aquinas speaks (C.G. 4, 11) of a hierarchy of emanation and return, self-absence and self-presence. In material beings, self-absence predominates: They show more than they can interiorize, i.e., they express themselves *ad extra* and for others more than they can reassimilate this self-expression unto "themselves." Presumably in man there first happens the so-called complete return to the self, not in the sense of a freedom from matter but as a relative triumph of self-presence over self-absence. Man has *logos*, and by saying that something *is* and is therefore distinct from him, he possesses himself over against that other, i.e., returns to himself. But the self to which he returns is always the one which speaks about, and so remains related to, the other. We shall see below that this complete self-return is precisely a unique way of remaining in self-absence.

We need not dwell again on the problem of Rahner's hypostasizing language about beingness as returning to *itself* versus the proper language of beingness as a *being's* return to itself. Rather, let us draw out some important conclusions concerning the proper object of knowing and the issue of prime matter.

If beingness is primarily and analogically self-presence and self-knowing, then, again analogically, the proper object of a knower is always that knower himself. In formal terms, the ontological intensity of the knower is the rule of his proper objects. Such intensity "is what decides *a priori* what its proper object is; this is what decides the question: what must the existent be with in order to be present-to-itself?"[85] "Hence there is a reciprocal and limiting *a priori* between knowing and known: the cognitive power determines *a priori* what can be its object."[86] Knowing first of all means an ability to know not the other but oneself; and likewise knowability is primarily the ability to be known not by another but by oneself.

Consequently, if the knowability of a being is in direct proportion to its self-presence, it is in indirect proportion to the being's self-absence. With that we gain a vantage point for a preliminary discussion of "prime matter." Materiality in the Scholastic tradition does not first of all mean quantity (which is secondary and derived) but rather lack of self-presence in one way or another. Rahner, it seems, broadens this concept of materiality to stand for all potency. Materiality is in indirect proportion to the simplicity of knowing and being known. But what about "something" which has beingness and yet does not know itself? Its presence is not unto itself; it is "otheredness," the empty, indeterminate dimension (*Worin*) of a being's lack of self-presence. Otheredness, of course, is always relative to some intensity of in-itself-ness, for absolute otheredness cannot exist. Everything that is strives to take possession of itself, to come to itself, and it *is* to the degree it does so. "Every action and operation, from that of the merely material [entity] all the way to the inner life of the triune God, are only variations on this one metaphysical theme, this one meaning of beingness: self-possession."[87] And materiality, which happens only *in* beings, is the measure of a being's lack of possession of itself.

Returning to the question of the proper object of knowing, we find a problem. If beingness means the analogical togetherness of knower and known, how can anyone know an object other than himself? In the limit case of God it is easy enough to see how he can understand the other precisely by understanding himself as the creative ground of the other. But in this case God's proper object is himself and not the other, and so we derive little help for the question about man. The horns of the dilemma are these: (1) To the degree he is self-present, man must be his own proper object; (2) but in fact man does know what is other than himself and in principle must do so to the degree he is absent from himself.

The solution forces itself upon us: man's presence-to-self intrinsically involves presence-to-the-other. His self-presence and self-absence do not cohabit side by side but interpenetrate. To be a human self is to be "othered"—indeed, the "complete return to the self" does not and cannot exclude this essential otherness. If this otherness is man's materiality as imperfect self-presence, and if (to anticipate) materiality is the basis of his corporeality, then otherness is man's essential, ineluctable, transcendental relation to his own body and to bodily things, so much so that if his soul be immortal, it can never exist in separation from corporeality. And conversely, in a reciprocal relationship with this corporeality as self-absence, man is in fact relatively self-present. If the name for self-absence be "sensibility" and that for self-presence be "thought," then the proper object of man's thought is the very sensibility he is, with all that it entails. But if thought means objectivity (knowing things as what *they* are "over against" us), then objective thought entails subjectivity (knowing ourselves as what *we* are "over against" the other). The *unity* of self-presence and self-absence in knowledge—what Rahner calls abstraction as conversion to the phantasm and what I prefer to call pres-ab-sence—must preserve this paradoxical bivalence. "Complete return to the self" can never annihilate self-absence but always remains presence-to-oneself *as* pres-ab-sence. And so long as man lives, self-absence (relative loss of the self in otherness) can not abolish self-presence but ever remains the relative self-absence that is intrinsic to man's self-presence.

Rahner's attempt to unfold the unity of man as a sentient-intellectual knower walks a thin line between materialism and Platonism. If anything, the more likely danger is a fall into Platonism (spirit "in" the world, as if it were only visiting matter "in the present state of life"). But finally Rahner's balancing act succeeds: "The free spirit becomes, and must become, sensibility in order to be spirit, and thus exposes itself to the whole destiny of this earth." "All thought exists only for sense intuition." "Abstraction and conversion are the same thing: man."[88]

The story of that brilliant balancing act runs under the title of the "abstractive conversion to the phantasm": abstraction paralleling self-presence or return to the self, conversion to the phantasm bespeaking self-presence *in* the self-absence of sensibility. There is in man no "juxtaposition" of sensibility and thought, with "conversion" as the glue that would bind them together. Man is *one* act of knowing which can be seen from two viewpoints. Man is sensibility (self-presence in self-absence), and he is intellect (self-absence in self-presence). Rahner approaches this unity in three steps: sensibility, abstraction, conversion to the phantasm. But greater clarity as well as succinctness of presentation can be achieved by uniting sensibility with conversion, and rearranging the order: abstraction and conversion-sensibility. Isn't that to jump *in medias res?* But since any point of the triad is the whole unity, anywhere we might begin would be *in medias res.* In fact, we have no absolute starting point since we are already doing the very thing we shall investigate.

Notes

1. On *ousia* as "beingness" (*Seiendheit*), see Martin Heidegger, "On the Being and Conception of *Physis,*" *Man and World,* 9 (1976), 237-38.
2. See Etienne Gilson, *Being and Some Philosophers* (Toronto: Pontifical Institute of Mediaeval Studies, 1949), p. 47; and Martin Heidegger, *The End of Philosophy,* trans. Joan Stambaugh (New York: Harper and Row, 1973), p. 9.
3. Gilson, *Being and Some Philosophers,* p. 74.
4. Heidegger, *The End of Philosophy,* p. 11.
5. Etienne Gilson, *The Philosopher and Theology,* trans. Céline Gilson (New York: Random House, 1962), p. 125.
6. John H. Finley, Jr., *Four Stages of Greek Thought* (Stanford, Cal.: Stanford University Press, 1966), pp. 5, 31, 29.
7. See Thomas Sheehan, "Heidegger, Aristotle, and Phenomenology," *Philosophy Today,* 19 (1975), 87-94.
8. Gilson, *Being and Some Philosophers,* pp. 166 and 174.
9. Etienne Gilson, *Elements of Christian Philosophy* (New York: Mentor/Omega, 1960), p. 107.
10. *Collected Papers of Charles Sanders Peirce,* ed. Arthur Burks, Charles Hartshorne, and Paul Weiss (Cambridge, Mass: Harvard University Press, 1931–1958), I, 19, cited in Leo Sweeney, S.J., *A Metaphysics of Authentic Existentialism* (Englewood Cliffs, N.J.: Prentice-Hall, 1965), p. 79, n. 32.
11. On "actuation" cf.: "It [*esse*] is the actuation which makes a thing be actually present outside nothingness and be a *being,* a term which means simply 'that which actually exists' " (Sweeney, *A Metaphysics,* p. 93).
12. Gilson, *Elements,* pp. 194, 144.
13. See Heidegger, *The End of Philosophy,* p. 16.
14. Gilson, *Elements,* p. 147, citing *De Pot.,* q. 7, a. 2.
15. S.T. I, 104, 1, resp., cited in Gilson, *Being and Some Philosophers,* p. 161. Cf. S.T. I, 8, 1, cited in Gilson, *Elements,* p. 196.

16. Gilson, *Elements*, p. 208, and S.C.G. I, 24, #4; 21, #9; 22, #3, Also *Elements*, p. 206.
17. Gilson, *Elements*, pp. 212 and 188.
18. Rahner, GW 65/100 (111 f.).
19. Gilson, *Elements*, p. 145.
20. Gilson, *Being and Some Philosophers*, p. 168. Cf. Heidegger, *The End of Philosophy*, p. 16. On *esse*/beingness as stable presentness, cf. *"Esse autem est aliquid fixum et quietum in ente,"* S.C.G., I, 20.
21. Rahner, HW 54/41 (58). The phrase "in the modern sense" appears in the first edition, GW 110, but is suppressed in the second edition at p. 167 and in the English translation, p. 157.
22. Rahner GW 65/100 (111 f.).
23. Ibid., 109/156 (166).
24. Ibid., 110/157 f. (168).
25. Ibid., 112/160 (170) and 116/165 (175).
26. Ibid., 112/160 (170). Do we hear such a hypostasization of essence in the following? "In order [for a being] to participate in [the pure Act of Being], the first condition is, *not* to be it. Now, not to be it is to be either nothing or something else. This possible something else is precisely that which can receive a particular act of being. The mode of participation that defines the being at stake is its essence, and the definition of the essence is called its quiddity. This is what we have stated by saying that every essence expresses a restriction of the Act of Being. As compared with this infinite act, essence is a very modest finite degree of perfection. But if it is like nothing as compared with God, it is a glorious thing as compared with nothingness. Essence is, for all that which is not God, the necessary condition of not being nothing" (Gilson, *Elements*, p. 209). See W. Norris Clarke, "What Cannot be Said in St. Thomas' Essence-Existence Doctrine," *New Scholasticism*, 48 (1974), 19-39, esp. 36 f.
27. For the example of the spring in the box, see Sweeney, *A Metaphysics*, p. 90, n. 49.
28. See William E. Carlo, *The Ultimate Reducibility of Essence to Existence in Existential Metaphysics* (The Hague: Martinus Nijhoff, 1966); and "The Role of Essence in Existentialist Metaphysics: A Reappraisal," *International Philosophical Quarterly*, 2 (1962), 557-94. Gerald B. Phelan, "The Being of Creatures," *Proceedings of the American Catholic Philosophical Association*, 31 (1957), pp. 124 ff. Donald O'Grady, "Further Notes on 'Being,' 'Esse,' and 'Essence' in an Existential Metaphysics," *International Philosophical Quarterly*, 3 (1963), 610-16; and "*Esse* and Metaphysics," *New Scholasticism*, 39 (1965), 283-94. Frederick D. Wilhelmsen, "Existence and *Esse*," *New Scholasticism*, 50 (1976), 20-45.
29. Rahner, GW 112/160 (171 f.).
30. Ibid., 123/174 (184). See GW 120/170 (180) on essences as potencies and limitations of *esse*.
31. Ibid., 113/161 (171) and the notes on those pages.

32. Ibid., 125/176 (186).
33. Ibid., 125/177 (187 f.): absolute ground; fullness; and 147/208 (216): one full ground.
34. Ibid., 127/179 (188).
35. Ibid., 114/162 (172).
36. De Anima, a. 6, ad 2, cited in Rahner, GW 126/178 (187); HW 54/41 (58).
37. Rahner, GW 131/186 (194).
38. At HW 63/49 (67) Rahner calls Beisichsein the Sinn des Seins.
39. Rahner, HW 123/98 (122); GW 44/72 (85); 48/78 (91).
40. Rahner, HW 150/121 (150).
41. Rahner, GW 41/69 (82); 50/81 (93); 11, n./26, n. (40, n.); HW 52/40 (57); 56/43 (61).
42. Ibid., 89/130 (141); 52/84 (96); 271/371 (371).
43. Ibid., 93/135 (146); 52/84 (96); 63/97 (110). HW 58, suppressed in second edition and in English translation.
44. Ibid., 45/73 (87); 52/84 (96); 93/135 (146).
45. Ibid., 46/75 (88).
46. Ibid., 49/80 (92).
47. Ibid., 204/283 (286).
48. Ibid., 41/68 (81).
49. Rahner's text is found at GW 128/181 (190). Aquinas' text is: "...non sic proprie dicitur quod esse sit, sed quod per esse aliquid sit," In De Div. Nom., VIII, 1, ed. Marietti (Torino, 1950), n. 751, p. 283, cited in Frederick D. Wilhelmsen, "Existence and Esse," New Scholasticism, 50 (1976), 26, n. 15.
50. Rahner, GW 135/192 (201) and 138/196 (204).
51. Rahner, HW 71/55 f. (74). Note the following instance of "confusion" between esse and ens. In the first edition of GW Rahner writes: 'Every judgment attains to esse mediately or immediately (even in the case of beings of reason)" (GW 119/169). In the second edition, p. 179, Metz adds with Rahner's approval: "...or, expressed first more precisely and more cautiously, to what really exists, to ens."
52. Rahner, HW 62/47 f. (65 f.).
53. Ibid., 65/50 (69).
54. Ibid., 2nd ed., p. 66, n. 1/Eng. trans., p. 48, n. 1.
55. Ibid., 2nd ed., p. 69, n. 7/Eng. trans., p. 50, n. 7.
56. For the term "ousiology," see Werner Marx, The Meaning of Aristotle's "Ontology," (The Hague: Martinus Nijhoff, 1954), ch. 6; and Introduction to Aristotle's Theory of Being as Being, trans. Robert S. Schine (The Hague: Martinus Nijhoff, 1977), pp. 14-42.
57. Gilson, Elements, p. 145.
58. For Seiendsein see Martin Heidegger, Was ist das—die Philosophie? 4th ed. (Pfullingen: Günther Neske, 1966), p. 31; in English, What is Philosophy?, trans. Jean T. Wilde and William Kluback (New Haven, Conn.: Twayne/College and University Press, n.d.), p. 97.
59. Rahner, HW, 2nd. ed., p. 69, n. 7/Eng. trans., p. 50, n. 7; cf. Gilson, Elements, p. 193.

60. For Aquinas and Avicenna on "essence," see Gilson, *Elements*, p. 145.
61. Rahner, HW 65, changed in 2nd. ed. at p. 69/Eng. trans., p. 50.
62. John D. Caputo, "The Problem of Being in Heidegger and Aquinas," *The Thomist*, 41 (1977), 62-91. Bertrand Rioux, *L'Etre et la verité chez Heidegger et saint Thomas d'Aquin* (Paris: Presses Universitaires de France, 1963), p. 254, cited in Caputo, p. 83. Emerich Coreth, *Metaphysics*, ed. and trans. Joseph Donceel (New York: Seabury Press, 1973), p. 29, cited in Caputo, p. 84. The last citations are by Caputo, p. 87-8. For a more developed statement of Caputo's position see his masterful work, *Heidegger and Aquinas: An Essay on Overcoming Metaphysics* (New York; Fordham University Press, 1982). That book appeared after the present work was completed and so is not considered here.
63. Rahner, GW 35-47/59-77 (71-90).
64. Ibid., 2nd ed., p. 71 f./57-59 initium. In HW, 2nd ed., 51, n. 2/35, n. 2, Metz summarizes the three paragraphs which he added, with Rahner's approval, to GW: "...The origin of metaphysics from out of the necessity of the question of beingness in human existence [GW, 1st ed.] can be formalized yet again into the origin of metaphysics from out of the necessity of the question about the question;...thus the ineluctable happening of the question *as such* in human existence becomes the 'origin' of every metaphysics [GW, 2nd ed.].... There too [2nd ed.] it is briefly shown how this absolute origin (which presents itself as a question by the fact that it is placed in question) is thematized necessarily as the question about beingness."
65. *In III Metaph.* lect. 1, n. 343, cited in Rahner, GW 35/59 (73).
66. Rahner, HW 46 f./35 (52).
67. Rahner, GW 283/390 (390).
68. Cf. Rahner, GW 17/34 (47) and the sentence added there by Metz.
69. Rahner, "Existential Philosophy," p. 130. See ch. IV, A.3 above.
70. T.S. Eliot, "Little Gidding," V, in *The Complete Poems and Plays of T. S. Eliot* (London: Faber and Faber, 1969), p. 197.
71. Rahner, GW 43/71 f. (85).
72. On the question of human "disposition" as "*a priori* passivity" (*apriorische Passivität*) see Karl Jaspers, *Notizien zu Martin Heidegger*, ed. Hans Saner (Munich and Zurich: Piper, 1978), p. 27.
73. Rahner, GW 37/62 (76), my emphasis.
74. Ibid., 17/34 (48).
75. Ibid., 12/27 (41).
76. Ibid., 20 f./38 (52). For other statements of the paradox, see GW 8/23 (37); 13/28 (42); 20/38 (52); 22/40 (54); 40/66 (80).
77. On "bivalence" see "*zweideutig*," GW 295/407 (405).
78. Rahner, HW 54/40 (58).
79. See Heidegger, SZ 183/228, 212/255, 316/364, and "Brief über den 'Humanismus,'" *Wegmarken*, p. 336 (1967 ed., p. 167); Eng. trans., *Basic Writings*, p. 216.
80. S.T. I, 84, 7, c., "*potentia cognoscitiva proportionatur cognoscibili.*"
81. Rahner, 41/68 (82).
82. Ibid., 292/402 (401).

83. Rahner, HW 59/45 (63).
84. Ibid., 62/47 (65): *gleitende Funktion;* GW 114/162 (172): *oszillierend.*
85. Rahner, GW 47/77 (90).
86. Ibid., 18/35 (49).
87. Rahner, HW 36 f./49 (67).
88. Rahner, GW 294/406 (405): destiny of earth; 295/407 (405f.): sense intuition; 296/408 (407): abstraction and conversion the same.

CHAPTER V

Towards Spirit in the World

Before we take up, in the following chapters, Rahner's metaphysics of human bivalence, let us step back to get a clear focus on his *topic*, to discern his *method*, and to gain an *overview* of how he will work out his project, lest the density and richness of the analysis that is GW obscure its aim and direction.

Within Scholasticism, the uniqueness of Rahner's approach lies in the fact that he makes metaphysics inseparable from a philosophical anthropology, or better, a metaphysics of knowledge. Not that these are two disciplines which he juxtaposes so that they might influence each other; rather, they are "the same." General metaphysics takes the transcendental turn in order to become, in the early Heidegger's term, "fundamental ontology," an investigation of man as the "foundation" of the knowledge of beingness. Can such a procedure be called Thomism by any stretch of the term? Rahner takes up this debate indirectly when he lays out the method of his treatise as a "retrieval" in the Heideggerian sense of *Wiederholung*. In this way Rahner cuts into Thomistic texts from a new angle and finds his way to their center by a new route—with results that are true both to Thomas and to contemporary exigencies. These three issues—(1) transcendental metaphysics, (2) as a "retrieve" of the "unsaid" in Aquinas, (3) in order to reorient Thomism—dictate the material we now take up.

A. PROBLEMATIC AND METHOD

1. Metaphysics as Transcendental Anthropology

Rahner's concern in GW is metaphysical knowledge (even if his final goal was to interpret it as the place of a possible revelation[1]), and metaphysics is an exclusively human pursuit. Only man is the need and demand for an interrogative knowledge about the reality *of* things, where the "of" points to a separation at the heart of human being, man's condemnation to mediate knowledge. Because man knows things only *as such* and so, he necessarily remains the questioner of their partially and imperfectly known reality. Metaphysics is an index of finitude.[2]

The metaphysical question, if it is not to remain naïve, must become the question about man the metaphysician. Our only access to beingness is *our* access as questioners of beingness. Hence it seems that the critically scientific way to do metaphysics is to turn the question back upon itself, to transform it reflexively into the question about the questioner of beingness, to make the inquiring subject the subject of inquiry. This does not mean turning away from beingness but turning to it critically by returning to the only place where it shows up for us. Such a critical, thematic, metaphysical question will thus be the reflexive elaboration of what we already know, indeed, of what we already are. And this move to the realm of "subjectivity" has been at least implicit in Western philosophy from the very beginning, from Parmenides' *noein* through Aristotle's categories to Aquinas' agent intellect. The progressive explicitation of it from Descartes' *res cogitans* through Kant's Copernican Revolution to Husserl's phenomenological reductions only heightens the task of elaborating a truly adequate notion of subjectivity. If metaphysics is not to be the discovery of a heretofore unknown continent but a *re*discovery such that "we can say that we are at home" (Hegel), then it should simply entail becoming what we already are and remembering what we already know.

Such indications seek to deprive the word "metaphysics" of the other-worldly connotations ("news from nowhere") which have brought it the scorn, bemoaned by Kant (KRV A viii), which continues to our own day ("a blind man in a dark room, looking for a black cat—which isn't there"[3]). Metaphysics does not mean leaving the world for some monastery of the mind, but rather keeps man precisely where it finds him: in the world. In a word, metaphysics as transcendental inquiry is a hermeneutics. It provides no "new" information but is the discovery and spelling out of what is already the case, so that understanding can explicitly appropriate itself. And by way of anticipation we may say from the start: It promises and delivers no intuition of pure beingness, no secular beatific vision of *esse qua esse*. If it makes any claim to be universal, necessary knowledge of a "more," it either will show that this is already operative in man's worldly knowledge, bereft of intellectual intuition, or will give up or modify the claim. The radical quality of Rahner's work consists in the merciless surgery he performs on our "metaphysical" illusions and in the modifications he introduces into our usual understanding of the science.

What, then, is the man who is the subject of this hermeneutics? We have seen that he exhibits a curious bivalence. Untransferably *in* the world, even if he be immortal, he is as well the ability to question that world in its entirety and to have a chiaroscuro vision of its unifying totality. Explication of man's questioning will not provide some "answer" to abolish its interrogative character, but will only unpack it, look at it, and pack it back in, perhaps with a better understanding of it than we had before.

Even before unpacking the structure of human questioning, however, the first step consists in closing all doors against flight into an illusory intuition of "reality as such." Sense intuition, experience of the world, the spatio-temporal realm of the imagination—these are man's only dwelling place even if he should point beyond them. They are the necessary starting point, the abiding ground, and the goal of all human knowledge, so much so that "if knowledge is primarily intuition, and if the only human intuition is sensibility, then all thought exists only for sense intuition."[4]

Even if we grant that man has a projective awareness of the unifying totality of things, is it proper to call this projection a "reaching beyond" things? Here is a dangerous phrase which might lead us to agree that, yes, all human knowledge begins with sense intuition and may even finally return to it, but in between it can take a metaphysical "look" at beingness itself. If the Thomistic word "phantasm" points to the world of sense intuition, the phrase *"conversion to* the phantasm" might nurture a furtive Platonic fantasy that one could excuse himself for a moment and slip out for a brief fling with Ultimate Reality before returning, refreshed and perhaps wiser, to the humdrum bonds of marriage to the world—but then again, only until death. However, in Rahner's telling, man is, for better or worse, wed to the world, in fact literally one flesh with it. And not even death can them part.

How then can we speak of "bivalence" without falling back into dualism? The philosophical claims for this structure stand or fall with evidence, and the first step in unpacking this structure (which it seems Rahner hurries over too quickly) should be a careful, step-by-step phenomenological showing of the evidence at the concrete everyday level of pre-predicative experience. Rahner prefers to begin at the predicative level, with only some passing references to pre-predicative experience in HW,[5] and his choice may be attributable to the fact that Heidegger had already worked out, thoroughly enough for Rahner's purposes, the phenomenal evidence for this bivalence in everyday life. Heidegger had shown that man is thrown into the world and that he finds himself (cf.

Befindlichkeit) already and ineluctably there with no exit. Yet, while bound to things, man also understands them, places them in the meaningful context of his purposes, relates them to his projects, and, in that relative sense, "transcends" them, even if there is no other place to go *but* the world. Both Heidegger and Rahner insist that in this bivalence man remains a unity, a "thrown project" or a "knowing sensibility." As that unity, man is *logos*—not primarily "reason" or "speech," but more fundamentally the condition of the possibility of both: presence to the world and relative absence from it, or, from another perspective, relative presence to himself while self-absent in the direction of the world. As bound to and yet relatively separate from things, man can bind and separate them in cognition, not only among themselves but also each one with its own specific reality at any given moment. Man can show them to himself and others *as* what they are, i.e., in their beingness, and he can concretize that showing in speech. Man is *to zōion to logon echon*, that is, the bivalent unity who can see and say beings-in-their-beingness.

We may now take—we have in fact already seen it—the next step in the explication of the nature of man. If the metaphysical question becomes the transcendental inquiry into man, then the conditions of the possibility of metaphysics are the same as the conditions of the possibility of the human bivalent unity. It is one and the same thing (1) to establish the possibility of metaphysics on the basis of sense intuition or the imagination and (2) to demonstrate that thought happens only in and on the world of sense reality.[6] The proposition works equally in the reverse: It is one and the same thing (1) to show that human imagination already is the possibilizing condition of metaphysics as worldly interrogative knowledge of beingness and (2) to prove that man can know a worldly being only because he already is interrogatively present to beingness as a whole. That is, transcendence (but not intellectual intuition) belongs to the constitutive grounds of knowledge of the world, in the same way that intuited sense reality remains the foundation of all human knowledge.[7] Spirit "would be blind without the intuition of sensibility."[8]

All talk of "reaching beyond" and "turning back to" the world is potentially misleading and should be dropped. The closet Platonism that lurks in such Scholastic language, even when explicitly repudiated, has to be flushed out once and for all by a purified understanding of these terms. In that regard a shift in terminology may be helpful, and Rahner attempts exactly that, even though he keeps a foothold in the old lexicon. He speaks of "an attempt which, at least in the new formulations which are determined precisely by the new questions asked, departs from the the traditional expression of Thomas' thought."[9] If we continue to use the traditional Scholastic phrases, it is only so as to remain in touch with Rahner's reinterpretation of them and finally to leave them behind and show the precise point of the break.

To summarize: When metaphysics becomes transcendental anthropology, the question about beingness becomes that of man as a unity of *synthesis* and *diairesis*, worldly *logos*, the power to distinguish and unite beings (*to on*) and their beingness (*ousia*). And this transcendental turn seems to remain within the aforementioned ousiological problematic while shifting emphasis from beings as the *subjecta* to man as the *subjectum*: from *ousio*logy to ousio*logy*.

2. The Method of "Retrieval"

The introductory pages of GW in which Rahner introduces some elements of his method, are as interesting for what they leave out as for what they include. There is a passing reference to Rousselot and Maréchal, a brief allusion to "points of contact" with "modern philosophy from Kant to Heidegger," and beyond that no thematization of the transcendental method which undergirds the whole effort.[10] Whether this *praeteritio* expresses the prudent caution of a doctoral candidate who had to present his dissertation to an unsympathetic director (the Thomist Martin Honecker, who in fact flunked the work) is for others to divine. In any case, Rahner apparently felt that the greater need was to defend his unique philosophical-historical approach to that text in the *Summa Theologiae* which is the jumping-off point of his treatise. In effect he advocates and defends the method of "retrieval" (*Wiederholung*) which he took over from Heidegger.

Although Rahner does not apply the word *Wiederholung* to his method (when he uses that word in his book it refers to the universal "repeatability" of quiddities in diverse subjects), there can be no doubt GW is a retrieval (in Heidegger's sense) of the hidden meaning of Aquinas' text. Heidegger's *Kant and the Problem of Metaphysics* (1929), the spirit and content of which shine through the whole of GW, offers a definition of retrieval as a method for reading the history of philosophy. But although the definition is a methodological one, it is rooted in the more fundamental notion of retrieval as the basic structure of human temporo-historical existence.

In *Being and Time* (1927) Heidegger had shown, on the basis of an existential transformation of the Aristotelian notion of *physis*, that the kinetic structure that is man's temporal essence is a dynamism of man's achieving actual self-presence by remaining in and renewing his privative absence or possibility. Since man's ultimate and on-going possibility is his being-towards-death or finitude, he attains authentic self-presence to the degree that he becomes that possibility, not by actualizing his death (this would end the possibility) but by taking over or "freeing up" (*überliefern*) that possibility for himself by consciously accepting it. The act of resolve is, to borrow Pindar's phrase, a matter of "becoming understandably what you essentially are" (*genoi hoios essi, mathōn*[11]). To take over that possibility in an understanding acceptance of it is not to actualize and thus end it. Because (for Heidegger) possibility is higher than actuality, one must liberate and enhance the possibility which confers genuine self-presence in self-absence. Freeing up possibility for oneself (*Sichüberlieferung der Möglichkeit*) has linguistic echoes of "retrieving the tradition" (*liefern*: to free up or deliver; *Überlieferung*: tradition) by bringing it over to oneself.[12] To unite the two senses of the German word, we may say that *Überlieferung* means creatively taking up what has been handed down. For Heidegger that requires, both in one's personal tradition as well as in the tradition common to one's culture, a "shake-down" or "deconstruction" of hand-me-down interpretations of the tradition, and concomitantly a "pulling out" or retrieving of the presently relevant meaning of the tradition from beneath the stale incrustations that have made it a matter of course.[13]

When this existential dynamic becomes a methodological tool, it signifies cutting through the philological commonplaces that establish what the text supposedly really means, in order to bring out the unsaid potentiality which can speak anew. Such an effort entails doing violence to a text (burrowing though its "said" to its "unsaid") in the same way that achieving authenticity in oneself comports a violence towards the trite, everyday understandings which cover over one's dynamic essence.[14] Again, the principle that possibility is higher than actuality guides the attack. Actuality in a sense represents the gains of the past, whereas possibility must be freed from within actuality to become the promise of the future. Why? Because human existence itself is possibility as the condition of present actuality. Implicit in the method of retrieval, moreover, is the presupposition that man has no Archimedean standpoint outside of his historicity whence he might discern once and for all, e.g., "what Aquinas meant." Rather, man's inescapable historicity imposes the task of constantly rereading the tradition in terms of contemporary questions. While philological exactitude is a prerequisite in such an endeavor (Heidegger to some degree prided himself on his philological abilities), that very philology is put into question and reciprocally determined by the text which one is reading, and particularly by the "unsaid." Besides Heidegger's own use of retrieval in reading the entirety of Western philosophy, we find examples, more or less faithful to the model, in Bultmann's demythologizing of the New Testament, Gadamer's hermeneutics of aesthetics, literature, and Greek philosophy—and Rahner's interpretation of Aquinas.

Heidegger delineates the method towards the end of *Kant and the Problem of Metaphysics:*

> We understand the retrieval of a basic problem to be the disclosure of its original and as yet hidden possibilities, such that, through the elaboration of these possibilities, the basic problem changes and thus for the first time is preserved in its problem-content. But preserving a problem means keeping it free and alive in those inner powers which, in the ground of its very being, make it possible as a problem. Retrieving the possible does not mean latching on to what is "fashionable" about it when "the prospects are good" for "making something" of it. That kind of possible is always much too actual, available for everyone in the going way of handling things. The possible in this sense precisely hides a genuine retrieval and, with that, a relation to history as such.[15]

Rahner's retrieval of the "unsaid" in Aquinas is not "historically" oriented in the usual sense of that term. To be sure, he draws directly on Thomas' works (and very sparingly on commentators), but not so as to gather inductively all possible texts and to classify them according to some extrinsic principle. "Such an approach cannot get back to the original philosophical event in Thomas."[16] That event is "the historical" *par excellence,* what phenomenology in general calls "the issue itself," and what Heidegger in particular delineates as the emergence of the beingness-of-beings. To attain that, Rahner employs what he calls a "philosophical-historical" approach (read: retrieval) with two discernible moments. The first is a matter of getting to the hidden, implicit center of Aquinas' issue, the unexpressed or unsaid "key" that controls the melody, so as to relive it (*nachvollziehen:* "retrieve").[17] This means abandoning oneself to the dynamism of the issue itself so as to live through it as it unfolds from that unexpressed center. While this first moment must always be checked against the explicit statements of the philosopher (Rahner frequently demonstrates his philological exactitude in GW[18]), it is fundamentally controlled by a second and reciprocal moment which pushes in the direction of the present.

Today's questions are what Rahner uses in order "to force the finished propositions in Thomas back to the problematic of their issue" (we hear echoes of "violence"). This contemporary systematic concern forces Aquinas' thought further than it was able to go under its own power, just as Aquinas did to Aristotle.[19] Indeed, Rahner says of himself, "the author would not know of any other reason to be occupied with Thomas than for the sake of those questions which stimulate *his own* philosophy and that of his time."[20] Even in this second moment, control is exercised by constantly checking the newly retrieved problematic against explicit texts in Aquinas. But only such a retrieved interpretation provides the norm for evaluating the adequacy of traditional interpretations of Aquinas. "Only by such a method can the eternal [Heidegger might say more modestly, "the abiding"] in a philosophy be salvaged from the irrelevance of the 'has-been.' "[21]

Rahner goes on to note a more mundane but nonetheless crucial methodological issue. Although his specific focus, he says, is on one topic within Thomistic metaphysics, namely, the conversion to the phantasm, this topic lies at the very heart of that whole metaphysics. He justifies plucking one text from the middle of the *Summa Theologiae* by the fact (at this point only a claim) that this one part will reveal the whole. In this regard he promises to consider the whole of Aquinas' metaphysics (= philological exactitude), even if only summarily, in order to show that this problem constitutes the hidden center of that same metaphysics (= retrieval).

As in all genuine philosophy, so too here the subject matter and the method are ultimately one. The reason: There can be no privileged access to the subject matter of philosophy, since one is already at and with the beingness upon which one will explicitly reflect. In analogous senses the subject matter and method of Rahner's work are the same: hermeneutics. Metaphysics is a hermeneutics (explicitation) of what man already is and knows. And the method for explicating man's condition is to cut through the surface of what he says and does, so as to unfold their hidden implications. Just as the body of his work will explicate one "doing" of man (the act of judgment), so at the beginning of his book Rahner chooses one "saying" from the tradition (not because it is traditional but because it embodies the issue) so as to perform a hermeneutical retrieval of its inner possibilities. His treatise begins, as he says, "by first trying to grasp its theme as a whole"[22] through the explication of a text. In what immediately follows I shall expand on Rahner's introductory textual commentary (GW 1-33/2-54 [20-68]) by drawing, in a preliminary fashion, upon the content of the whole of GW.

B. OVERVIEW: *SUMMA THEOLOGIAE I, 84, 7*

As the basis of his retrieval of Aquinas, Rahner selects from the heart of the *Summa* a brief text (Part I, Question 84, Article 7) which "recapitulates the whole paradoxical nature of this metaphysics of knowledge and poses it in its final sharpness." Although Rahner's introductory interpretation of the article comes before the body of his work and stands as a first delineation," a "preliminary and aporetic interpretation" in the service of merely ascertaining the scope of the problematic, nonetheless for all its tentativeness it contains *in nuce* the whole retrieval of Aquinas.[23] The book proper will start on a different basis, rearrange everything, and work in a specifically transcendental mode, but the preliminary interpretation already pushes Aquinas back to the hidden "unsaid" of his metaphysics: a transcendental turn to man.

The *Summa* article speaks explicitly in the language of an objectivist metaphysics even when it treats of man the knower. For one thing, it stands within a theological context which studies man's soul (known by its acts, specifically those of knowledge) as the place of a possible theological event: the revelation of God. For another, and again within the theological context, the *Summa* still discusses the possibility and meaning of intellectual knowledge in the objectivist framework of cognition of immaterial, universal, and necessary essences. It is first of all a metaphysics of the known object (Article One) even as it criticizes the object in terms of the possibility of knowing it.

But Rahner insists that an unspoken transcendental turn to the subject operates at the heart of the *Summa*'s objectivist language. For example, the third objection of Article Seven shows that the hidden issue there is the possibility of metaphysics, whereas, by apparent contrast, the body of the article is devoted entirely to the conditions of the possibility of sensation as the only human knowledge. We draw the conclusion: The hidden key in this text is the grounding of metaphysics in a transcendental critique of man. For all that, we cannot say that the transcendental turn is thematic in Aquinas, for he already presumes the possibility and the fact of explicit metaphysical knowledge as he develops the article about the grounds of human cognition. But if we pull these issues together, we begin to see both the uniqueness and the full range of Rahner's efforts. Aquinas writes an objectivist theology on the basis of an objectivist metaphysics which rests on an objectivist theory of knowledge. If Rahner can retrieve a transcendental turn from Aquinas' theory of knowledge, he can then project a transcendental metaphysics as the basis for a transcendental theology. In fact, that always was his overarching purpose. GW is his transcendental theory of knowledge, HW is his projection of a transcendental basis for receiving revelation (the possibility of theology on the basis of human language in the deepest sense), and the rest of his life's work was devoted to a transcendental rereading of Christian theology: "Dogmatic theology today has to be theological anthropology. . . . Such an anthropology must, of course, be a transcendental anthropology."[24] Our own concern, of course, is the limited one of critically evaluating the "laying of the foundations" for this project.

1. The Objections and the Topic

The objections or *videtur quod non* that open Article Seven provide a clear if preliminary notion of the issue at stake. The title of the article seems to focus on an epistemological problematic: "Can the intellect in act know anything through the intelligible species which it possesses, without turning to the phantasms?" However, the overriding importance of the objections is that, while they preface a discussion of human knowledge, they in fact contextualize that discussion within, and focus it upon, the proper question of the article: the possibility of metaphysics. Of the three objections, the first two come down to one issue: the promise of a Platonic non-worldly knowledge in which the mind would know through intelligible species and without conversion to phantasms. The third objection contests the primacy of sensible intuition in the name of a transcendent knowledge.[25]

The first and second objections raise the complex question of the intelligible species, which Rahner properly reserves for his later treatment of sensibility and conversion. Nonetheless, we can point to the issue at stake in the question of the intelligible species: If the intellect, both in potential and actual knowing, is distinct from the senses, then isn't it also separable from the senses? Intellectual knowledge, it might be claimed, happens in a kind of inverted Platonic cave where it is no longer sense knowers who stare at sensible reflections, but rather intellectual knowers who contemplate the walls of their inner consciousness, upon which spiritual rather than material reflections play: a movie in the monastery of the mind. Aquinas states the objection: "It seems that the intellect can actually know something through the intelligible species which it possesses, without turning to the phantasm" (objection one). Indeed, "if the sense imagination can actually imagine without the sensible object being present and given, so much the more can the intellect actually know something without turning to the phantasms" (objection two). These objections do concede that sensation is the starting point of knowledge (in Plato as *excitans*, in the Avicenna as *disponens*[26]), but once the cameraman comes off location, the mental movie can replace the actual experience.

The third objection highlights the apparent contradiction between, on the one hand, the restriction of man's intuition to sensible objects and, on the other, the trans-sensible nature of "metaphysical objects." Along with the entire tradition up through Husserl, Aquinas and

Rahner hold the classical position that knowledge is primarily intuition, the "immediate grasp of what is to be known in its own real and present self."[27] The objection presumes that we do in fact have metaphysical knowledge, and then states that metaphysical knowledge requires metaphysical intuition. But according to the objection, since no such intuition is available in worldly experience, metaphysical knowledge cannot be grounded in worldly knowledge. If the first and second objections were content with a movie in the monastery of the mind, the third objection invites us to flee the cinematic cloister for the great Hollywood in the sky. And there we would know something without turning to phantasms.

In short, all three objections hold intuition to be man's only form of knowledge, but such intuition is either a promise of or a threat to metaphysics, depending on whether it be intellectual or sensual. But Rahner, with Aquinas, is clear: all intellectual knowledge is essentially limited to the space-time world known in imagination. Following the Heidegger of the Kant book, he asserts that all thought is "ordered as a means towards sense intuition."[28] No more metaphysics, therefore, as taking a look at the other world. If there is to be metaphysics, it can draw on no intellectual intuition. On what then?

But these are only "objections," devices which frame the question. But they also give hints of how we might approach the issue. Negatively, we already foresee that a self-enclosed metaphysical vision, an intuition that is non-sensible, is nonsense. If the "meta" of metaphysics indicates a "more," we will find that "more" in no Cartesian interiority or Platonic beyond. If metaphysics claims immaterial, universal, and necessary knowledge, it will arrive at this knowledge in encounters with the material world, or it will surrender the claim.

When Aquinas turns to his own position (the *respondeo*), the issue, against all reductionism and Platonism, is the full unity of man as the basis for whatever metaphysics there may be: "It is impossible for our intellect in the present state of life, in which it is united with receptive corporeality, to know anything in act without turning to the phantasms." That is, the mind can know nothing without knowing it in and upon the world. Let us note two things.

First, Aquinas speaks of intellect "as such" in contrast to the senses (the world), and as "united with receptive corporeality" in the "present state of life." But what kind of unity is this *pro tempore* gluing of intellect to senses? For Rahner the point is that while we can speak of the distinctness of intellect from sensation (*chōriston kata ton logon*, Aristotle would say), the two are inseparable.[29] They cannot be defined separately from each other because they are not two things, but two aspects of the bivalent substantial unity that is man. Man is not a ghost in a machine or an angel in an animal, and his "faculties" of intellection and sensation cannot be understood by investigating, respectively, pure spirits and beasts. If he is a unity and not a compound, and if natures are known by acts, then we can sort out the distinct aspects of that unity only by studying man's *unified* acts such as knowledge. Aquinas' language could be misleading, and it should be translated in a direction which reinforces the substantial unity of man. Against all closet Platonism, we are to understand that "the present state of life" is the only state, that the unity of "soul" and "body" holds even in a state of immortality, that man is essentially (and not temporarily) delivered over to the world while always being able to make sense out of it.

Secondly, the transcendental turn begins to come into view. Whereas the third objection hinted that the fundamental issue of the article is the possibility of an ousiological ontology or general metaphysics (there is no special metaphysics in Aquinas[30]), the *respondeo* now launches the article into a hermeneutics of the unity of human knowledge under the rubric of a "metaphysics of the conversion."[31] If we pull these two facts together, we can draw the preliminary conclusion: The metaphysics of human sensibility *is* general metaphysics; transcendental reflection on man in the world *is* ontology. The article is—implicitly—a sketch of a "fundamental ontology."

This conclusion reveals the inner articulation of the *corpus* of the article. The first step consists in establishing the arena of fundamental ontology: the togetherness of knowing and beingness. The second step interprets that arena in terms of the bivalence of human knowing or, in Rahner's terms, sensibility and intellection as abstractive conversion to the phantasm. The third step shows what kind of metaphysics is possible on the basis of human bivalence. These three steps finally provide the substantial articulation of the body of Rahner's treatise: (1) The Foundations: Part Two, Chapter One, (2) Sensibility, Abstraction, and Conversion to the Phantasm: Part Two, Chapters Two through Four, and (3) The Possibility of Metaphysics on the Basis of the Imagination: Part Three.

2. Step One: The Arena of Fundamental Ontology

Properly speaking, the transcendental turn is not a shift from the object to the subject or, as we put it earlier, from *ousio*-logy to ousio-*logy*. The latter phrase is correct only if we realize that *logos* is no self-enclosed form of subjectivity. Better then, if more awkward, to say that the transcendental turn lands on the hyphen in between. The point is to recognize that the real issue in philosophy is neither beings-in-their-beingness nor man as subject, but rather their togetherness such that man's essence is the transcendence of all forms of monadic self-enclosure, while the beingness of beings appears only in such transcendence. We have seen that, since its inception, philosophy's proper subject matter has always been, at least implicitly, the question of the bond between beingness and man, between the meaningful presence of things and the human essence. Rahner expresses this togetherness as the questioning of beings "in" their beingness, where man is the interrogative place of the "in."

Aquinas expresses this correlation of man and beingness in the guiding sentence of the *corpus:* Every knowing power has an intrinsic homogeneity or transcendental proportionality with its possible objects (*potentia cognoscitiva proportionatur cognoscibili*). He asserts that this transcendental correlation applies wherever there is knowing: from God and angels, who contemplate themselves in their spirituality, to man whose proper study is his worldly self. We have already seen how this principle derives from Thomistic positions on beingness and simplicity, and we have an initial understanding of what that entails with regard to receptive knowledge, prime matter, and the analogical degree of the self-presence of beings. The point now is to stress that, within and because of this correlation, all talk about the luminosity or intelligibility of things per force entails talk about the place where that luminosity shows up. And since our present focus is on man, the task becomes that of establishing the proportionality that is specifically his. If he is an angel hiding in an animal, his proper objects must lie beyond what he can see and sniff. If he is a beast who cannot even imagine the angelic state, we needn't trouble him with anything beyond eating and rutting. But he is neither. He is the world come to a point where it has stepped back and can take the measure of itself without ever ceasing to be the world. The arena of fundamental ontology is none other than the space opened up by this step back, and carrying out fundamental ontology is nothing other than taking the measure of the clearing—but right up to its edge, to "the dark fold of the revealed world."[32] What, then, is known and questioned in this step back? What is the nature of the correlation which establishes both man's essence and his proper objects?

3. Step Two: A Hermeneutics of Bivalence

The issue here is to gather, from what man *does*, the phenomenal evidence for what he *is*. Rahner takes a stab at gathering such evidence from pre-predicative experience when, in HW, he points out that man transforms the physical-biological environment, of which he is merely a part, into the lived world of his concerns where mere things become objects in the sense of *pragmata*, from which he can take relative distance. But, like Aquinas, Rahner prefers to hurry over the everyday world of pre-predicative, lived purpose in order to engage man at the predicative level of making true judgments: "The ontological constitution of man [is] disclosed in certain characteristics...of a judgmental, universal knowledge attaining to the in-itself of the object differentiated from the subject...."[33] We have already said that Rahner largely presumes Heidegger's pre-predicative investigations in *Being and Time*. Now because Heidegger's language shines through Rahner's own analyses of judgment in Aquinas, and because both Heidegger and Aquinas are deeply rooted in Aristotle, we may fruitfully explicate Rahner's new formulations of intellect and sensibility by using the phenomenological terms that Heidegger retrieved from Aristotle. Whereas Aquinas preferred to speak the objectivist language of "knowing quiddities in matter," and whereas Rahner continues that discourse even as he transposes it transcendentally, I will use the Aristotelian language of *legein ti kata tinos* (knowing P of S) and translate the problematic of intellect and sensibility into Heidegger's lexicon of distance, presence, and their unity.

ues), we may agree that when we assert a P of an S, we always distinguish and unite the two. It is not the case that P and S are united only in affirmative judgments and separated only in negative ones. Rather, as Aristotle correctly notes, both *synthesis* and *diairesis* are found in every judgment, whether positive or negative.[34] And the place of this critical tension is the "as" (S *as* P) which becomes the "is" of apophantic discourse or *logos* (S *is* P). Before it means "word" or "reason" or "ground," even before it means "sentence" or "judgment," the term *logos* (originally an early Greek mathematical term for relation or bond) means the gathering of diverse elements into a unity of sense which preserves the togetherness and distinction of the elements.[35] And deeper than that, it points to the unified essence of man as the one who divides and unites. *Logos/legein* as the asymptotic bringing-together-into-sense is what Rahner calls the power to "objectify." But he means that term in the original and non-modern sense of gathering something into meaningful givenness in the specifically human realm where one deals with the thing as itself and as different from oneself. If, by a difficult and finally impossible abstraction, we were able to experience sensation at a purely animal level, we could say in Kantian language that sensation lets things be present "in" us whereas *logos* lets the sensible for the first time be present "for" us. But in fact *logos* permeates human sensibility from the start and operates over the whole range of human activities from sensation through intellection and from the pre-predicative through the predicative. To speak of *bringing* something present in sense means that, while of course things are already "there" apart from man, they enter human presence only with and on the basis of the kinetic tension that is *logos/legein*. This is the force of all of Heidegger's language of "coming-into-presence," and it underlies Rahner's discussion of abstraction and conversion to the phantasm. Neither terminology refers to letting something *be at all* for the first time; both refer to a thing's emergence into intelligibility in the broadest sense. And both are rooted in Aristotle's elusive discussion of *nous poiētikos*, the power which makes things actually transparent—that is, brings them into presence—for meaningful use, discourse, and thought.

To speak of a man as *logos* or agent intellect, therefore, is to say that he is a rupture in the solid flesh of being, an opening in which something new—the *krisis* of uniting and dividing—can take place. As an open horizon, a realm of mediation, a relative transcendence which steps back and takes the measure of things, man makes trouble for beings. He rearranges them on the map of reality by speaking of them *as* this or that and as *for* such and such a purpose. This strangest of beings, as Sophocles so beautifully expresses it in *Antigone*, has found his way to the "word," and nothing has been the same since.[36] With *logos*, things are forced into givenness and appearance (*alētheia*), and history, properly speaking, begins. Man's strangeness lies in the fact that he cannot know things by copying them indifferently like a self-conscious mirror. To be sure, as sensibility he is thrown into immediate cognitive awareness of things, but sense intuition requires more than itself: the revolutionary step back which questions and takes measure. While we can distinguish some such distantiation wherever there are the signs of cognition, even in plants and animals, in man the distance reaches a unique stage of double transcendence: beyond things to their spatio-temporal horizon (but surely animals do as much) and then *further* beyond to an empty awareness or anticipation of an objectless dimension in which things appear *as* something for the first time.[37] This latter domain may be no broader than one's current projects and expectations, those, for example, by which we see this bicycle as rideable and that pothole as dangerous. This second level of transcendence makes possible the "as-experience," which is embedded in the projection of an "itselfness" (the pothole is *itself* dangerous) even if the itselfness is ineluctably bound up with our purposes. The "as-experience" is the unspoken recognition of what the explicit "is" of apophantic discourse will articulate. *Logos*, as man's essential kinetic tension, gives rise to the word, which seals one's birthright as a human being.

From the joining of Ps and Ss we have arrived at a notion of man as the one who takes distance and can thus separate and join. And the arena of that tension we designate initially as the realm of "is" or being-ness. The central issue in *legein ti kata tinos*, saying this of that, is the "of" between P and S, the distance which is opened up, measured, and partially overcome in man's speech and symbols. Aquinas speaks of the "of" (P of S) in terms of quiddities "in" matter, with man as the one who judgmentally refers universals to their instantiations. But this language says much the same as Heidegger's retrieval of the unsaid in Aristotle. To say that the quiddity is broader than its instance and thus is "universal" or repeatable in an infinity of other possible instantiations is to speak of the distance which man is and measures, the gap between that which is immediately there and that as which we take it and could take others to be. To refer back to the earlier example: The point is to get to the store, and that bicycle, these feet, those roller skates might all be useful as means to that end. Moving to the predicative level, one might assert, "This bike is a vehicle," but without excluding one's car as another means. But more important than the repeatability of "vehicle" in a variety of possible subjects is the fact that one is *beyond* both bike and car, living in one's need to get to the store. In that regard one could pre-predicatively understand oneself as a "project," not just occasionally but structurally, one whose projectedness opens the space within which things become meaningfully accessible both in themselves and for one's current projected purposes. Or at the predicative level one might under-stand himself as "intellect," the ability to be beyond particulars in some kind of relative universal meaning which renders intelligible the imme-diate data he meets.

As much as man is beyond things in projectedness, he is thrown in with them in immediacy. This fact of being with things is never a dumb bumping-up-against-them. Things are always found—man always finds himself with things—in reciprocal relation to a projected purpose. Pre-predicatively he may see things "as for" this or that, even "as useless." At the predicative level we could say that man refers the relative universal (be it purpose or meaning or whatever) *to* things. This referral of the *katholou* to the *hekaston*, of the universal to its instantiation, with the concomitant understanding that the universal is broader than its in-stance, is precisely what *logos* achieves. This awareness of the dimension of the "broader" and hence of repeatability is what Aquinas calls "abstraction"—hardly a fortunate term. Aristotle, perhaps more felici-tously, prefers to speak of seeing or showing (*legein*) the universal in its distinct, not necessarily separable, "place" (cf. *chōriston kata ton logon*), and the particular in its place. The function of *logos* is to know the dif-ference.

From both sides of the human bivalence—distance and presence—what presses to the fore is their unity. Distantiation is always implicitly referred to something immediately present and is at the service of its givenness, and conversely, what is immediately present is always accessible in terms of a projected distantiation. Man as *logos* is an interplay of presence and absence: pres-ab-sence, original movement; and only thereby can he show and say beings-in-their-beingness. Neither distance nor immediacy "alone" can constitute the objectification which is the bringing of something to present sense. The distance, which Rahner reads in terms of agent intellect, allows a thing to be *brought* present for me in sense instead of just bumping up against me, whereas the immediacy of intuition *gives* me something which I can in turn hold at arm's length and understand as what it is and can be used for. If we could reduce things to their sheer thereness, the way Roquentin experiences the wet stone in *Nausea*, we would begin to experience the opacity of the world, its urge to close in upon itself against the force of man's rupturing of its silence and solidity. But even in such tactility we may not understand the senses as some sort of mute passageways through which things enter the antechambers of the mind. Sense is exteriority, the first moment of *logos* as *phantasia*, man's deliverance over to that opacity and apparently indifferent identity with the world, the index of his powerlessness to break open the earth and illumine its every crevice. On the other hand, to the degree we experience our relative distance from things, as the same Roquentin does while contemplating a chestnut root, we begin to experience the luminosity that transmutes mere stuff into things. We are caught between both, unable to reduce either moment of the tension to the other—as Eliot says, "In the middle, not only in the middle of the way / But all the way...."[38] The unique kinetic unity of man is a language that is never innocent or an innocence which is always guilty of speech. One flesh with the world, man inevitably keeps his good sense.

Rahner's hermeneutics of human bivalence stands in the tradition that would save and protect man's dynamic unity against all Platonic forms of dualism. In the somewhat static terminology of KRV (first edition) Kant spoke of the schematism in which categories get linked up with sense. In more kinetic terms Heidegger spoke of the unified generation of temporality as a dynamic of presence and absence. In the language of spirit "in" the world, Rahner reads man as a constant turn to the phantasm or, in perhaps better terms, as "cogitative sense." The issue is the same: the undivided center, always on the way to unity, which embraces the immediacy that is sensation and the projected distantiation that is agent intellect—in brief, the effecting of distance for the sake of rendering things humanly present. There are not two knowledges, one of the universal predicate, the other of its possible instantiation, which then collaborate in agreeing that P fits S. There is only the experience of having something present by holding it at arm's length. This is what Aquinas calls "looking at the universal as existing in the individual." We understand what he means: knowing innerworldly entities by being a thrown project.

The issue is the *scope* of this thrown project of unified bivalence, and in the next two chapters we shall emphasize first one side of the bivalence and then the other side, as we pose two questions. Chapter VI, in effect, asks: How far "beyond" the world does the project reach? And Chapter VII asks: Can the project ever leave the world? If we put these questions in Scholastic terms, they become respectively: What is the range of the agent intellect? and: How close to the world is the possible intellect? If we state the questions in terms of the earlier simile, where to know anything is to hold it at arm's length, then the questions become: How long must an arm's length be if I am to know this thing in my hand? and: Does *any* arm's length ever free me from the thing I am holding?

The two questions pose a delicate balance between intellectual distance and sensuous immediacy. A Platonist would absolutize the former and minimize the latter; an empiricist would do just the opposite; and a true positivist would not understand either question. How long is an arm's length for Rahner? Just as long as necessary in order to say that the thing in my hand *is*. And how close to the world is the possible intellect? So close that it *is* the world.

4. Step Three: The Possibility of Metaphysics

If metaphysics means intellectual intuition of suprasensible beings, then there is no metaphysics in Aquinas. If metaphysics means a *volte-face* from the world and a contemplation of the beyond, it is an illusion. On the other hand, if all human knowledge is always and only turned to sensibility, if man has no knowledge that is not a *convertere se ad phantasma*, how can man possibly know incorporeal—literally meta-physical—beings? This is the substance of the third objection in S.T. I, 84, 7.

There are at least three easy ways out of this problem. First, one could read the word *conversio* as meaning a "turning *back* to the phantasm" after having looked away to the realm of immaterial universals. This is the Janus-head solution: We start with a look at the world, then we take a look at beingness itself, and then we turn back and look again at the world. In this interpretation metaphysics would mean taking a quick and furtive glance over one's shoulder. A second solution would be to re-strict man to sense knowledge only during his "present state of life" be-fore the separation of soul and body, but then to reward him with a metaphysical intuition in an angelic afterlife (cf. *De Anima*, G, 5, 430 a 22-23). The conversion to the phantasm would then become only a tem-porary necessity during the present vale of tears. Or thirdly, one might follow the solutions opened up by Kant and the German Idealists, either by transposing metaphysics from the area of speculative knowledge to the area of practical "faith" (KRV B xxx), or by expanding the range of speculative knowledge so as to subsume finite man into the Absolute.

But none of these options work in Aquinas' framework. Rather, he says, "when we want to know non-worldly things, even though there are no phantasms of them, we must necessarily be turned to the phantasms of the corporeal world" (ad 3). The sentence constitutes a revolution in the meaning of "metaphysics."

The present state of life is the only state of life: Man is ineluctably bound to the imagination, and he retains his worldly orientation even "after" death. How then can man reach beings which, like God, do not belong to the realm of the physical and imaginable? Aquinas' answer—we only sketch it here and then take it up in Chapter VIII—revolves around three phenomena, called in Latin *remotio*, *comparatio*, and *ex-cessus*. Rahner shows how the first two reduce in fact to the third. Nega-tion (*remotio*) of any sensible characteristics in order to reach the suprasensible presumes comparison (*comparatio*) of the sensible and su-prasensible, but comparison in turn presumes that the suprasensible realm has been "reached" by a transcending movement (*excessus*). The possibility of metaphysics on the basis of man's ineluctable sense-orientation thus comes down to what is meant by this non-intuitive *ex-cessus*, taken as the *a priori* condition of human knowledge of the world.

In the next chapter we shall make the point that Rahner's language can be misread so as to encourage an understanding of the *excessus* as an act of leapfrogging the world so as to land in some Beyond. The word "transcendence" is culprit enough if it in any way abets the fantasy that man is able to see beyond the world or that he can in any way break with it. For all its possible defects, I prefer the image of holding the ma-terial object at arm's length and thus being able to see it *as* something. This stepping back in order to focus better on the material object—without ever breaking with it—is all the transcendence man ever has and all the metaphysics he can ever do. Because, according to Scholasti-cism, angels *can* do more than that, they are not metaphysicians and they do not exercise "transcendence." That word, or the phenomenon for which it stands, is unique to man and is the seal of his special kind of finitude. It points to that state of being which, properly speaking, is found only in man: movement as a self-conscious *tendere in actum*, a self-aware *actus existentis in potentia* (*In Boeth. De Trin.*, Lect. II, q. 1, a. 4). Metaphysics *in actu exercito* is nothing other than this "ontological movement" which is man himself. As a thematic discipline metaphysics is only "the progressive science of our itinerary towards being" (Blondel). If man is nothing but his *kinēsis*, his ontological movement, and if metaphysics is nothing but the kinetic thematization of that movement, then the concept of the science of being is revolutionized. Metaphysics is the very opposite of intellectual intuition. Metaphysics is the search, not the find, the demand, not the satisfaction. Make man an angel, give him an intellectual vision of beingness pure and simple, and you will have promoted him beyond any need for First Philosophy.

A metaphysics that explicates man's movement—what Rahner calls "metaphysics on the basis of the imagination"—is the science of the asymptotic and the measure of the unending. And that is also its purchase on human interest: nothing to do with bloodless abstractions and chaste desires for the angelic, nothing to do with fond hopes of resting beyond the world. Metaphysics is a matter of taking one's own pulse and feeling one's own passions. It is the systematic destruction of all systems that would freeze movement and pacify desire, even those which promise perfect *stasis* in a vision of God. In that sense it is arguably closer to Marx than to Plato and has more in common with Nietzsche than with Plotinus. It is wed to *this* world, and knows about God only by looking at the world. That may not be much, but it is all we have. "For us there is only the trying," says Eliot. "The rest is not our business."[39]

The next two chapters study human bivalence under the aspects of abstraction and conversion to the phantasm. (The discussion of sensibility, which Rahner puts before his chapter on abstraction, will be reserved for our chapter on conversion, for reasons that will become clear in the course of the argument.) The point of these chapters is to come to an understanding of how man's bivalence is precisely ontological *kinēsis*, what Rahner calls "movement in the broad sense" and what Heidegger calls "temporality." If, as we have argued, Rahner's philosophical goal is to build a general ontology on an interpretation of human bivalence, and if that bivalence is temporality or movement, then we can express Rahner's goal as the elaboration of the time-character of beingness in correlation with the temporality of man. But that is exactly what Heidegger set out to do in 1927. In the last chapter, therefore, we will ask about the possible consequences of Rahner's and Heidegger's temporal interpretations of man. Does Rahner's anthropology find its proper fulfillment in a metaphysics of beingness? Or does this interpretation of man already, if implicitly, lead him beyond the problematic of beingness and into an area which Heidegger has investigated explicitly as "the thing itself," *die Sache selbst*, of philosophical thought? That last chapter will ask whether the hermeneutics of human movement lays the foundations *for* metaphysics or throws man into a groundless dimension *beyond* all metaphysics.

Notes

1. Rahner, GW 8/23 (37).
2. See Martin Heidegger, *Kant und das Problem der Metaphysik*, 4th, enlarged ed. (Frankfurt: Vittorio Klostermann, 1973), p. 252 (from the Davos seminar, 1929).
3. B. Hagspiel, *Smiles and Chuckles* (Techny, Ill.: Mission Press, 1952), p. 1, cited in Leo Sweeney, S.J., *A Metaphysics of Authentic Existentialism* (Englewood Cliffs, N.J.: Prentice-Hall, 1965), p. 5, n. 6.
4. Rahner, GW 295/407 (405 f.).
5. Rahner, HW 68-71/54-55 (72-74).
6. Rahner, GW 31/51 (65), 32/53 (67).
7. Ibid. 22/40 (54), 23/41 f. (55 f.).
8. Ibid. 171/240 (245).
9. Ibid. xiii/lii (14).
10. Ibid. v/xlvii (9); and xii/lii (14).
11. Pindar, *Pythian Odes*, II, 72, in *The Works of Pindar*, ed. Lewis Richard Farnell, 3 vols. (London: Macmillan, 1932), Vol. III, *The Text*, p. 56.
12. Heidegger, SZ, 383 f./435.
13. Ibid., Section 6.
14. Ibid., 311/359.
15. Heidegger, *Kant und das Problem der Metaphysik*, 3rd. ed. (Frankfurt: Vittorio Klostermann, 1965), p. 185; *Kant and the Problem of Metaphysics*, trans. James S. Churchill (Bloomington, Ind.: Indiana University Press, 1962), p. 211.
16. Rahner, GW xi/1 (11). On the method of "retrieve" in Rousselot, see Ch. III, A, 1, above.
17. On "*nachvollziehen*," see Rahner, GW xiii/li (13). Cf. GW xi/1 (11), "*mitvollziehen*."
18. See, e.g., Rahner, GW 135, n./192, n. (200, n.); 265, n./363, n. (363. n.).
19. On Aquinas' "retrieval" of Aristotle, see Rahner, GW 13/28 f. (42).
20. Ibid., xiii/lii (14).
21. Ibid., xii/li (12).
22. Ibid., xv/lv (16).
23. Ibid., 8/21 (36): recapitulates; 18/34 f. (48): first delineation; 33/54 (68): aporetic interpretation.
24. Karl Rahner, "Theology and Anthropology," in *The Word in History*, ed. T.

Patrick Burke (New York: Sheed and Ward, 1966), pp. 1-2.

25. Rahner, GW 8-13/22-29 (36-43).

26. Ibid., 10, n./23, n. (38, n.).

27. Ibid., 11/25 (39), 188/262 (266): *"Erkennen ist primär Anschauung."*

28. Ibid., 12/27 (41); cf. GW 295/407 (406), but contrast GW 171/240 (245): *". . . dass der 'Geist' am Menschen . . . das Urspünglichere ist, . . . ursprünglicher durch das [Denken] bestimmt ist."*

29. Ibid., 15 f./31 f. (45 f.).

30. See ibid., 282/389 (388).

31. Ibid., 2/7 (24).

32. Alfred Corn's poem "Promised Land Valley, June '73" in his *All Roads at Once* (New York: Viking Press, 1973).

33. Rahner, GW 170/239 (244).

34. On *synthesis* and *diairesis* in each judgment, see *De Anima*, G, 5, 430 b 3. See also Martin Heidegger, *Logik: Die Frage nach der Wahrheit*, ed. Walter Biemel, *Gesamtausgabe*, II, 21 (Frankfurt: Vittorio Klostermann, 1976), p. 139.

35. See Martin Heidegger, "On the Being and Conception of *Physis*," *Man and World*, 9 (1976), 251-53.

36. See *Antigone*, line 354, *phthegma*.

37. Rahner, GW 23/41 (55).

38. T.S. Eliot, "East Coker," II, in *The Complete Poems and Plays of T.S. Eliot*, (London: Faber and Faber, 1969), p. 179.

39. Eliot, "East Coker," V. On "system," see Karl Rahner, "Living into Mystery: Karl Rahner's Reflections at Seventy-Five. A conversation with Leo J. O'Donovan, S.J." *America*, 140 (March 10, 1979), p. 180: "The true system of thought really is the knowledge that humanity is finally directed precisely not toward what it can control in knowledge but toward the absolute mystery as such; . . . the system is the system of what cannot be systematized."

CHAPTER VI
Human Bivalence as Abstraction

Rahner's *Geist in Welt* is a bipolar fundamental ontology. The objective pole is the theory of the meaning of being as such, and the subjective pole is the hermeneutics of man as metaphysical knower.

These two poles do not stand over against each other. In the transcendental framework which governs GW, the theory of the meaning of being as such is only the thematization of the conditions of the possibility of any and all human knowledge. The reflection on the possibility of man as man provides all that can be known in metaphysics.

The transcendental turn also adds a new twist to the question of the unity of metaphysics. Within his pre-transcendental medieval framework, Aquinas salvaged the unity of ontotheology via the unity of its object: *ens commune* with its first principles and causes. After the "Copernican Revolution" Rahner establishes the unity of metaphysics on the basis of the unity of metaphysical knowledge (to know the reality *of things* one must anticipate reality *as such*) and ultimately on the unity of the metaphysician himself.

But there is a further twist. Can we properly speak of the "unity" of the metaphysician himself when in fact man gives every evidence of being fragmented, kinetic, and unachieved—as Rousselot put it: a synthesis never fully made? Man is not so much a unity as a movement of continually attempting to unify himself, what Heraclitus called *Agchibasiē*, "approximation" (fragment 122), and what James Joyce called "almosting it" (*Ulysses*, Ch. 3). A first step towards discerning the unity of metaphysics will necessarily be a matter of clarifying what Aquinas and Rahner mean when they speak of the "complete return" of the self to itself in human knowledge.

If it can be shown that man is neither a complete and perfect unity, nor a duality of soul and body glued together in "the present state of life," but a kinetic bivalence, a self-unifying potentiality for unity, then it can be shown that the so-called unity of metaphysics is nothing other than the index and the manifestation of the finitude and movement that man as man is. Because man is movement and not repose, metaphysics will always be an anticipation, and never a grasp, of pure beingness. Because man is always in potentiality to self-coincidence, metaphysical knowledge will always remain faced to the world as it enacts its distance from the world.

The Thomistic names for this bivalence inscribed at the heart of man are "body" and "soul." Seen in terms of human knowing, the bivalence is called "abstraction" of the quiddity from the supposit by agent intellect and "conversion to the phantasm" or referral of that quiddity back to the supposit via possible intellect. Although in this chapter and the next we shall have to speak of these two moments separately, the overriding issue remains that of their unity as intrinsic moments of the one human knowing, two inseparable moments of the one objective knowledge of the world.

In that unity the agent intellect or abstractive power is man's structural ability to differentiate the universally known from its concrete instantiation, whereas the possible intellect or conversion to the phantasm is his constitutive power to be "receptive of the other . . . , a definition which formally applies to sensibility also."[1] The bivalence of sensible receptivity and intellectual spontaneity finds its unity in man as the spirit who "becomes, and must become, sensibility in order to be spirit,"[2] in man, that is, who remains the potentiality for a self-presence which is ever and constitutively in a state of relative self-absence.

The present chapter is devoted to Rahner's reading of "abstraction" as one moment in human bivalence. Division A lays out the problematic of abstraction: the issue of the "complete return" to the self, the question of proper metaphors for describing abstraction, and an overview of how Rahner will work out the question in GW. Division B follows Rahner's analysis of the function and range of abstraction: the anticipation of a "more" beyond the limitation of the quiddity, the question of whether the agent intellect reaches God, and certain conclusions which flow from Rahner's position. Throughout the chapter we shall attempt to show the points of contact, and the distance, between Rahner's and Heidegger's positions.

A. THE PROBLEMATIC OF ABSTRACTION

1. Human Unity as "Complete Return to the Self"

How can Rahner, following Aquinas (*In Lib. de Causis*, lect. 15) call human unity, in the knowing of an object, a *reditio completa*, a "complete return" to the self? We know of a double self-absence at the heart of human knowing: a self-absence in the direction of the sensibly known and, deeper even than spirit's ineluctable turn to the world, a further self-absence which Aquinas calls *excessus*. Does the phrase "complete return" harbor a refugee Cartesianism that would undo man's worldly character, or a crypto-positivism that would deny his transcendence?

In other words, the phrase "complete return to the self" raises two questions: first, whether the adjective "complete" can cancel man's thrownness into the world, and secondly, whether the "self" to which man returns might in fact be *not* a substantial entity but a *kinēsis* of self-exceeding. Similarly, the danger that lurks in the phrase "spirit in the world" is that we might conceive of that spirit as a Janus head which, as sensibility, looks towards the world and, as agent intellect, casts an eye at beingness as such. Let us at this point pose the alternative hypothesis of a "presence" to oneself which dissolves in the direction of two absentialities: sensibility as self-absence towards worldly beings, and the *excessus* as self-transcendence towards beingness as such. (We shall see below how these two absentialities are connected.) The complete return to the self would then become a task rather than a given: the task of personal reappropriation of one's constitutive self-transcendence as the condition of the possibility for an authentic, i.e., truly human, encounter with worldly beings.

On the one side of this kinetic bivalence, sensibility is the ontological (not physiological) condition of man's "ontological abandonment to matter," his "givenness over to the other," his "already complete openness to the world."[3] Indeed through the facticity and thrownness that is sensibility, man is not only open to the world but *is* the world in the undifferentiated unity whereby *sensum* and *sentiens* are one in act. Yet, inseparable from the world in this immediacy, man keeps his wits about him such that sensibility is never a dumb *factum brutum* but a conscious, aware illumination of the world. Man is the *act* of matter.[4] Sensibility remains a function of *logos*, the specifically human faculty, and cannot be properly understood by observing sense cognition in animals. Sensation does not get "spiritualized" subsequent to dragging its data before the tribunal of the mind, but rather is "always already spiritualized and standing under the spontaneous formative power of the spirit."[5] And if, according to our hypothesis, spirit is the *kinēsis* of self-exceeding, then human sensibility meets its data only by being a moment in man's movement towards beingness as such. Indeed, the whole unity of human knowledge—abstraction, conversion to the phantasm, even metaphysics itself—has already happened at the moment of sensation. Sensation in its full human breadth *is* judgment, abstractive referral of universals to singulars, and knowledge of beings in their unified beingness as a whole.

Rahner's radical rereading of sensibility draws directly upon Heidegger's analysis of human "affective disposition" (*Befindlichkeit*) as an intrinsic, structural, kinetic moment in the opening up of the realm of intelligibility which Heidegger calls the "there" (*Da*). As much as Platonism would flee the fact, man's *a priori* passivity before, or his disposition among, worldly beings is already one with the projected distantiation which makes metaphysics possible. Sensation is already a fully accomplished *synthesis* and *diairesis* and thus a primary and original disclosure (*logos*) of the beingness of beings. Its particular characteristic, however, is that it cannot of itself pull back from the accomplished concretion of P with S so as to recognize it as such. But on the other hand, neither can the distantiating projection by itself accomplish the bringing-present of what it has seen in separation (*diairesis*). Only the unity of sense and intellect in interpretative *logos* can perform the objectification of what man has already become in sensibility.

If, on the one side of the bivalence, sensation is man's "being with a thing in the here and now of the world,"[6] on the other side intellect gives him "his position as man in a self-liberation from his abandonment in the subject-object unity of sensibility."[7] Here we have "the being-present-to-oneself over against the other,"[8] with all the apparent connotations of a substantial subject looking at the world as through a window. But Rahner insists that the so-called liberation from abandonment to matter and the complete return to self "cannot have the sense of a complete liberation from the sentient possession of the world," "a flight which perhaps originates from sensibility, but does not remain in it permanently. . . ."[9] All monadic overtones must be purified from the word "complete" so that the "complete return" can become an analogical and heuristic concept which indicates a return to *whatever self-presence man structurally has*. And such self-presence will always be absential in the senses we noted above.

But even then Rahner's language might seem to encourage a kind of Platonic reading, for he speaks of man's "continual coming from the world," his "continual 'preceding from without' " and his "coming from sensibility."[10] But towards what? Not to some cozy spiritual self-containment, as if man commuted back home from work. There is no home. As much as man might yearn for what Eliot calls the "intense moment" of "Quick, now, here, now, always,"[11] he is in fact always and only on the way, always in the middle: *Nel mezzo del cammin di nostra vita*. Man is a continual coming *to* himself (*Zu-sich-selber-kommen*), an ever incomplete pulling of himself together (*sich zu seiner Einheit selbst einigendes Wesen*), what Heidegger calls "temporality."[12] To come from sensibility and the world to oneself means overcoming one mode of self-absence—that of one's sensible involvement in the world—by incorporating it into a deeper and more original self-absence. Man remains a potentiality for an asymptotically complete self-presence, a movement between the Absolute and absolute nothingness, one which "is possible only by the fact that it comes to itself in the receptive letting-itself-be-encountered by another as what is immediately and first apprehended."[13] The *reditio completa in seipsum* is no return home after day-labor in the world. Rather, it means the self as a movement of transcendence that keeps its distance from the world while remaining present to it.

If, in brief, the "one human knowledge is objective reception of the other, of the world,"[14] the question becomes: On what conditions is that possible? The Thomistic answer is initially "abstraction," even though the word itself and the metaphors and images that traditionally describe it may not provide the best path for approaching the problematic. In order to locate the issue that underlies the term "abstraction," we first look for some indications of the phenomenon, then we delineate the power which makes abstraction itself possible, and on that basis we gain a preliminary overview of Rahner's treatment of the problematic.

2. Indications of the Complete Return to the Self

The hermeneutics of knowledge as the entrée to metaphysics is rooted in the unity of man as presence-by-absence. So too the problematic of abstraction is rooted in that same ground, and there we must look for traces of the complete return to the self. In HW there are *pre*-predicative indications of it in the phenomenology of man as opposing to himself a world in which he lives and freely acts. But in GW Rahner investigates three *predicative* indications: the intellect's ability (1) to "liberate" a universal *from* particulars and to synthesize it *with* them; (2) to judge things and thereby place them in objective opposition to the knower; and (3) to grasp the truth of judgment, where "truth" means the relation of a knower to something-as-it-is (*das Ansich*). The three *indicia* in fact come down to one: knowledge, seen as universal, judgmental, and true.

The first indication is traditionally called the first act of the intellect, the formation of a universal concept or known intelligibility as the "what" of a possible "something," as transcendent of the individual in which it happens to be concretized, so as to be predicable of many other particulars. This is "the simple apprehension of a known, a quiddity (*intelligentia indivisibilium*, of the *quid est*)."[15] It is equally called the *concretio* of S and P or, with Kant, the "predicative synthesis." The second indication is traditionally called the second act of the intellect, the judgment, *enuntiatio, complexio,* or apophantic, affirmative, or veritative synthesis.[16] The two moments together constitute both abstraction and conversion: the formation of a universal concept in its possible concretion with a particular, and the referring of the concretion to a thing-in-itself, with the attendant differentiation of subject and object. The point is that "these two operations of the intellect should not be understood as two modes of the intellect's activity, each one existing by itself, but as moments of the one thought, each mutually conditioning the other...."[17]

The distinction and relation between *concretio* and *complexio* is not that of a part to the whole but of a possible to a realized synthesis of S and P. In fact, despite their titles as "first" and "second" acts of the intellect, the latter is prior to the former and is that from which we understand the first. We begin with the *concretio*.[18]

It might seem that everything is known by conversion to the phantasm (referral of a universal to a singular) *except* the universal itself. But in fact the abstracted universal is always related, immediately or mediately, to possible instantiations, insofar as reference to many possible supposits is essential to the P *as universal*, as a "one *of many*." Seen prior to the referral, the transcendental unity of form is indifferent to any particular "that" but not indifferent to "thats" as such. Its nature is to be able to exist, by an unlimited repeatability, in any number of "whereuntos" (*Woran*) to which it is essentially referred.[19] This fact reaffirms that man, as *logos* and not *nous*, always and only knows *ti kata tinos*, something about something.[20] Abstraction or "liberation" of a universal content is always already a concretizing synthesis of that universal with an empty "this." But this state of affairs entails two things: first, that "the subject with the content of his knowledge (the universal concept) already stands to some extent at a distance from the 'this' to which he refers the content of knowledge,"[21] and, secondly, that he in fact sees the possible reference of the P to an S. This liberation-and-concretion is simultaneously abstraction and conversion to the phantasm and thus complete return to the self as something distinct from the "this." Aquinas writes: "To know that which exists in individual matter *not as* it exists in such matter, is to abstract the form from the individual matter which the phantasms represent."[22] Rahner comments that (1) "the qualitative content remains in the individual matter, that is, in the phantasm known sensibly"; (2) "the knowledge of the 'not as' is all that abstraction as such accomplishes"; and (3) "abstraction as acquisition of the universal concept is the realization of this return (*reflexio*) of the subject to himself."[23]

But in real thought, that is, objective knowledge, the concretizing or predicative synthesis occurs only in the apophantic, veritative synthesis, the *complexio*. It is not the case here that two concepts (that of the S, that of the P) are referred to each other "in the mind," but rather that both of them are referred to a real thing that "is the case" (*ein Ansich*). True judgment recognizes in *concretio* and affirms in *complexio* what in fact is the case in the first order of reality where a particular thing does have such and such a quality. Distance (abstraction) and presence (referral) are operative with different emphases in both *concretio* and *complexio*. In *concretio* there is distance with possible referral; in *complexio*, actual referral from the vantage of distance. And with different emphases, both indicate the complete return to the self. *Concretio* highlights "liberation" of the self from the sense object by abstraction of its form, and *complexio* indicates "distance" by objectifying the sense object *as* really possessed of this form.[24]

This Scholastic analysis may be clarified further by transposing it into different terminology. Heidegger discusses analogous matters at the pre-predicative level in terms of the disposed understanding (*befindliches Verstehen*) or thrown project (*geworfener Entwurf*) as well as in terms of interpretation and assertion (*Auslegung, Aussage*).[25] More exactly, disposed understanding stands at the pre-predicative level as parallel to *concretio*, whereas interpretation and assertion represent differing degrees of "predication." In Heidegger, as in Rahner, the issue is the "as" and "as not."

In the disposed understanding of everyday life, an *implicit* "as" and "as not" are at work. We understand a thing (the S of later and derived propositions) in terms of its referredness to a purpose (the P of those later statements). And insofar as we grasp that thing within a totality of useful things, we see it *as not* exhaustive of that purpose (hence the P will become predicable of a many). The "as" and "as not" can be articulated in a threefold distantiation and referral which Heidegger calls the fore-structure, i.e., the measuring of the distinction-and-synthesis of thing and purpose.

Heidegger speaks first of a fore-having (*Vorhabe*) in which understanding is already projectively out towards the purpose and thus beyond the thing-to-be-referred (= distance, liberation). Yet at the same time the understanding *already has* grasped ("*pre*-grasped") the particular thing in question as projected towards that purpose (= referral, concretion). Secondly, Heidegger describes the same structure in terms of fore-sight (*Vorsicht*): projected understanding already sees *what* the tool is *for* (= distance, liberation) and sees the tool *as* for that purpose (= referral, concretion). And thirdly, moving towards conceptualization, understanding in its projective distantiation has already pre-thematically conceived (*Vorgriff*) the thing *as* both distinct from and united with its purpose.

These kinds of liberation and referral operate at the pre-predicative level. But interpretation (better: "spelling out," *Aus-legen*) quasi-predicatively explicates or articulates the reciprocal liberation and referral; and assertion (*Aussage*) most explicitly affirms the relations in terms of P and S. By this analysis Heidegger intended to show that assertion is a derived rather than an original modality of *synthesis* and *diairesis*, one, in fact, that flattens out and obscures the world of lived purposes in which the binding and loosing primarily take place. The more original as-structure operative in man's pre-predicative interpretation (*hermēneia*) of his lived world is thus called the "hermeneutical" as-structure, whereas that whereby he shows (*apophainesthai*) things in predicative speech is called the "apophantic" or "assertoric" as-structure. While Rahner does not have that specific critical goal in mind, he effects much the same thing when he shows that *concretio*—indeed, human sensibility itself—is already a primordial *synthesis* and *diairesis*, a showing of the "as" and "as not."

3. Towards an Understanding of Agent Intellect

We have seen that the question of the unity of human bivalence in GW reduces to the question of the togetherness of receptive objective knowledge and the complete return to the self in that knowledge. We also saw that the condition of the possibility of all this is *abstraction* of a universal and *referral* of it to a concrete instance. If we discuss these two separately, we may distinguish the agent intellect as the power of abstraction ("the capacity to differentiate what is known universally from another existent"[26]) and the possible intellect as the power of the conversion ("the referral of the universal to a 'this' "[27]). But if the traces of abstraction, referral, and complete return are somewhat clear, the metaphors and images for describing the unified phenomenon (and abstraction in particular) are not always helpful. Here again the ghost of Platonism rattles its chains.

From Aristotle's problematic text on the *nous poiētikos*, through Aquinas' discussions of *intellectus agens*, down to neo-Thomistic popularizations, imagery and metaphor abound and confuse, even when their literalism is disclaimed. Some images speak of "illuminating" the phantasm and seeing the intelligible species in it, others speak of "liberating" the intelligible species from matter and "impressing" it upon the possible intellect, others of metamorphizing the phantasm by "elevating" its qualitative content to the level of intellect, or even of "undressing" the species (*spoliare species*[28]) for spiritual inspection. Perhaps the culprit is this term *species intelligibilis*, a relic of dead Platonism. (Aristotle means something quite different by his *to eidos to kata ton logon*.[29]) The agent intellect purportedly produces it as an intellectual double of what is given in the phantasm, so that the possible intellect can take a look at it. (But Rahner asks: "What, for example, would an intellectual color be?"[30]) Perhaps we can see such unfortunate images crowd together in a passage, chosen almost at random, which is the *ne plus ultra* of Scholastic similes.

> When the agent intellect illumines phantasms and abstracts intelligibles from them, far from reducing physical natures to a sort of proletariat and ruining them for its own profit, the agent intellect overcapitalizes their original value and sets them up so prosperously that they can exchange the poor dwellings they inhabit in sensibility for the dwelling of spirit itself. This they do by means of the intentional species, the spiritual likeness of outer reality, which makes the latter intelligible and thus knowable, and hence the principle object and measure of intellection.[31]

Whatever its pedagogical value, this epistemological Leninism can be balanced off at the other end of the spectrum by an equally radical simile from Professor Randall: "The 'active intellect' is thus really the least important or significant part of the *De Anima*. To mix the metaphor, it is a Platonic wild oat coming home to roost...."[32] Randall sees Aristotle's text as a regress to a Platonic myth of illumination by an intelligible light, when in fact the answer to the question, "What makes us know? What actualizes universals?" is, according to Randall, simply *logos*, discourse or language in Mead's and Dewey's sense of the term.

If the truth lies somewhere in between these two positions, it may well lie more on Randall's side although not necessarily for Randall's reasons. The agent intellect is indeed *logos*, but in its more fundamental structural moment which renders possible *synthesis* and *diairesis* and thus speech and communication. In fact, as Rahner sees, it is formally the same as Heidegger's *Verstehen* or, if we use the word in its precise sense, *Existentialität*: the ability to project (i.e., to pre-have, pre-see and pre-conceive) beingness in its distinction from and composition with beings. "The agent intellect is to be defined as the power of anticipating beingness as such [*das Vermögen des Vorgriffs auf das esse schlechthin*]."[33] According to Rahner, Aquinas knew as much; but old flames die hard, and Scholasticism's unresolved love affair with Plato continues to bear such dubious fruit as "intelligible species," "illuminated phantasms," and the like.

Rahner tries to clear the air by retrieving from Aquinas a term for the

anticipatory projection of beingness: *excessus*, "excess," not an action occasionally performed, e.g., upon reception of sense data, but a structural ontological principle of man as man, "the necessary and always
already realized condition of knowledge...."[34] It is not that the impact of
the *sensum* sends the agent intellect scurrying away towards beingness as
such, but rather that man is nothing other than the kinetic excess or self-
absence which allows the *sensum* to encounter him at all. All the metaphors and images for agent intellect, if they be used at all, must be
interpreted in terms of the condition for the possibility of man's objective access to, his rendering meaningfully present of, whatever is receiv-
able in sensation. On one side of the human bivalence, such a condition
is the excessive anticipation of beingness pure and simple, whatever the
meaning and however broad the scope of that movement. Further investigation of the agent intellect as the power of abstraction may thus proceed as a discussion of excess as the condition of the possibility of access,
relative "absence" as the possibilizing condition of "presence."

4. An Overview of the Problematic of Abstraction

If natures are revealed by acts, then we can discover the nature of
man as a complete return to the self by studying the act of thinking as
objective knowledge, that is, as the universal, judgmental, and true apprehension whereby man grasps a universal in objectified synthesis with
a concrete state of affairs. As sense knowledge or receptive intuition,
man is the act of matter, so much given over to matter, in fact, that he *is*
it and thus can both receive another and be undifferentiated from it *as*
other (never, however, like the plant or animal, for man's fallenness
among things is always a *logos* activity.) We have tentatively seen abstraction to be the grasp of the "as" and "as not." We have also seen that
the condition of the possibility of abstraction (in Scholastic language, its
inner nature) is agent intellect as the prior grasp of a universally repeatable quiddity, while the condition of the possibility of the synthesis of a
universal with a concrete thing is the possible intellect as conversion to
the phantasm. In their unity they are the knowing of a P of an S,
grounded in man's excess-access, his distance from and presence to the
world. Rahner interprets agent intellect as the anticipation (*Vorgriff*) of
the beingness of beings in its unity and totality. Let us note that, in appropriating Heidegger's term *Vorgriff* to delineate *excessus*, Rahner does
so loosely. In Heidegger, *Vorgriff* is one way, along with *Vorhabe* and
Vorsicht, of articulating the full character of man's projective nature. In
Rahner, however, the term stands for projection as a whole. Hence, we
may translate *excessus* by the broader Heideggerian term "projection"
(*Entwurf*), which subsumes the three aspects of the fore-structure.

Rahner's explication of *excessus* as the condition of the possibility of abstraction proceeds in two steps: (1) a more precise elaboration of the *function* of this excess, and then (2) a precision of its *scope* or breadth, what Rahner, again in a loose borrowing from Heidegger, calls its *Worauf* or *Woraufhin*, its "whither" or "towards-which." (Note, however, that Rahner also uses the word in a different sense: the S to which the P is referred is called the *Woraufhin* of reference or, when the concrete particular is considered ontically, the *Woran* of a quiddity.[35])

The first step is carried out in two sub-steps. In the first, the projective excess is explicated as knowledge of the *intrinsic limitation* of the P in and by its instantiation in or concretization with any given possible S. This limitedness follows necessarily from the fact that objective knowledge is the referral of a universally known (hence intrinsically repeatable) form to a specific and intrinsically limiting instance. Simultaneous with, and as the condition of the possibility of, this limiting referral, man must be a projection beyond the limitation, an excess towards something which is at least relatively unlimited and which Rahner calls the negative (formal) illimitation of the form.

The second sub-step in delineating the function of the excess consists in reducing that negative (formal) unlimitedness of form to *esse*, first by showing that the judgment does in fact reach *esse* (*Ansichsein:* what is the case) and secondly by reducing essence to a modality of *esse*. Thus Rahner shows in a preliminary way that the projective anticipation at least *also* attains *esse* as its "whither," hence that "every intellectually apprehended object (every concrete object) is apprehended as a limited *esse*...."[36] By the end of the first step as a whole we should be able to affirm heuristically that "*esse* is first of all just the expression of the scope of the anticipation itself...."[37]

The second step in explicating the anticipation as possibilizing condition of abstraction consists in discerning the range of anticipation, i.e., asking whether man's excess transcends the spatio-temporal horizon of the beingness of beings. Rahner's intention is to show that the *esse* reached in the projection, as the being-in-itself-ness of the sensibly received other, is unlimited *esse* as such.[38] After demonstrating its formal and transcategorical universality, he will argue that the anticipated *esse* is beingness pure and simple, ultimately God. But it is worth pausing for a moment over this formulation which it is at the heart of the debate about the "forgottenness of being." Pure and simple beingness as such is called the totality (*das Ganze*) of all the possible objects of thought, where "totality" does not mean the sum (*die Summe*,[39] *die quantitative Zusammenstückung*[40]) of individual possible objects, but rather "the one original ground" and "the original unity" of all possible objects.[41] This

ontologically unifying ground (*das Sein*) is finally the theological totality of all that is (*das Seiende im Ganzen*), the unlimited beingness which
is called God.[42] Rahner's ontology, through a transcendental turn towards the metaphysics of knowledge, arrives (even before considering
the conversion to the phanatasm) at a natural theology. The project, in
Heidegger's term, is an onto-theo-logy, formally homologous with the
structure of every metaphysics from Plato through Nietzsche. (Heidegger will claim: "Even Nietzsche's metaphysics is *as ontology. . .at the
same time* theology."[43]). Let this passing reference suffice for now. At the
conclusion of this second major step, one should be able to affirm with
Rahner that *esse* is "the one full ground of all possible objects of knowledge as the index of the absolutely unlimited scope of the anticipation
[*Vorgriff*]."[44]

Rahner's treatment of abstraction thus proceeds as follows:
1. The Function of Anticipation
   a. Knowledge of the intrinsic limitation of form by supposit;
      knowledge of the negative formal infinity of form.
   b. Reduction of the negative formal infinity of form to *esse*.
2. The Scope (*Worauf*) of Anticipation
We shall now follow out the individual steps in Rahner's thickly woven
chapter.

B. ANTICIPATION AS THE GROUND OF ABSTRACTION

1. The Function of Anticipation

The quiddity as individuated in matter is potentially, but not actually, intelligible to the degree that the self has not yet appropriated the
distance whence it can objectively refer that quiddity to something
which in itself is the case. Beyond actual sensibility, man is a demand for
the higher order of actual intelligibility, and all images and metaphors
which describe his *nous poiētikos* or agent intellect point to the simple
fact of his ability to make (*poiein*) the potentially intelligible actually so
by making it universal. One such image is that of the "liberation"
(*Loslösung*) of form from matter, an image which Rahner uses with this
caution: The form "is liberated in such a way that it retains its ordination to
a possible 'this' and can be thought of as real only in a concretion."[45]

To specify this liberation we may ask one question in four ways: How
can the intellect know *in the form* the latter's relation to sense matter if,
of itself, the content of the form does not have such a reference? How do
other possible instantiations (*Diesda, tode ti*) present themselves to the
knower as possible concretions of the form? How can one see in the form

itself the fact that it is only accidentally the form of this particular instance? How can the form and the instance be differentiated if they are always given in sense as united?

As a provisional answer we may point to the contingency of the sensible concretion, to the limited mode that a form has in sensible things, and thus to its intrinsically broader scope. This is knowledge of the "confinement" of form by matter. We note two things: first, that the focus remains on the sensibly given, while the point is to come to know it as a limited realization of the form and thus to "universalize" the sensibly concretized form; secondly, that the fact that Rahner and Aquinas approach the agent inellect via a study of intelligibility as universality again underlines the man-centeredness, better, the transcendental nature, of that approach. Within the analogically correlative hierarchy of knowing and beingness there are, supposedly, levels of beingness ("separated forms") which of themselves have no ordination to material instantiation and thus "are in themselves actually intelligible without for that reason having to be universals."[46] But to see that Aquinas derives the concept of agent intellect from the human need for actual intelligibility as universality (a one of a many) "is to see intelligibility from the specifically human level of beingness and from human thought."[47]

But how is the limitedness or confinement of form known? When, beyond merely experiencing a limit or "stop," one comes to understand that limit *as* limit, as an obstacle to the attempt to exceed it, then one is already somehow beyond it in an *a priori* knowledge of a relatively "more." Indeed, if objective knowledge of the sensibly given requires knowledge of its "form" (actuality, perfection, reality), then such knowledge must entail that man as projective excess or agent intellect antecedently (*vor*) "grasps" (*greift*) the whole field of possibilities of that form. This horizon offers the possibility of experiencing the forms of sensible data as limited, and therefore the possibility of differentiating the data from and uniting it with the form. The antecedent "grasp" is called the *Vorgriff*—usually translated as "pre-grasp." Because that translation might carry misleading connotations of a grasp (of beingness) which precedes another grasp (of beings) while remaining in the same order, I prefer to render it as "anticipation." Although that word is etymologically only a Latinate equivalent (*ante* + *capere*) of the Anglo-Saxon "pre-grasp," it may better preserve the kinetic and asymptotic sense that Rahner wishes to convey. The *Vorgriff* projectively *points towards* beingness as a unified whole rather than grasping it, and this indication of a "more" is what allows man to see a limited "less." The anticipation of the goal or *Worauf* remains on the way towards that goal, and it is never a commutation back and forth between the end-point and the present milestone. What this anticipation "attains"—its "whither" or "whereunto"—is not another object of the same order as the one man is trying to know through abstraction, for if it were, yet another projective excess would be required to know *that* object, and so on to infinity. Rather, the ever kinetic and excessive anticipation remains the condition of the possibility of the one grasp of the sensible object. For all that, Rahner says, in the second order of reflection we inevitably speak of the whereunto as an "object" which is "attained" in the anticipation.

Not only does the anticipation of the goal of human movement allow disclosure of the one particular sense datum in question, but it also implicitly discloses everything that can be a possible object of knowledge: the breadth of form, the whole (*das Ganze*) of its possible objects,[48] insofar as the "more" which it indicates cannot be an absolute nothing, a *nihil negativum et absolutum*. This means that the projective excess anticipates both the beingness of the specific datum and the beingness of all possible data: beingness as a whole in its unity (*das Sein als solches und im Ganzen*). It also says that all objective knowledge falls short of the full possibility of knowledge that is co-disclosed in the breadth of the excess. All objective knowledge is a *Zugriff* (objective access to a particular thing) on the basis of an *Übergriff* (exceeding that particular thing and reaching towards beingness as such): access by excess, presence by absence.[49]

The major issue, of course, is that of the scope of the excess. If man is always finite, can the projection itself remain finite (only thus could it be human) and still "reach" beingness as such in its totality? Does the "attainment" of the unlimited (infinite) breadth of beingness in the *Vorgriff* undo the limitation (finitude) of man? No, the "attainment" always remains anticipation and thus a privative knowledge of unlimitedness. It is never all-at-once possession. Man as excess is what Aristotle calls *energeia ateles:* he is never at the goal (*telos*) in immediacy, but has his degree of being (*energeia*) only insofar as he has not yet arrived at the goal (*ateles*). This dynamic, atelic way of being a self entails an absential potentiality which ever gnaws at the heart of one's actuality. It is an absentiality which allows (indeed requires and is manifested in) man's need for receptive sensibility, but which is rooted in his more primordial *kinesis*. The Scholastic doorway to this topic is the question of the reciprocal limitation of form and supposite.[50]

The form represents the content of the predicate: that which is known of and referred to the supposite, the *ti* which is said *kata tinos*. As such, the form is universal, of itself unlimited, and therefore repeatable. But from another perspective, the form is limited by the supposite, whereas matter as the empty potentiality for any possible number of forms is it-self unlimited.

We see that form and matter by themselves have both an intrinsic lim-itedness and, in different ways, an intrinsic illimitation. Form in itself has a qualitative (that is, *qua* essence) limitedness insofar as it is this form (P[1]) and not that (P[2]). Matter as quantitativeness (see Chapter VII, B.2) is intrinsically limited both insofar as it can be matter only for forms which are not "repugnant" to being concretized in matter and in-sofar as matter "is always already individuated, and precisely for this reason can contain [of itself] no ontological actuality...."[51] It is only the "empty bearer" of form. On the other hand, both are, again for differ-ent reasons, intrinsically unlimited, although only relative to each other. The unlimitedness of matter is privative and "material"/potential—the deprivation of form—whereas the unlimitedness of form is negative and "formal"—its intrinsic repeatability in an unlimited number of suppos-ites. How are they related?

All knowledge is always through act, that is, it is knowledge of what *is*. And knowledge of matter is had only through form, that is, "at" the actual existing thing. Thus the privative unlimitedness of matter is known through and at the negative infinity of form. "Matter is not known in an apprehension apprehending it immediately, but as opposi-tion, as limitation of the form as universal."[52] In short, "man knows the finiteness and limitedness of a concrete, ontological determination (of a being) insofar as it is held in the broader 'nothing' of its potentiality; but this broader nothing itself is known only insofar as it itself is held against the infinity of the formal actuality as such (of beingness)...."[53] In Heidegger's terms: Man has access to any particular being only in a pro-jective excess towards the "horizon" which contextualizes *all* accessible beings in their mode of accessibility. But Rahner's statement ends on a note of undecidedness: "...the formal actuality as such (of beingness), *whatever this might be:* essence or *esse.*" We are propelled into the ques-tion of the scope of the projection and, as a step towards that, into the question whether the whereunto of that excess is best understood in for-mal, essential, quidditative terms, or in terms of beingness as being-actual.

Here we may be brief, since above, in Chapter IV, A.4, we have al-ready covered much of this transitional move to *esse*. The point is first to establish that the judgment attains to *das Ansich*, that which is the case; and then to specify the being-in-itself-ness of what is the case as being-actual.[54]

For Aquinas the realist, there was never any point to asking what the ontological status of the objects of our knowledge might be. He presumed it to be the actualness, the very being-actual (*Wirklichsein*) of the known object. The objects of knowledge had no other validity than that of the real world: what was knowable was the form of sensible things. The in-itself-ness of the in-itself (*das Ansichsein des Ansich*) was not that of separate forms. "So, for Thomas, knowledge appears from the outset as attaining to the things of the real world, and he sees no reason to extend the in-itself of the real world of objects by an ideal in-itself which is in principle independent of this world."[55] Even in the case of beings of reason, "every judgment attains to *esse* mediately or immediately," and "Thomas does not know any objects of knowledge except such as are related to *esse* in some mediate or immediate way."[56]

Rahner establishes the same point by a brief consideration of judgment. The true affirmation or *complexio* merely recognizes and affirms the first order of synthesis or *concretio* in the real world. In the first order of synthesis the this-here ("S") has the "in-itself" already belonging to it, and affirmation explicitly relates the known content (*das Gemeinte*) to the thing and thus recognizes the *Ansichsein des Seienden*. Pre-grasped as unlimited in the excess and affirmed as limited in the affirmation, the quiddity is the objective *Ansichsein*, the what-it-really-is, of the concrete thing. But this what-it-really-is is the beingness of the thing, and that is always to-be-actual (*Wirklichsein*) or to-be-real (*Realsein*) in the modern and non-Scholastic sense of "real." Thought, therefore, attains to beingness and not to ideally valid propositions. Although heretofore in GW Rahner has treated the unlimited form (actuality) that is reached in the pre-grasp in terms of essence, we may now see, on the basis of the reduction of essence to *esse* (cf. Chapter IV, A.4) that the "whither" of the projective anticipation is *esse* itself as unlimited. Abstraction of this *esse* is the condition of the possibility of knowledge of the limitedness of *esse* (form, essence) in the supposite. Just as the form or P was pre-grasped as negatively unlimited when it was apprehended as more than the supposite and hence as repeatable, so too *esse*, as the being-in-itself of the supposite, is anticipated as applicable to an unlimited number of instantiations, hence as one *esse* of many in formal and transcategorical universality. "But this means that in every essential judgment (e.g., the tree is green) a universal *esse* is simultaneously affirmed which, as one, is able to include in itself the quiddity of the subject and that of the predicate (being tree and being green), and to that extent is one and universal (that is, the beingness of many determinations),"[57] indeed, "in itself the fullness of all possible determinations absolutely, for in every judgment it is the same *Ansichsein* that is anticipated."[58] Whereas formerly Rahner demurred about the ontological status of the relative nothing which contextualizes all knowable objects ("...whatever this might be: essence or *esse*"), he can now affirm: it is *esse* in formal and transcategorical universality.

2. The Scope of Anticipation: On Heidegger and Kant

Rahner now takes up a series of objections to the unlimitedness of the *Worauf* of excessive anticipation. They all come down to two, which are attributed in the first edition of HW to Heidegger and Kant respectively. These attributions are dubious at best, especially in the case of Heidegger, and for that reason the second edition of HW omits the reference, even though it substantially retains the content of the objections.[59]

The first objection, in the name of Heidegger, has two moments. First: the anticipation attains to nothingness (*Nichts*) as the necessary condition of the negation (*Verneinung*) of any illimitation in the sensibly given; the "nothing-ing" (*Nichtung*) of the nothingness reveals the finitude of the given object. In GW Rahner translates his understanding of nothingness in Heidegger into the "privative infinity of matter," the mere possibility of what is to be actually apprehended. In the second moment of the objection, which follows immediately from the first, Rahner implies that Heidegger asserts that the actual being is known from its possibility.

Lest there remain any doubt how Rahner understands Heidegger's positions, we may refer to texts outside of GW and HW, where Rahner explains himself explicitly. In his essay "Existential Philosophy..." Rahner takes it that, for Heidegger, Dasein's transcendence "goes beyond the diverse beings to end up in nothingness, that every particular being is necessarily finite, participating in nothingness, and that 'pure being is identified with pure nothingness.' "[60] In the same essay he continues: "It seems, consequently, that this existential analytic of Dasein ought to have as a logical, even necessary, sequel not an ontology but an *ontochrony* (the expression comes from Heidegger himself), that is, a science showing that the meaning of all being as such and the meaning of being in the absolute, is nothingness."[61] And nine years later, in his essay "The Passion and Asceticism" (1949), Rahner provides one of the most telling of his infrequent references to Heidegger in the theological writings:

> The tragic-heroic philosophy of a Heidegger too has its idol: if man of himself alone exists only for death, then death must be the absolutely ultimate reality for this philosophy of a last resentment; since for this philosophy man's God must not be *more* than man himself, it adores death as its God and highest reality, for it is also the most empty; being and nothingness are the same.[62]

Leaving aside for a moment the question of the correctness of these interpretations, let us see how Rahner responds to "Heidegger's" two-fold objection. Regarding the first moment of the objection, Rahner answers easily and correctly that the projective excess cannot anticipate a *nihil absolutum*. For Rahner, if the excess anticipates a nothing, this nothing is only the negative infinity or intrinsic unlimitedness of actual beingness, something real, actual, and "affirmative," not potential and negative. And this "more" is enough of a basis for the negation of any unlimitedness in the sensibly given. In answer to the second moment of the objection Rahner asserts that the potentially knowable (matter as privative infinity) is actually known within the context of beingness as act, and not vice versa. The basis of both answers is the Scholastic principle of the priority of actuality over potentiality, as over against Heidegger's claim that "the potential is higher than the actual." Closer study of Heidegger's own claims in the matter may help to clarify things.

In the essay to which Rahner implicitly refers throughout, namely, "What is Metaphysics?" (1929), Heidegger shows that the nothingness (*das Nichts*) which allows the meaningful presence of beings is neither a being of reason (a "nothing" of which we could say "is") nor the logical negation of beings in totality. By beings in totality, of course, Heidegger means beings in their beingness, in their *esse* in Rahner's sense. To locate nothingness in the area of reason would be to put it under the power of logical negation, whereas Heidegger sees the phenomenon as lying deeper: "We assert that nothingness is more original than the 'not' and negation."[63] Heidegger justifies the assertion by three steps: (1) a phenomenological reading of man, in his ontological disposition (*Befindlichkeit*), as already with beings-in-totality; (2) a description of "dread" (*Angst*—in broader terms, the Greek *thaumazein*) as a particular mood in which nothingness is revealed, not at all as apart from beings-in-totality but as one with them; (3) a conclusion that dread, and the nothingness revealed in it, are prior to logical negation. Heidegger's analysis is either well known or readily available and therefore may be briefly summarized here.

First, although it is "impossible in principle" for man actually to grasp the sum total of all beings, he does in fact find himself, as ontological disposition (Rahner would say: possible intellect *quo est omnia fieri*[64]), with beings in their wholeness. "No matter how fragmented our everyday existence may appear to be, it always deals with beings in the unity of the 'whole' [= beingness], if only in a shadowy way."[65] Heidegger offers examples of how that is the case in boredom and love, and the reader can find fuller treatment in *Being and Time*, paragraphs 29-30.

Such moods both confront us with beings in their unified wholeness and "conceal from us the nothingness we are seeking."[66] At this juncture we can already form a negative heuristic notion: The nothingness which Heidegger seeks, even if it be bound up with beingness in totality, is not identical with it. There is no effort here to reduce pure beingness to a *nihil absolutum*. But there does seem to be a search for a possibilizing condition of beingness, one which, from the viewpoint of beings-in-beingness, would appear to be a nothingness.[67]

In his second step Heidegger briefly describes the phenomenon of dread (to be distinguished from such states as fear, anxiety, nervousness, and so forth[68]) in which things lose their significance, sink into indifference, and at one and the same time "recede" from us and close in upon us oppressively, robbing us of our power even to speak the "is." This event of the appearance of nothingness (Heidegger calls it *Nichtung*, the act of nothing-ing) neither annihilates nor negates beings but in fact for the first time repels man into beings as a whole in their unique open "is-ness." It reveals human existence to be precisely this projectedness-into-nothingness on the basis of which beings can appear (excess as the condition of access). Far from obliterating beings-in-their-beingness, Heidegger's nothingness opens the space for that phenomenon—but precisely by being distinct, although not separate, from it, i.e., by being its possibilizing condition. The nothingness of which Heidegger speaks, therefore, is the *need* which appropriates man into the questioning knowledge of the beingness of beings. It is the man's being appropriated by the disclosure of beingness.

What of this event-of-nothingness (*Nichtung*) in relation to logical negation (*Verneinung*)? "We can of course conjure up the whole of beings in an 'idea,' then negate what we have imagined in our thought, and thus 'think' it negated. In this way we do attain the formal conception of the imagined nothing but never the nothing itself."[69] But in the pre-predicative, hence pre-negational, experience of dread there is no annihilation or even logical denial of beings as a whole so as to attain nothingness. Beings remain, even when the nothingness is revealed; in fact they appear in their uniqueness for the "first" time in what Heidegger calls "the wonder of all wonders." "Quite apart from the fact that the explicit act of a negating assertion is foreign to dread as such, we also always arrive too late with such a negation which is supposed to bring about the nothingness."[70] What is the nothingness, if logical negation is too late for it? It is not a being, it is no thing about which we could say "is," it is not even the "is-ness" of whatever is. But for all that, it is "real" in the broadest sense, and not an absolute negative nothing. It is the very dynamism of what the early Heidegger calls being-in-the-world, not just being in a set of beings, not even just knowing the actuality of the beings one encounters within the world. It is part of a problematic that is different from that of beings, their beingness, and God as the ground of beingness. It is the heuristicon of the question, "If beingness is what allows beings to appear, what allows beingness itself to happen?" To answer that question in terms of the highest form of beingness (*ipsum esse subsistens*) is only to promote the question to a higher level without answering it. Since Heidegger is asking for the condition of possibility of all actuality, both limited and unlimited, he will assert that "possibility is higher than actuality" without denying that in the more circumscribed framework of beings-in-their-beingness actuality is higher than potentiality.[71] If we attempted to translate back into Rahner's language the sense of nothingness that is experienced in dread, we would say that the nothingness is the ever-receding *Worauf* which evokes man's projective excess and thus renders beings accessible.

It would seem, then, that Rahner's attribution of a *nihil absolutum* to Heidegger is a misunderstanding and that for this reason Metz dropped the reference to Heidegger in the second edition of HW. Heidegger and Rahner agree that the *Vorgriff* does not land in an absolute negative nothing but points to something "more real" (Heidegger: *seiender*) than what is to be thematically grasped. For Rahner, as we shall see in a moment, that greater reality is God. In the *Vorgriff* "the existence of an Absolute Being is also affirmed simultaneously [*ist doch auch die Existenz eines absoluten Seins mitbejaht*]."[72] The *Worauf* is finally, for Rahner, a theological being (*ens*) of the highest degree of beingness.

But in Heidegger's use of *Nichts*, the *Worauf* of the excess is a self-recessive hiddenness which, on the basis of philosophical experience alone, cannot be known to be a thing of any sort, but can only be "co-affirmed" (if we use this term at all) as what allows the appearance of "affirmable" beings. Drawing upon Greek terms, Heidegger will call the appearance of beings their *alētheia* or revealedness and will heuristically name that which allows this appearance *lēthē*. As intrinsically recessive in favor of the accessibility of beings, this *lēthē* can be "known" only by remaining ever worthy of question. If divine revelation has already disclosed who this *lēthē* is, then, Heidegger says, "One who holds to such faith can in a way participate in the asking of our question, but he cannot really question without ceasing to be a believer and taking all the consequences of such a step. He will only be able to act 'as if'...."[73] In that regard Heidegger was quoted in 1954 as saying: "Philosophy engages in a kind of thinking of which man is capable on his own. This stops when he is addressed by revelation." Indeed: "Within thinking nothing can be achieved which would be a preparation for or a confirmation of that which occurs in faith and in grace. Were I so addressed by faith I would have to close up my shop.—Within faithfulness one still thinks, of course; but thinking as such no longer has a task."[74] To which Rahner responded in 1969. Heidegger, he said,

> has taught us *one thing;* that everywhere and in everything we can and must seek out that *unutterable mystery* which *disposes* over us, even though we can hardly name it with words. And this we must do even if, in his own work and in a way that would be strange for a theologian, Heidegger himself abstains from *speech* about this mystery, speech which the theologian must *utter.*[75]

This later position of Rahner's may be a *retractatio* of his earlier reading of Heidegger. He may well have seen that when Heidegger cites Hegel's *Logic* to the effect that pure being (*das Sein*) and pure nothingness are the same (although not for Hegel's reasons),[76] nothingness does not mean a *nihil absolutum* or even the privative infinity that is the Scholastic *materia.*

But did Rahner see that *das Sein* in Heidegger is not *Seiendheit,* the Scholastic *ipsum esse subsistens* which "all men call God"? We here come upon Rahner's answer to the second moment of what GW takes to be Heidegger's position. The possible, Rahner says there, is known only from the actual; beings as the potentially intelligible are known only in terms of beingness as actual intelligibility. We have seen that Heidegger's statement that "the possible is higher than the actual" does not deny this but in fact shifts the ground of the discussion, for it arises from his non-ousiological position. All ousiology knows the potential from the actual (beingness), and Aquinas knows actual *esse* only as the actuality of beings, even of the highest being in which substance and essence are beingness-as-act itself. Metaphysics, Heidegger writes, "tells us what beings are by conceptualizing the beingness of beings. In the beingness of beings metaphysics thinks *das Sein* but without being able, in its mode of thought, to reflect on the truth of *das Sein.*"[77] The "truth of being" in Heidegger is the prior event whereby beings-in-beingness becomes phenomenologically accessible. It is the self-recessive *lēthē* whereby *alētheia* happens. Compared with the beingness *of beings,* it is as possibilizer to the possibilized, or (if we use these words in a non-ousiological, non-Scholastic sense) as "potential" to "actual." Far from being the "mere possibility of what is to be apprehended" (thus Rahner),[78] this nothingness is the appropriation of man's excess for the sake of the appearance of beings-in-their-beingness. Nothingness is the *archē* and the *aition*— dare we say the "actualizer"?—of beings-in-beingness.

Within this context, the term *ontochrony*, which Rahner says stems from Heidegger himself, does not mean that nothingness swallows up beingness (*on*, *ousia*) like Chronos devouring his children. Heidegger's first sketch of a new "ontology" on the basis of human *kinēsis* went under the title of "phenomenological chronology," by which he meant a theory of the time-character (*die Temporalität*) of beingness.[79] Husserl, in *Logical Investigations* VI/6, had demonstrated that phenomenological intuition renders beings present in their categorial beingness. Thus he had implicitly uncovered the major premise of the tradition, unspoken since the Greeks, that *ousia* or beingness (whether *idea, energeia, esse, das Kategoriale,* or whatever) is the meaningful "givenness" of things. But this allowed the step which Husserl did not take, viz., asking the phenomenological *Wie-Frage* about how that givenness is given: the question of the possibilizing condition or "meaning" of beingness. Heidegger took it as his task to push the noetic-noematic *nous-ousia* correlation back to the prior movement which is the very enactment or *Vollzug* of the phenomenological bond between man and beingness. Since movement is fundamentally a matter of presence-by-absence (in Aristotle, *energeia atelēs* or *energeia* that is still caught in *dynamis*), Heidegger sought to reawaken the question of "time," not as Aristotle's number of movement according to before and after but as the unique movement of sense which happens in man, where relative self-absence or nothingness (he calls it the *nihil originarium*[80]) renders possible the present beingness of things. Thus, while the tradition from Plato through Aquinas to Husserl had been clear about the beingness *of beings* or the givenness of what is given, it had overlooked the question of the givenness itself: how nothingness, held open but never controlled by man's transcendence, allows the presentness of whatever appears. This unique question of "time," originally called a phenomenological chronology, becomes the "being question," the temporo-kinetic determination of the meaning of beingness, *ontochrony.* This phrase, then, cannot mean "a science showing that the meaning of being as such and the meaning of being in the absolute, is nothingness" as Rahner understands it.[81]

To be sure, all of these remarks somewhat anticipate what we can discuss more fully only in the concluding critique. But if the discussion is proleptic, it is not entirely out of place, for we are at the threshold of Rahner's identification of unlimited beingness with God. We want to let the question surface for a moment: Is the totality and unity of beingness the best place to locate the issue of the divine? Does the *question* of beingness point in a different direction? Or is it simply a matter of substituting the name "God" for the *lēthē?*

But, before following Rahner towards his onto-theo-logical affirmation, we take up the second objection against the unlimited scope of the *Vorgriff*.

This objection, like the former, can be divided into two subsets which share one general viewpoint, namely, that the scope of the *Vorgriff* is intrinsically finite, a "relative negative infinity." The first edition of HW designates the first subset as Kantian: The anticipation reveals that the beingness it attains is ultimately finite and, specifically, limited to space and time. Rahner takes up this argument in both GW and HW. The second subset is not attributed to any particular philosopher and differs from the former in this respect: the *Worauf* of the anticipation is indeed ultimately finite, but its finitude remains hidden to the *Vorgriff*. Rahner treats this objection only in GW.

Rahner develops the Kantian objection as follows. The agent intellect is not a sense faculty; hence it transcends spatio-temporal data. But it reaches only as far as the horizon of all possible sense intuitions (the forms of sense); and in terms of that limited horizon of beingness, anticipation knows sensible data as limited and objective.

Against this position Rahner poses an argument from retorsion: There is an intrinsic contradiction between what the statement holds (*Inhalt*) and what it performs (*Vollzug*). To know that the totality of possible objects is intrinsically limited, one must have grasped this limitation *as* limitation and thus have already reached beyond it. To what? Either to beingness as unlimited or to "nothing." In the former case Rahner has won his point directly. In the latter, he refers the question back to his answer to the "Heideggerian" objection: the anticipation co-affirms reality and therefore "more" reality than is had in the sensible datum. To affirm *esse* as finite means to have pre-apprehended not a nothing but a "more" which is more reality, *esse* as absolutely unlimited in itself. "The pre-grasp of 'nothing' would be the necessary but untenable presupposition for limitation of the *Vorgriff* to the forms of space and time," and Heidegger is thus "the logical outcome of the Kant who stands over against German Idealism."[82]

The second subset, treated only in GW, differs from the first only in asserting that the ultimate finiteness of the whereunto of the anticipatory excess remains hidden to that excess. This objection has a general and a specific moment. In general it holds that the whereunto, without itself being known as finite, reveals the even greater finitude of the object which it surpasses. Therefore, knowledge of the finiteness of the whereunto is not a necessary condition of the possibility of knowledge of the finiteness of the object, although the latter is necessary for objective knowledge. Then specifically, the objection offers an option. This finite—but in its finitude hidden—*Worauf* can be only one of two things: either beingness in totality or a limited region of beingness in totality. In the second case we are to understand that some region of beingness would be, vis-à-vis man, metaphysically irrational.

Rahner offers two refutations directed at the general statement of the objection, and two more directed respectively at each of the specific possibilities of the range of the *Worauf*. In general (1) the *Vorgriff* has already been shown to reach beingness as absolutely unlimited in itself; and (2) it is not clear where the finiteness of beingness could "subsequently" emerge except in a *Vorgriff*, and such a *Vorgriff* reaches unlimited beingness. Regarding the specific moment: If the range of this finite—but in its finitude hidden—*Worauf* is beingness in its true totality, then, concerning the hiddenness, how could it be pre-apprehended without *manifesting* itself as finite? And, concerning the finitude, if it manifests itself *as* finite, then isn't one already beyond the finitude and into unlimitedness?

The arguments of hiddenness and limitedness reduce to the argument of nothingness versus reality, and the discussion of reality leads to the conclusion that the whither of the anticipation is an intrinsically unlimited reality. The unlimitedness of this beingness as "absolute" (*schlecht-hin:* pure and simple) is what makes the man who stands before it to be *spirit*, whereas the fact that he "has" it only in anticipation and not in a thematic grasp is what defines him as *finite* spirit. In Aquinas' phrase taken from Aristotle, man is "somehow" (i.e., in *excessus*) "all things" (all beings in their simple and unifying beingness, what Rahner calls *esse schlechthin*). Man does not have infinity and simple beingness in his grasp, but is a dynamic desire for it. He knows infinity and absolute beingness only as it is registered in his *movement* towards it, that is, only by experiencing himself as transcending all of his thematically knowable objects. And if the whither of that transcendence is not finite, material, quantitative beingness in space and time, if it is unlimited beingness, metaphysics must somehow be possible.

3. The Scope of Anticipation: God as Absolute Beingness

It remains for us to study Rahner's claim that God as unlimited, absolute beingness (*absolutes Sein*) is co-affirmed in the anticipation. We recall the progression of Rahner's argument so far: Objective knowledge requires complete return to the self, which in turn entails abstraction, the inner possibility of which is excess towards an unlimited whereunto. This whereunto or *Worauf* is thus far only a heuristic expression of the scope of the anticipation, and heretofore (the English translation of GW does not always make this clear[83]) Rahner has spoken of this *Worauf* only as *esse schlechthin* (actual beingness pure and simple) and not as *esse absolutum* (absolute actual beingness). Moreover, this "objective" is never an object in the first order: "The anticipation, as the condition of the possibility of objective knowledge, never of itself presents an object as it is in itself."[84] And further, even in the second order of reflection, the "objective" of the excess can never be an object of an intellectual ("metaphysical") intuition because, for one thing, it is never something grasped but always the heuristicon of the scope of anticipation; and for another, only finite real beings can be the objects of human intuition. Thus, if it is never given among the finite real things which alone man can intuit, and even if it were realized in an *esse absolutum*, it could never, as far as philosophy knows, be intuited objectively by man. How then does God as the absolute being show up in the anticipation? Rahner's demonstration takes three steps: negative, positive, and cautionary.[85]

First, negatively. The fullness of beingness is never given to man objectively; that is, it is never grasped as a represented object, and that for the following reasons. (1) The *Vorgriff* by definition is never a grasp (*greifen, erfassen*) of beingness but only an anticipation or projection of it for the sake of the grasp of a material object. (2) Because this *Vorgriff* happens only in and with a conversion to a definite reality which limits *esse*, the anticipated beingness is never known (*gewusst*) in the first order of reality but only co-known (*mitgewusst*), and indeed co-known as always limitable and concretized by a quidditative determination in a concrete thing—hence as limited beingness. (3) Even when this beingness is made an "object" in the second order of reflection, it is so known only again by a concretion, whether in and to a definite form (in which case it is limited to a definite degree of beingness) or to all possible forms, "any-quiddity" (in which case it is *esse commune* for *ens commune*). If, then, an absolute beingness must necessarily exclude the possibility of any limitation, the beingness anticipated in the excess shows itself to be non-absolute.

Then, positively. To begin with, Rahner repeats that the anticipation is always already realized (even in doubting, we affirm an *Ansich* and thus beingness) as the condition of the possibility of any knowledge. The following steps then show how God appears in the projective excess. (1) Because it does not reach to a *nihil negativum* but to reality—indeed, reality without limit—the anticipation implicitly affirms that anything which *can* stand within its scope would be at least objectively possible. (2) But then if there were a being which absolutely possessed beingness, it would fit the scope of the unlimited anticipation and in fact would completely fill it. (3) The anticipation, therefore, implicitly affirms such an absolute being as at least possible. (4) But the anticipation reaches out only to actual beingness (*auf wirkliches Sein*[86]) and not to merely possible beingness; hence such an absolute being cannot be grasped (Rahner says *gefasst*) as merely possible. (5) Therefore, the anticipation co-affirms the existence of an absolute being (*die Existenz eines absoluten Seins*) and in this sense—and only in this sense—"goes towards God" (*geht auf Gott*).[87]

Finally, cautionary. In the first place, this co-affirmation of the existence of an absolute being is not an immediate and objective representation of that being, not at all a bringing of it to present givenness in its own self. Rather, only by anticipation of *esse commune* as the whereunto of the excess does man simultaneously but implicitly co-affirm the actuality of God as *esse absolutum*. If the *excessus* were to grasp God, its scope would be filled up and the projection would dissolve itself into a secular beatific vision of the divine. "But, on the other hand, insofar as in human knowledge, which alone is available to philosophy, the anticipation is always broader than the grasp of an object itself because of the conversion to the phantasm, nothing can be decided philosophically about the possibility of an immediate apprehension of absolute *esse* as an object of the first order."[88] In the second place, Rahner's demonstration does not constitute an *a priori* proof of God's existence, for the anticipation and its whither are co-known and co-affirmed only in the *a posteriori* grasp of a real finite being in the world. Rahner's remarks about God and the *Vorgriff* only transpose onto the transcendental level of a metaphysics of knowledge what Aquinas attempted to do in his pre-transcendental ontology of the real. The five *indicia* for the existence of God argue that this or that real being requires, as the condition of the possibility of its reality, an unlimited absolute beingness. Rahner merely says: the *affirmation* of this or that real being requires, as the condition of its possibility, the co-affirmation or anticipation of absolute beingness by the agent intellect. And presumably this *a priori* transcendental awareness of the absolute does not preclude, but in fact calls for, a later, *thematic* "proof for the existence of God" in the usual sense.

But Rahner's positive statements call for some further cautionary remarks of our own. Just how much has he demonstrated about the relation of the *Vorgriff* and God? And once again, what are the steps of that demonstration? Even though Rahner attempts a transcendental deduction, the language of "beings" and "beingness" might lead us to believe that he has proven more than he intended. Be that as it may, I shall again run through the second or positive step of his discussion, but this time with a different but parallel terminology. Instead of "beingness," let us say "meaningfulness." Instead of "beings," let us say "meaningful beings." And let us replace "*das Vorgriff auf das Sein*," i.e., the anticipation of beingness, with "the demand for meaningfulness."

The premise of Rahner's demonstration is that man is the demand for meaningfulness as the condition of the possibility of access to beings, and that there is no limit to this demand since man can still ask about the meaning of such a supposed limit and thereby be interrogatively beyond it. On that premise Rahner proceeds as follows. (1) Because this demand reaches towards unlimited meaningfulness and not towards the irrational (*nihil negativum*), it implies that whatever could fall within its scope would be meaningful. (2) If there were a meaningful being that were meaningfulness itself—let us say, *ipsum intelligere subsistens*—it would completely satisfy the demand. (3) Therefore, the very fact of the demand for meaningfulness at least implies the possibility of such a being. (4) But this demand demands actual and not merely possible meaningfulness; hence an absolutely meaningful being cannot be grasped as merely possible. This requires substeps: (4a) Wherever man meets beings, he is the demand for their meaningfulness. (4b) This demand is always a demand for actual meaningfulness. (4c) The demand knows no limits. (4d) Therefore, in the unlimited expanse of encounterable beings, there is an equally unlimited actual meaningfulness. (5) Therefore, the demand co-knows unlimited actual meaningfulness and in this sense "goes towards God."

Three remarks about all this are in order. In the first place, how does one make the move from actual meaningfulness to a *being* of actual meaningfulness, that is from an *intelligere* to an *intelligens*? Answer: In an ousiological framework, which always seeks the *ousia* of an *on* or the "X-ness" of any given X, both beingness and the being are given together, as we have already seen. Just as Rahner can "confound" *das Sein* and *das Seiende*, so too here he can say equally *ipsum intelligere subsistens* and *ipsum intelligens subsistens* under the rubric of a "pure intelligibility" which covers both the act and the one exercising it.

In the second place, what is the force of the words "co-known" and "co-affirmed"? It cannot be emphasized enough that the knowledge these words refer to remains kinetic and dynamic, anticipatory and interrogative. They do not denote an objective thematic knowing and affirmation but a non-objective, unthematic awareness which always remains *in via*. "Man knows infinity only insofar as he experiences himself *surpassing* all of his knowledge in anticipation...."[89] Man remains the *quodammodo*, that is, *in excessu*. He has access—in the strict sense of presence—only to worldly beings-in-their-beingness, and that only on the basis of an ever kinetic excess. The projective character of agent intellect remains a *docta ignorantia*, an interrogative knowing whose objective is a known unknown. "Co-knowledge of absolute beingness" is no quasi- or crypto-intellectual intuition but an affirmation that man as we know him is a demand unsatisfied, a question that has no answer. It would be more true to say that he feels only the kinetic unlimitedness of his projectivity than to claim he knows the perfect self-subsistence of an objectivity. When he completely, that is, authentically, returns to himself, he finds that he is the ineluctable "skeptic" who keeps on looking (*skeptesthai*) without ever seeing; he is the *quest* for reality, who never, as far as philosophy knows, gets his hands on a self-coincident reality. For man, "there is only the trying."[90]

Thirdly: Is it proper, then, to say that man "co-affirms the existence of an Absolute Being"? Would it not be better to speak of an ever recessive *evocation* of man's excess, which, in comparison with beings-in-their-beingness, would be both "less real" (no form of *Seiendes* or *Seiendheit: nihil*) and "more real" (that which lets the actual-in-its-actuality *be*)? Could philosophy know the "name" of this evocation and still remain philosophy? Could theology call it "pure actuality" and remain true to the mystery of the faith? For Heidegger, knowing the "name" would mean closing up the shop ("A 'Christian philosophy' is a square circle and a misunderstanding"[91]). On the other hand Heidegger allows: "There is, to be sure, a thinking and questioning elaboration of the world of Christian experience, i.e., of faith. That is theology. Only epochs which no longer fully believe in the true greatness of the task of theology arrive at the disastrous notion that philosophy can help provide a refurbished theology...which will satisfy the needs and tastes of the time."[92] Rahner, on the other hand, says that the theologian must speak, from out of faith, about the mystery which Heidegger refuses to name. The question is whether ousiology, even in the language of "pure act," can provide the adequate syntax for such a discourse.

4. Confirmations, Clarifications, and Conclusions

Up to this point, Rahner's treatment of abstraction has been "guided more by the dynamism of the matter itself" rather than by explicit texts in Aquinas.[93] Having arrived at his conclusions by a transcendental analysis of judgment, Rahner now turns to Thomas both to confirm his own interpretations and to clarify Aquinas' positions with regard to the first principles of knowledge, the three levels of abstraction, and the light-imagery of agent intellect. This lets Rahner draw conclusions about the complete return to the self. His textual analyses are dense and not central to our purposes, so we may be brief.[94]

Aquinas defines the agent intellect as the power to form first principles of transcendental validity, all of which are grounded in beingness. These "most basic principles of beingness and thought" are the principles of all science, and the agent intellect, as Rahner shows from a variety of texts,[95] is in turn their ground. Does the agent intellect "abstract" first principles? Rahner answers with a yes and a no. On the one hand, the first principles express the scope of the agent intellect, and, on the other, the agent intellect uses them as instruments for abstraction. How can the first principles be both the means and the result of abstraction? Rahner responds: The first principles are the first and proper result of the agent intellect, and all other abstractions are only consequences of this fundamental abstraction. Since the first principles are founded upon the "first conceptions," of which the most fundamental is *ens*, knowledge of them must be founded on knowledge of *ens*. But the "being" which the agent intellect as *excessus* anticipates is universal metaphysical beingness without qualification: *esse*. "Consequently, if the function of the agent intellect was defined as the apprehension [*Erfassen*] of the first principles by the abstraction of the concept of *ens*, this means that the agent intellect attains to *esse*."[96]

Consideration of the three levels of abstraction likewise confirms Rahner's position. The three levels are: abstraction of the universal essence from a concrete "this" (*materia signata*); abstraction of "intelligible common matter" (the quantitative) from the qualitative sensible common or individual matter; and abstraction of the transcendental determinations of *ens* as such (not just *ens* concretized in matter) from intelligible matter. At the first level, for example, one abstracts a *round red thing* from *this* round red thing. The second level provides the objects of the mathematical sciences insofar as it attains a universal which retains an intrinsic ordination to some "this" in which it can be realized, and in fact is itself quantitative, that is, related to "being as the principle of number." Whereas the second level prescinds from sensible (but not from intelligible) common matter, the third level leaves behind *all* common matter and attains to such transcendental determinations as being, one, potency, and act. It might seem to be abstraction of a form in absolute precision from matter, but in fact we have seen that no abstraction can prescind from possible relation to matter, for otherwise the transcendental determination which it delivers could not be known as applicable to matter. Rahner argues minutely and at length that this third level of abstraction is not an act of thought which represents a quiddity, but simply and solely a moment in judgment. He adduces two lines of proof in Aquinas.[97]

In the first line of proof he interprets texts in which Aquinas relates the third level of abstraction, in explicit distinction from the other two, to judgment. In the second and more interesting line of proof, he shows that in Aquinas the mode of merely representing a quiddity (the *modus significandi*) never reaches the transcendental level.[98]

In the first line of proof, texts from *In Boethii de Trinitate* (5,3 and 6,2) and *De Malo* (16, 12, c.) show that the intellectual apprehension or first act of the intellect cannot as such be the "term" of a metaphysical judgment, and that "it is in judgment alone that beingness and its transcendentals reveal themselves."[99] But these texts provide no reasons why this is the case. The second line of proof establishes that the reason for the inability of the simple apprehension to be a term of metaphysical judgment lies in the very essence of that first act of intellect. Simple apprehension issues in the *modus significandi*, which concerns the designating of things. Analysis of language shows that the *nomen* or *oratio*, whether concrete or abstract, always contains a reference to matter (an abstract name describes some way in which a singular can be abstractly; a concrete name obviously points to a particular thing of a specific kind). How then does the third level of abstraction know the represented *significatum* differently from the way the first act of intellect *de facto* represents it in its *modus*? Or again, how does abstraction separate the *significatum* from its *modus significandi* without the former losing all objective reference? The point is to "abstract" at a third level from all the relations to matter contained in the *modus significandi*. Obviously the first act of intellect, which produces the *nomen* with its relatedness to matter, cannot achieve this abstraction. Then there must be a negation which removes from the *modus significandi* all that is inadequate to a metaphysical object. But Thomas always asserts that negation is founded on some kind of affirmation, and here that would mean: on some antecedent knowledge of that which is metaphysically prior to the negation. Clearly this remainder cannot be grasped as something represented, for otherwise the metaphysical object could be apprehended without the negation, and the latter would be superfluous. The only alternative is that the abstraction of metaphysical content is the very same as the non-representational, non-objective anticipation of beingness at the metaphysical level. There the metaphysical content is liberated from concretion by negation, without being eliminated as really possible.

From both lines of proof, therefore, a single conclusion emerges: The abstraction of metaphysical being happens only in the judgment; indeed, only in judgment and not in simple apprehension is absolute *esse* attained. Therefore, the agent intellect as the condition of the possibility of judgment is the power to anticipate beingness as such, and it grounds the first and second levels of abstraction.

When we turn to the question of the light imagery which describes the function of the agent intellect, we discover behind Rahner's apparently innocent reinterpretations the full force of his retrieval of the unsaid in Aquinas. We noted above some of the traditional similes used for the action of the intellect upon the phantasm (elevation, liberation, metamorphosis, and so on), but it is the imagery of light which is most common to the *philosophia perennis* from Plato to Hegel, not only for describing intellection but above all for speaking of beingness. The radicalness of Rahner's rereading of Aquinas can be seen gathered up in the brief section in which Rahner shifts the symbolics for agent intellect, and therefore beingness, from light to *movement*. And we may be able to see as well a certain amount of tension at the ousiological joints of his transcendental structures, as Rahner intimates more than Aquinas' language will allow him to say. To work all this out we must investigate first the nature of the light-imagery, then its reinterpretation, and finally what the force of this retrieval may be.

If in Heraclitus and even in Parmenides the imagery of light always seems bound up with that of darkness, it is in Plato that the full brightness of the sun breaks through. In the *Republic* the Form of the Good is compared to the sun as that which gives revealedness (*tēn alētheian*) to the thing known and knowing power to the intellect (VI, 508 e). The Good is itself the most apparent or luminous of all things (*to phanotaton*, 518 c), thus the cause of all that is right and beautiful (*orthōn te kai kalōn aitia*, 517 c). This light shines upon both Forms and intellect (cf. *kuria alētheian kai noun paraskomenē*, ibid.), making the Forms luminous and the intellect sunlike (*hēlioeides*), that is, able to see in the light of the sun.

With Aristotle's text on the *nous poiētikos* we move from this bright sunlight back into the shade when we read that the intellect makes (*poiein*) all things luminous somewhat the way light makes potential colors into actual colors (*De Anima*, G, 3, 430 a 15 ff.). Plato had already spoken of "making" (*poiēsis*) as a bringing from non-being into being (*ek tou mē ontos eis to on*: *Symposium* 205 b), that is, bringing something out of the darkness of unintelligibility into the light of intelligibility. If we translate the Greek *poiein* into the Latin *agere* and *facere*, then the *intellectus agens* as *quo est omnia facere [intelligibilia]* can be compared to a light-source which illuminates the sensibly known, renders it visible—that is, actually intelligible—for the possible intellect. To carry over the Platonic image, the agent intellect is to the possible intellect as the sun is to the eye. Both are a means by which (*quo*) something gets known. Moreover, if the tradition likewise describes beingness in terms of light (Rahner: *Sein* as *Lichthaftigkeit*), then the agent intellect's degree of beingness can be called its degree of light. Always in act, it is "always light," the always-already-achieved condition whereby the sensibly known is brought out of unhiddenness into appearance as universally intelligible.

It is while reinterpreting this actuality of the agent intellect that Rahner shifts the traditional symbolics from light to movement. The nature of agent intellect consists in a *kinēsis* towards beinginess as a whole, towards total intelligibility. Although "always in act," the agent intellect is imperfectly in act. In the light-metaphor we might say that it is chiaroscuro rather than perfectly luminous. In the movement-metaphor we would say that it is kinetic rather than achieved. Combining both we may say: It is a continual process of coming out of the dark (*lēthē*) into the light (*alētheia*). In any case, as imperfect and kinetic the agent intellect both requires the sensibly known and renders it intelligibly present. And it proffers this intelligibility by giving the data a share in man's movement towards a never-fully-grasped total meaningfulness. In other words, within man's more original kinetic self-absence—his movement beyond himself in a demand for intelligibility—there is opened up the need for the "other absence," that is, his deliverance over to the sensible being which he must receive in order to be his own primordial movement. When received, the sensible enters into man's movement towards intelligibility and thus is "known universally." The universality which the agent intellect bestows on the data is a participation in its own movement towards its *Worauf*. Only in the excess/anticipation does intelligibility happen in the human realm.

Moreover, within this anticipation we have now located the place of the *a priori* in Aquinas. "The opposition between Augustine and Thomas does not lie between aposteriorism in Thomas (of an 'empirical' abstraction) and the *a priori* vision of divine ideas in Augustine, but between an apriorism of the intellectual light as a formal *a priori* of the subject in Thomas, and the apriorism of an idea objectively existing in itself in Augustine."[100] Rahner summarizes this apriority of Aquinas in the language of movement:

> It is the spontaneity of the human spirit, which spontaneity is dynamically ordered to the totality of possible objects and as such already anticipates in its dynamic orientation the totality of all objects according to their most universal metaphysical structure (*sub ratione entis*), and yet still needs the determinations of sensibility in order to present an object to the possible intellect at all, and in it these metaphysical structures of the object.[101]

The language of movement comes from Heidegger, who delineates sense (*Sinn*) as the *Woraufhin* of a projection whereby an encountering being can be grasped as what it is and is for. The ground of sense is the movement of "temporality," the process whereby man constitutively and constantly becomes what he already is, namely, projection. As ever becoming, or coming towards, himself as this possibility (*das sich auf sich Zukommen-lassen*[102]), man is the existential "future" or becoming. But this becoming is only a continual return to, or abiding with, what he already properly is: movement. ("*Das Vorlaufen in die äusserste und eigenste Möglichkeit ist das verstehende Zurückkommen auf das eigenste Gewesen,*"[103] the latter read as "*wie es je schon war*"[104]). This movement of excess, of becoming one's alreadiness, opens the horizon of meaningful accessibility (coextensive with the scope of the anticipation) in which beings can be encountered and known. We see here the "double absence," one moment inside the other, of excess in agent intellect and access in sensibility. For Heidegger, in constantly returning to what he already is (*Zurückkommen* in the primordial sense), Dasein is simultaneously a return (*Zurückkommen* in the secondary sense) to the things rendered intelligible by his excess. ("*Das faktische Dasein kommt. . .aus diesen Horizonten zurück auf das in ihnen begegnende Seiende.*"[105]) The self-presence of Dasein—what Rahner calls the spirit's "complete return to itself"—would more properly be called absence, i.e., the ever kinetic anticipation of a receding dimension that is never grasped. And what Rahner calls "absence" or spirit's self-alienation in sensibility would in Heidegger's language more properly be called presence to the world in the sense of rendering it meaningfully present. "Spirit in the world" means access via excess, presence by absence.

But Rahner's retrieval of the unsaid in Aquinas puts some pressure on the ousiological seams of the transcendental garment in which Rahner wraps the Angelic Doctor. The above analysis indicates that the language of Scholasticism disguises Rahner's debt to Heidegger, even granted that Rahner transposes Heidegger's issue from the pre-predicative to the predicative level. This indebtedness is partially confirmed by Rahner's rereading of the symbolics of light and sight in terms of movement and excess-access. Yet Rahner continues to speak the ousiological language of beingness, or self-presence, of spirit "in" the world, of complete return to the self, even when that last phrase is never understood as a *per se cognoscere seipsum* but always as a *Zu-sich-selbst-kommen* in presence to material things. If Rahner transforms the agent intellect into *kinēsis* or "temporality" in Heidegger's sense, he does not do *kinēsis* full justice insofar as he holds to a movement beyond the ontological (material beings in their beingness) to the theological (the divine being in his beingness)—a strategy that stays within the parameters of ousiology. Heidegger would say that if *kinēsis* be taken seriously, then it always comports a *lēthē*, not more beingness. In that perspective, there could be no real *lēthē* in Rahner, even if Rahner speaks of *die Verborgenheit des Seins*,[106] because faith already knows too much, even in its *docta ignorantia*, and has passed on the news to philosophy. The result would be what Heidegger calls a philosophy of "as if." Yet Rahner says that the believer is the true skeptic.[107] This conflict is what gives rise to the question about pressure on the ousiological seams. Does Rahner tear the garment and surpass ousiology? Or has he stretched the garment to fit Heidegger too?

In any case, we may let Heidegger speak for himself. In 1971, when the present writer asked him whether he thought his own work was compatible with Rahner's, he answered with a simple sentence that can have many meanings: *"Ich bin sehr skeptisch."*

Notes

1. Rahner, GW 92/135 (145 f.).
2. Ibid., 294/406 (405).
3. Ibid., 79/118 (129): abandonment; 79/117 (129): givenness over; 206/285 (289): complete openness.
4. Ibid., 58/91 (104).
5. Ibid., 223/308 (310).
6. Ibid., 39 f./66 (79).
7. Ibid., 80/119 (130).
8. Ibid., 91/133 (144).
9. Ibid., 80/119 (131) and 164/230 (236).
10. Ibid., 80f./119 (131): from the world; 163f./230f. (236 f.): from without, from sensibility.
11. Eliot, "East Coker," II, in *The Complete Poems and Plays of T.S. Eliot* (London: Faber and Faber, 1969), p. 179.
12. Rahner, GW 163/229 (235): *Zu-sich-selber-kommen;* also at 176/247 (252). The phrase *"zu seiner Einheit..."* is added by Metz, GW, 2nd ed., p. 245, Eng. trans., p. 239. On "temporality" as self-unification (*"sich selbst ursprünglich einigende Einheit"*) see Martin Heidegger, *Metaphysische Anfangsgründe der Logik im Ausgang von Leibniz*, p. 264, *The Metaphysical Foundations of Logic*, p. 204f.
13. Rahner, GW 176/247 (252).
14. Ibid., 91/132 (143).
15. Ibid., 136 f./193 (202).
16. See Karl Rahner, "Aquinas: The Nature of Truth," trans. Andrew Tallon, *Continuum*, 21 (1964), 63; and Martin Heidegger, *Kant und das Problem der Metaphysik*, p. 34; *Kant and the Problem of Metaphysics*, pp. 34 and 33.
17. Rahner, GW 136, n./194, n. (202, n.).
18. Ibid., 81-83/120-23 (132-34).

19. Ibid., 66/101 (114).
20. Ibid., 99/143 (154): *Wissen von etwas über etwas.*
21. Ibid., 83/122 (134).
22. *"Cognoscere id quod est in materia individuali non prout est in tali materia, est abstrahere formam a materia individuali quam repraesentant phantasmata"* (S.T. I, 85, 1, c., cited in GW 151/214 [221]).
23. The first two quotations are from GW 151/214 (222), the third (italicized in the original) from GW 82/123 (134).
24. Rahner, GW 83-86/123-126 (134-37). Rahner treats *concretio* and *complexio* in Aquinas at GW 86-91/126-32 (137-43).
25. Heidegger, SZ, sections 29-33. For the Aristotelian roots of this analysis, see Heidegger, *Logik: Die Frage nach der Wahrheit,* (see Ch. V, n. 34, above), sections 11-13.
26. Rahner, GW 92/134 (145); cf. 132/187 (196): power of abstraction.
27. Ibid., 82/121 (132)
28. Guerric of St.Quentin, O.P., who taught theology at Paris from 1233–1242: *"Intellectus humanus, quia permixtus est sensui, accipere potest speciem spoliatam quia adjunctus est aliis viribus interioribus et exterioribus mediantibus quibus potest spoliare species"* (Codex Vaticanus Latinus 4245, Folio 66ra, transcribed in Leo Sweeney, S.J., and Marvin Kessler, S.J., "Human Knowledge According to Guerric of St. Quentin, O.P.," *Arts Libéraux et philosophie au moyen âge* (Montréal: Institut d'Etudes Médiévales; Paris: J. Vrin, 1969), p. 1136 f., lines 123 ff. See Fr. Sweeney's review of Martel's *La Psychologie de Gonsalve d'Espagne* in *Speculum,* 46 (1971), p. 167.
29. *Physics* B, 1, 193 b 1, for example. Heidegger translates this as *"das Aussehen, das gemäss der Ansprechung gemeinte,"* that is, "the appearance, meant in accordance with the statement." See "On the Being and Conception of *Physis,*" *Man and World,* 9 (1976), 251.
30. Rahner, GW 97/141 (151 f.).
31. L.M. Régy, O.P., *Epistemology,* trans. Imelda Choquette Byrne (New York: Macmillan, 1959), p. 250.
32. John Herman Randall, Jr., *Aristotle* (New York: Columbia University Press, 1960), p. 102.
33. Rahner, GW 142/201 (208).
34. Ibid., 128/181 (190).
35. Ibid., 63/98 (110).
36. Ibid., 147/209 (216).
37. Ibid., 127/179 (189).
38. Ibid., 109 f./157 (167).
39. Ibid., 100/145 (155).
40. Ibid., 147/209 (216).
41. Ibid., 147/209 (216): one original ground; 100/145 (155): original unity.
42. Cf. GW 159/224 (230): *Gesamtheit möglicher Gegenstände, totius entis universalis.* HW 77/59 f. (78 f.): *die absolute Weite aller möglichen Gegenstände; absolute Weite des Erkennbaren.* GW 142/201 (208): *Vorgriff auf das esse schlechthin.*

43. Martin Heidegger, *Nietzsche*, 2 vols. (Pfullingen: Günther Neske, 1961), II, 348.
44. Rahner, GW 147/208 f. (210).
45. Ibid., 96/139 (150).
46. Ibid., 95/138 (149) with textual references to Aquinas in footnote.
47. Ibid., 94/137 (148).
48. See ibid., 100 f./145 f. (156).
49. Rahner, GW 8/21 (35). On the anticipation as conscious, see GW 152 f./214 f. (222) and HW 78/60 (79).
50. Ibid., 102-08/148-54 (158-65).
51. Ibid., 103/149 (159).
52. Ibid., 107/153 (164).
53. Ibid., 108/154 (165).
54. Ibid., 108 ff./154 ff. (165 ff.).
55. Ibid., 115/165 (174 f.).
56. Ibid., 119/169 (179) and 117/167 (176).
57. Ibid., 121/172 (181).
58. Ibid., 125/177 (186).
59. The attributions to Heidegger and Kant appear explicitly in HW 79-81 (the title "Heidegger und Kant" appears at the top of p. 80), but the pages are somewhat revised and the references dropped in the second edition (German 80-83, English 60-63). The parallel pages, with no explicit mention of Heidegger or Kant, are GW 130-31/184-86 (193 f.).
60. Rahner, "Existential Philosophy," (see Ch. III, n. 4, above), p. 135.
61. Ibid., p. 136.
62. Karl Rahner, *Theological Investigations*, III, 77.
63. Martin Heidegger, "What is Metaphysics?" trans. David Farrell Krell in *Heidegger: Basic Writings*, ed. David Farrell Krell (New York: Harper and Row, 1977), p. 99.
64. Rahner, GW 172/242 (247) with textual references in the footnotes.
65. Heidegger, "What is Metaphysics?" p. 101.
66. Ibid., p. 102.
67. The nonreducibility of *das Nichts* to a *nihil negativum* is shown in Heidegger, *Die Grundprobleme der Phänomenologie*, pp. 442-45, *The Basic Problems of Phenomenology*, pp. 311-13, and in Heidegger, *Metaphysische Anfangsgründe*, pp. 271-73, *The Metaphysical Foundations*, 209-11.
68. See Heidegger, SZ, Section 40.
69. Heidegger, "What is Metaphysics?" p. 101.
70. Ibid., p. 104.
71. Heidegger, SZ 38/63, and *Metaphysische Anfangsgründe*, p. 280, *Metaphysical Foundations*, 216f.
72. Rahner, GW 128/181 (190).
73. Heidegger, *Einführung in die Metaphysik* (see Chapter one, p. 5, Eng. trans., p. 7). Rahner assisted at the lecture course which underlies this publication: SS 1935.
74. Cited in Hermann Noack,"Gespräch mit Martin Heidegger," *Anstösse:*

Berichte aus der Arbeit der Evangelischen Akademie Hofgeismar, 1 (1954), 31-37, Eng. trans., "Conversation with Martin Heidegger, Recorded by Hermann Noack," in Martin Heidegger, *The Piety of Thinking*, ed. and trans. James G. Hart and John C. Maraldo (Bloomington, Ind.: Indiana University Press, 1976), p. 64.

75. See the Foreward to this volume.
76. Heidegger, "What is Metaphysics?" p. 110, citing Hegel, *Science of Logic*, trans. W.H. Johnston and L.G. Struthers, 2 vols. (London: George Allen & Unwin, and New York: Macmillan, 1929), I, 95 (original in *Werke*, III, 78).
77. Heidegger, *"Nachwort zu: 'Was ist Metaphysik?'* " in *Wegmarken* (Frankfurt: Vittorio Klosterman, 1976), p. 304 (p. 100 in 1st ed.), Eng. trans., Martin Heidegger, *Existence and Being*, trans. Werner Brock (Chicago: Regnery-Gateway, 1949), p. 351.
78. Rahner, GW 130/184 (193).
79. See Heidegger, *Logik* (see Ch. III, n.29), p. 199 and SZ 19/49.
80. Heidegger, *Metaphysische Anfangsgründe*, p. 252, *Metaphysical Foundations*, 195f.
81. On *"phänomenologische Chronologie"* see Heidegger, *Logik*, p. 199.
82. Rahner, HW 81; dropped in the second edition and therefore in the English translation.
83. Some instances of possible confusion between *"absoluter"* and *"schlecht-hin"* are: GW 98/143 (154): "of being absolutely" in para. 2 translates *"des Seins schlechthin"*; 108/155 (166): "what is absolutely" in para. 2 translates *"das Absolutsein"*; 128/181 (190): "Absolute Being" in para. 2 translates *"absolutes Sein"*; 131/186 (195): "what is absolutely infinite" in para. 2 translates *"das schlechthin Unendliche."*
84. Rahner, HW 82/63 (83)
85. Rahner, GW 127-29/179-83 (189-92). (Prof. Metz has added the paragraph which, in the English, runs from p. 182 to p. 183. The concluding paragraph of the section is from the first edition.) The corresponding passages are HW 81-83, changed somewhat in the second edition, German 83-84, Eng. trans., 63-64.
86. Rahner, HW 82, first edition only.
87. Rahner, GW 128/181 (190): *Existenz;* HW 82/64 (84): *"geht auf Gott,"* changed in the second edition to: *"zielt auf—Gott."*
88. Rahner, GW 128f./181 (190).
89. Ibid., 131/186 (195), emphasis added.
90. Eliot, "East Coker," VI.
91. Heidegger, *Einführung in die Metaphysik*, p. 6, Eng. trans., p. 7.
92. Ibid.
93. Rahner, GW 132/187 (196).
94. On the first principles, GW 143-49/203-11 (210-12). On the three levels of abstraction, GW 132-42/188-202 (197-209). On the light imagery, GW 149-61/211-26 (219-32).
95. Rahner, GW 143/203 (211) and footnotes thereto.

96. Ibid., 146/207 (214).
97. The first line of proof: GW 136-38/192-96 (200-04). The second line of proof: GW 138-42/196-201 (204-09). Professor Metz has added the paragraphs which, in the English, extend from p. 201, paragraph 2, to the end of the section (German, second edition, pp. 208-09).
98. Heidegger treats of the *modus significandi* in *Die Kategorien- und Bedeutungslehre des Duns Scotus*, in *Frühe Schriften*, ed. Friedrich-Wilhelm von Herrmann, *Gesamtausgabe*, I, 1 (Frankfurt: Vittorio Klostermann, 1978), esp. Pt. II, *"Die Bedeutungslehre,"* pp. 303 et seq.
99. Rahner, GW 138/196 (204).
100. Ibid., 283, n./390, n. (389, n.). Cf. 155-56/219-20 (225 f.).
101. Ibid., 129 f./224 f. (231).
102. Heidegger, SZ, 325/372.
103. Ibid., 324/373.
104. Ibid., 325/373.
105. Ibid., 366/417.
106. See the title of HW, Pt. 3.
107. Karl Rahner, "Thomas Aquinas on the Incomprehensibility of God," lecture delivered at the University of Chicago, November 8, 1974, cited from the manuscript, p. 30.

CHAPTER VII

Human Bivalence as Conversion to the Phantasm

The question of the possibility of metaphysics has become the question of the unity of the human bivalence, here read as the unity of abstraction and conversion-to-the-phantasm. Seen in terms of knowledge, that bivalence is a tension between the self-exceeding that is registered in agent intellect and the worldly presence that is performed in possible intellect. And since man's knowledge expresses his beingness, that latter is revealed to be a tension of presence-to-the-other in receptive sensibility and presence-by-absence in spontaneous intellection. The "self-alienation" of sensibility is in fact man's only way of returning completely to his absential, kinetic degree of self-presence.

The danger is that this bivalence will fall apart into a dualism: man with himself (soul) and apart from himself (body), intellection accompanied by sensation, or sensation repeated at the level of intellection. But there can be no dualism if man is but one knower and not two, and if he can know only something universal about something material. We attempt to reserve man's fragile bivalence by saying that he is movement, but movement remains the most difficult phenomenon that Western thought has ever tried to conceive. Philosophy usually loses the phenomenon by either reducing it to its unifying goal or denying the goal in favor of an irrational becoming which never comes to be anything. But these options are two sides of the same devalued coin: the loss of the essence of movement.

Although we cannot finally decide what human *kinēsis* is until we have investigated the problematic of possible intellect and sensibilization, we can begin with some formal indicators. To say that man is movement is to affirm that he is a directionality which already "has" its goal (*en-tel-echeia*) but in imperfect possesion (*a-telēs*). He is a "unity" which is ever coming towards its oneness (a uni-fication, a *Zukommen*), a potentiality always on the way to a receding term which has already

but incompletely appropriated that potentiality. In brief, man is becoming what he already is. He is a twofold self-absence which carries
within itself its own therapy insofar as absence *qua* otheredness (receptivity of the sensible) nurtures absence *qua* selfhood by turning man to
the world for fulfillment. Is this therapy worse than the disease? Lest
our formula seem to cure becoming at the expense of becoming, we
must stress that, if man is authentically to be what in fact he is, if he is to
become his becoming and not reduce it to being, then he must abandon
the dream of undoing his movement by actualizing its potentiality and
instead must cultivate his becoming *as* becoming. The therapy pre-
scribes that he personally assume the task of generating (*zeitigen*)[1] his
becoming by enriching his otheredness, on the premise that this authentic temporality (*Zeitlichkeit*) contains whatever measure of selfhood
man is allotted.

   And in Rahner the therapy entails the *generation of sensibility*
whereby man's "alienation" and his becoming are confirmed rather
than overcome. If man is not a mind in a mammal, living on the promise
of liberation from animality, then the active intellect can never swallow
up or banish possible intellect, spirit can never leave the world. Rather,
possible intellect must be cultivated as the production of the sensibility
in and through which man becomes himself. More precisely, the task is
to find the midpoint where man lives between the pure luminosity of
full self-actualization and the abyssmal dark of absolute fragmentation.
The first edition of Kant's KRV found this unifying center in the transcendental imagination, and Heidegger, as we have seen, discovered it
in primordial temporality. Rahner locates it in Scholasticism's "cogitative sense."

   The present chapter will show, from within Scholasticism, what that
midpoint is and how it makes sense knowledge possible. First we study
spirit's sensibilization, its generation of its own worldliness. Second, we
follow Rahner's difficult excursus on the relation of activity and passivity in inner-worldly, efficient causality. This will allow us, third, to
broach the question of sensibility and the intelligible species.

A. SENSIBILIZATION

1. Being the World: The Necessity and the Possibility

   Rahner makes an important distinction at the beginning of his treatment of possible intellect. Throughout his metaphysics of knowledge he
has followed the Scholastic paradigm of coming to know essences from
acts, specifically the essence of the "soul" from its cognitive perfor-

mances. From what we have seen so far, the essence of man is the bi-valent unity which is expressed in agent intellect as excess towards beingness and in possible intellect as conversion to the phantasm. The essence of man, then, is "spirit which of itself exists in potency to be ac-tually present to itself,"[2] and Rahner can therefore simplify matters by referring to the essence of man as "possibility" or "possible intellect." This *broad* sense of possible intellect is, of course, to be kept clearly dis-tinct from the same term when used of that structural faculty of human cognition whereby man turns to the phantasm. "Therefore, when we speak of the possible intellect in what follows," he writes, "it is meant as a totality in which the substantial ground [of the soul] lets the intellect (possible and agent) flow from itself as its potency.... We are only ask-ing about the relationship of the (possible) intellect, understood in this broader sense, to sensibility."[3]

This distinction is legitimate and enlightening, especially insofar as its stresses the kinetic nature of man. "The human spirit is desire, striv-ing, action [*Begierde, Streben, Handlung*]. For in itself it is *possible* in-tellect [in the broader sense], that is, something which reaches its full actuality from its potentiality.... Hence, being appetite in itself, the in-tellect is in movement towards its end and goal...."[4]

However, in our own exposition of Rahner, we shall *not* follow his us-age but shall use the term "possible intellect" only in the narrower sense. Not only does this better accord with normal usage, but in fact it will al-low us to emphasize what Rahner wishes to convey, by using terms like movement, *kinēsis*, and even "temporality" for the pres-ab-sential es-sence of man. The point is this: Man is the being that is ever unifying it-self into its unity (Metz glosses: *sich zu seiner Einheit selbst einigendes Wesen*)[5] and that, in becoming itself, must generate and hold unto itself that which is distinct from itself. This "other" is man's own bodiliness, first of all in its ontological modality. The prior moment of becoming what one already is (pres-ab-sence) necessarily generates the possibility of presence to worldly beings. Man is a self-becoming (*dieses Zu-sich-selber-kommen*) only by receptively encountering material beings (*in dem hinnehmenden Sichbegegnenlassen eines anderen*).[6] The unity of these two moments—the spirituality of sensibility or the sensibility of spirit—is the "cogitative sense" as conversion to the phantasm.

"Sensibilization" is a word that Rahner borrows from Heidegger's *Kant and the Problem of Metaphysics*. There, on the premise that the Kantian problematic of synthetic *a priori* judgments is one of ontologi-cal cognition, i.e., knowledge of the beingness of beings, Heidegger de-lineates the five-stage progression of the Transcendental Aesthetic and the Transcendental Analytic of KRV. First, he sorts out the essential elements of pure knowledge: pure intuition and pure thought. Secondly, he shows that the unity of ontological knowledge (the ontological synthesis of pure thought and pure intuition) happens in the transcendental imagination through the categories. The third stage of Heidegger's analysis moves from the fact of ontological synthesis to its possibility. The issue is still the transcendental imagination, but now its possibility as unifying unifier is shown by the two transcendental deductions in the first and second editions of KRV. Once the fact and the possibility of the transcendental imagination have been shown, the fourth stage seeks the *condition* of that possibility, i.e., the ground on which it stands and functions. If the transcendental imagination is the possibility of transcendence or excess towards the beingness or beings, the condition of that possibility is the schematism as the sensibilization (*Versinnlichung*) of pure concepts, i.e., the "procedure of imagination in providing an image for a concept" (A 140/B 179 f.). If a schema is a rule whereby a many can be brought to a unity, and if schematism is a kind of sensibilization, then pure or transcendental schematism provides concepts with *a priori* determinations of the pure "inner" intuition of time. In so doing, schematism as the internal structure or condition of possibility of the transcendental imagination constitutes ontological synthesis *qua* transcendence towards the beingness of beings. The fifth stage shows that this "temporalized" transcendence forms the horizon for the possibility of general metaphysics.

Even from this brief sketch we can see the parallel steps that GW takes. The premise is the same: an investigation of judgment as an ontological performance, by a hermeneutic of its conditions of possibility. And the central issue is the same: the unifying center of sensible receptivity and intellectual spontaneity, the spiritualization of sensibility or the sensibilization of spirit. And finally the up-shot is the same: Transcendence towards the beingness of beings is rooted in the primordial movement ("temporality") whereby self-becoming generates the possibility of worldly encounter. It seems that Heidegger's retrieval of the unsaid in Kant is guiding Rahner's retrieval of the unsaid in Aquinas, even if the steps and the language are different. We may sort out Rahner's reading of the necessity and possibility of the sensibilization of spirit by once again taking a look at agent and possible intellect.

Agent intellect as excess towards the beingness of beings indicates the unique form of kinetic self-subsistence that is man. This is not the stability of a Cartesian subject but the self-unification of a moving potentiality which opens up the sphere of intelligibility within which material things can and must be encountered as intelligible. Man is the power to make all things intelligible (*quo est omnia facere*)—in the light-imagery, the luminosity which illuminates phantasms. But that means that the range of intelligibility covered by the movement of agent intellect is the same as the range of worldly encounterability. And for Rahner this latter is covered by the possible intellect (*quo est omnia fieri*), which is man's power to become, in sensibility, all the beings rendered intelligible by agent intellect. The agent and possible intellects are therefore distinct but complementary, indeed co-extensive. The breadth of the "reaching-towards" (*die zugreifende Weite*) of excess is equal to the scope of what can be intelligibly received (*die empfangende Weite*) in worldly access.[7] Reach and receptivity—for Heidegger, projection and thrownness—measure the scope of the finite clearing of intelligibility. As regards the "receptivity," whatever beings I encounter will always be met in their intelligibility. As regards the "reach," I must have always already anticipated the intelligibility of whatever beings I may meet. Translated back from the essence of cognition to the essence of man, this formulation reveals primordial "temporality": I open the clearing of intelligibility because I am always coming towards (*Zukünftigkeit*) what I already am towards (*Gewesenheit*), and thus I render possible worldly encounter (*Gegenwärtigen*).[8]

Kinetic spirit, therefore, generates not only its excess towards intelligible beingness but equally its own possibility of material receptivity: sensibilization. If we remain for a moment within the parameters of the medieval cosmos, we could say that sensibilization is the specifically human characteristic of spirit. Because the angel is perfectly self-present, its proper object of knowledge is itself, and there can be no receptivity. Human self-presence, however, remains kinetic and therefore is achieved through the other. Man is the midpoint between the angelic separated form and the form that is exhausted in material determinations. Man is "that being which is present to itself in the knowledge of the other."[9] But the point is that man's otheredness or necessary state of receptivity is not due to the fact that he has a body that bumps up against other bodies. Indeed, it is just the reverse. The *a priori* generation of sensibilization—necessitated by the pres-ab-sential nature of his spirit—is what issues in man's body and allows sense knowledge.

To that extent, and only to that extent, Thomas compares [the human soul] with prime matter and calls it a "clean slate." Not as though, like prime matter, it were completely indeterminate in itself and received every determination only from another and absolutely passively. It really apprehends itself in every act of knowing; and what is really intelligible is its own light [movement] which it imparts to its objects actively and spontaneously, so that all of this is not given to it from without. Nonetheless it does apprehend all this only insofar as a sensible object of itself can and must manifest itself to it, for the intellect of itself is only in potency to apprehend itself: it is possible intellect [in the broad sense of "kinetic spirit"].[10]

Although human spirit can be itself only by becoming sensibility (*das Sinnlichwerden*), its sensibilization is not imposed from without but generated from within. The fact of this necessity—we leave aside for a moment its possibility—can be seen in Aquinas' position on the relation of soul and body. Thomas usually approaches the unity of body and soul from the viewpoint of man's spirit as the act of matter. As the *de facto* subject of sensible activity, man needs corporeal organs in order to be complete (cf. C.G., II, 68 *ad fin.*). "Insofar as [the soul] acquires immaterial knowledge from material knowledge, it is clear that it cannot be complete in its kind without a union with the body" (*In De Anima* 1, c.). Not only is the soul united *de facto* with the body, but it even has a transcendentally appropriate (*conveniens*) union with corporeality. If the degree of beingness (hence, self-presence) determines whether and to what degree a being requires a potentiality in which to fulfill itself, man as potentially intellective needs a body for self-presence and knowledge, and indeed "must produce this [body] of itself by way of formal causality. . . as the intellect's own realization of its essence."[11]

But if Aquinas establishes the *necessity* of sensibility from the very nature of man's kinetic spirit, he does not specifically show the *possibility* of sensibilization, and here Rahner's retrieval, now guided by Heidegger's work on Kant, once more comes into play. Drawing on the Thomistic discussion of *resultatio* ("emanation"), Rahner brilliantly elaborates a position on the possibility of *a priori* sensibilization, the generation of sensibility in man, even though he admits that "this kind of production of one's own being can only with difficulty be comprehended within the usual categories commonly used in Thomas."[12]

Rahner defines this kind of generation in general as "the unfolding of a being from its central point into the plurality of its powers"[13] and as "the metaphysical constitution of a being through the origin of its powers from its substantial ground and from one another. . . ."[14] It is a question neither of the cause-effect relation in which one finished being produces another, nor of a subsequent union of independent powers. Rather, self-generation refers to the constitution of a single being in its unity, an emergence of plurality from out of a single origin (in Aquinas: *origo, fluere, resultatio, emanatio*) so that a being comes to itself (*das Zu-ende-kommen; ad completionem subjecti*).[15] Although Aquinas does not adequately clarify the distinction between self-generation and efficient causality, Rahner says that in the former the productive and receptive principles are identical such that the origin "receives in itself what emanates as its fulfillment. . . ."[16] Moreover, such generation is not an event which happens once "at the beginning" and then is finished.

"Rather, the powers are held constantly in this relationship of emanation from the substantial ground and from one another"; indeed: "The human spirit exists permanently in letting its powers emanate and only in this way."[17]

Most importantly, Rahner calls this generation "motion in the broader sense."[18] As if to parade the connection with Heidegger, Rahner appropriates (correctly) a term from *Being and Time* to define the general concept of motion: "There is motion and time only when there is a stretching-forth-of-self [*Sichvorstrecken*] towards something in such a way that this stretching-forth-of-self primarily grounds the momentary 'state.' "[19] For Heidegger, the "stretching-ahead" (*Erstreckung*) of Dasein is a characteristic of its primordial temporality and has nothing to do with the natural motion of mere things. He calls it the "temporal happening" (*das Geschehen*) of Dasein, understood as Dasein's stretching itself ahead insofar as it is already stretched out ahead (*das erstreckte Sicherstrecken*).[20] We recognize here the structure of becoming what one already is.

In the present context Rahner says that "motion takes place in each of its partial movements by the fact that the moving thing anticipates the outermost term of the movement and thus in this anticipation always already bears the term within itself."[21] This means that emanation holds within itself the lesser or intermediate moments of the generation by reaching out to the more perfect term. If we take this a step further than Rahner does, we could say that sensibilization—as the *a priori* generation of the possibility of rendering material beings present (*Gegenwärtigen*)—is a continuation of the movement of excessive presab-sence (*Zukünftigkeit, Gewesenheit*). In Rahner's language, intellect in the broad sense of kinetic spirit is the source which from out of itself generates sensibility, while sensibility is the receptive origin of kinetic spirit. The "prior" movement of agent intellect (becoming what one already is) and, within that, the movement of generating sensibility (as the ability to render beings present) "can be understood only as partial movements of the one movement of the metaphysical self-realization of the one human spirit."[22] Moreover, just as in Heidegger the moment of "futurity" (*becoming* what one already is) has priority in the generation of original temporality ("Temporality is generated primarily out of the future"[23]), so too in Rahner, self-becoming (here: intellect) keeps primacy. "Wherefore, the one movement is directed towards the final goal of its constitution, hence to that which is more perfect in it. For Thomas this is the intellect"[24] meant as "the complete potentiality for being-present-to-itself."[25] This is what gives orientation and consistency to the whole emanation. Insofar as this presence-to-self has its origin in its mere potentiality (possible intellect [in the broad sense of kinetic spirit]), it can constitute itself as complete potentiality only in that, in striving towards the intellect, the substantial ground produces originally a power for the receptive intuition of another, a sensibility.[26]

Without calling it by Heidegger's names, Rahner has found the unifying center of human bivalence—what he will later designate as cogitative sense—to be the same that Heidegger retrieved from Kant: "temporalized" transcendence. He now proceeds to show that the temporal generation of sensibility from an intrinsically temporal spirit is already the realized conversion to the phantasm.

2. Sensibilization as Cogitative Sense

Rahner proceeds in three steps. First he states his thesis about the nature and function of cogitative sense as the unity of human bivalence. Secondly, he shows by a transcendental deduction that sensibilization is the condition of the possibility of cogitative sense as the unity of abstraction and conversion to the phantasm. And finally he focuses on cogitative sense itself in a "review and verification"[27] that ties together the whole treatment.

We recognize here a progression that parallels Heidegger's own in *Kant and the Problem of Metaphysics* (cf. the previous section). (1) Rahner's first step parallels Heidegger's second stage: Heidegger interpreted the Kantian *transcendental imagination* as a hypothesis that explains the ontological synthesis of pure thought and pure intuition, while Rahner posits the *cogitative sense* as the point of identity of abstraction and conversion to the phantasm. (2) Rahner's second step parallels Heidegger's third stage: Heidegger showed that by the double deduction Kant demonstrated the transcendental imagination as the possibility of the ontological synthesis, whereas Rahner shows that the kinetic spirit's desire for absolute beingness renders both possible and necessary the spirit's own sensibilization as the basis for acts of judgment. (3) Finally, Rahner's third step parallels Heidegger's fourth stage: For Heidegger it was the Kantian *Urteilskraft*, and for Rahner it is the *cogitativa*, that is the sensible power of spirit.

Step One: The Thesis. The terms "sensibilization of spirit" and "spiritualization of sense" point to one center. Sensibility is not primarily an *a posteriori* reception from without but an *a priori* generation, by spirit, of an emptily but nonetheless already possessed world. "If this sensibility appears now as emanating from the spirit, if it is shown to be produced by the spirit as its active principle, then this means likewise that the spirit already and always has in itself its possession-of-the-world as produced by it."[28] Equally, if sensibility always stands under the law of its origin, then it always brings intellect with it and is a certain—deficient, but real and not analogical—participation in intellection. "Thus, sensibility is the power of intuition of the spirit itself in its specifically human form."[29]

Conversion to the phantasm, we have said, means knowing the intelligible universal only in the sensibly known; it is already, then, the sensibilization of spirit and the origin of sensibility. But the intelligibly knowable is only the agent intellect in its *a priori* movement, which becomes known as the "intelligible form" of the sensibly given. Therefore, the conversion to the phantasm is itself the "illumination" or "abstraction" of the sensibly known, that is, its incorporation into the clearing of intelligibility opened up by agent intellect. Abstraction and conversion to the phantasm are thus intrinsic and inseparable moments in a single process. The conversion to the phantasm is the agent intellect's illumination or intelligible informing (*Durchformung*) of the sensible, at once prior to and coincident with abstraction. By "seeing the intelligible species [the universal] *in* the phantasm" (S.T. I, 86 1, c.), the conversion is prior to the "first apprehension." Yet by apprehending the individual as a *limited* instance of the universal within agent intellect's movement to absolute beingness, conversion coincides with abstraction.

But, so the thesis maintains, this coincidence *is cogitative sense.* In Aquinas, the "particular reason" or cogitative sense is unique to man (different, therefore, from the "estimative power" in animals) and "collates particular intentions" and "apprehends the individual under a particular nature. . . , knows this man as this man, and this wood as this wood."[30] The cogitative sense does not provide more sense knowledge (information that eluded the five senses and the common sense) but rather a different kind of knowledge—in the words of one commentator, "the unity of the sensible thing, a unity that is no longer merely local and temporal. . . but is ontological and existential. . . ."[31]

For Rahner, the cogitative sense is the unified center of spirit and sensibility. As a sense power it is the "particular reason" which grasps particular, individual intentions, while on the other hand "it is the point where spirit breaks through into sensibility, or better said, the first emanation from spirit to sensibility."[32] As a continuation of spirit into sense, it sees the individual in its common nature and thus "offers [for intellection] an already differentiated unity of the individual as such and the universal. . . ."[33] Thereby it makes the sensible "more powerful" (*virtuosior*) and "suitable" (*habilia*) for intellection—these being but other terms for abstraction.[34] The intellect, of and by itself, cannot know the material individual, but as cogitative sense it *can* know the individual, although not in its undifferentiated individuality, that is, not *as* an individual apart from the universal. In cogitative sense, as Aquinas puts it, "the mind. . .mingles with individuals" (*De Veritate*, 10, 5, c.). Rahner comments, "Hence, when Thomas says that the intellect knows the individual with the help of the cogitative sense, that can be meant only in this way: that in the cogitative sense the individuality and the common nature are given in a differentiated unity for the intellect, which keeps the cogitative sense with itself as *its* power and by that very fact always knows what is given in it."[35]

Rahner summarizes his thesis that cogitative sense is both abstractive illumination of and conversion to the phantasm. It "is not merely a turning of the spirit to sensibility which is logically prior to the actual knowledge of the universal and makes it possible, but is precisely that movement of the spirit in which the sensible content is informed, as it were, by the *a priori* structure of the spirit, by its 'light'—that is, is seen within the beingness as such which the spirit anticipates, and is thereby known in its universality."[36]

Step Two: The Deduction. Rahner proceeds now not from texts in Aquinas but from a transcendental analysis of the kinetic nature of human spirit. For one thing, Aquinas did not explicity show the derivation of abstractive conversation to the phantasm from the sensibilization of spirit, even if his texts on the phantasm as instrumental cause and on abstraction as preparation of the phantasm can be interpreted in this direction.[37] Rather, following the transcendental procedure of deducing powers from acts, Rahner will attempt to show that the original unifying unity (*ursprüngliche Einheit*[38]) of sense and spirit grounds the possibility of agent and possible intellect. So far we have seen that the nature of human spirit requires (i.e., constitutes itself in and fulfills itself by) the production of sensibility from out of itself. But Rahner has also posed the thesis that conversion to the phantasm is identical with abstraction. The point of the deduction is to use the first point to illuminate the second, to show that the emanation of sensibility from spirit (sensibilization) *is* the ground of the unity of abstraction and conversion (cogitative sense). We may be brief, for the procedure is simply a matter of drawing conclusions from what has already been seen.

The range of agent intellect, we have said, is co-extensive with that of possible intellect. As an anticipation of the intelligibility of all that is, man is likewise a dynamic orientation to the totality of intelligible beings. It is from this fact that Rahner will grasp emanation as the ground of cogitative sense. All operations of the spirit—including, pre-eminently, sensibilization—are moments in spirit's movement-towards-beingness, the movement that clears the realm of intelligibility. If in striving towards its own fulfillment spirit necessarily generates, bears, and informs sensibility, then it likewise incorporates sensibility into its movement. In so doing it knowns a priori whatever may be given in sensibility as something already standing within the scope of intelligibility. In other words, spirit's very movement, insofar as it must and does generate sensibility, is abstraction. In that sense, sensibilization itself is the ground of abstraction. And insofar as the anticipation must retain sensibility, spirit's movement is likewise conversion to the phantasm. In that sense, the sensibilization of spirit is also the condition of the possibility of conversion.

> Insofar as the spirit is the origin that lets sensibility emanate, the sensibly known is always already *abstracted*, since it is apprehended within beingness as such towards which the spirit is tending in the production of sensibility. Insofar as sensibility is the receptive origin of the spirit, a conversion to the phantasm is always already accomplished, since beingness in its totality is had only in a sentient, intuitive possession of the world.[39]

The generation of sensibility is spirit's production of its own otheredness as a priori possibility of the worldly encounter it needs. And the worldliness it generates is always within spirit's openness for beingness in totality. "The world is already open in principle, and in fact opened by the spirit for itself," and "the spirit-produced world as sensibly open already and always stands in the spiritual openness of beingness in its totality." Moreover, insofar as any given act of sensation always participates in the anticipation of beingness which produced it, "the act of sensibility is itself a moment in an act of the anticipation of beingness, and so its object is always abstracted already."[40]

Rahner draws the conclusion of his deduction: "The emanation of sensibility from the spirit is the decisive conversion to the phantasm, and insofar as this generation takes place in an anticipatory desire for beingness as such, this conversion to the phantasm is already and always essentially abstraction, the illumination of the phantasm by the light of the agent intellect."[41] And if cogitative sense is the unity of abstraction and conversion, then sensibilization is the condition of its possibility.

Step Three: Review and Verification. Cogitative sense as the manifestation of spirit in sense, as the center of spirit and sense, is the place of the abstractive conversion to the phantasm, what Heidegger would call the *Da* or "there" (Rahner says, the *Ort*[42]) of beingness. Cogitative sense *is* the conversion to the phantasm, the "place" where spirit is turned to sensibility and sensibility is held in spirit. Without cogitative sense, man knows nothing. As "the continuation of spirit in sensibility," cogitative sense receives unto itself all of Thomas' terms for intellection (*ratio, dividere et componere, inquirendo et conferendo*, and so on). It already is all that human intellection is: the knowing of something universal about something material "in an already differentiated unity."[43] Yet it is called a sense power because the universal nature is always and only given there with the individual. In fact, cogitative sense and imagination are two names for one thing, and although Aquinas distinguishes them as two powers, Rahner leaves it an open question whether this distinction "is really demanded by the inner dynamism of the Thomistic metaphysics of knowledge, or is more a piece of tradition handed on uncritically."[44] Rahner also merges the common sense with imagination and cogitative sense into "internal sensibility," which he says would be better called "the imaginative power of the spirit." Moreover, Rahner ratifies Edith Stein's translation of *ratio particularis* as *Urteilskraft*, "the power to think of the particular as contained under the universal..., the power of judgment as the power to synthesize the universal *a priori* of the spirit with the *a posteriori* sensibly given...."[45]

If the above reveals the dominating presence of Heidegger's Kant book in the analyses of GW, so too does Rahner's elaboration of the unifying center of man as "freedom." Drawing upon Heidegger's *Vom Wesen des Grundes* (1929), Rahner argues that "the possibility of abstraction and the complete return is grounded in the freedom of spirit."[46] Granted that spirit must become otherness in sensibilization in order to know the other, spirit likewise produces otherness only in striving towards itself. In that sense spirit has always surpassed the other—and thus the spatio-temporal world—in anticipating beingness as such, even if it can never withdraw from that world. "Thus the spirit remains free as it lets itself emanate into sensibility," and "insofar as it lets sensibility emanate, spirit has always already transcended the breadth of sensibility." Even when Rahner calls spirit "a form of matter which is subsistent in itself," we know that its self-subsistence remains kinetic, a "desire for beingness as such, which desire it itself is." "It produces this being-other in its striving-towards-itself." Man as freedom remains in the world and, in an ontological sense, temporal.[47]

B. INNER-WORDLY EFFICIENT CAUSALITY

The last three sections (§§ 8, 9, 10) of Rahner's chapter on the conversion to the phantasm pose a particular problem for interpretation. In the first place, they offer the very thickest analyses in his treatise, and here, more than anywhere else in GW, one has the impression of riding a bicycle through sand dunes. Yet one's efforts are richly repaid, not so much with more material beyond what we have already seen, as with a deeper confirmation of that material from other aspects of Thomistic metaphysics. Secondly, the analyses are among the most "Scholastic" of the book—for example, the self-contained essay on inner-worldly efficient causality in § 9. And yet what might appear to be a medieval analysis of the Rube Goldberg mechanisms whereby agents influence and patients suffer, turns out to be a remarkable reinterpretation of the doctrine of causality in terms of a metaphysics of intentionality, homologous with Heidegger's treatment of the doctrine of schematism and image in his Kant book. Finally, although the analyses come at the end of the treatment of conversion to the phantasm, they stand in fact at the service of the question of sensibility, which Rahner treated two chapters previously. It is for this reason that I have reserved all treatment of sensibility for these later paragraphs.

Sections 8–10 may be delineated roughly as follows. The first section simply gives the state of the question of intelligible species by locating it within the broader problematic of "determination from without" or inner-wordly efficient causality (transient causality). The second section—for this reader, as thick as molasses—is an almost independent treatise on such causality, but in the modality of a retrieval which Rahner time and again admits "can only with difficulty be comprehended within the usual categories commonly used in Thomas."[48] The third section supplies the results of the second section to the problematic of intelligible species and to "those questions which were left unsettled in the first section of the chapter on sensibility." As a whole, the three sections "offer the opportunity to summarize and review what our investigations have shown to be the Thomistic doctrine of the conversion of the intellect to the phantasm."[49]

My own exposition of all of this will, for now, focus on only the first two sections (§ 8 and 9) of Rahner's chapter on the conversion to the phantasm. The application of these analyses to the questions of sensibility and the intelligible species I reserve for the concluding division of this chapter, where I will incorporate the analyses that Rahner presents in his chapter on sensibility. Moreover, in this present division of the chapter I put the major emphasis on Rahner's reinterpretation of the doctrine of causality as a metaphysics of intentionality. We begin, then, with a brief statement of the *status quaestionis*.

1. Contextualizing the Problematic of Intelligible Species

We already have a preliminary notion of what the intelligible species *is not*: an "object" (*id quod*) which the intellect could inspect without returning to the phantasm, an "image" of the sensible thing, a "movie in the monastery of the mind" (cf. above, the first and second objections in S.T. I, 84, 7). As to what in fact it *is*, we may begin with some formal indicators. It is not an *id quod* but an *id quo*, a means by which intellection is performed. Specifically it is "the conscious ontological determination of the knower himself, one which, along with being that, shows itself to be the ontological determination of the known other object."[50] Already, then, we have staked out the area of this problematic: the phenomenological correlativity of *noēsis* and *noēma*, intellect and intelligible object.

But that formal indication also poses a problem for understanding the intelligible species, and we may state the problem in a number of ways. First, in terms of apriority and aposteriority, "the question arises how the species can be both at once: a creation of the spontaneous activity of the spirit and yet of such a nature that as such it can manifest the external object as passively received."[51] On the one hand, the intelligible species is a passively received, concrete determination of the intellect to a particular object received *ab extra*. On the other hand, it is produced by the spontaneous excess of the intellect in its freedom from sensibility and the phantasm, and thus expresses the law of spirit's active *a priori* structure. Even if we leave aside the Thomistic problem of how the intelligible species remains "habitually" in the possible intellect after actual thought, there remains the problem of the relation of the intelligible species to the phantasm.

Rahner sharpens that problem in two ways. Just as Aquinas compares the intelligible species to the phantasm as form to matter, so he does the same for the relationship of agent intellect and phantasm. Thus the intelligible species would seem to be the agent intellect, or more broadly, "the actualization of intellectual knowledge as such"[52] (*intellectus fit in actu per speciem intelligibilem qua informatur*). But if the intelligible species would then be the illumination or information of the phantasm, it is at the same time and in a fundamental sense the possible intellect, that which produces sensibility "not merely as a general, empty power, but in its concrete determinateness in each instance" so that "the spirit 'suffers' a determination which goes beyond the producing of sensibility in general."[53] The problematic is sharpened, therefore, by placing intelligible species in the context of the passive and active nature of the intellect itself. And there is a further sharpening: If it can be shown, as Rahner does in some detail,[54] that the soul is the actuality of *all* its material determinations, both its corporeality and any incidental determinations which accrue to that body, then the soul actively produces each particular instance of sensible affectation even though it receives such impressions from without. But then "how can the determinateness of a being from without (the material element) be actively produced by the receiver from within, and thus be the formal element?"[55]

These difficulties can be stated both in the framework of a realistic metaphysics and in the transcendental context of a metaphysics of knowledge. In the former the problem is to reconcile the soul as the form of the body and the cause of all its material determinations (i.e., the soul as the essential ground of the whole man) with the issue of accidental determinations received from without (i.e., the accidental affects of the body). In the transcendental metaphysics of knowledge the problem is how the intelligible species can be both the creation of the active, spontaneous spirit and the manifestation of a passively received object. Rahner, of course, takes up the second way of stating the problem, on the premise that realistic ontological concepts can be gained only in correlativity with their corresponding concepts in a metaphysics of knowledge.[56] But the step towards solving the problem of intelligible species is, in section 9, a realist treatment of inner-worldly efficient causality, the problem of how one separately existing entity can produce new determinations in another separate entity without the second entity being rendered totally passive. Rahner will discover an active self-production of passively received determinations and thus will have a paradigm for solving the paradoxical nature of intelligible species.

2. An Ontology of Inner-Worldly Efficient Causality

Rahner moves now through a series of complex, interconnected steps, the crucial ones being the first: the various ways (specifically: as emanating and received) that an influence can be in the receiver or patient.[57]

The Kinds of Agency. The first and foundational task is to clarify the arena of agency. Rahner proceeds by way of a textual analysis of seemingly conflicting descriptions of agency in Aquinas.[58] On the one hand, St. Thomas affirms, agency is in the agent (*Cum actio sit in agente et passio in patiente...* [*II Sent.*, 40, 1, 4, ad 1]), and on the other, agency is in the patient (*Actus activi et motivi fit in patiente et non in agente et movente* [*In III de Anima*, lect. 2, n. 592]). Rahner will now show that these two sets of statements are mutually inclusive. The chart on the following page may help to clarify the issue.

We can distinguish three modes of inherence of the agent's influence (*das Insein der Einwirkung*)[59] in the medium or matter of the patient, and they are indicated by the letters B, C, and D in the diagram below. The first two, B and C, indicate the inherence of the agent in the medium of the patient *during* the actual impression and change, whereas

AGENT APART FROM THE CHANGE	AGENT DURING THE CHANGE		
(A)	(B) Emanating, not-yet- received influence		
	(C) *Passio:* Received influence during the change	(D) *Qualitas Passibilis:* Received influence after the change	(E)
	PATIENT DURING THE CHANGE	PATIENT AFTER THE CHANGE	PATIENT APART FROM THE CHANGE

the third, D, indicates the agent's abiding influence after the actual impression and the change are over, that is, *after* the agent has withdrawn. If we leave B aside for a moment in order to focus on the patient, we can discern in both C and D, but most obviously in D, an active reception (*Übernahme*) of the impression by the patient according to the principle that the patient receives according to the mode of the patient. In D we clearly see an *active production* of the received determination on the part of the patient: The influence continues to be received, after the impression, as a connatural, more or less permanent quality or form of the patient. Thus the inherence is called an "undergone quality" (*qualitas passibilis*). Now in C, that is, during the change, such an active production is also at work, even if the on-going presence of the impression or inherence (B) tends to disguise it. Here in C, even though there is an active production operative, it is called simply an "undergoing" (*passio*). In both C and D the same principle is at work: Something (the agent) can determine something else (the patient) only if the form of the patient produces the determination. That is, each being is responsible for, or is the act of, all that it becomes. To be sure, this activity is more discernible in the "undergone quality" (D). Such a quality cannot become connatural to the patient if it is merely borne and "had" in the patient; rather, it must be actively produced by the patient from out of its own ontological ground. But likewise in the *passio* or "undergoing" (C) the active assumption of the influence does not occur *after* the influence of the agent, for an influence *is* influence only when it *is* assumed. In both cases, C and D, although the influence originates from without, the active effecting of the influence on the part of the patient (*die Erwirktheit der Einwirkung*), whereby the influence becomes the determination *of* the patient, is called the "reception" or "taking over" of the determination.[60]

But now the central problem emerges, and it has to do with the difference between B and C, agent and patient, during the change. We have distinguished a continuing reception of the influence (D), one which began during the impression and continued after it. And we have sorted out an active reception during the change (C). But Rahner wants to isolate an activity of the agent itself *in* the medium of the patient (B) yet considered *apart from* the active reception (C) on the part of the patient during the change. The reason, of course, is that when this paradigm is applied to knowledge, B and C will constitute the area of external perception, and Rahner wants to isolate two moments in the sensible species: the species as self-realization of the sensible object (B), and the species as the self-realization of sensibility itself (C). Even apart from the problem of cognition, the hypothesis of a distinction here will allow Rahner to explain the two sets of statements in which Aquinas discusses agency: the one which sees the influence residing in the agent (B), and the other which sees it as actively received by the patient (C).

In order to draw the distinction between B and C, Rahner resorts to a text of Aquinas that could easily confuse the reader. He adduces the passage for one purpose only: to illustrate that in Thomas (and in fact apart from Thomas' discussion of sense knowledge) a distinction *can* be made between B and C. Rahner is willing to admit that the content of the text—the specific instance of this differentiation—may not even be possible in nature or at least in contemporary physics. Hence, the text is trotted out simply to support Rahner's retrieval. It could as well have been left aside, and the point made without textual support. Be that as it may, the text allows Rahner to pose the limit case of an action of the agent which *inheres in* the patient without yet being *assumed by* the patient.

According to Thomas, colors expand from the colored body in the medium of the air. But the air undergoes no "natural mutation," the colors are not in the air, in the translucent medium "according to a natural *esse*," the color *non denominat aeram*: it is indeed in the air [B: inherence], but without being able to be predicated of it [i.e., not yet received], that is, without becoming even only a transitory ontological determination [a *passio*] of the air. But this denies the reception [C] of the color by the permeable medium. . . . Nevertheless, even here Thomas maintains that there is an inherence of the influence [B] of the colored body in the air.[61]

Here, apart from reception in the strict sense (C), we notice that the action of the agent expands in and remains in the medium of the patient in a *kind* of inherence. (Risking confusion, we note that this is also called "reception," but in the *broad* sense, which is to be distinguished from the proper reception *by* the patient). This inherence is logically prior to assumption in the strict sense whereby the agent's influence become a determination of the patient in C or D.

What can we say about this B, this unique form of inherence?[62] First, it is "in" the agent, belongs to the agent as its perfection or self-realization. Secondly, it can be an influence insofar as it is "in" the patient by expanding in its medium. Thirdly, the special mode of inhering in the patient without being strictly assumed by the patient—this unique way of being both in the agent and in the patient—is called by Rahner "emanating-not-yet-received influence" (or more exactly, we may say "prescinding from" reception rather than "not yet" received), and it belongs to every influence as such insofar as it is logically prior to the assumption whereby it becomes the ontological determination of the patient. Fourthly, this emanating not-yet-received influence corresponds to the first set of statements whereby Aquinas maintained that agency is in the agent. Fifthly, this kind of influence is what Aquinas calls *intentio, esse spiritualis*, and *receptio spiritualis*. It will correspond, as we see below, to one moment of the sensible species, viz., the self-realization of the sensible object. Sixthly, the import of all the above for the metaphysics of knowledge lies in the fact that we have distinguished (1) the external object of possible knowledge as existing independently of knowledge (A: the agent apart from effecting change) and (2) the object of knowledge *as known*, at which point it is "in" the knower (B) without yet becoming the ontological (received) determination of the knower (C). And (3) the area of overlap (B and C) is, for the purposes of sense knowledge, the realm of the common medium or neutral ground for both knower and known. This area must now be defined from both sides (emanating-not-yet-received influence and received influence) and from the common ground itself.

Emanating-not-yet-received Influence and the Self-realization of the Agent.[63] Here we take up one moment in efficient causality, the B-moment where emanating influence can be seen as distinct from its re-

ception as *passio* in the patient. In terms of knowledge we are talking
about the sensible species as the self-realization of the sensible object
(the agent) in the medium or potency of sensibility (the patient).

Insofar as the agent lets the influence emanate from its own ground,
that influence is the self-realization of the agent, a perfection of and
thus "in" the agent itself. But the reason for this emanation is precisely
the agent's deficiency in self-presence. The less a being is self-present
and the more it is othered, the less its self-produced activity can belong
to itself and the more it must be "lost in the other and an emanation
(*emanatio*) away from itself into the other."[64] Thus the agent realizes itself in the only interiority it has, the otherness it shares with the patient, the patient's matter. There it expands and maintains itself, indeed
in its full essence. "What is 'in' the patient is therefore the agent itself in
its completed essence, the emanation of the agent's own interiority, its
self-realization in that interiority which alone is possible to a being
which is exterior to itself."[65] The rule here is that in material beings, self-
realization of this sort can happen only by the agent expanding itself in
the matter of the other. This, moreover, is a particular case of, and
hence is reducible to, "intrinsic causality," the kind of causality whereby
a being constitutes itself. Specifically, as *actio qua perfectio agentis*, it is
a particular case of formal causality.

Let us now apply what we have said about the agent's self-realization
to the particular case of sensibility. The word "species," Rahner points
out, is not to be taken as indicating some kind of "intentional representation" of an object, as if (in a kind of critical realism) a "subjective" influence of the object is felt, and from it, somehow or other, the knower
infers and apprehends an external object. No, the species, as far as we
can define it heuristically at this point, is "the ontological ground of the
fact that a definite cognitive faculty apprehends a definite object of
knowledge."[66] And "sensible species" must be an actuality of the thing itself, something "in" the thing. This means that the thing itself projects
itself into the medium of sensibility (the "self-givenness" of the object).
Yet Aquinas does say that the sensible species is an "effect" of the object
and "represents" the object. Rahner takes this to mean that the sensible
species is not something static and always already "had" by the knowable object, but rather that it is different from the actuality of the object
"in itself" by being the actuality which the object *produces anew in sensibility* as a new self-production which influences the patient. In terms
of the diagram, this would be the difference between A and B.

Expansion of the Influence in the Matter of the Patient. [67] The operative
principle, we have seen, is that something can determine a being (the

patient) only if the patient produces that determination. Therefore, the
patient cannot be determined by something external to its own potentiality. Hence the determining influence must at one and the same time
be outside the patient (otherwise there would be no receptivity *ab extra*)
and "in" the patient (lest there be no relation to its potentiality). We
conclude: The determination must be the patient's *self*-determination in
a real principle of absolute indeterminacy belonging to the self-
constitution of the patient: prime matter. This is an absolutely passive
(thus, indeterminate) principle which is intrinsic to the patient. It is
purely receptive, never a *productive* bearer of a determination produced
by a form. Rather, the produced determination expands in this indeterminacy as its "wherein." And the agent's emanating influence can in-
here in this without yet (or prescinding from) being a determination of
the patient. All of this implies, of course, that the inner-worldly causality of one thing upon another is possible only if both are material. If
prime matter is the necessary "wherein" of the reception of inner-
worldly determinations, receptive knowledge of an object is essentially
sensibility. Man, therefore, has sense organs because he must know receptively, and not *vice versa*.

It remains to be asked why the emanating influence must, and how it
can, "expand" in the medium of the patient. The first question can be
answered briefly: The agent must expand in the matter of the patient
because of the agent's own ontological deficiency, its lack of full self-
presence. In answering *how* such expansion is possible Rahner provides a
more developed understanding of the nature of matter.[68]

Matter as the ground of the plurality of repeatable forms is both one
and many. Its oneness is not a numerical unity; hence it is not a oneness
that could be repeated. Rather, its oneness is a question of wholeness,
magnitude (*quantitas*) as such, which is the basis of the repeatability of
form. This *materia quantitate signata* is the original ground of both spatiality and (in the narrow sense) temporality, and thereby the ground of
concrete space and time. Quantity as such is not immediately space in
the sense of locality (*Ortlichkeit*), that is, a definite space relative to a
network of relations external to the spatial thing. Rather, the "intrinsic
spatiality" of quantity is what is responsible for the individual spaces of
material things. Although the issue is hardly explicated in Aquinas, the
same holds for temporality as a factor in individuation. *Quantitas per se*
can be articulated into spatiality (*quantitas dimensiva*) and temporality
(*quantitas successiva*), these in turn being the basis of individual spaces
and moments.[69] The whole of matter can be "divided" by forms into
many "whereins" of their instantiation, but not by dividing the unity of
matter itself. Material bodies thus have an intrinsic solidarity with one

another insofar as they are one in matter. The "division" of the whole of matter by individual actualizations always of itself leaves matter "untouched" as a potentiality for more forms, since, even when limited by a particular form, the specific matter has a potentiality for absolute quantity. Moreover, and of signal importance for sensibility, this potentiality of a specific matter for a "more," for absolute quantity, is the *real quantity of the other*. But this means that the self-realization of the agent, which can happen only by expansion in the matter of the patient, expands in the quantity of the patient, which in turn *is* the greater potentiality of that very agent.[70]

The Relation of the Self-determination of the Agent and of the Patient. [71] We now ask in what way the patient (which actively produces the determination it receives from without) needs the influence of the agent in order to so determine itself. We have seen that the negative infinity of form can have two meanings: form's ability to be repeated in many "whereins," and form's ability to produce many determinations of itself in essential and accidental emanation. In the second sense we can see a certain "positive indeterminateness" on the part of the form, always, of course, within the limits of its genus. That is to say, the form is not determined to this rather than to that accidental determination of itself; it is indifferent to one contrary determination vis-à-vis another. Form in fact is ordered to the *whole scope* of its possibilities, and only for that reason can it let the contrary determinations emanate and replace each other. As a corollary we note that no single realization can ever exhaust the whole range of possible realizations.

In the light of this "indifference," it becomes clear (1) how the patient requires an *external determination* of its potentiality to a definite possibility as over against another possibility, and (2) how, even in this act of being determined from without, the form of the patient remains free for yet further determinations. The accidental determinations which the patient's form receives from without do indeed emanate from the ground of the patient, but *the fact that they are thus and so* depends on outside agency. In this sense alone is the form of the patient "passive" to the outside agent. The role of the agent, then, is not to be the ground of the ontological unfolding of the patient, but only to determine which of the possible self-realizations of the patient is in fact to be realized in this case. The agent's role is to be the ground of the patient's being thus and so in a particular accidental self-realization. The agent, in short, is a *specification* of the patient's becoming, although not in such a way that the patient determines the *esse* of the accident while the agent determines its quiddity.[72]

But how can the agent's specification of the patient's self-realization avoid rendering the patient a purely passive and receptive being? How does the patient remain an active receiver? Rahner finds the answer in the area of the relationship of form and matter.[73] Matter does not produce an effect in form; rather, form "informs" matter by being its act. Yet this outpouring of form into the otherness of matter *"is* already essentially the [form's] being-determined by the matter, since the form of itself is nothing but the act of matter."[74] We can speak, then, of an activity of matter upon form, but only in the limited sense of determining the form "for its actualization of the potentialities of matter."[75]

Application of these principles to the case of the patient shows how the patient remains active and receptive at the same time. The self-realization of the agent in the matter of the patient specifies the matter and thus indirectly specifies the direction of the self-realization of the patient's form. In that sense the patient's form "undergoes" (suffers, is receptive of) the matter by actualizing itself as the ground *of this specificity* in the mode of formal causality.[76] Thus the determination of the patient from without is identical with the patient's own act from within as formal ground of its own self-production. This is not a reaction subsequent to a merely passively received influence but is the *active selfproduction* of the given determination specified by the external agent.[77]

This analysis also allows us to see how the emanating and received influences are related to each other in their respective intrinsic quiddities. Causality is not some merely quantitatively functional connection between cause and effect but rather always is of a qualitative and quidditative nature. How do the two self-realizations relate to each other?[78]

The agent's self-realization as the actuality of matter is possible only because the patient's matter already has a potency for the actualization of the agent. That is, the self-actualization of the matter was already produced by the patient's form, and the patient retains this potency permanently. The patient, so to speak, "holds out" to the agent the possibility in which it can realize itself.[79] Thus the patient can realize by itself only what coincides quidditatively—indeed is one flesh—with the agent's self-realization. "Therefore, the received and the emanating influences cannot be distinguished in their intrinsic quiddity, but only by the fact that the agent realizes this quiddity as its own in the matter of *another,* while the patient realizes the same quiddity as its own in its *own* potency borne by itself."[80] To act and to be acted upon, to move and to be moved, are the same, with the difference that the mover maintains itself in the moved, the agent in the patient.

Therefore, whereas up to now we have discussed the emanating and the received influences as quantitatively (numerically) different but qualitatively the same in the one medium, we now must ask: What is their relation during the undergoing of the impression? Can the same matter be medium for two qualitatively different forms?[81]

The agent and the patient subsist in the one matter of the patient. Therefore, one and the same actuality determines two different beings, agent and patient. "In the 'one' matter, in which everything material subsists, *every individual is already the other* because of its ground."[82] Thus there are two productions of the one actuality in the one potency of matter. Each, of course, has a different character, and thus they mutually condition each other. In the first place, they have different finalities. The patient's form always actualizes the received influence because only the patient's form is substantially united with this definite matter. The agent's form, on the other hand, realizes itself in the matter of the patient because it seeks a "wherein" in which to sustain its realization; that is, it reaches out to what it is not substantially united with. In the second place, they are mutually dependent. The agent depends on the matter of the patient for self-realization, and the matter of the patient depends on the patient's form. Therefore, the agent's self-realization depends on the fact that the patient's form actualizes the patient's matter. And during the impression the actualization of the patient's matter by its form is the agent's self-actualization. And the whole process can be read in the reverse. In the third place, despite the dual origin, what emanates from the two substantial grounds is one and the same actuality. "The influence is also strictly identical with what *emanates* from the productive substantial ground of the *patient* itself. . . ."[83]

Thus far, Rahner's sketch of an ontology of inner-wordly, efficient causality. As we now move towards applying all of this to the metaphysics of knowledge, we may begin to translate the above into the problematic of sensibility in the form of theses. (1) The knower, under the influence of an external object, produces its determination and thereby produces the self-realization of the sensible itself. (2) This self-realization of the sensible object participates in the ontological intensity of the knower, is therefore "reflected against" the knower, and thus is sensibly known by the knower. The sense knower (3) lets the self realization of the object arise in the knower's otherness, (4) knows the object's self-realization as other and not as "species," (5) does not co-perform or "re-realize" the origin which belongs to the object's self-realization as emanation from the object, (6) does not, therefore, grasp the actuality of the object as produced by the object, and therefore (7) grasps the actuality of the object as other than the knower.[84]

C. SENSIBILITY AND INTELLIGIBLE SPECIES

Rahner's exposition of causality provides us with the vantage point from which we can properly enter into the question of sensibility and, with that, resolve the paradoxes of the intelligible species. In what follows we synthesize §10 of his chapter on conversion to the phantasm with the second chapter of the body of his treatise, "Sensibility." Our treatment unfolds in three steps. First it is a matter of gaining a starting point for the notion of sensibility at all. Secondly, we shall apply the results of the investigation into causality to the question of sensible knowledge of the other. Here we shall bring together the relevant sections of the chapter on sensibility with paragraphs 1 to 3 of §10. Thirdly, we may see how Rahner resolves the problem of the intelligible species.

1. Towards an Ontological Concept of Sensibility[85]

The final goal of Rahner's efforts here is to show how and why sensibility is defined—ontologically and essentially, not merely descriptively—as "to receive after the mode of an intention" (*recipere ad modum intentionis*).[86] And because all receptivity is essentially sensible and material, this definition will hold "of any receptive knowledge as such at all."[87] Rahner is after a metaphysics and not a gnoseology of sensibility. He seeks an adequate *a priori* deduction of sensibility based on the fundamental presupposition of his entire work: the analogical identity of knowing and beingness. His claim is that only such a metaphysical approach can (1) establish the *a priori* activity of sensibility in knowledge, (2) show the relation between sensibility and its determinations in terms of immateriality and thus knowledge, and (3) as a consequence clarify the traditional metaphors which accrue to the sensible species.

In nailing down the point of departure for the concept of sensibility, Rahner poses this thesis: a non-creative, receptive knowledge which has its first and immediately (i.e., intuitively) apprehended object as something other than itself must be sensibility: Man is a sentient knower, essentially material, the act of matter or the form of the body.[88] The steps of the deduction show how this sensibility must be, in limited ways, both *a posteriori* or passive and *a priori* or active vis-à-vis the given material sense object. The activity is spelled out ultimately as the pure forms of intuition, which are grounded in the fact that man already emptily possesses the world through sensibilization. The overarching framework of the treatment is what we have called the "double absence" in man: the being-ahead-of-himself (*Sich-vorweg-sein*) of agent intellect and the being-away-from-himself-by-being-with-the-other (*Weg-von-sich-beim-*

andern-sein) of sensibility.[89] And we must show how and with what results the former is the condition of the latter.

In the framework of the analogical identity of knowing and being-ness, to know is to be present to oneself to some degree; and the first and proper object of knowledge remains oneself and specifically one's own intensity of beingness. A God of perfect self-coincidence would know the other precisely by knowing himself. A man, however, even if his cog-nitional object is finally himself, does in fact have the other as his first object. Yet even if it is an outside cause that increases man's intensity of beingness, i.e., brings him to more self-presence, nonetheless that in-creased intensity always gives man *himself*. This says that man must be so structured ontologically as to be *a priori* given over to otherness if he is to apprehend a concrete other thing. This otherness or state of being-the-other is *a priori* and not brought about by the fact that other beings elicit man's attention. Prior to empirical encounter with particu-lar other beings, man is *a priori* separated from himself (has entered otheredness). This is what Heidegger calls *Befindlichkeit* as *a priori* af-fectability. This absence is: a real constituent of the knower; not some-thing self-subsistent of and by itself but rather "real non-beingness"; and that whereby and wherein a being is "alienated" from itself. It is Scholasticism's prime matter. Self-presence in this particular form as being-with-otherness is the ontological condition for receptive mate-rial knowledge of the other: sensibility.

Sensibility may be defined dialectically from two sides. Positively, it is a midpoint between total abandonment to otherness and indepen-dence or assertion of form against matter. Negatively, it is neither total self-presence over against the other nor complete self-absence lost in the other. Likewise it is neither perception of its own affective states "within" nor perception of an unconnected world "without," for man's interiority *is* his exteriority and *vice versa*. In summary: If knowledge is self-presence and if man's only intuition (i.e., his first and immediate knowledge) is of material things, then he must be sensibility as self-absence in the direction of the other. And although we speak of a "dou-ble self-absence"—of spirit as movement towards beingness and of spirit as sensibility for the other—they are not separate but in fact confirm each other and ultimately are "the same." "The fact that spirit at the hu-man level of beingness must [as *excessus*] produce from itself sensibility as its own potency, different from itself, is, of course, the index of its on-tological weakness."[90] That does not mean that sensibility is a drag on perfect self-presence, as if, were it lopped off, man could "really" return to himself. Rather, it is man's only way of returning to his kinetic self, which ever remains a coming-to-himself. Sensibility is a reinforcement of the movement by which alone man is himself, and (if we could make this artificial distinction) his ontological weakness is primarily registered in his *excessus* and not in his sensibility. Sensibility is his therapy.

Central to the problematic of sensibility is the Thomistic species-concept. Popularizations run the risk of losing the original Aristotelian sense whereby the *eidos* (species) *is* the thing itself *as known* (the *eidos* is separable, therefore, only in man as *logos*). The usual popularizations turn it into a mental "double" of the object, a representation separate from the thing and possessed of only "mental existence." Here the Scholastic tendency towards hypostasizing concepts can undermine a proper understanding of sensibility. One commentator goes so far as to call the species "a creature of God, intended to expand the limited being of some of His creatures. . . ."[91] The result is what Rahner disparagingly calls "a 'critical realism,' according to which a 'subjective' influence of the external object is felt and from that, through inference or some other way, the external object is apprehended."[92] But neither can we reduce the essence of knowledge to a positivism whereby "an act produced by the knower . . . merely leaps out, as it were, to the 'in-itself' [*das Ansich*] of an object. . . ."[93]

Claiming, in effect, that Aquinas preserves the original Aristotelian sense of species, Rahner steers a middle course between "critical realism" and "positivism." On the one hand Rahner will hold to a species-concept, but without the Rube Goldberg mechanisms whereby objects leave wax impressions on (or transmit intentional photographs to) the senses. On the other hand Rahner will maintain that sensation does indeed attain the thing in itself ("Thomas is a 'naïve' realist if one wants to call his metaphysical realism that"[94]) but only on the basis of a species which the thing itself realizes in sensibility. The crux of the matter is to work out the species-concept in a way that preserves both the activity and the passivity of sensibility. For Rahner that entails an *ontology* of the species. It was for the sake of such an ontology that he took the detour through an ontology of inner-worldly efficient causality, with its emphasis on *passio* or "undergoing" as the activity of the patient, and on emanating-not-yet-received influence as the activity of the agent. Our task now is to apply those analyses more fully to the case of sensibility.

2. Sensibility and Knowledge of the Other

If Rahner will hold with Aquinas that sensation does attain the thing in itself, then two series of problems cluster around the role of the agent (the sensible object) in sensibility: problems with regard to the sensible species and problems with regard to the patient (the knowing sensibility). The first set: If the object itself is sensibly known, then doesn't the sensible species become superfluous? or a mere stimulus before sensation? or somehow a mental double (cf. *similitudo*) which would deny direct knowledge? And what does it mean to say that sentient knowing is "receiving a species without matter" (*suscipere speciem sine materia*[95])? Finally, what is the significance of Aquinas' distinction between the "impressed" species operative in sensibility and the "expressed" species that is not? The second series of problems concerns the assertion that the sensible object, which is "outside the soul" (*extra animam*[96]), becomes actually known "in" sensibility. What is this "inside" and "outside"? How can Thomas speak of the sensible species as an "effect" and a "representation" of the object "in" the senses and still hold to knowledge of the thing itself? The two series of problems, of course, coalesce, and they overlap with the question of the role of the patient's sensibility. But if we distinguish for a moment the sensed and sentient, we may initially approach these problems from the side of the object and apply here the results of the investigation into causality.

First, a clarification of expressed and impressed species. The Thomistic thesis that there is an impressed but not an expressed species in external sense perception is an assertion that the sensed object is grasped in its immediate, real self. In a general and preliminary statement, we noted that the species-concept stands for "the ontological ground of the fact that a definite cognitive faculty apprehends a definite object of knowledge."[97] Also in general, an "expressed" species brings a knower to consciousness of an object "which in its own self is not present in the knowing; therefore, neither is such an object intuited."[98] But an "impressed" species functions when knower and known are one in their own reality. Thus, "when an object is intuited, that is, when it is present in the knower in its own real beingness, there is no expressed species, thus neither in the beatific vision of God nor in sense intuition."[99] To say, then, that an impressed but not an expressed species is formed in sense preception is to affirm the "realism" of sensation and not to place some intentional double between the object and the knower. But this attainment of the object in itself is not to be taken in the general, undifferentiated sense that all knowledge (including that with an expressed species) attains what is the case. Here, rather, the object is immediately present and intuited. The sensible species is the self-givenness of the object, "an actuality of the thing itself," "something in the thing itself."[100] We recognize here what the analysis of causality called emanating-not-yet-received influence as a self-realization of the agent—on the diagram given above, the B-moment. The sensible species, we may say, is not a hypostasizable "thing" but a dynamic self-actualization of the agent. However, insofar as this self-actualization (*Selbstvollzug*), even if it can be distinguished from reception by the patient (the C-moment), nonetheless happens only "in" the medium of the patient, we are pushed into the second series of problems and the question of what this "in" might be.

If, from the side of the object, the sensible species is called an "effect," a "representation," and a "likeness" (*similitudo*), and if the emanating influence happens only in the medium of the patient, then we already have a clue that the species is a "new" self-realization of the agent insofar as the object "projects" itself into the medium of sensibility. It is not "a static determination which always belongs to the thing" in its A-moment, not "its already and always possessed static being."[101] Although the species—now understood dynamically—is no "image" of the object but is the object's very giving of itself, that self-givenness happens only as the agent's extension and realization of itself *in* the patient. But that "inside" is no private chamber over against the world: "The sensible object does not penetrate into the interior of sensibility, but sensibility . . . has already moved out into the exterior of the world. . . ."[102] The soul already *is* the world, even if only in empty anticipation, and in this sense alone is the sensible species—while remaining "in" the agent and thus in the real world—also "within the soul." When Aquinas speaks of the sensible object as "outside the soul," he means the agent in its A-moment, apart from any influence upon the patient. But even there the agent remains (in a sense we shall discuss below) "within" the soul in the soul's empty possession of worldliness as such.

The species-concept, as we have clarified it thus far, also explains two Thomistic formulations: natural *esse* versus spiritual *esse*, and the "reception of the species without matter." When Thomas says that the sensible species has a spiritual or intentional *esse* or that it is an intention, he does not use these phrases to indicate some "ideal" beingness as opposed to natural beingness. We know, for example, that according to Aquinas, color in air (an emanating-not-received influence in the medium of a patient) is called an "intentional beingness." Nonetheless, it remains real and physical and is not immaterial in the proper sense of "ideal" in the Husserlian sense. Natural *esse*, therefore, does not mean "real" as contrasted with "spiritual/ideal" beingness, but beingness in the A-moment. And spiritual or intentional *esse* indicates the beingness that something has—whether in nature or in knowledge—when it has projected itself into the B-moment of causality. In terms of knowledge, we may say proleptically that the B-moment entails the object's entrance into the concrete sphere of self-presence of the knower and thus comports a shared degree of self-presence. In that sense, natural *esse* or the A-moment in knowledge indicates "that inferior physical beingness which is not present to itself in self-reflection."[103]

Likewise, the phrase "receiving a species without matter" does not indicate some "ideal" activity outside of time and space. But neither does it mean that the species—granted, in its real, physical beingness—is somehow separated from matter. If it were that, the species would be a self-subsistent form, hardly knowable by sensibility; and Aquinas always says to the contrary that the sensible "species without matter" retains the conditions of matter (*cum appenditiis materiae*[104]). Rather, the phrase again points both to the B-moment of agency, where the emanating influence expresses and flows from the agent's *form* (even when it operates in matter), and, as we shall see in a moment, to the C-moment, where the object is consciously known and participates in sensibility's limited self-presence as the *act of* matter.

The above remarks, beginning on the side of the sensible, have applied Rahner's analysis of causality to the A and B moments of the object-to-be-sensed. The purpose of the application was to show that and how the object itself (and not some mental double) is what gets intuited. There is no preparatory stimulus on the part of the object, *after which* sensibility goes into action and reacts to some impression made upon it. Were that the case, then "what is perceived would be precisely the ontological actuality produced by such a reaction, hence it would be [sensibility's] own reality, not that of the other."[105] But if the sensible species is read as a dynamic self-realization of the object in the medium of sensibility (where the "inside" is already "outside"), then the object itself is that which is intuited.

As we shift now to the other side of sensation—to the sentient subject—we see that sensibility must be *passive* to a degree: It knows the *other*, not its own states. The reason why it must know the other is, of course, due to the subject's deficiency in self-presence; the subject requires an externally produced increase in its beingness in order to return to itself. And, in general, the way in which man can be open to such an other has been designated as sensibility's prior entry into otherness.

Granted that, the point now is to discover precisely how the sentient subject is *active* in sensibility. If its passivity guarantees conscious intuition *of the other*, its activity guarantees *conscious* intuition of the other. We can enter into this question by asking why there is no "agent sense."

There are, Aquinas says with Aristotle, no material objects which are "potentially sensible," but only "actually sensible" ones. We translate: There are no material beings which do not, of themselves, lend themselves to being present to the sentient subject. If there were, a faculty would be required, analogous to agent intellect, whereby such objects would be elevated to a state of actual sensibility. But then that new state would not belong to the objects of themselves, and sense knowledge would not intuit things in themselves. To say that all material beings are actually sensible of and by themselves is to affirm that in the A-moment "outside the soul" material beings *offer themselves* to the *possibility* of sensation. But in this A-moment, things are not always being actually sensed (e.g., the tree which crashes in the forest). Rather, they become actually sens*ed* in the medium of sensibility. What then of the object's actual sens*ibility*?

> If, nonetheless, the sense object as such (as "outside the soul") is to be actually sensible, then... that can be understood only in such a way that the sensible object, insofar as it is outside the soul, projects into sensibility (wherefore sensibility itself must be "outside itself") and in this medium, and only in it, acquires through its own operation that intensity of beingness which implies consciousness. Thus it can be in itself actually sensible, although that only in the medium of sensibility. . . . [106]

Because sensibility itself is already functioning "outside itself" in empty possession of worldliness, whatever enters its horizon is thereby actually sensible, and no "agent" faculty is required to elevate objects to a state of self-presentation.

But then the *activity* of sensibility begins to come into view. The self-presentation of the object is not its mere local presence before the eye or in the hand, nor is it something merely passively borne by sensibility. (If it were, the object would of itself be able to enter consciousness apart from the medium of the patient.) Rather, sensibility itself actually bestows upon the actually sensible object that intensity of beingness whereby the thing enters the sphere of knownness in the simultaneous B and C moments of sensation. "So once again we are brought to the thesis that the self-realization of the sensible object must be identical with the self-realization of sensibility. . . . "[107] The identity of the B and the C moments is what is meant by the Thomistic axiom: The sensed in act and the sentient in act are the same. And we may note here the proper meaning of Aquinas' term "likeness" (*similitudo*) as a description of the sensible species. Once again it is worth saying: This "likeness" is no "double," no "intentional representation" of the thing, somehow numerically identical with the object "outside." Of sense knowledge Aquinas says: "It is not to be understood as though the agent produced in the patient a species that is numerically identical with it; rather, it generates one like it, *generat sui similem*" (*Quodl.* 8, 3, c.). Rahner comments: Granted that in the A-moment the object has its own quiddity or "species," that object must generate a new self-realization of this species (the B-moment) that "reveals this [object] in its inner essence."[108] In the B-moment, the species is the revealedness or disclosure of the thing to sense; in Heidegger's use of the terms, the sensible *eidos* is already *alēthes*, disclosed. When dehypostatized and rendered dynamic, the *similitudo* is a matter of bodily presence and givenness. And this givenness must be co-performed by the active reception of it on the part of the patient.

We may likewise approach and in fact deepen the question of the activity of the sentient subject by considering again in what way sensation is an "undergoing" or *passio* rather than an "undergone quality."[109] An "undergone quality" or D-moment, we recall, happens when the agent has withdrawn. After the actual transmutation, the agent's influence is actively received by the patient as a more or less permanent quality or determination. If sensation were a matter of an undergone quality (D), it would take place *after* an impression by the sensible object; thus the sense impression would be reduced to a mere stimulus, and sensation would be a matter of perceiving one's own states. But Thomas holds that sense perception is an "undergoing" (*passio*) rather than an undergone quality (cf. *III. Sent.*, 14, 1, 1, sol. 2, c.), and the question becomes how the B and C moments are related while the emanating influence lasts and while the patient itself actively produces or "receives" the influence.

Heretofore we have considered only the B-moment as an *intentio* or spiritual *esse*. But Rahner shows, by another passing reference to medieval physics (light in air rather than color in air[110]), that the received influence or C-moment is likewise called an intention. It, too, like the emanating-not-yet-received influence, depends on the natural *esse* of the agent for its beingness (not just for its genesis), and it, too, ceases when the agent withdraws. Now, by investigating how and why sensation is a *passio*, that is, how and why the intention in the C-moment depends on the physical presence of the object, Rahner deepens the discussion of the activity of sensibility.

Two questions are posed: (1) Why does the agent's particular determination (d¹—let us say: pain) stop determining the patient once the agent withdraws? (2) During the undergoing of d¹, why is the patient unable to be affected by the opposite determination (d²—pleasure)? If, in sensation (as contrasted with the example of light and air[111]), the patient is of a higher level of beingness than the agent, then it *could* produce d² and yet does not. Why?

One could answer both questions in a way which reduces the sentient subject's activity. For example, in response to the first question one might say that d^1 stops determining the patient because d^2 or d^3 comes along and affects it. And one could say that sensibility does not produce d^2 because, at the moment of undergoing, the patient is actively directed to d^1. Rahner, however, takes a different tack. If the patient keeps d^1 only so long as its agent is present (first question) and if, during the presence of *that* agent, the patient does not get determined by d^2 (second question), the reason is *not primarily due to any agent* but rests with the nature of the undergoing on the part of the patient. We must search for the answers, then, in the *active* structure of the C-moment.

In the first place, we know that the general reason why any patient actively receives any determination is that the patient is already of itself ordered to self-realization and needs only an external specification or determination of this broad potentiality. In that sense (and *only* in that sense) the patient in its broad potentiality for self-realization is "above" any and all determinations, in a state of "indifference." Secondly, when in fact the patient is specified by an agent to d^1, it continues to have its broad and indifferent potentiality for other determinations (d^n), but this potentiality of itself is not a sufficient reason for choosing d^2 over d^1, since any specific "d" would only be a partial realization of the broader potentiality. If, then, the patient keeps d^1 as a mere *passio* which falls away when the agent withdraws, or if the patient holds onto d^1 during the *passio* instead of receiving d^2, the reasons are to be found in the patient's superiority (in its broader potentiality) to all external specification. "Hence an undergoing is given only where the further potentiality of the patient as such comes to appearance and where, as such, it is itself already given during each individual determination taken singly."[112] The broader potentiality is not for d^1 as contrasted with d^2, but a potentiality for all d's. And it is a *real*, *active* (not a "mere") potentiality, and one which is never exhausted in any particular determination. Conclusion: Sensation is a *passio* which holds d^1 only during the presence of the agent and which holds d^1 rather than some other determination during the undergoing, *not* primarily because of the passivity of the senses before the object *but* because sensibility "is already beyond [any determination] by maintaining itself in its further potentiality. . . ."[113]

With this analysis we arrive at the idea of the pure forms of intuition and the apriority of sense knowledge. If knowledge is by self-presence, then the senses, by receiving any determination as a mere *passio*, are the first level of immateriality and self-presence, because sensibility "produces its own actuality as already reaching beyond this determination."[114] The *passio* is a limited exercise of freedom insofar as, in it, sensibility produces its total, greater, real potentiality as more than any specific determination. In actualizing any particular determination, sensibility posits itself as able to be determined by *many* determinations, even if this possibility is empty and anticipatory. Sensibility is in a limited way immaterial and therefore self-present or conscious. Moreover, anything which pertains to the realization of sensibility's broader potentiality is itself consciously known: the *passio* itself, the specific determination which shows up in it, the form of the external agent of that determination, and even the real further potentiality of sensibility itself. The *a priori* further potentiality, which is always related to a particular determination and yet is always a real, broader potentiality that outrides the determination, is "pure intuition as conscious empty anticipation of [all] possible determinations...."[115] While this pure sensibility can be actually sentient only if specified from without, its very apriority is what allows the external determination to be received as a *passio* and to be intuitively known. Indeed, the productive reception of the sensible object *within* sensibility's broader *a priori* receptivity is what allows the self-realization of the sensible to be one with the self-realization of sensibility in the medium of the senses.

From this vantage point we can briefly indicate how space and time are the *a priori* structures of sensibility.[116] Pure intuition as the broader potentiality of sensibility is a potentiality for material forms, that is, for the determination of *materia quantitate signata*, which we have seen to be the original ground of spatiality (*quantitas dimensiva*) and temporality (*quantitas successiva*) and thus of individual spaces and moments. In the chapter on sensibility Rahner comes at this issue from a transcendental analysis. The principle is that the "ontological structure of a knowing entity is the *a priori* norm of its possible objects."[117] In his self-absence in otheredness, man is delivered over to matter which, as indeterminate and not ordered to any specific form, is the basis of motion, the change of one thing into another. Motion, therefore, is the *a priori* structure of sensibility; and this fact determines that the object of sensibility must be "the mobile" with its essential characteristics of space and time. But man is not just propelled into an unconnected succession of changes from one state to another. As self-present in otheredness, man is already (as sensibility and distinct from intellect) a *synthesis of mobile beings*, one which bestows upon the corporeal a greater unity than it has in itself. As the act *of matter*, sensibility is *a priori* given over to the mobile; as the *act* of matter, sensibility is the *organization* of the mobile.

But the material is intrinsically the quantitative, "the juxtaposition [*Nebeneinander*] of the same."[118] The *a priori* form of sensibility is, therefore, spatiality. But the material, as the mobile, likewise has the quality of forming time—not Aristotle's "numbered succession" (*arithmos kinēseōs*), which remains derivative, nor even the succession (*Nacheinander*) of a series of moments which would supposedly form motion and thus time. *Original* time is indeed intrinsic to motion, but distinct from the soul's numbering of motion. It is intrinsic to a motion which is not composed of successive moments but in fact first *forms them.* "Hence, it is not composed of past, present, and future, but lets these come to be for the first time."[119] That is, motion—and temporality in the *original* sense—is an *expectare aliquid futurum* (see *IV Sent.* 17, 1, 6, sol. 3, ad 1), a stretching of oneself ahead in such a way that the absence is what allows the present moment. This is not a movement from one actuality (the present) to another actuality (the future), but a stretch from potency towards act, a *tendere in actum* and an *ordo ad ulteriorem actum.* Motion is not a succession of moments (*nunc*) where the present is a cobblestone I stand on now as I step towards the next cobblestone. Rather, it is a matter of being appropriated (cf. *ordo*) from out of potency towards actuality, such that the present "precipitates" from out of that appropriation. "The present of the motion (its momentary state) is thus a vindication of its past in reaching-out towards the future, and only in this reaching-out-of-the-past-into-the-future does the present maintain itself."[120] We know that this future is the asymptotic self-presence which in fact is the origin of motion, and that the "past" which gets vindicated is man's already-being-ordered-to, or appropriated by, that origin. The mobility of sensibility is within the mobility of kinetic spirit, which in turn is appropriated by its recessive term. Rahner's "ordination" (*ordo*) translates Heidegger's "facticity" (*Faktizität*). It is in this radical sense that motion forms original temporality.

This is confirmed when Rahner collects temporality and spatiality, as *a priori* forms of intuition, under the imagination, which we have seen to be the midpoint of man, his center as "temporal transcendence."[121] If, as we have shown above, there can be no agent sense, the reason lies in the fact that man as a bivalent whole is that kinetic possibility which, both as agent intellect and as possible intellect or sensibility, is always and only faced to the world and, as appropriated beyond his spatio-temporal objects, has already opened the arena of their intelligibility. Within this horizon of possibility, which he is, man actively renders present, i.e., is one with, the beings he encounters.

3. The Intelligible Species

Rahner's analysis of causality and its application to sensibility give us the necessary clues for solving the problem of the intelligible species.[122] The issue, we recall, is this: If the intelligible species is not an *id quod*, something which exists on its own and fills knowledge with content, if it is rather the possibility of setting the phantasm over against the intellect so that the knower is ontologically determined to cognition of a particular object, how can the intelligible species be more than merely the *a priori* structure of the agent intellect without being something formed and received passively from without? Connected with this problematic are two positions formulated by Aquinas: (1) that the intelligible species remain in the possible intellect after actual thought,[123] and (2) that after separation of the soul from the body the intelligible species remain in the soul "in the treasury of the species."[124] In order to answer these questions Rahner draws again upon the analyses of sensibilization and sensation, and in the light of them makes a new distinction.

The phantasm in the broadest sense is the determination of sensibility, and we know that this is not something merely passively received but rather actively produced by sensibility upon specification from without. But sensibility itself is produced by the spirit in emanation. Therefore, given the hierarchy of emanations, the phantasm is generated by the intellect without need of some merely passively received influence. "The phantasm is produced by the spirit itself which reaches its end insofar as it forms itself into matter and lets sensibility emanate from itself in its full actuality in each instance."[125] And in so doing, the intellect has already accomplished the abstraction in the conversion to the phantasm.

Now, precisely because of spirit's free activity in producing sensibility as well as the particular sense determinations (in the C-moment), spirit actively determines itself logically prior to receiving the phantasm, the determination from without. This self-determination is what Rahner calls, in his new distinction, the intelligible species in the *broad* sense, "the self-determination of the free spirit in itself in the production of the phantasm. . . ."[126] *If* one wanted to discuss the question of retention of intelligible species in a separated soul (and Rahner adduces that position only as a limit case), the reason for such retention of the individual species—what Rahner calls intelligible species in the *narrow* sense— would lie in this free self-determination. When Aquinas asserts that separated human souls retain a relation to objects previously known, he says that this is through a *vestigium* or *habitudo* or *affectio*. Rahner interprets: ". . . we must understand this *cognitio* (*affectio*) not so much as content (*cognitum*), but rather as act. . . . According to Thomas, consequently, there remains in the spirit as such a relation to the earlier known individual because [spirit] once produced this knowledge as act."[127] But this means that even the separated soul would not be totally free of conversion to the phantasm insofar as, with any intelligible species, the intellect "always and already keeps it abstract in itself. . . ."[128] With regard to the other problem: "If species expresses the possibility of setting the phantasm over against the knowing subject, then it is self-evident that the permanent possession of this possibility of itself (its habitual existence) does not yet imply an actual knowing" apart from the conversion.[129]

The freedom of the spirit and its movement towards itself thus provide us with a concept of an intelligible species which is not passively received from without and yet is distinct from merely the *a priori* structure of agent intellect. Spirit's *movement* towards itself is what generates sensibility, and yet even in that free movement the spirit requires a quidditative determination of its sensibility from without. The issue of the intelligible species—as both free and determined—points to the unifying theme of the whole of GW: free spirit, determined in the world.

Notes

1. Cf. Rahner, GW 61/95 (108): *per generationem*, citing *In De Anima* lect. 12, n. 374.
2. Ibid., 176/247 (251).
3. Ibid., 175/246 (251).
4. Ibid., 203/281 f. (285).
5. Ibid., second edition, p. 245, glossing GW 171/239.
6. Ibid., 176/247 (252).
7. Ibid., 172/242 (247).
8. Heidegger, SZ 327/374.
9. Rahner, GW 174/244 (249).
10. Ibid., 175/245 f. (250).
11. Ibid., 180/252 (257).
12. Ibid., 247/340 (341).
13. Ibid., 185/258 (262).
14. Ibid., 187/260 (265).
15. Ibid., 184/257 (262), citing S.T. I, 77, 6, c.
16. Ibid., 184/257 (262).
17. Ibid., 186 and 187/260 (265 f.).
18. Ibid., 185/259 (263): *motus-Begriff im weiteren Sinn*.
19. Ibid., 72/109 (121).
20. Heidegger, SZ 375/407.
21. Rahner, GW 186/259 (263).
22. Ibid., 187/261 (265 f.).
23. Heidegger, SZ 332/380.
24. Rahner, GW 187/261 (266).
25. Ibid., 189/263 (267).

26. Ibid.
27. Ibid., 217/299 (303).
28. Ibid., 190/264 (268 f.).
29. Ibid., 190/265 (269).
30. *In VI Ethic.*, lect. 1, n. 1123 (*collectiva intentionum particularis*) and *In De Anima*, lect. 13, n. 398 (*apprehendit individuum ut existens sub natura communi*).
31. L.M. Régis, *Epistemology*, trans. Imelda Choquette Byrne (New York: Macmillan, 1959), p. 272.
32. Rahner, GW 196/272 (276): *die Einbruchsstelle des Geistes in die Sinnlichkeit*.
33. Ibid., 195/271 (275).
34. *S.T.* I, 85, 1, ad 4, cited at GW 193/269 (273).
35. Rahner, GW 197/273 (277).
36. Ibid., 200/278 (282).
37. Rahner does this at GW 207-10/286-90 (290-94).
38. Ibid., 202/280 (283).
39. Ibid., 207/286 (289).
40. Ibid., 206/284 f. (288).
41. Ibid., 205/284 (288).
42. Ibid., 217/299 (302).
43. Ibid., 218/301 (304).
44. Ibid., 222/306 (309).
45. Ibid., 224/308 f. (311): *Einbildungskraft des Geistes*, etc.
46. Ibid., 215/296 (299). Martin Heidegger, *Vom Wesen des Grundes* in *Wegmarken*, ed. Friedrich-Wilhelm von Herrmann, *Gesamtausgabe*, I, 9 (Frankfurt: Vittorio Klostermann, 1976), pp. 123-75, Eng. trans. *The Essence of Reasons*, trans. Terrence Malick (Evanston, Ill.: Northwestern University Press, 1969).
47. Rahner, GW 212 f./293 f. (297).
48. Ibid., 247/340 (341); cf. 243/334 (335) and 248/342 (343).
49. Ibid., 225/310 (312).
50. Ibid., 225/311 (313).
51. Ibid., 240/330 (332).
52. Ibid., 10/24 (39).
53. Ibid., 234/323 (325).
54. Ibid., 235-40/323-30 (325-31).
55. Ibid., 239/329 (331).
56. See Rahner HW 157, omitted in the second edition and in the Eng. trans. The parallel sentence in the English *Spirit in the World*, p. 331, paragraph 2, has been added by Professor Metz (GW, second edition, p. 332 f.).
57. Rahner, GW 242-46/333-39 (335-40).
58. Ibid., 241 f./332 f. (334).
59. Ibid., 243/334 (335).
60. Ibid., 243/335 (336).

61. Ibid., 244 f./336 f. (338).
62. Ibid., 245-46/337-39 (338-40).
63. Ibid., 246-47/339-40 (340 f.).
64. Ibid., 247/340 (341), citing S.C.G. IV, 11.
65. Ibid., 261/358 (359); cf. 247/340 (341) and 254/349 (350).
66. Ibid., 53/85 (97).
67. Ibid., 247-50/340-44 (341-45).
68. Ibid., 250 ff./344 ff. (345 ff.).
69. Ibid., 251, n./346, n. (346, n.).
70. Ibid., 254/349 (350): *die reale Räumlichkeit des anderen Körpers; die grössere Potentialität des Tätigen.*
71. Ibid., 255-67/350-66 (349-66).
72. Ibid., 255-58/250-54 (349-54).
73. Ibid., 258-61/354-58 (354-58).
74. Ibid., 259/355 (355).
75. Ibid.
76. Ibid., 260/356 (357).
77. Ibid., 260/357 (357).
78. Ibid., 261-67/358-66 (358-66).
79. Ibid., 262/359 (359): *vorhält.*
80. Ibid.
81. Ibid., 264/362 (362).
82. Ibid., 265/363 (363), emphasis added.
83. Ibid., 266/365 (365).
84. Ibid., 267/365 f. (365 f.).
85. Ibid., 48-51/78-82 (91-95).
86. See the texts at GW 273/374 f. (374).
87. Rahner, GW 275 f./378 (377).
88. GW 151/213 (221): *nicht-schöpferische...Sinnlichkeit;* 170/239 (244); 176/247 (252). All these texts summarize GW 48-51/78-82 (91-95).
89. Ibid., 50/81 (94).
90. Ibid., 151/213 (220).
91. Régis, *Epistemology,* p. 213, where he likewise writes: "Knowledge, we said, was invented by the Creator to remedy the finite and limited character of certain creatures and to permit them to imitate divine infinity."
92. Rahner, GW 53/85 (98).
93. Ibid., 52/84 (96).
94. Ibid., 53/85 (98).
95. Ibid., 57/90 (103).
96. Ibid., 60/93 and 94 (106) citing S.T. I, 79, 3, ad 1. Cf. also 61/95 (108).
97. Ibid., 53/85 (97).
98. Ibid., 53/84 (97).
99. Ibid., 53/84 f. (97); cf. 55/87 (100).
100. Ibid., 55/87 (99).
101. Ibid., 55/88 (100) and 62/96 (108).
102. Ibid., 61/95 (107).

103. Ibid., 57/90 (102).
104. Ibid., 58/91 (103) citing S.T. I, 79, 3, c. and *I Sent*. dist. 8, q. 5, a. 2, c.
105. Ibid., 59/92 (105).
106. Ibid., 60/93 f. (106).
107. Ibid., 60/94 (107).
108. Ibid., 62/96 (109).
109. Ibid., 267/366 (366).
110. Ibid., 268/367 (367) for this and the following paragraph.
111. The reader is forewarned that Rahner uses this example of light not for its own sake but simply to clarify agency in knowledge. Indeed, GW 268-69/368-69 (368-69) is dedicated to excluding the light example from the point Rahner is making.
112. Rahner, GW 270/370 (370).
113. Ibid.
114. Ibid., 271-372 (372).
115. Ibid., 272-373 (373).
116. Ibid., 63-79/97-116 (110-28).
117. Ibid., 63/97 (110); cf. 65 f./101 (113).
118. Ibid., 66/102 (114).
119. Ibid., 72/108 (120).
120. Ibid., 73/111 (122).
121. Ibid., 67-71/103-07 (115-19) and 74/111 f. (123).
122. Ibid., 276-80/379-83 (378-83).
123. See ibid., 228 f./315 (317f.) and footnotes thereto.
124. Ibid., 278/381 (380).
125. Ibid., 277/379 (379).
126. Ibid., 278/381 (381).
127. Ibid., 278 f./382 (381).
128. Ibid., 278/381 (380).
129. Ibid., 30/50 (64).

CHAPTER VIII

The Possibility of Metaphysics: Heidegger and Rahner

In his introductory interpretation of S.T. I, 84, 7, Rahner showed that the question about the conversion to the phantasm was simultaneously the question about the possibility of metaphysics (see Chapter V, B. 1). The last fifteen pages of GW are devoted precisely to that question: "The Possibility of Metaphysics on the Basis of the Imagination." For Rahner, imagination in the broad sense is the same as sense intuition, experience of the world; and man as spirit *in* the world is always turned to, and can never perform an about-face from, this intuition which "does not transcend time and the continuum."[1] How then is metaphysics, as knowledge of the suprasensible and specifically of God, to be possible?

GW is a metaphysics of human knowledge and not of beingness as such. Yet the work cannot pass over the crucial issue of the possibility of a metaphysics that is inscribed in the nature of the human knower. Rahner, therefore, proposes to "summarize once again in thesis form and in its objective context" the question of how human bivalence guarantees the possibility of the science of the common and the ultimate. He understands this science in the traditional sense, i.e., as ontotheology, but he sees that science "newly defined" by Aquinas' location of it in the realm of a human intellection "permanently dependent on sense intuition." And not only are the *contents* of metaphysics readjusted, but its "sense, method, and limits" as well. In effect, Rahner is claiming that Aquinas, in a generally objective mode, had already, before Kant, carried out a critique of the limits of speculative reason and had saved metaphysics for speculative reason in the bargain.[2]

Although Kant is Rahner's unmentioned adversary in the concluding pages of GW, I propose here to bring Rahner into dialogue with another thinker on his other flank: Heidegger. That dialogue has already been woven through all of Part Two of this essay, and the purpose of this last chapter is to bring it into the open and to focus it on the question of the possibility of metaphysics. The chapter has three Divisions: (A) First, we shall see how Rahner, against Kant, establishes the possibility of metaphysics on the basis of sense intuition; (B) secondly, we shall show how Heidegger's strategy is quite different: not to establish metaphysics but to "overcome" it; and (C) thirdly, we shall ask what is at stake in Heidegger's effort to surpass metaphysics.

A. RAHNER: THE GROUNDS FOR METAPHYSICS

1. The Problem of General and Special Metaphysics

A perennial problem in metaphysics is that of the unity of the science of being (ontology) and of God (theology). Whereas that unity was only posited but not elaborated by Aristotle, Aquinas claimed to have achieved it under the rubric of the "science of the first being" (*scientia primi entis*) as the principle and cause of being as being. For Aquinas, as for Rahner, "there cannot be a 'special metaphysics' in the sense of a science which would have definite metaphysical objects given to it as already known, and then would investigate and define them more precisely in their essence."[3] The division into general and special metaphysics, prepared by Suarez and effected by the seventeenth and eighteenth centuries, can have no sense for a Thomistic vision which sees that "the science of the first being and the science of the common being are the same" and that "the consideration of common being pertains to that science to which pertains the consideration of the first being."[4] Let us review this issue in Aquinas.

At first sight metaphysics seems to have two "objects" (or as the medievals would say, "subjects," *subjecta*): God as the first and highest being, and being-as-such or common being. For St. Thomas, however, God as absolute being is not the *subjectum* of metaphysics at all, but is known therein only as the ground or principle (*principium*) of *ens ut sic*, which remains the object of the science. In his commentary on Boethius' *De Trinitate* Aquinas had distinguished two kinds of principles: those which are not complete natures in themselves but simply principles for other things (e.g., the matter and form of material bodies) and those which are both complete natures in themselves and principles for other things (e.g., God and the heavenly bodies). The former have no science unto themselves but are treated only in the science which considers the things of which they are principles (there is no science devoted just to material form as such; it is treated as a principle of material beings in the philosophy of nature). The latter, however, can be treated in two sciences: one which takes them as principles for what derives from them, and one which treats them in themselves as the proper subject matter. But God, as a metaphysical being, i.e., one which cannot be experienced through sense intuition, cannot be the object of a reason ineluctably turned to such intuition, and therefore cannot be the object of a metaphysics based on the imagination. But since a science fulfills itself by knowing the principles or grounds of its subject matter, God comes into consideration in metaphysics because and insofar as "common being...already presupposes [him] as its ground, without this ground itself being an object which could be investigated by itself." God is the proper object not of natural or philosophical theology but of revealed theology. The general ontology of common being must in fact attain God, but only as the principle of its proper object: common being. Any so-called special metaphysics of God, whether in the classical modern form (e.g., Wolff) or as a neo-Scholastic natural theology, "is therefore either a repetition of general ontology or a usurpation of what can be possible only in a theology of sacred Scripture."[5]

To say that God-as-principle is the "end" of the disclosive anticipation which reveals beings in their common being is not to say that God is reached as the last in a series, i.e., after man has already understood being as such. To be sure, Aquinas holds that man's first-known object is a material quiddity, an S-as-P, and that only later does man become thematically aware of what in fact is more intelligible in itself, e.g., God. However, in the very act of knowing a material quiddity, the most intelligible *in se* functions as the *principle whereby* the S-as-P is known, and thus is simultaneously and implicitly—but not objectively—co-known in that very act. "This principle of knowledge which is co-apprehended in the apprehension of the sensible object is the light of the intellect; in it the 'eternal intelligibilities' are co-apprehended as the 'first intelligibles.' "[6] Implicitly co-known in every act of knowledge, these metaphysical principles are thematically known as "objects" only in a later, second-order reflection.

We have already seen how man co-grasps or anticipates the whole range of the metaphysical in the very consciousness he has of the movement (agent intellect) which is his nature. If man knows the metaphysical realm only as the ground of common being, and if common being is elaborated in the first principles which in turn are grounded in the agent intellect (cf. Chapter VI, B. 4), then man knows the metaphysical by knowing himself. To *do* metaphysics in the first-order dimension is consciously to let oneself be appropriated by the atelic movement that defines one. To *elaborate* a metaphysics in the second order of reflection is simply to spell out propositionally the movement that one is. "Metaphysics is only the reflexive elaboration of all human knowledge's own ground, which as such is already and always co-posited in this knowledge from the outset."[7] For Rahner, of course, man as lived metaphysics is a God-ward movement that illuminates things for possible knowledge. "All knowledge is possible only in the anticipation of absolute *esse;* and hence the implicit affirmation of absolute beingness is the condition of the possibility of any knowledge." And the thematic science of metaphysics is possible only "insofar as a metaphysical realm manifests itself through the light of the intellect."[8]

Again we see the necessary unity of ontotheology, but now from a transcendental perspective. Aquinas rooted that unity in the object of metaphysics (being as such), whereas Rahner grounds it in the nature of the subject who does metaphysics. Ontotheology must be, at least heuristically, one science because man is *an intention of unity:* a self-unifying bivalence which reveals beings in their beingness by anticipating the ever receding term of his movement, or more succinctly, a movement which grasps things by reaching towards God. But there is no anticipation of God except in the grasp *of material things*, no vision of the suprasensible at all but only a vision—from a distance—of physical things. If man does metaphysics by living his own movement, he knows that movement only as the condition for knowing the world objectively. Man has no "special metaphysical" objects, and for that reason there can be no special metaphysics. His movement merely allows a knowledge of beings-in-their-beingness, and a reflection on that can establish only a general metaphysics, a "conceptually formulated understanding of that prior understanding which man as man *is*."[9]

2. The Possibility and the Limits of General Metaphysics

At this point Rahner poses an objection to the position he is propounding.[10] If it is true that man knows the movement of his agent intellect and the realm opened up by it *only* as the condition of the possibility of knowing the physical world, then it would seem that the scope of agent intellect is limited to the beingness of physical things and that therefore physics (the philosophy of nature) would be the apex of philosophy. Let us elaborate first the objection itself and then Rahner's response.

It is in fact Aquinas' position that the agent intellect is given "first of all only and exclusively as a condition of the possibility of physics" and that "there is metaphysics for man only insofar as he has already made use of it for his physics: a realm of the metaphysical is opened up to man only insofar as this is necessary for him to be able to be in the world."[11] But that position would seem to lend itself to the following conclusions. If it is true that for Aquinas there is no agent intellect without a conversion to the phantasm, if the agent intellect is always and only a formal *a priori* at the service of sense intuition, we might conclude that this *excessus* must—and indeed can only—reach as far as physical being. Its scope would be that of the imagination, i.e., the pure intuition of space and time. To put it another way, if the agent intellect provides no material intuition of metaphysical objects and if it is always the intellect of a sentient spirit, then it would seem that it is able to disclose *nothing but* "the conditions under which the objects of sense experience as such stand."[12] Human knowledge of physical reality would be shown to be possible— and there would be no remainder. Physics would be first philosophy.

Rahner's answer is built around the third *responsio* in the article on conversion to the phantasm. There Aquinas said that in order to know the incorporeal dimension, of which there are no phantasms, we must be turned to the phantasms of the corporeal world (*necesse habemus converti ad phantasmata corporum*) and come to a knowledge of the incorporeal by comparison, excess, and negation (*comparatio, excessus, remotio*). We may distinguish three moments in Rahner's commentary on this text: a preliminary clarification of the three Latin terms; a demonstration of the possibility of metaphysics within conversion to the phantasm; and a critical discussion of the limits of that metaphysics.

In the first moment of Rahner's commentary there are two questions: What is the relation between *comparatio, excessus,* and *negatio* on the one hand and the knowledge of God as cause (*Deum . . . cognoscimus ut causam,* ad 3) on the other? and, What is the relation of the three terms among themselves? In answer to the first question Rahner notes that we do not first of all—before comparison, excess, and negation—know that God is, and only subsequently come to know him as cause by comparison, excess, and negation. Rather, God is known for the first time and as cause of things only in comparison, excess, and negation. This is what is meant in saying that God enters the purview of metaphysics only insofar as he is the principle of being. But this also means—here Rahner finds the turn to the subject in Aquinas—that

> the fundamental act of metaphysics is not some causal inference from a being as such to its ground, which also would not have to be more than a being, but the opening of the knower to beingness as such as the ground of both the being and the knowledge of the being.[13]

In answer to the second question Rahner states that, although comparison, excess, and negation are all necessary to opening the metaphysical realm, they "are not simply coordinate acts of the spirit" but in fact exhibit a hierarchy among themselves, with excess having the primacy. To "compare" the metaphysical and the physical realm presumes that the metaphysical dimension has already been opened up—by excess. All "negation" of the physical realm likewise presumes a prior anticipatory affirmation. "So only the *excessus* remains as the first and primary act which, as a condition of the knowledge of the world, is to make metaphysics possible."[14] The point, then, is to define how it makes possible a metaphysics which, while always at the service of physics and worldly being, in fact exhibits a remainder beyond the physical.

The second moment of Rahner's commentary seeks to find within sense intuition itself those aspects which point to a remainder or a "more," beyond physical being, in man's knowledge. He begins with a hypothesis which prefigures the scope of the argument.[15] If there *were* a metaphysics possible on the basis of sense intuition, (1) it could appeal to no suprasensible intuition of metaphysical objects; (2) it could be based on only a formal and not a material *a priori*, one in fact which would ground knowledge only of the world; and (3) it would have to be in correlation with sense intuition: The metaphysical realm would be opened only in the conversion to the phantasm, just as the latter would be possible only on the basis of a disclosed metaphysical realm. But beyond the hypothetical, what is it about sense intuition that points to a metaphysical remainder?

Here Rahner summarizes the thrust of GW as a whole. Thematic metaphysics is simply man's appropriation of his own nature as movement *in* the grasping of S-as-P. The S points to the receptive, sentient nature of knowledge, the "as-P" points to the universality and objectivity (the truth) of the judgment, and the "as" indicates the distance from the object which man must have (therefore, it indicates his consciousness of himself as kinetic: *reditio in seipsum*) in order to posit the S-as-P in reality. In other words, the possibility of objectifying the sense data in a true judgment which affirms a P of an S is grounded in the two moments of man's excess: the moment whereby the P, which is had in concretion, is known as limited by and as surpassing the S; and the moment whereby the knower is conscious of himself as distinct from the object (and so is able to objectify it) by being himself an excess towards absolute beingness. "With that, a being [*ein Sein*] beyond the realm of the imagination is [co-]affirmed, and this [co-]affirmation is the condition of the possibility of objective knowledge of the world because it takes place in *that* anticipation which first makes possible such an objective possession of world."[16]

In judgment as a manifestation of "the dynamic desire of spirit for beingness as such,"[17] God is not intuited, not conceived or represented, but is given as anticipated and thus is *co*-affirmed as what allows us to affirm worldly being. Here is no realistic, inductive metaphysics in the usual sense (for man's movement is *a priori*) and certainly no back-door intellectual intuition (there is only a front door—sense intuition—and the agent intellect is the formal principle for opening it). Yet there is a remainder beyond physical being, one that is anticipated in and through man's kinetic nature. The appropriation of man by the ever receding term of his movement constitutes the possibility of whatever metaphysics there is. And therefore a second-order reflection on man in his fullness, a hermeneutics of his ever unresolved movement, is all there is to ontology. "According to Thomas the reflection on that which makes metaphysics possible is already itself metaphysics, and basically is already the totality of what is accessible to metaphysics."[18] Fundamental ontology *is* ontology. The hermeneutics of man's facticity, of his appropriation into asymptotic movement, is the whole shot. And even if as Rahner holds, the three moments of excess-comparison-negation reveal, in their unity, an implicitly known unlimited metaphysical beingness, still these aspects of man's movement "give us the metaphysical realm not in its own self, but only as the 'principle' of the real object of the one human knowledge: the world."[19]

The third moment in Rahner's commentary concerns the limits to the metaphysics disclosed in the human excess.[20] At stake is not a supposed limitation to the quantity of possible sensible objects, and not just the fact that the conversion to the phantasm limits man to sense objects. At stake, rather, is the limitation inscribed in the very finitude of man's movement and, along with that, the correlative limitation intrinsic to the way he knows beingness as such. Just as the possibility of metaphysics was established by a transcendental reflection on man's knowing powers, so too the limits of metaphysics will be established in the same way. In this area Rahner is content with a few remarks on the *nomina transcendentia*, the transcendentals, which are the intrinsic moments of man's "concept of beingness" (one, true, good, etc.).

Rahner is not concerned with the number or derivation of the transcendentals (these problems were not central to Thomas' metaphysics either) but rather with the formal indication that the realm of the transcendentals globally—and not of the categories—is what constitutes the object of metaphysics. That much is already said in Aquinas' assertion that we know only the "thatness" and not the "whatness" of separated substances. We know only their existence and what it implicitly entails: the transcendental determinations in that degree of beingness which we can analogously postulate of immaterial substances. Beyond that, all is *tenebrae ignorantiae*, the darkness of ignorance (*I Sent.*, d. 8, q. 1, a. 1, ad 4). Here lie the limits of man and his metaphysics. All he knows of beingness is gained from the empty infinity of his movement and from the common being and its transcendental modes which are known in that movement. To light one's way by one's kinetic idea of beingness is to strike a match in the dark. But that is all man can do. In any case this "idea of beingness" has the structure of a kinetic *pros ti*, a referral to the receding term of man's dynamism. The analogy of beingness, Rahner says, "is not merely a construction designed to help towards the conceptual, negative definition of the essence of God, but already has its starting point where the experience of the world is transcended in an anticipation through excess and negation."[21] In fact, the concept of beingness is not first univocal and later seen to be analogical. It is analogical first and foremost and is rendered univocal only in the turn to the phantasm.

Of the categories, Rahner has little to say (Professor Metz adds some paragraphs to the second edition of GW) other than that they are primarily concepts of natural philosophy, not of metaphysics, and that their possible applicability in metaphysics would be known by a proper transcendental deduction of them, which, necessary as it might be, was never attempted by Aquinas. "Thomas is satisfied with a critique of the individual concepts in the particular instance of their application beyond physics,"[22] and for the rest he locates the content and limits of metaphysics in the beingness (with its transcendental modes) that appears in man's excess.

Rahner draws together his remarks on the possibility and limits of metaphysics in a concluding summary which at once recapitulates the whole of GW and pushes it beyond itself.[23] First, the retrieval of the transcendental starting point: However little it is expressed explicitly by Thomas, he says, metaphysics is a matter of placing *man* in question. Secondly, the meaning of man's worldliness: Although the world must be the starting point for the question of beingness, it is never the world of brute fact but always one "transformed by the light of the spirit, the world in which man sees himself, the world *of man*." Thirdly, the meaning of human transcendence: Every one of man's acts is borne along by "the desire for beingness as such," but in such a way that "the free spirit becomes, and must become, sensibility in order to be spirit, and thus exposes itself to the whole destiny of the earth." Thus, fourthly, man's self-unifying bivalence (*Zweideutigkeit*): "Man is always exiled in the world and is always already beyond it." He is ordered in his knowledge to material quiddities, and yet somehow he is all things; he is an anticipation of God while ever remaining a sentient knower. Both sides of the bivalence condition each other. All thought is for sense intuition, yet all sense intuition is possible only by man's distance and movement (*reditio*). Fifthly, the implicit and explicit knowledge of God: Reflective metaphysics shows that "every venture into the world is borne by the ultimate desire of the spirit for absolute beingness." God is implicitly known in man's movement and can be explicitly affirmed in reflection on that movement.

Rahner's sixth point hints at the usefulness of GW for a fundamental theology. "We would not be true to the ultimate purpose of this whole Thomistic metaphysics if we did not let its intrinsic movement reach that point towards which it is ultimately striving. Everything. . . is situated by Thomas within the context of a theological endeavor."[24] Here Rahner anticipates the outline of HW: ". . . God manifests himself in such a way that he is able to be heard in the word of his revelation. . . . In order to be able to hear whether God speaks, we must know that he is; lest his word come to one who already knows, he must be hidden from us; in order to speak to man, his word must encounter us where we already and always are, in an earthly place, at an earthly hour." Abstraction thus places man before the *hidden* God, conversion places man in the here and now where that hidden God may *speak*. "Abstraction and conversion are the same thing for Thomas: man." And man is the act of metaphysics. Insofar as faith holds to the revelation of God in the man Jesus, the Thomistic metaphysics of man "is Christian when it summons man back into the here and now of his finite world into which the eternal has entered so that man might find him, and in him might find himself anew."

B. HEIDEGGER: BEYOND METAPHYSICS

Chapter III above was dedicated to how Rahner understood Heidegger in 1940. In that chapter I held my own criticism to a minimum precisely in order to see what Rahner himself perceived as usable—and what he found unusable—for his own GW. Elsewhere throughout this essay Heidegger's positions have emerged for the sake of comparison or criticism, and throughout I have let his thought guide our path through Rahner, just as, so I claim, it guided Rahner's own thought in a large if not wholly thematic way.

The purpose of the present division is to lay out the general lines of Heidegger's thought for itself rather than as seen through Rahner's eyes. This will prepare for a last confrontation between Heidegger and Rahner in Division C. At issue here are the following topics: the difficulty of locating exactly what it is that Heidegger claims as his "issue for thought"; an examination of Heidegger's central debt to Husserl; a sketch of what Heidegger meant by the "meaning of being"; and some remarks on the non-metaphysical issue that has gone forgotten in Western philosophy.

1. Locating Heidegger's Topic

Bergson has written that every great philosopher thinks only a single thought—an inexhaustible one—and spends his whole life trying to express it. *Et c'est pourquoi il a parlé toute sa vie.*[25] Over the half century of his professional life Martin Heidegger continued to insist that his thinking was concentrated on one topic only, *die Sache selbst*, the "issue." He also insisted that this topic was utterly simple. However, the task of defining and articulating that one simple issue has proven to be no easy matter either for Heidegger himself or for his commentators. In fact it is something of a minor scandal in philosophy that those who claim to understand Heidegger often seem to be able to express their understanding only within the peculiar and sometimes ideosyncratic language of the master himself. It may well be that, as Professor Biemel writes, "[Heidegger's] language is his thought, and if we give up his language, we give up his thought."[26] Nonetheless the fact remains that outsiders are often denied access to Heidegger's thought precisely because of the difficult language in which it is expressed and because of the dogged repetition of that language by the commentators. Not only that, but such repetition runs the risk of obscuring the delineation of Heidegger's topic itself.

In what follows, I will try to take a path that lies somewhere between repeating the same terminology as Heidegger's and creating an entirely new one. This middle path is the simple one of attempting to "translate" Heidegger's language into speech which may be more accessible to those who stand outside the circle of Heideggerians of the strict observance. Whether the effort succeeds or fails—whether in fact it falls back into the very problem it is trying to overcome—must be decided by the reader.

It is a truism that the subject matter of Heidegger's thought is the "question of being" (*die Seinsfrage*), but like most truisms, it is both correct and potentially misleading. Indeed, it could be argued that one might enhance clarification of Heidegger's topic by retiring the terms "being" (*das Sein*) and "the question of being" from the discussion.

There are a series of problems, right at the entrance to Heidegger's thought, that can mislead the uninitiated. In the first place, this phrase "the question of being," which is usually taken as the statement of Heidegger's topic, is in fact a condensation, a kind of shorthand or abbreviation, of a longer and more telling phrase. For another thing, that longer phrase underwent some changes throughout Heidegger's career: from the question of the "meaning" of being, to the question of the "truth" of being, to the question of the "place" or "clearing" of being.[27]

These three terms—meaning, truth, place/clearing—have a sense that is different from the ordinary. "Meaning" (*Sinn*) does indeed point to the "understandability" (*Verstehbarkeit*) of something—in this case, the understandability of being. But for Heidegger, understandability is bound up with man's intrinsic movement and temporality and thus has connotations of a kinetic-temporal "opening up" of possible regions of sense. Meaning, for Heidegger, is not some static quality of things, something that can be read off of them by an equally static intellect. Rather, it is *emergence* into intelligibility (where "intelligibility" is to be taken in the very broad sense of "meaningful accessibility" [*Zugänglichkeit*], whether that be practical, aesthetic, theoretical, or whatever). Likewise the word "truth" means something different from the traditional meaning. It indicates "disclosure" rather than the usual sense of conformity to rational standards. And again, this disclosure has a kinetic feel about it: the act of pulling something out of the obscurity of non-understandability and bringing it into the clarity of intelligible accessibility. Finally, the word "place" (*Ortschaft*) or the more kinetic word "clearing" (*Lichtung*) point to the same phenomenon of disclosive movement. "Clearing" indicates the event of opening up the domain of intelligibility, whereas "place" points to that domain itself. Taken together, both words refer to what Heidegger calls the *Entwurfbereich:* the projective character of movement (*Entwurf*) as opening up the "place" of intelligibility (*Bereich*).

By fleshing out Heidegger's phrase "the question of being" into its fuller forms, we have gained a preliminary perspective on his topic: It has to do with a *movement* which issues in *intelligibility.*

But even in its fleshed-out forms, Heidegger's statement of his topic runs a second risk of being misunderstood, and for reasons which cluster around the difficult word "being." As we have seen, the word "being" (*einai, esse, das Sein,* etc.) is the general name used by the philosophical tradition to indicate the highest principle of reality, regardless of the metaphysical transformations that that principle undergoes from Plato through Hegel. In Chapter IV I argued that the general title of "being-ness" (*Seiendheit*) can be given to all these forms—even to Aquinas' *esse*—insofar as they share in common the naming of what it is that makes beings be beings: their being-*ness.* And I have argued that the study of beingness both in its universal traits (ontology) and in its ultimate instance (theology) is what constitutes metaphysics. When metaphysics says "being," it means "beingness." But when Heidegger says "being" he sometimes means "beingness" and at others times means the *prior disclosive movement* which issues in the beingness-of-beings. Because of this ambivalence in the use of "being," Heidegger's question runs the risk of being misunderstood as a metaphysical inquiry when in fact it is about something prior to the metaphysical realm. Rahner falls into this error when he writes: "Metaphysics is what Heidegger is about, what he means to do."[28]

Let us attempt to diagram the two different meanings of "being" and thus to distinguish Heidegger's topic from the tradition's.

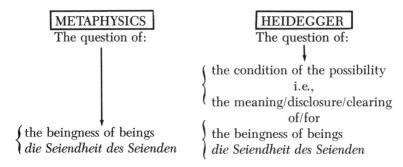

Heidegger's topic is the prior event of the "opening up of the space" within which beings can appear in their beingness (i.e., their intelligibility, in the sense I indicated above). This prior event—which, we must stress, always includes the movement of human transcendence—is what Heidegger means by "being" (*das Sein*) in the proper sense, i.e., "being-as-being" (*das Sein als Sein*). In order to stress the kinetic character of this event Heidegger sometimes uses the old German word *das Seyn* (be-*ing*). Or, because in philosophical usage the word *das Sein* is usually reserved for the tradition's topic of the beingness-of-beings, Heidegger once used a cancellation sign to bring out *his* meaning of the word: S̶e̶i̶n̶, i.e., "not *Seiendheit!*" If we bring these words together, we can state Heidegger's topic as follows:

The question of	*das Sein* *das Seyn* *das* S̶e̶i̶n̶ etc.	of	*die Seiendheit des Seienden* *das Sein des Seienden* the *esse entium,* etc.

Confusion is well nigh inevitable, and Heidegger's last and best move was to drop the word *das Sein* as much as possible from usage.[29] In what follows I shall continue to use the word, but always within inverted commas ("being") to refer to *das Sein* as Heidegger means the word to be taken. This is only a preliminary, formal-heuristic decision, and we shall have to flesh out the content of this "being" in what follows.

By means of this second clarification, which concerns the ambivalence of the word *das Sein*, we have taken another step towards locating Heidegger's topic. In the first clarification we said that Heidegger is concerned with the *movement* that issues in the *intelligibility/*

accessibility of beings. Returning to some of Heidegger's own language we may now say that Heidegger's topic is the *kinetic meaning/disclosure/ clearing* that issues in the *beingness/intelligibility/accessibility-of-beings*.

There is yet a third possibility of misunderstanding, the hypostasization of "being" into a quasi-Platonic entity that subsists above and beyond man and somehow lives a life of its own: It claims man, calls to him, sends itself to him, hides itself from him. Heidegger's own language often seems to encourage such hypostasization, and the English translation of *das Sein* by the capitalized "Being" can abet this kind of misreading.

Such reification loses sight not only of the kinetic nature of "being" but also of the analogical character of beingness. Ever since 1907, when he first read Franz Brentano's dissertation and raised his own question about the unified meaning of beingness, Heidegger's concern was never about some kind of univocal "thing" subsisting on its own. Over and above the beingness of man, implements, nature, artworks, ideal objects, and so on, there is no second level of "being itself" as the "real thing." Rather, the "itself" (in German one can also say *überhaupt*, "at all") points only to the analogical unity and condition-of-possibility of all modes of the beingness-of-beings.

In order to stave off the possibility of hypostasization, we may attempt another translation, this time into a more phenomenological lexicon. Instead of saying "beingness," let us speak of "givenness." Beingness is the givenness of entities (in some form of human awareness) as what and how they are at the moment. Moreover, instead of saying "being" to indicate *das Sein* in Heidegger's sense (that is, the prior condition for the emergence of the beingness/givenness of entities), let us speak of the "giving of the givenness-of-entities" (*Es gibt das Sein-des-Seienden*). Such usage may let us see that Heidegger's topic is not the givenness of beings; rather, that is the topic of metaphysics in all its forms. Heidegger's question is about the very "giving" of any and all modes of givenness. He asks about the event that opens up the "space" within which the intelligible givenness of things happens. It is this event that Heidegger has in mind when he speaks of the *"Es Gibt,"* the fact that there-is-given (without explanation) the various modes of the givenness of things.

Another way to preclude the hypostasization of Heidegger's "being" is to emphasize the "sameness" or "identity" of "being" and man's essence. We are not to think of "being" as some kind of object towards which the Dasein-subject strives. Rather, there is only a single, tri-dimensional movement that we may call the happening-of-sense. Within that movement we can experientially identify:

(1) the temporalized movement of man's transcendence, which we have called his "excess,"
(2) the movement of entities into their intelligibility, which we have called their "accessibility" or simply "access," and
(3) the privative absentiality of the "*telos*" of man's movement, which we may call "recess" (*Entzug*); or equally, the fact that man does not initiate his movement but is pulled or appropriated (*vereignet*) into it.

In speaking of this tri-dimensional phenomenon called "being" it is important to stress that, for Heidegger at least, there is no "thing" or "person" that appropriates man. There is just the happening-of-sense, the facticity of the event itself: the movement for which man is essential but over which he does not dispose.

The problem, of course, is how to speak of the "identity" of man-and-"being" without hypostasizing "being" and sending man chasing after it, and without making "being" into some sort of human project over which man exercises control. Heidegger puts the matter simply and directly:

> We always say *too little* about "being itself" when, in saying "being," we leave out presence *to* man's *essence* and miss the fact that this essence itself goes to make up "being." Likewise we always say *too little* about man when, in saying "being" (not just man's being), we posit man in and for himself and only later bring him, as thus posited, into relation with "being."[30]

At any rate, we have taken yet another step towards clarifying or locating Heidegger's topic. The movement that issues in the accessibility of entities—that is, the *de facto* giving of the meaningful givenness of entities—is intrinsically bound up with the movement of man's transcendence.

A fourth area of possible misunderstanding draws the previous ones together. It is the matter of Heidegger's audacious claim that the question of "being" has been entirely forgotten in the Western tradition of philosophy. In that regard Professor Helmut Franz recounts an anecdote about a 1958 philosophy conference at which Heidegger had discussed this issue. A Protestant participant asked Heidegger whether it were not the case that at least Martin Luther had not forgotten "being." Heidegger quipped in response: Would you care to guess how many Catholics ask me the same thing about Thomas Aquinas?[31]

This exchange can help bring us to the heart of an eventual debate be-

tween Rahner and Heidegger. One could ask whether, after the painstaking work of Gilson and others, it is not the legitimate claim of
neo-Thomism that Aquinas raised metaphysical questioning to a new
and indeed revolutionary height by his thematization of the primacy of
esse, the existential act of to-be, over form and essence. The neo-Thomist
can point to text after text in Aquinas that speaks of this primacy; surely
there is no forgottenness of being here![32] And indeed, the various attempts to rescue Aquinas from Heidegger's indictment generally consist
in demonstrating (irrefutably, as far as I can see) that in St. Thomas not
only does *esse* have primacy, but indeed essence is reducible to it.

And yet Heidegger, who is far from ignorant of Aquinas' metaphysical revolution and of its rediscovery in this century, nonetheless
maintains that in St. Thomas, as much as in Plato or Nietzsche, "being"
is forgotten. From what we have seen above, a possible explanation of
Heidegger's claim begins to take shape. If *esse* is one historical thematization of the generic issue of beingness, then for all its "existentiality,"
esse as understood by St. Thomas does not break out of the fate of metaphysics: the fact that it overlooks the prior event of the *opening up of* the
realm of *esse*/beingness/intelligibility.

As a young highschool student Heidegger studied a brief treatise entitled *Vom Sein: Abriss der Ontologie* by Carl Braig, Catholic theologian
of the Tübingen school. The work opens with a long citation from St.
Bonaventure's *Itinerarium mentis in Deum*, V, 3, 4, which said in part:
"*Mira est caecitas intellectus, qui non considerat illud [esse], quod prius
videt et sine quo nihil potest cognoscere.*" ("How amazingly blind is our
intellect. It does not consider that one thing—*esse*—which it sees first of
all and without which it could not know anything.")[33] It remains
Aquinas' lasting achievement that he removed the scales from philosophy's eyes and thematized that *esse* in the most striking way. But it is
Heidegger's claim that Aquinas missed something, that he suffered from
a second-level blindness, as it were, and in fact from a blindness that was
not his fault. Not only that, but such blindness cannot even be recognized, Heidegger claims, from within metaphysics.

The issue we are discussing is usually called the "forgottenness" or
"oblivion" of "being" (*Seinsvergessenheit*), although I think that the
German is better paraphrased as the "hiddenness" of "being." I shall return to this matter below, but some indications of the meaning of the
phrase are in order here. We may distinguish two moments in this "hiddenness" of "being," namely, (1) an intrinsic unknowability and (2) an
extrinsic overlooking of that intrinsic unknowability.

Intrinsic unknowability: The primary meaning of the "hiddenness" of
"being" is the sheer unexplainable facticity of the tri-dimensional pro-

cess of the happening-of-sense (the giving of the givenness of entities in conjunction with human transcendence). Or to put that in other terms: Whereas we do in fact perceive and know entities and their modes of givenness, and whereas we immediately experience our transcendence, we do not know, cannot argue to, and (if we stay with our experience) cannot postulate any supposed "moving source" of that givenness and that transcendence. In fact, it is misleading to speak of "the *giving of* the givenness of entities," as if there were some thing or event behind the givenness of entities. Rather, the only thing man experiences in that regard is the *sheer facticity* of the "that-there-is-given" of the meaningful givenness of entities in conjunction with human transcendence.

Extrinsic overlooking: Granted the unknowability, unexplainability, and unpostulatability of anything like a "source" of the happening-of-sense—indeed, *because* of that state of affairs—man for the most part overlooks ("forgets") the sheer facticity or "intrinsic hiddenness" of the process of "being." Forgetfulness of [the hiddenness of] "being" is quite common in everyday life; it is equally common in the thematic science of metaphysics, which seeks for and claims to find a final ground or explanation both for the beingness of beings and for human transcendence. But such overlooking or forgetting happens *not* because of a psychological or educational defect in man, something that might be overcome through, say, a good course in philosophy. Rather, the overlooking (= second moment in the hiddenness of "being") is due to the intrinsic facticity of the happening-of-sense (= first moment in the hiddenness of "being").

The above distinction comes into its own when we ask: What might it mean to overcome *Seinsvergessenheit*? Such overcoming, if it is possible, could never be a matter of undoing the facticity (or intrinsic hiddenness: *lēthē, Entzug,* recess) of "being"—if only because man does not dispose over that facticity. Nor could it be a matter of doing away, once and for all, with one's own or anyone else's overlooking of the hiddenness of "being"—if only because such overlooking is due not to a defect in man but to the very nature of "being."

Rather, the overcoming of *Seinsvergessenheit* means, negatively, ceasing to overlook the facticity/hiddenness of "being," that is, awakening from the dream of metaphysics, which believes that thinking can trace beingness back to God. And positively, the overcoming of *Seinsvergessenheit* does not mean abolishing the facticity/hiddenness of "being" but accepting it, "going along" with it by living out one's own (inexplicably evoked) transcendence. In fact, we should not speak of "overcoming" *Seinsvergessenheit* as if there were the promise of a secular beatific vision of being-as-such. Heidegger is talking about the exact opposite: the acceptance of one's groundless movement into an ever-darkening *tenebrae ignorantiae.*

The two moments in the "hiddenness" of "being" are clearly laid out by Heidegger in the following text:

> The thinking that begins with *Sein und Zeit* is, on the one hand, an awakening from the overlooking of [the hiddenness of] "being". . . . On the other hand, and precisely *as* such an awakening, it does not extinguish the hiddenness of "being." Rather, the point is to place oneself in, and to stand within, that hiddenness. To awaken *from* the overlooking and to awaken *to* the hiddenness is to awaken to *Ereignis.*[34]

The *Ereignis* mentioned here is the factical tri-dimensional happening-of-sense. To awaken to that factical happening means simply to accept—i.e., to become—what one already is and is involved in.

There is a fifth (and for our purposes here, a final) possibility of misunderstanding Heidegger's topic, and it concerns the much-discussed difference between the early and the later Heidegger. Any talk of a "Heidegger I" and a "Heidegger II" makes sense only if, as Professor William J. Richardson has masterfully shown, the earlier prefigures the later, and the later fulfills the earlier. If every great thinker thinks but a single thought, then the task is to find that thought in its totality at each phase of the thinker's development, even where it achieves only a seminal form of expression. In Heidegger's case that means finding the "later" thought of *Ereignis* in the "earlier" analysis of human transcendence, rather than separating his works into a first phase where supposedly Dasein is the center and a second phase where supposedly "being" comes to the fore. The principle holds: Talk of man and talk of "being" are always redundant, not because man is "being itself," but because in each case the one is found only in and with the other.

These remarks bring us to the question of the "turn" (*Kehre*) in Heidegger's thought. This "turn," which usually is dated to around 1936, has been the subject of much scholarly controversy. I shall risk stating my own position on the matter and leave that position to be justified or not by what follows.

In discussing the turn in Heidegger's thought, one may distinguish at least three possible meanings of the term. (1) For our purposes the least significant of the possible meanings concerns the shift in Heidegger's language and style that became noticeable in the 1930s, when a more "poetical" way of speaking—even, some might say, a "mystical" language—began to replace the language of SZ. (2) In another interpretation, the turn means the supposed emergence of a "new" topic in Heidegger's thought around 1936: *Ereignis.* (3) Finally, the turn can be taken as what Heidegger called a "transformation in man's being" (*Verwandlung des Menschseins*),[35] one which is often called "the step back" (*Schritt zurück*).

We may omit discussion of the first suggestion, not because it is unimportant but because its importance comes from the other interpretations of the turn.

Regarding the second meaning of the turn—the apparent emergence of a "new" topic in Heidegger's thought—we must say that it is just that: apparent. Not only did the term *Ereignis* begin to emerge as early as 1928, one year after the publication of SZ (in a seminar on Aristotle's *Physics* that Heidegger gave at Marburg[36]), but more importantly the subject matter to which the term refers was present in Heidegger's thought from the early Twenties in such issues as *Faktizität* and *kinēsis*. Heidegger's topic remained the same from his Privatdozent years after World War I through his last writings. That topic was *movement* as the emergence of sense in man's experience. The term *Ereignis* only clarifies and stabilizes earlier attempts to articulate that topic. That process of clarification certainly entailed a shift in language as well as an effort to overcome the inadequate, "horizonal" framework of the earlier writings. But these shifts are, in relation to the topic itself, *relatively* unimportant.

The third and most important meaning of the "turn" is what we may call "man's turn towards *lēthē*," or what Heidegger calls simply the "transformation of man's being." What kind of turn or transformation is this?

In the *Nicomachean Ethics* (K, 7, 1178 a 3 f.) Aristotle says: "It would be out-of-place [*atopon*] if man were to choose not the life of his true self but that of something else." Heidegger's thought is simply at the service of reawakening man to his true self and his true place (*topos*). What is unique about the content of Heidegger's thought is the fact that he finds man's *topos* to be neither a self-contained place nor a static self. Rather, man's properness or authenticity (*Eigentlichkeit*) consists in his being-appropriated into a movement the term of which he cannot grasp. That movement with its unknowable source is what allows men to grasp present beings, and the point is to let oneself go beyond beings-in-their-beingness in the direction of that unknowing. This release means that man must "reappropriate his appropriation," but without hoping to bring it under control. And this entails letting go of the securities of the substantial ego and its tidy world. To do that is to have "taken the 'turn.' " Heidegger's thought is entirely at the service of such a "transformation of man's being," and this is the only "turn" worth talking about.

What we have said so far in an effort to locate Heidegger's topic sharpens the issue mostly in a negative and heuristic way. We have suggested that the way to get at Heidegger's topic is to make some formal distinctions in the very title of his thought, with special attention to the difference in meaning between "beingness" in the tradition and "being" in Heidegger's sense. We have pointed out the danger of hypostasizing "being," as well as the necessity of understanding "being" in connection with the essence of man. Finally we discussed the controversial issue of the "forgottenness of "being" and, implicit in that, the question of the turn. In a preliminary way we have seen that Heidegger's topic is the kinetic-disclosive event whereby beingness (the meaningful givenness of things as what and how they are) happens at all. If beingness or givenness is the way in which beings show up, Heidegger is asking about the movement in which the givenness-of-beings is given (*es gibt*): the "being" that issues in beings-in-their-beingness.

All such ways of putting Heidegger's question indicate a preliminary shift of focus away from beings and towards beingness. Of course, metaphysics is already aware of beingness—as the way in which *beings* are present. Heidegger, however, wants to investigate beingness in and of itself, and specifically in terms of its "essence" or the conditions of its possibility. And since, as the tradition implicitly knew, beingness is necessarily tied into man's essence, the question becomes that of man's unique relation not only to beings but to the very happening of beingness. But clearly this question is not to be interpreted as pointing towards divine creation. Rather, it indicates the issue of the disclosive bond between human transcendence and the emergence of beings-in-their-beingness, a conjunction that is operative wherever man is man and beings appear, but that gets covered over both in everyday life and in the thematic science called metaphysics. If the bond is proper or essential to man, then he will come into his own only by re-appropriating it, becoming that which in fact he already essentially is. And if it could be shown that the bond is a phenomenon of movement, then man would become his authentic self—and beings would show up as they originally are—when man gives himself over to the movement which is his nature. Already appropriated into movement, man would become himself by *letting* himself be thus appropriated. The central issue is the facticity of this appropriation-into-movement.

But these formal indications of Heidegger's topic require concrete demonstration, and that means some intermediate steps. If phenomenology is always about the *immediate presence or givenness* of whatever is at issue, how could Heidegger possibly go "behind" that presentness to ask how *it* comes about—if he intends, as he claimed, to remain a phenomenologist to the end? Clearly beingness itself—and not just beings—

must become a phenomenon, something experienced as immediately present to man. But at the same time, the realm of presence, to which phenomenology confines itself, must be expanded beyond present givenness by being questioned as to its condition of possibility. The first of these services was performed for Heidegger by Edmund Husserl's ground-breaking work *Logical Investigations*. The second was to be reserved for Heidegger's own SZ.

2. The Debt to Husserl: Phenomenological Access to Beingness[37]

Although Heidegger began reading Edmund Husserl's *Logical Investigations* as early as 1909, upon entering Freiburg University, it was some years before its import for Heidegger's own question about the unified meaning of beingness became apparent to him. The crucial text was Husserl's Sixth Investigation, Chapter 6, "Sensuous and Categorial Intuitions." The very title of the chapter signaled at one and the same time Husserl's connection with and his break from Kant. The whole second part of the Sixth Investigation was entitled "Sense and Understanding," and the reference to Kant was clear. Likewise, discussion of "sensuous intuitions" recalled KRV. But the topic of "categorial intuition" heralded Husserl's revolutionary break from Kant's critical philosophy.

For Kant, categorial intuitions were impossible insofar as the categories of the understanding function only to bring the hyletic data into categorial form so that an object is known in a synthesis of intuition and concept. All intuition is immediate, but the categories in KRV are functions of mediation for synthetic unity. But Husserl's chapter broadens the range of intuitive givenness beyond the realm of the senses and sense data. Husserl's aim in the Sixth Investigation is a phenomenological clarification of truth (i.e., true knowledge) by means of a phenomenological analysis of the identity-synthesis, specifically by analyzing how categorial as well as sensuous meaning-intentions are fulfilled. If the clarification is to be phenomenological, that is, a matter of immediately seeing the issue, then the categorial content of the meaning-intention must itself become a phenomenon, an immediate, intuitable given, analogous to the immediate givenness of sense data. And because intuition bespeaks an "immediate presence to...," then the dimension of the categorial must enter presentness.

What is this dimension of the categorial? It is one of the tradition's names for beingness, that which makes a thing accessible to understanding as what and how it is. Both Kant and Husserl stand within that heritage of metaphysics which sees the doctrine of beingness (*Seinslehre*) as a doctrine of categories (*Kategorienlehre*). In that tradition, beingness is always—explicitly or not—correlative to a revelatory enunciation (*logos*) and specifically to a categorial-predicative enunciation (*logos apophantikos, apophansis*). To that degree, ontology is the theoretical disclosure of beingness-as-categorial. To be sure, in this sixth chapter of the Sixth Investigation Husserl was not explicitly interested in elaborating the categories the way metaphysics from Aristotle to Hegel had done, but only in establishing the analogy between sensation and categorial intuition. Thus, although the categorial intuition appears in the work, it did not become an explicit ontological thematic there.

Husserl discusses the phenomenological presentness of the categorial dimension in terms of a "surplus" (*Überschuss*) of meaning over and above the preceptual sensuous presentation. For Kant, only the sense data are given, and the category (e.g., "substance") is simply a form for organizing that data. Husserl, however, demonstrates how the propositional categorial form of a statement can attain to intuitive fulfillment. When one says, "Rome is beautiful" or just "*Bella Roma!*" he knows that city *as* beautiful. The entrance of the "as-factor" indicates the surplus of meaning beyond sense intuition. "Rome *as* beautiful" = "Rome *is* beautiful." But there is nothing in sense perception corresponding to form-words like "is." Rather, the surplus of meaning requires another act, the categorial, in order to be seen. This categorial act, to be sure, is founded on sense preception, but it also lets the sensuously appearing object be manifest *as* what and how it *is*, i.e., in its mode of beingness beyond the purely formal sense available in the copula. And since, for Husserl, intuition is the model for knowledge (because true knowledge must have the character of fulfillment and identity), Husserl will have to broaden the scope of intuition beyond the perceiving of individual objects and make it include general and categorial objects in a categorial intuition. The object of the latter is "what is universal, what is merely documented in [sensuous] intuition."[38]

As far as Heidegger was concerned, this discovery of the surplus of intuitable categorial meaning, and the rendering of this surplus as equally present as are sense data, marked the major achievement of the Sixth Investigation. Beingness—that wherein one knows a thing as what and how it is—*is given as a phenomenon* and is not derived from the Table of Judgments as in Kant. As a phenomenon it is immediately present; indeed, it is the immediate meaningful presence of the data of sensuous intuition. There are, therefore, two levels of givenness, and man has immediate access to both. Roughly diagrammed:

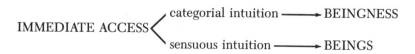

IMMEDIATE ACCESS ⟨ categorial intuition ⟶ BEINGNESS

sensuous intuition ⟶ BEINGS

With Husserl's discovery of beingness as the (immediately present) presentness of things, the young Heidegger at last had a clue for returning to Plato, Aristotle, and the whole tradition of metaphysics so as to read traditional *beingness* in terms of *time*, and specifically in terms of the one temporal moment of the *present*. To say that something "is" is to say that it "is-present-now." All of metaphysics implicitly reads beingness in terms of the (analogical) *present givenness* of beings. But that insight stayed within the rules of Husserlian phenomenology and simply applied them to the history of metaphysics. In fact it simply thematized what traditional metaphysics, mostly implicitly but occasionally explicitly, knew. However, Husserl's discovery also opened up for Heidegger the question which his master, like all metaphysicians, did not pose. Now that the strangle hold of the apophantic assertion in ontology was broken, now that beingness was rescued from the copula and rendered present as an immediately intuitable phenomenon, Heidegger could ask *how beingness itself is given* in such a way that it can be intuited. If beingness is the meaningful givenness of beings, and if this givenness of . . . is itself given as a phenomenon, then one can ask *how* it becomes present. Is it by categorial performances of subjectivity? Or is this what the Greeks called the *alētheia* or self-disclosure of things in a non-subjective framework?

To use language that Heidegger developed after World War I, Husserl had uncovered the *Bezugssinn* operative in all traditional ontology: the meaning inherent in the relation between the beingness-of-beings and man. But the *Vollzugssinn* remained to be settled: the meaning of the "how" in which the *Bezugssinn* is carried out. For Husserl, the *Vollzugssinn* was finally a matter of the performances of transcendental subjectivity. For the Greeks, the question never emerged, just as the question of the *Bezugssinn* remained implicit: The Greeks *lived* the experience of presence. But for Heidegger, the *Vollzugssinn* essentially had to do with man's disclosive *kinēsis*, his existential presence-by-absence in which there opens up a correlative world of finite sense. Man finds himself in the realm of actual present meaning by being beyond himself, relatively self-absent, in the direction of his possibilities and especially his ultimate possibility, death. He is "appropriated" into his absential possibilities, and this appropriation contributes to making possible the happening of the beingness of whatever there is.[39]

With his reading of *Logical Investigations* Heidegger had found the clue to transcending the problematic of the beingness-of-beings (metaphysics) so as to raise the question of the kinetic-disclosive "meaning," the "condition of the possibility," of beingness as such. For all his disregard for the tradition, Husserl had brilliantly uncovered its major premise, unspoken since the Greeks (and even there only whispered), that the true field for philosophy was the question of the correlation between *einai* and *nous* (Parmenides) or between *eidos* and *logos* (Aristotle), between the beingness/appearance of beings and man's nature as essential to and bound into that appearance. By interpreting beingness as immediate phenomenological presentness, Husserl had freed the beingness-issue from its captivity in Kantian formalism and had opened the way to the promised land of the question about the *possibilizing condition* of beingness. But Husserl eventually was refused access to that promised land because of his self-restriction to the issues of consciousness and objectivity. It was to be Heidegger's privilege to enter that territory and work out its topology. This he did by pushing the *eidos-logos* correlation of immediacy and presentness back to the prior question of the *kinēsis* or movement that is the very enactment (*Vollzug*) of the bond between man and beingness. Since *kinēsis* is primarily a matter of presence-by-absence (in Aristotle's terms: *energeia* that is still bound up with *dynamis*; hence, *energeia atelēs*), Heidegger would enter the promised land by reawakening the question of absence ("future," "past") as the condition of the presence (beingness) of beings.

3. The Kinetic Meaning of Beingness

It is well known that SZ was projected in two parts, the first of which was to determine, on the basis of a new understanding of man as movement (temporality), the time-character or kinetic meaning of all modes of beingness, while the second part would use this time-character as the clue for reducing traditional ontology to its underlying temporal content. The second part would confirm by historical "de-construction" what the first part had established by phenomenological "construction": a new doctrine of the "analogical unity" of beingness. This analogical unity would no longer be some *ground* of the beingness-of-beings as in metaphysics; for Heidegger it is a tri-dimensional, factical *groundless movement*. Unlike the traditional report that focused exclusively on beingness *qua* stable presentness, Heidegger would show that the absential moments of *kinēsis* are the co-efficients of—that which allows—the presentness of beings. This entails taking a step behind traditional ontology in the direction of a new "fundamental ontology" that would reveal the premetaphysical "source" of metaphysics. In short, SZ had one purpose: to understand the meaning of the intelligible presence of entities as a movement ("time") that happens in conjunction with the movement of man's transcendence ("temporality"). Each of the two parts of the work had three projected divisions, but the published volume got no further than Part I, Division 2.

Part I as a whole is entitled: "The Interpretation of Dasein in Terms of Temporality [= Part I, Divisions 1 and 2] and the Explanation of Time as the Transcendental Horizon for the Question of the Meaning of Beingness [= Part I, Division 3]." SZ I.1 would establish that the structure of human existence is care (*Sorge*); SZ I.2 would interpret the meaning of care as kinetic temporality (*Zeitlichkeit*); and SZ I.3—the unpublished division entitled "Time and Beingness"—would show how *Zeitlichkeit* in its horizon-forming function called *Temporalität*, determines the analogically unified movement-character (time-character) of the process that issues in beingness.

The density and complexity of individual analyses within SZ can tend to block a clear view of the overarching argument of the whole work. To state the content of the book simply: Man as "excess" (ahead of himself and already situated among things) holds open the area of "access" to (or understandability of) beings in their modes of beingness. As an "excess" that makes "access" possible, man contributes to opening up the *Da* or arena of intelligibility. (By "intelligibility"—*Verstehbarkeit*—we do not mean just "theoretical knowability" but, more broadly, the "accessibility of beings in meaningfulness" in all its possible modalities.) Because it is man's movement or temporality that structures this open area of sense, we may call the *Da* the "time-being" (*die Jeweiligkeit*).[40]

SZ I.1 reads human being as constituted by three moments, all of which come together in the definition of man as care.[41] These three moments are: *Existentialität*, *Faktizität*, and *Sein bei*—roughly: "ek-sistentiality," "*de-facto*-ness," and "being-with."

(1) In "ek-sistentiality" Heidegger wants us to hear the "ek," the standing "outside" and "ahead" of oneself. This does not indicate occasional sorties from a self-contained Cartesian ego but rather the simple fact that man has no "inside," that he is always "outside" in the sense of living in his worldly possibilities. Even though, under the pressure of everyday living, we tend to read ourselves "backwards" as substantial things (this is what Heidegger calls the non-proper or *uneigentlich* self), we are in fact a movement forward, a project, an ability to.... As we are projected forward into our possibilities, there opens up a "space" for ourselves and things. We risk schemes, work for goals, overspend our account; we are beings of excess who live into the distance. In a very real sense we can never make ends meet. And precisely because we are kinetically ahead of ourselves, we can understand things "as for" this or that *purpose* registered in our *aheadness*. That is, our understanding has a *futurity* to it.

(2) In fact, however, our projects are not entirely free, unconditioned, and at our will. We are already pulled into our aheadness in and

through what we may call *de-facto*-ness. We are already thrown into a family, a language, a social structure, the whole panoply of things and situations which we did not choose and which condition our actions and choices. From the first instant of our lives we are already confronted by a history as long as our gene-structure. This means that the "past" does not lie behind us but already *stands in front of us*, molding our choices, embodying and enworlding us. To say this in a temporal modality: Our conditioned, situated understanding has an *alreadiness* to it.

(3) The previous two moments are really reducible to one, which Heidegger calls "being-ahead-of-oneself-and-already-in-a-world." Man, in other words, is a situated understanding (*befindliches Verstehen*).[42] Moreover, these two-as-one make possible man's presence to (*Sein bei*) any and all particular things. This "being-with" is not the same as *de-facto*-ness, which is only the general condition of being ineluctably thrown into the world of things. Rather *Sein bei* indicates the actual "picking up" of particular things, the using of them for this or that purpose. In the *everyday* modality of the natural attitude, "being-with" things signifies a kind of absorption in or fascination by them, in such a way that one overlooks the world of sense *within which* these things appear. The everyday way of being with things is called "fallenness"—not a very happy term insofar is it has lent itself to a host of misinterpretations (for example, connections with "fallenness from grace," "negativity," and so on). Better, then, to leave aside for now this *one* modality of being-with, and to talk about being-with in its general and formal state. It indicates "rendering things present in their meaningfulness," whether for practical activity, theoretical contemplation, interpersonal involvement, or artistic appreciation. Being-with-something is always a matter of treating it *as* this or that, *for* such and such a purpose. Therefore, being-with points implicitly to the situated projection that man himself is and to the "futurity" and "alreadiness" that encompass and allow for any "present" involvement. Moreover, insofar as we are with things *as* what and how they *are*, the moment of being-with always reveals a being in its current mode of *beingness*.

Heidegger pulls these three moments together in his definition of Dasein as "care": Man is already ahead of himself—*de facto* existentiality—in such a way that he can meaningfully encounter particular things. In a briefer formulation, man is excess that makes possible access. The whole of excess-and-access is called "transcendence," and the up-shot of the analysis thus far is that in the movement of man's essence there is the opening up or dis-closure (Greek: *alētheia*) of the world of sense. We may let this much suffice for Part I, Division 1, of SZ.

Part I, Division 2, entitled "Dasein and Temporality," first of all shows what the ultimate term of man's situated projectedness, his "aheadness," is. That term is death, but not in the simple sense of his future demise at the end of his days. Death is man's ever-present finitude, the darkness which at every moment shoulders up against his light. In that sense, man is always "at the point of death" (*zum Tode*), already situated there, and he is already becoming his death in each of his daily projects. This fact remains true even when we avoid it. Such avoidance is only evidence of our penumbral awareness of what Eliot calls "the eternal Footman" who holds our coat and snickers.

We can, if we listen to our own movement, hear a protreptic to accept the inevitable and to take ourselves for what we are. Heidegger calls this the "call of conscience," and he analyzes it in the second chapter of Part I, Division 2. This call, if heeded, issues in a decision simply to be what we already are, our true and proper self. But the individual, personal (i.e., existenti*el*) decision to *become* what we already are rests on and is made possible by the meta-individual, essential (i.e., existenti*al*) structure that we *already* are. In other words, the decision to accept the inevitable is not a resignation to despair but a reappropriation of our own essence—an *amor fati*, but one which brings us to what Aristotle called, in a different framework, the "true self" (*Nic. Ethics*, K, 7).

For Heidegger, that proper, authentic self is movement. The analysis of death and conscience thus reveals the *temporal meaning* of the moments of care, which Heidegger treats in the third chapter of Division 2.[43]

(1) As ahead of himself, man is becoming not just particular possibilities but his most proper possibility of death. This "becoming" or "coming towards" (*Zu-kommen*) is the existential meaning of the "future" (*Zukunft*). Man's true futurity is not something up the road and someday to be achieved, but rather is the ever-present and never completed achieving of himself as finite.

(2) But what man is becoming is ultimately that which he already— i.e., essentially—is: his finitude, concretized in his dying. In the existential schema of temporality, "the past" as something by-gone is replaced by the "already essentially operative." This is what Aristotle called *to ti ēn einai* and what Heidegger, combining the German words for "essence" and "already is," calls *Gewesenheit*: "alreadiness." Unlike the past (*Vergangenheit*), man's existential alreadiness lies in front of him, just as his existential futurity does. In fact, the two are one in the kinetic tension of becoming-the-already, the movement which we have called "excess."

(3) The usual understanding of "the present" as a "now" which constantly slips away into the past while being replaced by yet another

"now" is existentially transformed into the disclosive activity of "rendering things present in meaning." When man accepts his essence, i.e., becomes his structural becoming, the world of present meaning is transformed from that of the everyday natural attitude into one that is aware of the movement that makes it possible. The wager is that we shall see things freshly by seeing them against the background of what is really at stake in human existence.

The major conclusion in Part I, Division 2, of SZ is that the structure of man's care finds its ground or meaning in the structure of kinetic temporality as self-transcendence and disclosure. Human being is nothing other than this disclosive transcendence: letting things be accessible in meaning by becoming what one already is.

After SZ I.2 had shown that primordial "time" is the unified structure of man's self-transcendence (and in that regard it is called *Zeitlichkeit*, "temporality"), the next but unpublished division, SZ I.3, was going to specify and work out what was already implicit in the foregoing, namely, that transcendence as excess-access forms the horizon within which one can understand the analogical unity of all modes of accessibility (beingness). In its horizonal function, primordial time or movement was to be called the *Temporalität*, the time- or movement-character of pres-ab-sence.

But what exactly is meant by this "time" that characterizes beingness? It is not the linear or cyclical *chronos* (the numbering of motion according to before and after) that the West has explicitly known at least since Aristotle. For Heidegger, "time" is the movement whereby the world of sense is opened up. All *kinēsis* according to Aristotle is a *metabolē ek tinos eis ti*, a change-over from something into something, the emergence of something heretofore hidden.[44] When Heidegger interprets *kinēsis* not "naturalistically" but as the happening of sense, it means the same as *alētheia*, the emergence (as if from hiddenness) of beings-in-their-beingness. For Heidegger this is likewise the meaning of *physis* when its unsaid meaning is retrieved from the pre-Socratics: the emergence of the world of sense within which particular beings (*ta physika*) show up for use or discourse or intellection. And since sense happens only in and with man, the movement of things into intelligibility (indeed, the very movement that is *alētheia* itself) is scored on man's correlative pres-ab-sential movement, his excess. When man is appropriated (*vereignet*) into his own movement, the "clearing" or open domain of sense happens and entities "enter" it. The event of intelligibility (*alētheia*) in its specific kinetic structure, which includes the movement of the human essence, is the single topic of Heidegger's thought.

Therefore, SZ I.3 was to look away, as it were, from the specific structures of human transcendence in order to focus on the "analogical unity" of "being," i.e., the movement that issues in the beingness/ intelligibility-of-beings. This would not mean leaving man behind, but looking at what the movement of his transcendence "co-constitutes." Regardless of what kind of entity is disclosed in its meaningful presence, the analogously same kinetic process is at work. Just as, in the traditional doctrine of motion, privativeness allows for presentness (Aristotle: a moving entity is present *as moving* only insofar as it has *not yet* arrived at its essential completeness: *energeia ateles*), so likewise in Heidegger's phenomenology a being is meaningfully present as what and how it is only in virtue of the privative self-absence (excess) of man. But man does not first of all "will" to be in movement and therefore self-absent. He does not stand outside of his movement, give it a push, and then climb aboard. The element of *de-facto*-ness reveals that man is willy-nilly pulled along in his movement, appropriated into it in spite of himself. The movement is governed by its own intrinsic recessiveness—a non-hypostasizable "nothing" that always outrides every moment in the movement while, so to speak, "pulling" the movement on.

As regards the disclosive factor in movement, we may say that the *kinēsis*, controlled by its own intrinsically recessive "origin" (*archē* as *lēthē*), is what is responsible for man's excess. This recessive origin, in conspiracy with the human transcendence that it occasions, opens the realm of sense in which entities are disclosed in their meaningfulness. The relation between excess (factical-existential transcendence) and recess (*lēthē*) is a sameness or identity (*to auto, autotēs*): Recess is responsible for excess, and excess, by resonating with recess, "lets" recess be efficacious. And this identity is what allows access. The identity of recess-excess-access is man's proper "place," and, as Aristotle says, it would be out-of-place (*atopon*) for man to choose something else as his real self. To be what he essentially and already is, man must reappropriate his factical appropriation into the movement that is governed by recess.

To describe man's condition as appropriated, Heidegger sometimes speaks of him as "called forth" or "claimed" or "drawn out." But we must avoid—at least from the standpoint of philosophy—any hypostasizing of this state of affairs, lest one posit a someone who calls or a something that draws. The intrinsically recessive dimension of movement is known *only* as it is registered in man's ineluctable exceeding of himself; and as regards this recessiveness "in itself," it would be better to speak of it as *nothing*.

Heidegger insists that the movement of recess-excess-access (*lēthē* evoking *transcendence* for the sake of *alētheia*) happens without discernable reasons. It is a groundless "play," a happening of which we can say little more than "it happens" (*es gibt, das Ereignis ereignet*). Heidegger's attempt to get beyond metaphysics (rather than to build new foundations for it) consists in his efforts to redirect man's awareness to this groundless, factical happening and then to draw the consequences.

According to Heidegger, the archaic Greek thinkers had indeed experienced *alētheia*, as the accessibility (openness) of beings, without thematizing the *lēthē* (unknowable recess appropriating excess) as what renders that possible. Because this possibilizing dimension is intrinsically withdrawn and hidden, it lends itself to being overlooked, even though it constitutes the essential withdrawnness of man himself. When it is forgotten, man finds himself fallen in among beings-in-their-beingness without being aware of the very dimension which allows that fallenness or natural attitude. The fact that metaphysics thematizes the *beingness* of beings and traces that back to God does not break out of this fallenness but only reinforces it. To surpass (*überwinden, verwinden*) metaphysics would mean to awaken to the dynamic context within which metaphysics, and the everydayness which it thematizes, are embedded. This is the task of getting to the abysmal "non-ground" of metaphysics.

4. The Non-Metaphysical "Non-Ground" of Metaphysics

Part II of SZ was projected as a phenomenological de-construction of the history of ontology in a backwards direction from Kant through Descartes to Aristotle. The purpose was to show that ever since classical Greek thought, the meaning of beingness has been interpreted in terms of time—but only one moment of time. Heidegger writes: "The outward evidence for this fact is the determination of the meaning of beingness as *parousia* or *ousia*, which in ontological-temporal terms means 'presentness.' Beings are understood in their beingness-as-'presentness,' i.e., they are understood with regard to one definite mode of time: the present."[45] Correlative with this state of affairs is the Greek understanding of man's *logos* as the function of "making things *present*." This one-dimensional "temporality" of man's *logos*-activity reflects the one-dimensional "time-character" of beingness. In fact, there is no real temporality or time here at all, but rather a presentness seeking to imitate, and reduce itself to, eternity. In this classical Greek vision, reality in the full sense is an eternal (divine) self-coincident presentness, and everything strives towards and is a *mimēsis* of that perfection. Time and movement are indices of the weakness and relative non-being of the world.

However, on the basis of the temporo-kinetic meaning both of man's

being (SZ I.1-2) and of all possible modes of beingness (SZ I.3) Heidegger hoped to unpack traditional ontology in SZ II in order to show the
"primordial 'sources' from which the traditional categories and
concepts—often genuinely—have been drawn."[46] And in interpreting
the mono-temporal basis of traditional ontology he hoped to confront
"the possibility of disclosing a yet more original, more universal horizon
from which we may draw the answer to the question, What does 'being'
mean?"[47]

This last sentence points behind Aristotle and beyond the scope of
Part II of SZ. It intimates that in pre-classical Greece, in such thinkers as
Heraclitus and Parmenides, the original and full *kinetic meaning* of the
intelligible presentness of beings might be rediscovered. But a certain
caution is in order here. Heidegger does not claim that the pre-Socratic
thinkers *thematized* the kinetic dimension of pres-ab-sence, but only
that they lived within it, saw it with peripheral vision, presumed but
never directly questioned it. Nor does Heidegger claim that the pre-
Socratic thinkers were thematically aware of the movement of human
transcendence. He says that they initiated only the "first beginning" (*der
erste Anfang*) of genuine thought, and the task he sets himself is that of
filling out that thought in a new beginning (*der andere Anfang*) in
which man would wake up to the "nothing" that evokes human transcendence and thus opens up the world of sense. The point of this new
beginning is not to go backwards in time and resurrect archaic Greece
(an impossibility, in any case) but to let oneself be appropriated into the
movement of one's groundless transcendence. The so-called step back
(*Schritt zurück*) is not a historical regress to the origins of Western
thought but an awakening to that movement. Neither the "destruction
of the history of ontology," which was planned for SZ II, nor the "retrieval" of the unsaid in pre-Socratic fragments, which was reserved for
Heidegger's later writings, is related to the past. In both cases, as
Heidegger writes, "the criticism is aimed at 'today.' "[48]

Metaphysics from Plato to Hegel is focused on beingness as the stable
presentness of entities. Heidegger's purpose is not to "destroy" that metaphysics but to embed it in the *kinēsis* that makes it possible and thus to
"overcome" it. But neither did Heidegger intend to promote metaphysics by laying new foundations for more and better versions of it. Along
with transforming our understanding of man from the one who possesses *logos* to the one who is appropriated into *kinēsis*, Heidegger's
search for the *meaning* of beingness is one in which the traditional question about the universal and ultimate ground of beingness gives way to
an adventure where "All is movement" (*Alles is Weg*).[49] The quest for
ground and certainty is transformed into *amor fati*. In a fictional dia-

logue that he wrote in the Forties, Heidegger has the following exchange take place between two persons:

—I hardly know anymore who and what I am.
—None of us knows that, as soon as we stop fooling ourselves.
—And yet we have our path....[50]

In Heidegger there is finally no laying of the groundwork *for* metaphysics, but only a protreptic to find the groundlessness *of* metaphysics: an uncontrollable movement and even, as Heidegger says, citing Heraclitus, a "game" (cf. *paizōn*, fragment 52).

But even though Heidegger's purpose is neither to condemn metaphysics nor to praise archaic Greece, he did take it upon himself to understand the pre-Socratics' unthematic awareness of "being" as *kinēsis* and its subsequent devolution into metaphysics. His own inquiry into the kinetic meaning of beingness, he says, entails an inquiry into the history of the inquiry itself. [51] And so we too now attempt a sketch of the main features of that history.

The "First Beginning." How does Heidegger read the implicit understanding of "being" that dominated the origins of philosophical thinking before Socrates? Some remarks on the non-philosophical vision of reality in archaic Greece will provide us with an *entrée* to Heidegger's interpretation.

Prof. John H. Finley, in his informative *Four Stages of Greek Thought*,[52] lays out with considerable force the implicit visual horizon within which the early Greeks, and especially Homer, moved. He finds in archaic Greece "an outgazing bent of mind that sees things exactly, each for itself, and seems innocent of the idea that thought discerps and colors reality," "a gaze that sees the world with sharp and bright particularity."[53] The age in which such a mind thrives "is one that lives with the color of the world as people directly feel it; it does not brush aside the show and impression of things in favor of ideas and definitions that are felt to express reality more purely."[54] This wholistic, archaic Greek mind which has not yet isolated that part of itself which deals with recurrences and logical sequences, lives in "a time when meanings seem within people's reach," not by analysis but by a simple openness to the meaning of daily concerns.[55] This simple and great age lies "before the complexities of nature and society separate man in a pursuit of special powers that destroys the former faith in the full consciousness."[56] And corresponding to that consciousness, things are "inherently noble and beautiful, not because we think them so" but because they themselves are suffused with "brightness" and "bright particularity," a "flashing concreteness and beautiful knowability," and they "remain each distinct while jointly comprising the brilliant world."[57]

Moreover, this very luminosity was seen as a call to archaic Greek man. "The [heroic] heart that leaps to the invitation of sparkling appearances is the heart that would itself perform as handsomely." Indeed, to be truly a man means to feel "the fierce tug in the brilliant world that draws to brilliant action."[58]

But such an age, filled with a surity that has nothing to do with Cartesian certitude, is brief. The shift from the eighth century of Homer to the fifth century of the Sophists constitutes both a preservation of this brilliance and a dimming of it to "clarity." Finley sees in the classical age of Athens a turn "from shape to concept, from story to analysis, from mythological to conceptual ways of thinking." For example, "In turning from the wide reaches of Homer and Aeschylus, Sophocles substituted depth for scope, representativeness for movement, lapidary form for long horizons."[59]

But the brilliance and concentrated simplicity of archaic Greece remains a dream that will not die, and in a particularly striking passage Finley speaks of the possibility of retrieving it.

> The pristine freshness that in Homer clothes the world and the innumerable people and objects in it once shimmered for each of us. However far we have traveled from that first shining sight, it can still awaken recognition. Hence Homer keeps reality, not at bottom because his blind gaze still saw the Mycenean past which the Greeks had lost for five centuries, but because everything that he describes keeps a flashing concreteness and beautiful knowability such as we once felt. But whereas we through education were led on to more complex and intellective realities, he traced to its proper conclusion the clarity with which he started.[60]

These remarks about the extra-philosophical context of archaic Greece are a fitting prelude to understanding Heidegger's approach to early Greek thinking and its vision of reality. Heidegger's effort is not just to capture anew the freshness and luminosity that characterized the early Greek poets and thinkers, but to retrieve from that experience a dimension of it which went unspoken.

In order to sort out both the "said" and the "unsaid" of the archaic vision, Heidegger concentrates on two Greek words: *physis* and *alētheia*. The later Latin translations of these words as *natura* and *veritas* obscure the original archaic experience embodied in the Greek, which was a unified experience of (a) movement, (b) stability, and (c) appearance. At some risk (for we introduce the word *eidos*/eidetic, which comes from later, classical philosophy) we may unite the three in one phrase and say that the experience was of the *kinetic-stable-eidetic* beingness of beings. With the proper precautions, let the phrase stand; and let us unpack its three moments, beginning from the last.[61]

(1) Beingness is a matter of the *appearance* or *phainesthai* of beings. Beings are *phainomena*, "self-manifestations" which exhibit what Finley calls brightness, nobility, and beauty. They come out of the dark and show themselves (*alētheia*); they are understood as "that which stands in the light," that which is suffused with glory (*doxa*) and which shows a radiant face (*eidos*).

(2) Insofar as beings *stand* in their luminosity, their beingness is a matter of stability (*stasis*), of having come to a stand, of and by themselves, there in the light. Beings are "the stable," what Aristotle would later call the *synestōta* and *synistamena* (*Physics*, B, 1, 192 b 13 and 193 a 36), indeed even *hypostasis*. Even if this "standing" be called a "lying there" (*hypokeimenon*), the same vision is at work: The luminous things of the world have "staying power" in the realm of the time-being, even if they will eventually pass away.

(3) But as standing in appearance, beings are implicitly understood as *having emerged* into this stable self-manifestation. This emergent character is captured by the word *physis* (upsurgence, emergence) and by the "*a–*" of *alētheia* (coming-out-of-hiddenness). But the process always harbors a referral to that from which things have emerged and to which they remain related, a *lēthē* or, in later language, a *dynamis*, a hidden *empowering* of their movement which permeates them in their on-going emergence into the light. Beings not only come into presence (*genesis*) but also recede from presence (*phthora*), and even while in presence they maintain their referral to the recessive dimension which gave them forth and claims them back. The *kinēsis* which issues in stable appearance preserves as well a privativeness which never allows the being's appearance to exhaust its reality.

Moreover, all three moments are implicitly correlative with the essence of man, understood (e.g., in Parmenides) as *nous*, "apprehension" or "letting something be seen." According to Heidegger this word *noein* implies (1) opening the clearing of finite, intelligible presence into which beings can emerge, (2) holding beings in that clearing and thus reinforcing their staying power, and (3) preserving the radiant appearance they offer. The whole process of kinetic-stable appearance is not a "naturalistic" one which happens in some Mesozoic era before man, but a "phenomenological" one, the event of sense which happens only in and with man's essence as *noein*. Without Dasein, no *physis* or *alētheia*.

Heidegger claims that all this was already understood, if only penumbrally, by the archaic Greek poets and thinkers. To thematize this implicit vision is merely to re-open the archaic world again, as Professor Finley has done, and perhaps to enhance thereby our reading of its poetry and thought. This is the relatively easy task of reconstituting the "first beginning." But this is not enough for the "turn" in understanding "being" that is Heidegger's goal. It leaves us with a vision of the natural attitude at its best, where man is "all eyes" and is caught up in seeing the world as just "there" in its emergent, stable radiance. But for Heidegger the point is to burrow down to what lies unsaid even in this re-thematized view. And in fact, in discussing *lēthē*, the recessive dimension of emergence, Heidegger was on just that path. We already know what he is looking for: an understanding of man as kinetically tied into that recess and as appropriated by it unto his own uncanny excess. But that is the task of "beginning anew," and we shall take it up in a moment. However, our purpose now is rather to follow out the devolution of the archaic "natural attitude" into its metaphysical thematization by Plato and Aristotle.

The Start of Metaphysics.[62] According to Heidegger it is with Plato that the rich multi-dimensionality of the emergence of sense gets repressed in favor of one moment in the process: the eidetic appearance of a being as *what* it is, its *eidos*. The *eidos* eventually loses its reference to the being's emergence into stability, and it becomes instead "that as which" a being presents itself for possible intellectual viewing by man. Thus, when *eidos* assumes the role of the primary characteristic of the beingness of beings, *physis* and *kinēsis*—emergence out of the *lēthē*—get covered over. With that, any hope of grasping the correlative kinetic nature of man is lost. Now beingness is read in terms of stability and appearance, and man is interpreted as the one who renders beings *present* in that stable appearance. And since only what is unmoving and eternal is, for Plato, truly stable, only the eternal shows itself as true being (*ontōs on*). Temporal, moving beings get relegated to the status of *mē on*, not-really-being.

Concomitantly a new term emerges to designate the beingness of beings: *ousia*, presentness-in-reality, a presentness over which the mind can in some way dispose (*verfügbares Anwesen*), if only by being able to line up with it in a correct (*orthotēs*) vision. If we look forward in history from this vantage point, we can see that all metaphysical thought after Plato will be governed by the notion of permanent presentness (*ousia*) in all the forms it will take in later thinkers. If we look backwards from Plato to archaic Greece, we can see, to be sure, that Platonic stability and essential appearance do preserve some continuity with pre-Socratic thinking insofar as they represent moments in (and specifically, the consequence of) the emergent process of sense. But in Plato the consequence of the process (*eidos*) has swallowed up and suppressed the antecedent emergence (*kinēsis*).

Aristotle represents a decisive shift away from Plato's emphasis on *idea/eidos* but does not thereby recover the original Greek meaning of kinetic-stable-eidetic beingness. For Aristotle, a being in its movement and becoming is no longer, as it was for Plato, a *mē on*, a not-really-being. Rather, it is the primary instance of *ousia*. The characteristics of a being are four. (1) A being (*to on*) is that which is stably present, "standing" or "lying" there in reality (*hypostasis, hypokeimenon*). (2) A being is that which rests, in the sense of having completed its substantial *genesis* within its *peras* or formal boundaries; but even in this repose of the state of actuality, the being is an in-gathered movement, for, as Aristotle puts it, "*Energeia* in the strict sense seems to be the same as *kinēsis*" (*Meta.* Theta, 3, 1047 a 32). (3) A being is that-which-has-been-brought-forth, whether by "nature" (*physis*) or "art" (*poiēsis*). And (4) a being is that which, as brought forth into repose, shows itself by standing out in evidence: A being *is* in its *eidos* or *morphē*. To summarize these four characteristics, we may say that for Aristotle a being is an *ergon*—a "work" in the unique Greek sense of that which *appears* as having been *brought forth* and *rendered stable*. A being is "e-ventuated evidence," a kinetic-stable appearance.

From this understanding of what a being is, we can see why Aristotle calls beingness *energeia*, that is, an entity's "presentness-in-reality as an (emergent, stable, appearing) *ergon*." And since the word *telos* means much the same as *ergon*, we can understand why Aristotle equally names beingness *entelecheia*: an entity's "presence in the fulfilled state of (emergent, stable) appearance."

We can see that to a certain degree Aristotle regains the kinetic dimension of the implicit pre-Socratic understanding of the "being"-process. But insofar as Aristotle's *kinēsis* follows after and to some extent is controlled by Plato's *idea/eidos*, it falls short of the pre-Socratic experience. *Kinēsis* in Aristotle is always for the sake of *eidos*. All movement is read from and for an entity's emergence *into presentness*, and the *logos* that reveals the *ousia* of something always has the function of "rendering an entity *present* in its meaning."

To be sure, Aristotle gave the primacy in *ousia* to that-*which*-is-present ("first *ousia*") rather than to that-*as-which* the being presents itself ("second *ousia*"). "But both of these stand on the past-Platonic side of *ousia*." They are differentiations within beingness and hence remain modes of being-present. The emergence that issues in *ousia* lies back behind *ousia* and is not recovered by Aristotle. The *hoti esti* (existence, thatness) of an entity shows itself along with the *ti esti* (essence, whatness)—both as modes of *ousia*. Henceforth throughout its history metaphysics will give one or the other of these the primacy within *ousia*, but metaphysics will not question back *behind* the beingness that differentiates itself into whatness and thatness. As we saw earlier, even Aquinas' thematization of the primacy of *esse* remains caught within the general ousiological perspective of Western metaphysics. To question, as Aquinas does, beyond the *esse entium* and to arrive at *ipsum esse subsistens* is not to question behind *ousia* but only to point towards the highest instance of it. To step, interrogatively, behind *ousia* would be, of course, to step out of metaphysics and into its groundless, kinetic "source."

We need not trace the development of metaphysics from classical thought through medieval philosophy to the modern world. It is enough that we indicate here, in summary fashion, the "repressed content" of Western thought, especially within the explicit thematic of metaphysics. We have said that the full tri-dimensionality of "being" or *alētheia* includes recess-excess-access: *lēthē* evoking man's transcendence for the sake of *on alēthes*, disclosed entities. As regards that tri-dimensionality we may say:

(1) In the first beginning of Western thought among the pre-Socratics
  (a) the dimension of excess was hardly named;
  (b) the dimension of recess was named (for example, in Heraclitus' *physis kryptesthai philei*) but not thematically thought through; and
  (c) the dimension of access was thematized as the emergence of beings into stable appearance.

(2) With the start of classical metaphysics in the works of Plato and Aristotle
  (a) the excess-dimension began to emerge (but within the ousiological framework), for example, in Plato's notion of *eros;*
  (b) the recess-dimension was neither named nor thought; and
  (c) the access-dimension began to lose its kinetic sense and to become a matter of presentness-in-reality (*ousia*), with a differentiation into essence and existence. The ousiological task of metaphysics became the ontotheological one of finding the common and the ultimate instance of *ousia*, whether that was interpreted in terms of essence or existence.

(3) The fulfillment of metaphysics, in Heidegger's interpretation, consists in the uttermost reduction of beingness to presentness in the age of "technicity" (*die Technik*) where

(a) the excess that is human transcendence is reduced to the mono-dimensionality of rendering all things accessible for possible consumption;

(b) the recess or intrinsic hiddenness of the factical happening-of-sense is entirely overlooked; and

(c) accessibility-for-consumption becomes virtually the only operative meaning of beingness.

Overcoming Metaphysics. The new beginning that Heidegger seeks to prepare through his works would consist in the recovery of the full gamut of the process of "being." Such a recovery is what Heidegger means by the "turn," which, as we noted, does not consist in a shift in Heidegger's language and style in the Thirties nor in the supposed emergence of a new topic in his thought. The turn, rather, is what Heidegger means by overcoming (*überwinden*) or surpassing (*verwinden*) the forgottenness of the factical tri-dimensionality of "being." Overcoming metaphysics by recovering the full scope of the disclosure-process does not mean that man "grasps" the hiddenness/facticity of "being" but rather that he allows the disclosure-process its "predilection for hiddenness," its "*kryptesthai philein.*" Man does this by following, by giving into, his own transcendence or excess, within which there is already registered the hiddenness/facticity of the whole process.

This kind of "letting go" (*Gelassenheit*) is what the "turn" is about: man's lived awareness of the pres-ab-sentiality that is already operative both in his own kinetic structure and in the kinetic structure of the emergence of accessible entities, but that is obscured by fallenness, metaphysics, and technicity. To "take the turn" is to wake up to and stand within the groundlessness and finitude of the "being"-process. After one takes the turn, presumably factories will run as before, cities will still be what they are, people will no doubt continue to work for an exploitative wage. But, according to Heidegger, somehow (he does not and cannot say how) all these doings will be significantly different, if only because they will be suffused with an awareness of and careful respect for the full, finite threefoldness of the happening-of-sense.

C. A PROTREPTIC: ON LEAVING METAPHYSICS TO ITSELF

To confront Rahner's philosophical efforts in GW with the whole of Heidegger's thought has an element of unfairness about it, if only because Rahner's philosophical position—even though his later concentration is on theology—shifted somewhat in his later years. To be sure, HW, which appeared two years after GW, is only a recapitulation of GW and an extension of its theory of cognition and metaphysics to the question of man's openness to a possible revelation, and in that latter work we find no real shift in Rahner's positions on beingness, metaphysics, and man. But within Rahner's theological essays, particularly those that stem from after the Fifties, one can discern a gradual de-emphasis of the earlier discussion of God as pure and absolute beingness, and a tendency to speak of God in terms of "mystery" or even "the holy mystery." In fact, in one of Rahner's latest works there is a conscious and decisive abandonment of the word *das Sein* when it comes to discourse about the divine. Whether this strategy is merely pedagogical or in fact represents an awareness on Rahner's part that the language of *das Sein* makes his work vulnerable to the critique of onto-theology, cannot be decided here. But we may listen to the text in which he makes this move explicit.

In the context of asking how one might name the term of man's transcendence, Rahner in *The Foundations of Christian Faith*[63] writes:

> We could, of course, follow the venerable tradition of the whole of Western philosophy, a tradition to which we are certainly responsible, and simply call it "absolute being" [*Sein*] or "being in an absolute sense" or the "ground of being" which establishes everything in original unity. But when we speak this way of "being" and the "ground of being," we run the deadly risk that many contemporaries can hear the word "being" only as an empty and subsequent abstraction from the multiple experience of the individual realities which encounter us directly. For this reason we want to try to call the term and the source of our transcendence by another name.... We want to call the terms and source of our transcendence "the holy mystery."

A glance at Rahner's Preface to the present essay confirms the suspicion that, as much as the language of mystery stems from his Christian experience, he does intend the reader to see the connection with what Heidegger has to say about "mystery" (*das Geheimnis*) in his own writings. In his essay *On the Essence of Truth*, first published in 1943 but drafted two years before Rahner came to study with him, Heidegger spoke of "the mystery" as the self-concealing dimension of the disclosure-process, as the *lēthē* in *alētheia*.[64] This was also what Heidegger had in mind when he spoke of philosophy as a nostalgia for the "all" that claims and calls to man (see Rahner's citation of this at the end of Chapter III above). Clearly in his later texts Rahner invites the reader to see at least a formal homology between the Christian God and the *lēthē*-dimension of disclosure in Heidegger's thought. In the Preface to the present work Rahner writes that it is the task of the theologian to speak about the unutterable mystery, even though Heidegger insists on silence with regard to it.

From the viewpoint of scholarship the issue is whether Rahner's theory of man and cognition, and his grounding of metaphysics on that base, do or do not fall under Heidegger's indictment of ontotheology and the forgetfulness of the hiddenness of "being." But I am not interested here in an external comparison, a tactic of lining up two thinkers and checking their sentences and paragraphs against each other. The preceding chapters have done that, with results that the reader can decide for himself. The point now in the following pages—which are more in the form of a protreptic than a formal drawing of conclusions—is to discuss the issue, not texts. Putting Rahner and Heidegger into dialogue in the preceding chapters has had only one purpose: not to find out which thinker is "better" than the other, but to find out what man is about. For Rahner, man is about God; for Heidegger, man is about *a-lētheia*. The issue in what follows is not what a certain theologian and a certain philosopher have said, but what we might learn from them. We are not asking about Rahner and Heidegger but about ourselves.

1. Naming the Unnamable

Man is the hermeneutical animal in at least two senses. His fate is that he can deal with himself and other beings only mediately, only from a vantage of distance that is a constant effort to recover presence. He has to spell things out (cf. *aus-legen*), to deal with them *as* such and so, in order to know them or use them. This necessary activity indicates that his own essence is mediate, caught between directly given things and the movement which renders them intelligible. As such a mediation, he is always an interpreter, a hermeneut, one who understands things by introducing them into the kinetic projection that he himself is. The hermeneutical animal is likewise the one who has *logos*—or better, "is had" by *logos*. He ineluctably binds things (cf. *legein*) into unities of sense, but only because he binds them into the movement whereby he is already stretched out beyond himself, bound for the ever receding term of his movement. In this first sense, man is the hermeneutical animal because he is the kinetic animal, the one who lives ahead of himself in movement.

In a second sense, man is the hermeneutical animal insofar as the reflexive appropriation of his movement is itself only the spelling out, the thematization, of what he already is. Such explicitation shows that man—the kinetic-mediating-interpreting animal—is likewise the "metaphysical" animal, the one who is always reaching out beyond (*meta*) the sensible entities he meets (*ta physika*), reaching for the source of their appearance at all (*hē physis*, in the sense of *archē*). In this second sense of "hermeneutical," one is confronted with the question of how one might thematically name the structure that one already is. To call that structure "movement" is to raise the question of what defines the movement, and hence to promote the question of naming a step further: how to name the ever recessive "term" of that movement.

To return for just a moment to Rahner and Heidegger: If the arguments of the present essay are valid, there is more than just a formal parallel between GW and SZ; there is a convergence of thought on one and the same issue, namely, the appropriation of man into a movement, the receding term of which eludes his grasp. It does not matter that Heidegger conducted his analyses into man's pre-predicative comportment whereas Rahner chose to begin with the judgment. It *may* matter that Rahner arrived at his kinetic reading of man's essence from a text that was already shot through with theological presuppositions that, in turn, rested on a metaphysics of stable presentness (*ousia*) rather than on a vision of the movement that issues in *ousia*. The question about naming the term of man's movement becomes, in that case, a matter of how seriously one takes the issue of *kinēsis*.

For better or worse, Rahner's GW imports into the discussion of man and metaphysics the presupposition that cognition is first and above all a matter of *intuition*. Riding behind that presupposition is the Aristotelian understanding of the divine as a self-intuiting intuition, a perfect self-coincidence in a unity of being and self-knowledge. The transcendental turn in GW is thus scored on a hidden premise: that man is an intuition *manquée*, that he is movement only insofar as he approximates the ideal state of beingness, which is the perfect self-presence of the divine.

Although GW purports to operate entirely in a transcendental mode, even when it is retrieving the unsaid from a pre-transcendental text, it is difficult for the reader—this reader, at least—to overlook the fact that in GW Rahner is already apprised, from another source, of the nature of being-as-such. That other source is not just Aristotle, but the Christian theology that adapted Aristotle's language to name the God of its faith. GW is not, then, an innocent work, a "presuppositionless" inquiry, but an inquiry already guided by the knowledge garnered from belief in the Father of Jesus Christ. For all its dedication to the transcendental turn and to the questioning of beingness, it already knows the answer before it starts. It is, in the broadest sense, an "apologetic" work, an exercise in *fides quaerens intellectum*. Rahner admits as much on the first page of the treatise when he says that the *Summa Theologiae* (and implicitly his own book) is what everyone knows it to be: a treatise written from within the wisdom derived from divine grace. To say this much is not to point out a defect in GW—Rahner in fact sees the theological contextualization of his book to be an advantage—but simply to indicate what kind of philosophy Rahner is about. Rahner is to be taken seriously when he writes in the Preface to the present essay, "I am a theologian, and so much a theologian that I make no claim to being a philosopher." It seems that this self-description applies as well to the Rahner who authored GW.

This is not the place to enter into the long-standing debate over the possibility or impossibility of a Christian philosophy. But neither, on the other hand, do I take it as self-evident that the believer who philosophizes is only engaged in an "as-if" activity (Heidegger). To be sure, there is a cheap and disreputable "Christian philosophy" that merely works backwards from the answers to the questions, but this is not the kind of work that either Aquinas or Rahner turned out. If anything, both Aquinas and Rahner knew that the God of their faith was no answer at all but an "incomprehensible" that in no way absolves man from earthly existence and questioning. Rahner says as much when, discussing the incomprehensibility of God in Aquinas, he draws the consequences of that incomprehensibility for the nature of man: "Man is the question for which there is no answer. . . .The Christian is the true and most radical skeptic."[65] That is, man is the entity who constantly finds himself in the presence of a faceless, ineffable, unnamable, undefinable, silent and withdrawing mystery.[66] Yet, Rahner says that the theologian must speak about this ineffable.

It is clear that Rahner sees Heidegger's thought, correctly understood, as a propaedeutic to theological discourse. Once Rahner came to see (as he did not in his 1940 article on Heidegger) that what Heidegger called "the Nothing" (*das Nichts*) was not a *nihil absolutum* but rather the withdrawing, self-hiding dimension of the disclosive process—i.e., the mystery—he felt free to adapt Heidegger's thought to his own theological ends. This is most clear in the introductory chapters of *Foundations of Christian Faith.*

On the other hand, there are ample statements from Heidegger to the effect that philosophy has no significance for theology. But what does that mean? Is Heidegger saying that theology should avoid metaphysics (= philosophy)? Or that *his* philosophy (= non-metaphysics) knows nothing of the God of revelation? And finally one can ask how much it should matter that Heidegger affirms that his own thought is neutral vis-à-vis revelation. Surely Heidegger is not the last word on his own thought, any more than Aristotle was on his. Rahner is as much within his rights when he retrieves from Heidegger a transcendence towards God as the unnamable mystery, as Heidegger is within his rights when he forces Heraclitus to yield up an awareness of the *lēthē*. (Heidegger writes: "Did Heraclitus intend his question as we have just been discussing it? Was what this discussion has said within the range of his concepts? Who knows? Who can say?"[67])

But everything is not a free-floating construction in GW. Rahner's engagement with what Heidegger said is as rigorous as Rahner's effort to get him to say more than Heidegger thought he could. At the same time, we may say that, in retrieving from Heidegger an awareness of God in man's transcendence, Rahner's language falls behind his insights.

The insight that prompted GW was a non-philosophical, non-metaphysical belief in the God of Christian faith. The language in which Rahner chose to articulate that insight was the ousiological grammar of beings and beingness, transcendentally transformed. Rahner's "turn to the subject" within the ousiological tradition was already a momentous advance. It was based on the conviction that philosophy and theology will be "taken seriously only if and insofar as they can show the listener that he already has something to do with this question [of transcendence]."[68] While all that may be to the good, the traditional language of "actuality" did not and does not allow a proper articulation of the dimension of mystery that is the beginning and motive of such philosophizing in the first place. This is especially evident in what we termed the "confounding" of entities and beingness (see Chapter IV above). Therefore, Rahner's later shift from the language of beingness to that of mystery seems to me to represent far more than a rhetorical strategy; it is rather a rending of the ousiological garment, a surrender of its language and viewpoint in order to attempt to find words adequate to an insight that transcends the metaphysical experience. Rahner's break with metaphysics is, to be sure, neither clean nor consistent. Rahner will continue to speak now and again of "infinity" and "infinite actuality" when he means the mysterious incomprehensibility of the God of faith. He will still waver in his terminology for the divine: a being (*Sein*) of perfect self-presence (*Bei-sich-sein*). Are these the careless slips of a theologian who is not fully aware of when his philosophy edges beyond ousiology and when it falls back into it?

Rahner, it seems, is simply not concerned with this matter. That indifference may be in the strength as well as the danger of his theology. The strength lies in the insight, which comes from outside philosophy, that man is claimed from beyond himself. The danger lies in the fact that Rahner's slips back into the grammar of ousiology may end up forfeiting the mysteriousness of the mystery that he believes in. An adequate language may not guarantee an insight, but it can protect it. That insight, according to Rahner, is that the whereunto (*Wohin*) of man's transcendence "presents itself to us in the mode of withdrawal, of silence, of distance, of being always inexpressible, so that speaking of it, if it is to make sense, always requires listening to its silence."[69] Naming the unnamable includes a good deal of silence about that unnamable, perhaps even, as Heidegger puts it, "silence about silence." The language of ousiology, based on presentness and actuality, unaware of the absence that allows for presence, has too much to say about God. Perhaps, then, the way to talk "about" the ineffable is to keep silent with regard to it, to leave metaphysics to itself.[70]

2. Atheology

What does Rahner's transcendental analysis of the movement of agent intellect show about its term? It is quite an easy—and erroneous—slip from anticipation (*Vorgriff*) to objective knowledge, from projectivity to intuition. While it is true that Rahner constantly warns against this slippage, the warning seems too little heeded by many scholars who would follow in his footsteps. Even the translation of *Vorgriff* by the English "pre-apprehension" (which seems to indicate one apprehension that precedes another) is momentously misleading and abets the misunderstanding that man intuits (grasps) God as the condition for his sensible intuition of worldly entities. The English translation of GW, at p. 181, says that man's pre-apprehension "attains to God," whereas Rahner prefers the language of going towards (*gehen auf*) or aiming at (*zielen auf*) the unity of beingness and knowing. The purpose of Rahner's entire philosophical effort is to show that man has only one apprehension—of worldly things—and no prior apprehension (pre-apprehension, pre-grasp) of God. To surrender Rahner's understanding of man as movement is to lose the brilliance of the revolution that he brought about within ousiology and the breakthrough he made—partially and tentatively—beyond ousiology. To apply this to Rahner's theology: If all dogmatics is to become theological anthropology, and if that means transcendental anthropology, then all dogmatics is to be read in terms of *kinetic* anthropology. Man projects, anticipates, the unity of self-presence without ever attaining it. In a real sense "God" appears precisely by not appearing, for man is the question to which there is no answer. "The infinite horizon of human questioning is experienced as one which recedes further and further the more answers man can discover."[71]

The achievement of Rahner in attempting to name the unnamable while leaving metaphysics to itself consists in his resolute turn to man, his return of Christian philosophy and theology to the point where they begin and also must end: human experience. If there is a failure of Christian philosophy and theology in the two millennia of their existence, it lies in a forgetfulness of finite, human experience as the only place where one can stand, whether or not a revelation from the beyond is given. It may well be that the very power of the experience *of revelation* is responsible for this forgetfulness. In that case, Rahner's turn to the *experience* of revelation is a momentous accomplishment. But the nature and structure of this "experience of . . ." is such that man is aware of himself, even under the pressure of grace, as an asymptotic nostalgia, an ever-unfulfilled act of unification, or, as Rousselot put it, a synthesis that is never made. Rahner calls this condition man's *unfulfilled* transcendentality,[72] echoing Heraclitus' *agchibasiē* (fragment 22) and James Joyce's "almosting it." What, then, is the experience of God? It is certainly not an intuition, grasp, or apprehension (prior or posterior). It is more a hope than it is a surety or a vision. It is more authentically found in the experience of the insecurity and groundlessness of experience than in the supposed sighting of the stable ground that holds everything together.

The Greek name for the entity of most stable self-presence was *theos* or *theion*: God, the divine. This still point of the turning world, this resolution of all oppositions, is a dream that dies hard. Christianity was happy to take it over into its own vocabulary as a name for what it had experienced in an entirely different way and in a very different world. Thus, "theology," a word born of Plato, became Christianity's tender for its self-interpretation, even though everything that Christianity stood for was set against the promised security and rational accessibility attested to by this word. And in the wake of that borrowing came "philosophy," the desire for the contemplative vision of *theos*, which God alone properly has and, because he is not jealous (*Meta.* 983 a 4), is happy to share, within limits, with man. The movement of man's desire, the experience of his incompleteness, had its goal set for it: the intuition of stable, eternal self-coincidence. Wisdom became the correlation between the visionary "believer" and his God, the *theōros* and his *theōrēma*. Faith became a matter of theology.

Rahner has never traced such a devolving history, but his philosophical and theological accomplishment points to an alternative, a way of overcoming it. That way is a return to man's experience of himself as movement. Rahner has turned the discourse about God (theo-logy) back to a discourse about man (kineo-logy). "Man knows infinity only insofar as he experiences himself *surpassing* all of his knowledge in anticipation. . . ."[73] and "A person knows explicitly what 'God' means only insofar as he allows his transcendence beyond everything that is objectively identifiable to enter into his consciousness. . . ."[74]

This return to discourse about man is one that Heideggerians would do well to heed. There is an unfortunate tendency in Heidegger's own works, and in the work of his commentators, to hypostasize "being" into an autonomous "other" separate from entities and from man and almost endowed with a life of its own. The following statement, in which Heidegger virtually summarizes his thought, illustrates that tendency: " 'Being' itself recedes, but, as this recess, 'being' is precisely the pull that claims man's being as the place of 'being's' own arrival."[75] Such a way of speaking seems to promote "being" (*das Sein*) to the level of a Platonic super-entity; it also can mislead the naive reader into thinking that Heidegger promises an "advent of being" that would issue in some kind of intuitive presence, a secular beatific vision. But *das Sein* is surely no thing or event, off by itself, which "recedes" and "claims" man so that it can show up for itself. As Aristotle clearly says (and Heidegger quotes him), being (whether beingness or "being") is not a separate entity (cf. *Physics* B, 1, 193 b 5: *ou chōriston on*), but rather is the disclosive structure of entities, distinguishable from them but neither separate from nor reducible to them. Moreover, it is distinguishable only by man (cf. ibid., *alla kata ton logon*), specifically through man's kinetic structure of excess and access. It would be better, then, to speak of the "withdrawal of 'being' " by speaking only of the registration of "being" in man's own movement. Thus, Heidegger's statement quoted above, correctly translated, would mean: the disclosure of entities has a privative dimension that is registered in man's transcendence in such a way as to allow the disclosure of entities. That is, the analogical unity (or "meaning") of the beingness of entities is the hidden but disclosive movement conjoined with, and indeed initiating, the world-disclosive movement of man.

A philosophical effort to name the unnamable while leaving metaphysics behind might conceive of itself as an "atheology." This would be a mode of discourse (*logos*)—or better, a silent attunement to one's own movement (*logos* as *kinēsis*)—that recognizes that the *theos* of traditional metaphysics and Christian theology is hardly adequate to the mystery inscribed in that movement. Atheology is a refusal of all claims to know already that the world is grounded in self-identical cognition. It radically calls into question the ontology of coincidence that rules from the *noēsis noēseōs* of Aristotle, through what Rousselot called "the intellectualism [= intuitionism] of St. Thomas," down to the being-as-*Bei-sich-sein* of Rahner. In Heidegger's terms, it would be a kind of thinking that is captured by difference rather than identity, by movement rather than *stasis*.[76] From an atheological perspective, Rahner's retrieval of the unsaid in Aquinas did not go far enough. Rahner recaptured a hidden theme in Aquinas that is finally only a transcendentalized Aristotelianism. But Rahner did not go deep enough into the pre-philosophical roots of Aristotle (I mean the archaic Greeks) or into the pre-theological roots of Aquinas (I mean Jesus). To have taken those further steps to have meant a decisive move out of metaphysics as natural theology, the rational search for the stable ground of all that is. Instead, Rahner—at least in *Geist in Welt*—delivered the possibility of regrounding theological metaphysics on a transcendental-anthropological base, even a kinetic base, but one which finally did not undo the ontology of identity that is the heritage of Western thought since Plato.

Whatever the transformations that Rahner made in his thought after GW, specifically while engaged in Christian theology, the achievement of his first book remains precarious, always in danger of falling back into an a-kinetic ousiology. Its accomplishments, as far as they go, are momentous. He removed the Platonic masks from Aquinas—and left us with a radically reinterpreted Aristotle. But to have removed the Aristotelian masks from Aquinas would have left us with—what? Perhaps the experience of Jesus. But—one last move—to remove even the mask of Jesus might have left us, for better or worse, with ourselves: the radical question that finds no answer.

To carry out a retrieval is to take utterly seriously the historicity of man, not as a movement towards a guaranteed end but as an asymptotic measure of the unending mystery that lurks within one. If the ineluctability of man's historicity raises the specter of relativism, then relativism must be faced. Terror before relativism is terror before man himself. Only by living through that terror do we find what is to be found and do we leave in silence what eludes our grasp.

Such an atheology might harbor the possibility of belief, not as a prevision of *theos* but as a resolute commitment, a surrender, to an unceasing exploration that constantly returns us to where we started: the darkness of interrogative knowing. In *Geist in Welt* there is too much presupposed, unquestioned baggage for such an atheology. For those who choose to carry that baggage, the book is a major accomplishment. For those who do not carry that baggage, the task of finding out who man is remains open.

Notes

1. Rahner GW 281/387 (387). *Imaginatio non transcendit tempus et continuum:* S.T., I, 84, 7, obj. 2.
2. Ibid., 281/387 f. (387).

3. Ibid., 228/389 (388).
4. Respectively: *In VI Meta.* lect. 1, n. 1170, and *In IV Meta.* lect. 5, n. 593.
5. Rahner, GW 282/389 (388 f.).
6. Ibid., 283/390 (390).
7. Ibid.
8. Ibid., 284/391 (390).
9. Added in the second edition, p. 47; the corresponding page in the first edition is GW 17/34.
10. Rahner, GW 285-94/393-404 (392-403).
11. Ibid., 284/391 (391).
12. Ibid., 285/392 (391 f.).
13. Ibid., 286/394 (393).
14. Ibid., 287/395 (395).
15. Ibid., 287 f./396 (395).
16. Ibid., 289/398 (397).
17. Ibid.
18. Ibid., 290/398 (398).
19. Ibid., 290/400 (399).
20. Ibid., 291-94/400-04 (399-403). The last paragraph of this section in the Eng. trans. (pp. 404-05) was added by Professor Metz in the second edition, p. 403 f.
21. Ibid., 292/402 (401).
22. Ibid., 294/404 (403).
23. Ibid., 294-96/406-08 (404-07), simply entitled "*Der Mensch*" in the first edition.
24. Ibid., 295 f./407 f. (406) for this sentence and the following.
25. Henri Bergson, *Oeuvres*, Edition du centenaire, ed. André Robinet (Paris: Presses Universitaires de France, 1970), p. 1347.
26. Walter Biemel, "Heidegger and Metaphysics," in *Heidegger, the Man and the Thinker*, ed. Thomas Sheehan (Chicago: Precedent, 1981), p. 163.
27. Martin Heidegger, *Vier Seminare* (Frankfurt: Vittorio Klostermann, 1977), pp. 73 and 82.
28. Rahner, "Existential Philosophy," p. 128.
29. See Thomas Sheehan, "Getting to the Topic: The New Edition of *Wegmarken*," *Research in Phenomenology*, 7 (1977), 299-316, esp. pp. 302-06.
30. Martin Heidegger, *Wegmarken*, ed. Friedrich-Wilhelm von Herrmann, *Gesamtausgabe*, I, 9 (Frankfurt: Vittorio Klostermann, 1976), p. 407 (1967 ed.: p. 235); *The Question of Being*, trans. William Kluback and Jean T. Wilde (New Haven, Conn.: College and University Press, Twayne, 1958), p. 75.
31. Helmut Franz, "Das Denken Heideggers und die Theologie," in *Heidegger und die Theologie*, ed. Gerhard Noller (Munich: Kaiser, 1967), p. 262 f..
32. See Johannes B. Lotz, "Das Sein selbst und das subsistierende Sein nach Thomas von Aquin," in Günther Neske, ed., *Martin Heidegger zum siebzigsten Geburtstag* (Pfullingen: Günther Neske, 1959), pp. 180-94. John N.

Deeley, *The Tradition via Heidegger* (The Hague: Martinus Nijhoff, 1971). John P. Doyle, "Heidegger and Scholastic Metaphysics," *The Modern Schoolman*, 49 (1972), 201-20. See also Chapter V, n. 62..

33. Carl Braig, *Vom Sein: Abriss der Ontologie,* (Freiburg: Herder, 1896), p. v.
34. Martin Heidegger, *Zur Sache des Denkens* (Tübingen: Max Niemeyer, 1969), p. 32; *On "Time and Being",* trans. Joan Stambaugh (New York: Harper and Row, 1972), p. 29 f. My own translation here paraphrases the original slightly.
35. See Martin Heidegger, "Vorwort" in William J. Richardson, *Heidegger: Through Phenomenology to Thought,* 3rd ed. (The Hague: Martinus Nijhoff, 1974), p. xxi.
36. On the appearance of *Ereignis* in 1928, see Thomas Sheehan, "Getting to the Topic," pp. 312-13.
37. For this section see Edmund Husserl, *Logical Investigations,* trans. J. N. Findlay, 2 vols. (London: Routledge, Kegan, Paul, 1970), II, 773-802; Martin Heidegger, *Vier Seminare,* pp. 110-28; Jacques Taminiaux, "Heidegger and Husserl's *Logical Investigations,*" trans. Jeffrey Stevens, *Research in Phenomenology,* 7 (1977), 58-83.
38. Husserl, *Logical Investigations,* II, 778.
39. See Thomas Sheehan, "Heidegger's 'Introduction to the Phenomenology of Religion,' 1920-21," *The Personalist,* 60 (1979), pp. 312-24, esp. pp. 318-19.
40. Heidegger used *"Jeweiligkeit"* in the brief lecture in which he first summarized the contents of *Being and Time.* See Thomas Sheehan, "The 'Original Form' of *Sein und Zeit*: Heidegger's *Der Begriff der Zeit* (1924)," *Journal of the British Society of Phenomenology,* 10 (1979), 78-83, esp. p. 82.
41. Heidegger, SZ, Section 41.
42. Ibid., 192/237 and 327/375.
43. Ibid., Section 65.
44. Martin Heidegger, "On the Being and Conception of *Physis* in Aristotle's *Physics,* B, 1" *Man and World,* 9 (1976), p. 229.
45. Heidegger, SZ 25/47.
46. Ibid., 21/43.
47. Ibid., 26/49.
48. Ibid., 22/44.
49. Martin Heidegger, *Unterwegs zur Sprache,* 3rd ed. (Pfullingen: Günther Neske, 1965), p. 198; *On the Way to Language,* trans. Peter Hertz (New York: Harper and Row, 1972), p. 92.
50. Martin Heidegger, *Gelassenheit* (Pfullingen: Günther Neske, 1959), p. 35; *Discourse on Thinking,* trans. John M. Anderson and E. Hans Freund (New York: Harper and Row, 1966), p. 62.
51. Heidegger, SZ 20 f./42.
52. John H. Finley, *Four Stages of Greek Thought* (Stanford, Cal.: Stanford University Press, 1966).
53. Ibid., pp. 3 and 29.
54. Ibid., p. 31 f.
55. Ibid., p. 32.

56. Ibid., p. 32 f.

57. Ibid., pp. 3, 27, 29, 54, and 5, respectively.

58. Ibid., pp. 28 and 29.

59. Ibid., pp. 58 and 52.

60. Ibid., p. 53 f.

61. See Martin Heidegger, *Einführung in die Metaphysik*, 2nd ed. (Tübingen: Max Niemeyer, 1958), ch. IV, nos. 2 and 3; *An Introduction to Metaphysics*, trans. Ralph Manheim (New Haven, Conn.: Yale University Press, 1959), pp. 98 et seq.

62. See Martin Heidegger, *Nietzsche*, 2 vols. (Pfullingen: Günther Neske, 1962), II, 399ff.; *The End of Philosophy*, trans. Joan Stambaugh (New York: Harper and Row, 1973), pp. 1 ff.

63. Karl Rahner, *The Foundations of Christian Faith*, trans. William V. Dych, (London: Darton, Longman and Todd, 1978), p. 60. German edition, *Grundkurs des Glaubens: Einführung in den Begriff des Christentums* (Freiburg: Herder and Herder, 1976).

64. *Vom Wesen der Wahrheit* in Martin Heidegger, *Wegmarken* (Frankfurt: Vittorio Klostermann, 1967), p. 89; in the *Gesamtausgabe* edition of *Wegmarken* (ed. Fr.-W. von Herrmann, 1976), p. 194. English translation by John Sallis, "On the Essence of Truth" in Martin Heidegger, *Basic Writings*, ed. David Farrell Krell (New York: Harper and Row, 1976), p. 132.

65. Karl Rahner, "Thomas Aquinas on the Incomprehensibility of God," lecture delivered at the University of Chicago, November 8, 1974, cited from the manuscript, pp. 17 and 30.

66. Rahner, *Foundations of Christian Faith.*, pp. 44 and 64.

67. Martin Heidegger, *Early Greek Thinking*, trans. David Farrell Krell (New York: Harper and Row, 1975), p. 120; German: *Vorträge und Aufsätze*, vol. III (Pfullingen: Günther Neske, 1967³), p. 75.

68. Rahner, *Foundations of Christian Faith*, p. 68.

69. Ibid., p. 64.

70. The phrase "leaving metaphysics to itself" (*"die Metaphysik sich selbst zu überlassen"*) comes from Heidegger, *Zur Sache des Denkens* (Tübingen: Max Niemeyer, 1969), p. 25; English trans. by Joan Stambaugh, On *"Time and Being"* (New York: Harper and Row, 1972), p. 24.

71. Rahner, *Foundations of Christian Faith*, p. 32.

72. Rahner, "Thomas Aquinas on the Incomprehensibility of God," p. 22.

73. Rahner, GW 131/186 (195), emphasis added.

74. Rahner, *Foundations of Christian Faith*, p. 44.

75. Martin Heidegger, *Nietzsche*, vol. II p. 368.

76. Cf. Martin Heidegger, *Identität und Differenz*, (Pfullingen: Günther Neske, 1957); English trans. by Joan Stambaugh, *Identity and Difference* (New York: Harper and Row), 1969.